MAKING MUSIC

The Guide to Writing, Performing & Recording

Edited by

GEORGE MARTIN

WILLIAM MORROW AND COMPANY, INC
NEW YORK 1983

This book is for my family – with my love

205963

Produced and designed by Shuckburgh Reynolds Ltd
Copyright © Shuckburgh Reynolds Ltd
with the exception of pages 74 to 77 Copyright ©
Stephen Sondheim

Library of Congress Catalog Card Number: 82-63154
ISBN: 0-688-01465-8
0-688-01466-6 (pbk)

Printed and bound in Spain by Printer Industria Grafica
SA, Barcelona. D.L.B. 1867-1983

First Edition
1 2 3 4 5 6 7 8 9 10

MAKING
MUSIC

Contents

Recording Music

The Music Business

Introduction

● Of all the arts, music is the most sublime, and touches the heart of every human being. Even those rare ones who boast that they are tone deaf have, at some time in their lives, been moved by music of one sort or another. It is also supportive to other arts; ballet, theatre, drama, comedy, film, television. All feed on music to give them life.

At the present time music is available to everyone on a scale which would be incredible to anyone living 100 years ago. Indeed, we have such a feast of good sounds that we are liable to chronic indigestion unless we are circumspect about our consumption. The wall-to-wall carpeting of Muzak that appears to be one of the penalties of modern civilization, can only dull the sensibilities of its audience and stifle the creative urge that I am sure is within most of us. We have the paradox that while more music is available in the world, fewer people get together to make it in their own homes. In the days before television had eaten its way into every household, families accepted as a matter of course that everyone would join in music making at times, and particularly on festive occasions. They knew, as I do, that it is fun to make music together. It does not matter that one is not Pavarotti or Sinatra or even Rod Stewart; sharing music heightens the enjoyment. And it can be any kind of music, from sing-alongs of pre-war songs to attempts at the classics. One of my funniest memories was attempting to sing with friends some two and three part inventions by Bach, most of which took us well out of our range, so that we ended in screeches and growls. Cleo Laine was under no threat from us!

In this book I have set out to cover all aspects of modern popular music making, drawing on the experience of many of its greatest exponents. Versatile I may be, but I freely admit that I am not an expert in many areas, so it occurred to me to ask my friends who are expert to help out.

Now I am lucky enough to have worked with and had as friends some of the greatest writers, performers and back-room boys in the business,

and their contributions are the very essence of this book. At first I was diffident, even embarrassed, to ask a friend to contribute a chapter for me. But a lot of the work was realized by means of interviews, and they became absolutely fascinating for me. The more I listened, the more I realized that I was learning a great deal in a privileged way. People I had known for years opened up and gave their inner thoughts and nuggets of experience in a surprising and delightful manner. And in so doing, they surprised themselves.

Obviously there cannot be exhaustive coverage of so many subjects in one book. Instead, often the topic is presented from many different points of view and anyone wishing to delve deeper will find a recommended section of reading at the end of the book. As you will see, there are three main sections – writing, performing and recording. So many people are puzzled by the creative process in music, and the irony is that often the very composers are not entirely clear how they generate wonderful works. In a process of self-analysis, all give hints about methods of working, emphasizing the hard work in the craft,. but the sixty-four thousand dollar question remains, how does one write a truly great and original song? Divine inspiration is still an essential element, and there is no short cut to genius. In a similar way, performing becomes a matter of enjoyable dedication. It is hard work becoming adept at any instrument, but that does not mean it need not be fun. In the record business, too, long hours of intricate work are often necessary and the glamorous show-biz world often turns out to be fairly hum-drum.

But it is all rewarding, and I hope that we give encouragement to the music makers. Not to be the world's greatest, but to enjoy the creative process and to give enjoyment to others. Through this joy good music will come, and with good music goes good life. Let us change the tired old slogan "make love, not war" to "Make Music for Peace". I believe it is a powerful force.●

George Martin

Acknowledgements

● So many people have worked so hard and freely on this book that I scarcely know where to begin my thanks. Each and every one of the contributors has given unstintingly of their time, effort and great experience. I cannot thank them adequately. Moreover, a few took extreme pains in providing material, writing, correcting, and virtually conducting master classes by proxy. Behind the front line of master artistes has been deployed a back-up team that was worthy of them. I would like specially to thank Chris Meehan, who played a major role in developing the idea and has been a lynchpin throughout the production of the book. Thanks also to David Reynolds whose dogged persistence and hard work overall made it possible, and Roger Pring, Dinah Lone, and David Mallott, whose artistry and design were meticulous. Sandy Loewenthal's groundwork and advice was always invaluable, as was the editing assistance from Brian Jones, Chris Petit and Miren Lopategui. Thanks to Roger Watson, who acted as my clone in America when sometimes I could not be there. I am indebted to Bob Barratt, Andy Bereza, B.J. Cole, Ray Cooper, Geoff Emerick, Simon Frith, David Harries, Simon Woodroffe and Hans Zimmer who all went out of their way to be helpful, providing pictures, captions and detailed advice. And a special thank you to Linda McCartney for her superb photographs and *Melody Maker* who provided many other pictures. The unrewarding task of typing was cheerfully managed by Lesley Gilbert, as well as by my own assistant Shirley Burns, who has spent many hours chasing people in the nicest possible way. Enthusiasm by all, stars and back-room boys alike, for this, their book, has been heart-warming indeed. G.M.●

Extract from *Ain't No Mountain High Enough* (page 51) Copyright © Nickolas Ashford and Valerie Simpson reproduced by kind permission of Jobete Music.

Extract from *My Sharona* (page 52) published by kind permission of Chappell Music Ltd.

Music from *Love Plus One* (page 53) by permission of Brian Morrison Music Ltd.

Extract from *Sad-Eyed Lady of the Lowlands* (page 53) reproduced with kind permission of Warner Bros. Music.

Music from *Blue Rondo à la Turk* (page 54) Copyright © 1960 by Derry Music Co., U.S.A.; printed by kind permission of Valentine Music.

Lyrics from *Blue Rondo à la Turk* by kind permission of Intersong International Ltd.

Lyrics from *Oh What A Beautiful Morning* (page 74) Copyright © 1943 by Williamson Music, Inc., New York, N.Y. Copyright renewed. Used by permission. All rights reserved.

Lyrics from *Maria* (page 75) Copyright © 1957 by Leonard Bernstein and Stephen Sondheim. Reprinted by permission.

Lyrics from *Summertime* (page 75) Copyright © 1935 by Gershwin Publishing Corp. Copyright renewed. Used by permission of Chappell & Co., Inc.

Lyrics from *America* (page 76) Copyright © 1957 by Leonard Bernstein and Stephen Sondheim. Reprinted by permission.

Lyrics from *What's the Use of Wond'rin?* (page 76) Copyright © 1945 Williamson Music, Inc. Copyright renewed. Used by permission of T.B. Harms Co. – sole selling agent.

Lyrics from *Where Is the Life That Late I Led?* (page 77) Copyright © by Cole Porter. Sole selling agent T.B. Harms Company. International copyright secured.

Lyrics from *It Was Just One of Those Things* (page 77 – "Our love was too hot not to cool down") Copyright © 1935 Harms, Inc. Copyright renewed. All rights reserved. Used by permission of Warner Bros. Music.

Lyrics from *Gee Officer Krupke* (page 77) Copyright © by Leonard Bernstein and Stephen Sondheim. Reprinted by permission.

Extract from score for *Tug Of War* (page 80) reproduced by kind permission of MPL Communications Ltd. Copyright © 1982.

Lyrics from *This Is It* (page 100) reproduced with kind permission of Warner Bros. Music.

Lyrics from *Good Vibrations* (page 101) Words by Brian Wilson and Mike Love copyright © 1966 Irving Music Inc. Reprinted by permission of Rondor Music London Ltd.

Extract from *Eleanor Rigby* (page 102) and extracts from score for *Eleanor Rigby* (page 268) and *I Am The Walrus* (page 269) reproduced by permission of Northern Songs Ltd. and Maclen Music Inc.

Contributors

Adam Ant first emerged during the punk boom in the late 1970s, but it was not until he worked briefly with Malcolm McLaren, who masterminded the career of The Sex Pistols, that his fortunes began to change. With a new musical and visual style, based on a flamboyant romanticism, he quickly achieved worldwide chart success. Recently he has been concentrating on his own video promotions which he regards as an essential new part of the music business.

Guy Barker played first trumpet with the British National Youth Jazz Orchestra at 16 and studied at the Royal College of Music before becoming a session musician. As well as playing and recording with such popular artists as Petula Clark, Joan Armatrading, The Boom Town Rats and The Pointer sisters, he has worked with jazzmen like Dizzy Gillespie and Clark Terry.

Bob Barratt made his reputation in production at EMI where he worked with artists like Cliff Richard, Vince Hill and Gene Vincent. He has also written 250 songs which have been recorded by singers ranging from Danny Williams to Brigitte Bardot. His best known song is probably The Yellow Pages jingle, *Let Your Fingers Do The Walking*.

Jeff Beck came to prominence as a guitarist in the mid 1960s when he replaced Eric Clapton in The Yardbirds. Since then he has formed a number of his own bands as well as joining ex-Vanilla Fudge members for Beck, Bogart and Appice. Jeff's award-winning album *Blow By Blow*, recorded in 1975 confirmed his position as one of the world's outstanding performers in his field.

Andy Bereza was born in 1949, studied at Chelsea College and in the late 1960s began building mixers in a converted garage. These designs became the Allen & Heath range, which he developed for five years. He joined TEAC, introduced TASCAM multitrack into Europe in the mid-1970s and originated the Portastudio. He became a consultant for Fostex and is now managing director of the Bandive, Turnkey company.

John Borwick, born and educated in Edinburgh, gained a physics degree before spending four years as a signals officer in the RAF. He spent 11 years as a BBC studio manager and instructor of studio operations. He has been Audio Editor of *Gramophone* since 1964, has written several books and presented numerous broadcasts. From 1971 to 1978 he was Senior Lecturer (Recording Techniques) in the Music Department of the University of Surrey.

Richard Branson was born in England in 1950. He founded *Student* magazine when he was 17 and the Virgin mail order record business in 1969. In 1971 he opened the first Virgin retail shop in London's Oxford Street, a business which quickly grew to a chain of 25 shops throughout Britain. In 1974 Virgin Records was founded, and immediately signed Mike Oldfield whose *Tubular Bells* became a mega-hit. Since then Virgin Enterprises has become a multi-million pound international business.

Gary Brooker, a founder member of the influential Procol Harum, wrote the music for *A Whiter Shade of Pale*, one of the most memorable records of the late 1960s. During its 10 year history the band moved further towards classical forms and consolidated its reputation for innovation. Since 1977 Gary Brooker has combined a solo career with playing keyboards for Eric Clapton's band.

Warren Cann was raised in Canada and California, majored in electronics and turned to music when his eyesight prevented him from becoming an air force pilot. After playing with every type of group from heavy metal to strip club bands, he arrived in England in 1972 with about £80 and his drums. Two years later he helped to found Ultravox.

Eric Clapton was the leading blues guitarist of the 1960s British movement. He taught himself from the records of the American blues masters and came to prominence with The Yardbirds. He then played with John Mayall's Bluesbreakers, the legendary Cream, and Blind Faith, first of the supergroups. In 1970 he formed Derek and the Dominoes and recorded *Layla*, his biggest hit. Since the mid-1970s he has expanded his international reputation with a series of albums and tours.

Tim Clark joined Island Records in 1965 and for three years worked as a van salesman selling

Jamaican ska and rocksteady records around London. In 1968 he became a production assistant and worked his way up to be Island's marketing director, a post he held for six years, before being managing director until his departure in 1980.

B.J. Cole, who was born in Middlesex in 1946, took up pedal steel guitar at 15 and worked with various country bands in the mid 60s. He is a veteran session musician and has been a founder member of various bands including Kiki Dee's, Cochise, Andy Fairweather Low's and Hank Wangford's. In 1977 he founded Cow Pie Records to foster original British country music. He also produces The Hank Wangford Band.

Ray Cooper became a drummer with John Dankworth in the mid-1960s after being an apprentice engineer, a music student and an actor. He is a specialist in Latin American percussion, has played sessions with The Beatles and The Rolling Stones, and toured with Blue Mink and Elton John. He is currently working with George

Harrison and is also a director of Hand Made Films.

Chick Corea, the son of a jazz musician, is famous for his keyboard playing on a series of albums with Miles Davis, including *Bitches Brew*. His own bands have included the experimental quartet, Circle, and the popular and influential Return to Forever. His collaboration with vibraharpist Gary Burton on *Crystal Silence* prompted many other jazz musicians to investigate line-ups that by-passed the conventions of jazz. Their two subsequent albums both won Grammy Awards.

John Dankworth was born in 1927 and studied clarinet at the Royal Academy of Music before becoming a multi-award winning band leader and jazz saxophonist. He has written for theatre, television and commercials. Film compositions include "Saturday Night and Sunday Morning", "The Servant" and "Accident". He works mainly with his wife, the singer Cleo Laine, acting as her musical director, orchestrator, composer and record producer.

Carl Davis was born in New York and, after studying composition, settled in London where he became known for his work for television. In 1980 he won a British Academy Award for Original Television Music, and won further British Awards in 1981 for the film "The French

Lieutenant's Woman''. His greatest recent success was the score he composed for the newly restored five-hour 1927 silent film classic "Napoleon", which has been performed to great acclaim in Britain and France.

Simon Draper was born in South Africa in 1950, moving to England in 1970 where he became chief buyer for the Virgin mail order and retail chain. In 1972 he founded the Virgin record label with Richard Branson and handled A & R and several other functions. He has been managing director of Virgin Records Ltd since 1978 and is a partner in Branson's Virgin Enterprises.

Herman Edel has had a wide background in US radio advertising promotion, theatre direction and production, and movie theatre management and promotion. With George Martin he founded Air-Edel music in London. He is the president of Music Makers Inc., and the founder of HEA Productions and LA/NY Music. He is also the present mayor of Aspen, Colorado.

Terry Ellis is the co-founder and co-chairman of The Chrysalis Group, one of today's most successful independent entertainment companies. With his partner Chris Wright, he has developed a small management and agency company into a multi-media concern

that has recently expanded into the film, television and video markets. Chrysalis has

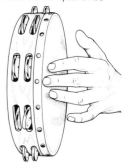

already released its first two films, "Babylon" and "Dance Craze", as well as the first video album, Blondie's *Eat To The Beat*.

Geoff Emerick became an engineer at EMI in 1966 after joining them in 1962. He first worked with The Beatles on *Revolver*, joined their company, Apple, in 1969, then moved to Air Studios in 1973 to continue his collaboration with George Martin. He has since worked with Paul McCartney, Cheap Trick and Ultravox. He has also just co-produced Elvis Costello's album *Imperial Bedroom*.

David Enthoven started EG Management with mainly folk artists like The Strawbs and Julie Felix. They were joined by Emerson, Lake and Palmer and T. Rex, and in 1972 by Roxy Music. Between 1974 and 1981 David Enthoven took a break and returned with Squeeze.

Simon Frith teaches sociology at Warwick University and is the author of *Sound Effects: Youth, Leisure* and the Politics of Rock 'n' Roll. He has written for many magazines, and is currently rock critic of the *Sunday Times* and a columnist for *The New York Rocker*.

Tristan Fry was born in 1946 of musical parents. After a five year spell as side drummer at the London Philharmonic, he joined John Dankworth's band and also became involved in television and film work. He has played with many contemporary musicians such as The Beatles, Elton John and Frank Sinatra. He is a co-founder with John Williams of Sky.

Steve Gadd was born in 1945 in Rochester, New York. He had formal tuition in percussion from the age of seven and studied at the Manhattan School of Music and the Eastman School of Music, graduating with a degree in percussion. Widely held to be the best and most versatile drummer in the world, he has recorded with numerous artists, including George Benson, The Brecker Brothers, Chick Corea, Paul McCartney, Carly Simon, Paul Simon and Weather Report.

Maggie Garrard was born in Belfast in 1951. She became a BBC sound engineer (as was her father) and for three years worked for Radios 1 and 2 before joining an EMI production company where she engineered and produced commercials, inflight programming and music sessions.

She has been a producer with Air-Edel Associates Ltd for over five years and was made Managing Director in 1981.

Harvey Goldsmith had ambitions to be a pharmacist until he started organizing dances and concerts at Sussex University. A visit to the USA in 1966 helped to persuade him to go into concert promotion. Since then he has become Europe's top pop promoter. He is proudest of his world promotion first: taking Elton John to Russia, the first rock star from the West ever to tour the country.

Roger Greenaway, born in Bristol in 1938, contemplated a career as a footballer but became a singer with The Kestrels instead and started writing with colleague Roger Cook. Their first of many hits was *You've Got Your Troubles* and they subsequently had a five year period during which not one week passed without a Cook-Greenaway song in the British charts. Greenaway also co-

wrote the first commercial jingle to become a hit, *I'd Like to Teach the World to Sing*.

Dave Grusin, after studying music at college, gained his first practical experience as pianist, arranger and conductor for The Andy Williams Show. After a period scoring television sitcoms, he moved into films and has worked on many major features including "The Graduate", "Reds" and "On Golden Pond". He continues to work as a record arranger and session player for many top artists, and, more recently, has begun to concentrate on his own recording career.

George Hamer comes from a musical Liverpudlian family. He learned the clarinet and the tenor saxophone, and gained his early musical experience in Germany during his army national service. He worked for big bands including Cyril Stapleton's, and was a copyist for composers like Bernard Hermann before becoming a session fixer.

Herbie Hancock's earliest musical experiences included piano lessons from a church gospel pianist and performing with the Chicago Symphony Orchestra at the age of 11. By the time he left college with a major in electronic engineering he had added jazz, R & B and electronics to his repertoire. From 1962 to 1969 he played with Miles Davis before forming his own bands which developed his experiments with avant-garde jazz, jazz-rock and funk.

Dave Harries was educated at Guildford Technical College and R.R.E. College of Electronics, Malvern. He worked at EMI Studios in Abbey Road before joining George Martin at Air in 1970. He became manager of Air Studios in 1973 and in 1978 he built the Montserrat Studios with George Martin.

Mike Hedge began as a roadie with The Pink Floyd and worked for four years as their road manager, later becoming their co-stage manager. He also stage managed many other acts including Wishbone Ash and Squeeze, with whom he worked for two years, before becoming their tour manager and then their manager. In 1981 he went into partnership with David Enthoven at EG Management.

Jerry Hey is a top session trumpet player and leader of The Seawind Horns, the Los Angeles based horn section. He attended the University of Indiana and moved to Hawaii in 1965, where he played in a band called Ox which later became Seawind. He returned to Los Angeles in 1975 and has since played on numerous recordings working with, amongst others: Quincy Jones; Michael Jackson; George Benson; Herbie Hancock; Earth, Wind and Fire; Michael McDonald; George Duke and Donna Summer.

Glynne Jones was born in Swansea, Wales, and started work as a lecturer in Fine Arts. He sang with the BBC Wales Choir and began to do solo singing as well as becoming interested in composing and arranging. For the last 12 years he has coached many singers and groups for record companies. He has also written a number of songs which have been recorded.

Quincy Jones was in a band with Ray Charles at 14; by 15 he was playing trumpet for Billie Holiday, and at 18 was touring with Lionel Hampton. He has arranged, composed and produced for artists like Ellington, Basie, Dinah Washington and, more recently, Michael Jackson, as well as recording and performing in his own right. His film compositions include "The Pawnbroker" and "In the Heat of the Night". He was also the first black vice-president of a major record label.

Skaila Kanga was born in Bombay and came to

live in London at the age of four. After studying piano at the Royal Academy of Music, she began playing harp with Tina Bonifacio when she was 17. She has freelanced with most of the major British Orchestras and now works as a recording artist in both the popular and classical fields. She is a member of The Nash Ensemble and of a successful duo with harmonica virtuoso Tommy Reilly.

Bernard Krause was a radio producer in New York before briefly becoming a member of The Weavers folk group. Since 1965 he has been president of a media music company that concentrates on producing music for cinema, television and commercials. He is also a solo recording artist, and was a member of Beaver and Krause, an electronic music composition duo which recorded seven albums.

Cleo Laine is Britain's best known female vocalist, the only singer ever to be nominated in the popular, classical and jazz categories of America's Grammy Awards. She has starred in many stage and television productions, both musical and dramatic. However, she is best known for her work with John Dankworth whose band she joined in 1952 and whom she married in 1958.

Julian Littman started his career as an actor before turning to music. He played the London pub circuit with Charlie Dore and made two

albums with her. He went on to do three major tours with Gerry Rafferty, and has recorded and toured with Steve Harley, Richard and Linda Thompson, Rachel Sweet, Toto Coelo, Bananarama and many others. He is now trying to reestablish his acting career without giving up his life as a musician.

Julian Lloyd Webber has toured all over the world as a concert cellist and has performed on nationwide television in the United States. In the last three seasons he has appeared to great acclaim with all the major London symphony orchestras. His album *Variations* sold over 350,000 copies in Britain alone. He has also worked with jazz violinist Stephane Grappelli and has had a concerto written for him by Joaquin Rodrigo.

Sandy Loewenthal formed his first group at school with Chas Cronk of The Strawbs, with whom he also wrote songs. After switching from lead guitar to keyboards, he played in various bands in Europe and America before taking a music degree at Dartington College. He

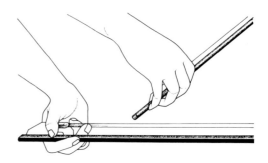

is currently a session player and arranger, and is co-founder of the production company Teamwork.

Paul McCartney, born in Liverpool in 1942, was a founder member of The Beatles and with John Lennon wrote a series of songs that established The Beatles as the best known group in the world. Since the break up of The Beatles in 1970 he has played with his own band Wings. His post-Beatles compositions include *Mull of Kintyre*, the biggest selling

British single ever. He received the MBE in 1965 and is married to the photographer Linda Eastman.

Tony Marshall took up the guitar in his teens and turned professional at 20. After freelance club work and teaching privately and in schools, he played and recorded with such diverse acts as The Ray Ellington Jazz Quartet, Blodwyn Pig and Brand X. He has also made three world tours with Roger Whittaker.

Dave Mattacks joined Fairport Convention as a drummer in 1969 after an apprenticeship with big bands in Northern Ireland and Scotland. Since going freelance in 1974 he has been a top session drummer for, among others, Gary Brooker, Joan Armatrading, George Harrison and Paul McCartney.

Christopher Neil became involved in record production through writing and recording demos. Before that he had been a singer with a touring English pop band in the 1960s, then an actor on television and in musicals like "Hair" and "Jesus Christ Superstar", in which he played the lead. Since his initial hits with Paul Nicholas, Christopher Neil has helped to establish such international artists as Dollar and Sheena Easton.

Keith Nelson was raised in California, where he learnt to play the guitar and banjo, before moving to

London in 1968. Since then he has played and recorded banjo with numerous artists and bands, including Billy Joel, Charlie Dore and Olivia Newton-John.

David Paich is a leading session keyboard player and a member of Toto, the highly respected Los Angeles-based band which has been together for ten years since it started as a high school rock band. David Paich has recorded with many artists and bands including Steely Dan, Elton John, Quincy Jones and Michael Jackson. He is the son of Marty Paich, the arranger and pianist.

David Platz formed the independent publishing company, The Essex

Music Group, 27 years ago. He is the publisher of songs by The Rolling Stones, Black Sabbath and David Bowie, and he has received 26 Ivor Novello Awards for British songs.

Chris Poole worked as a journalist for the British trade music press before joining Decca Records as a public relations officer. For the last four years he has been head of the press office at Chrysalis.

Phil Ramone was a solo classical concert violinist before he turned to contemporary music. During the Kennedy and Johnson administrations he was the White House consultant for all cultural events. He was also sound consultant on many top Broadway productions. Since the 1970s he has been involved in radio, television, film and record production working with artists like Paul Simon, Billy Joel and Barbra Streisand. In 1980 he won a Grammy for Producer of the Year.

Tommy Reilly trained as a violinist and turned to the harmonica while a prisoner of war in Germany. The first Harmonica Concerto was composed for him during The Festival of Britain in 1951, and since then a number of famous composers have written especially for him. Although he has worked with such personalities as Bing

Crosby and Marlene Dietrich, most of his time is devoted to classical playing and recording.

Tom Scott was born in Los Angeles and took up the saxophone at an early age, gaining experience playing and recording with various jazz groups. In the early 1970s he emerged as bandleader of The L.A. Express, an innovative force in jazz fusion. Most of his time now is taken up with cinema and television work, and session playing for artists like Blondie, George Harrison, Joni Mitchell and Quincy Jones.

Paul Simon enjoyed brief teenage success in 1958 with schoolmate Art Garfunkel as Tom and Jerry. In 1964 they reunited as Simon and Garfunkel to become among the most successful artists in the world. Their collaboration culminated with *Bridge Over Troubled Water*, one of the best selling albums ever. Paul Simon continues to write and perform as a solo artist and his latest album, *One Trick Pony*, is from a film he wrote and in which he stars.

Christopher Small was born in New Zealand in 1927 and obtained BSc and BMus degrees and LRSM diploma there. He has taught in schools and colleges in New Zealand and England, and now teaches at

Ealing College of Higher Education, London. He is the author of *Music, Society, Education (John Calder, London, 1977, Riverrun Press, New York, 1982).*

Stephen Sondheim was born in New York in 1930 and wrote the lyrics for the musical "West Side Story" at the age of 26. His early mentor was the lyricist Oscar Hammerstein II, who, according to Sondheim, determined his professional career. Subsequent Broadway hits include "Gypsy", "Sweeney Todd" and "A Little Night Music". He is generally acknowledged as the greatest lyric poet of post-war theatre.

Sting was born Gordon Sumner in Wallsend, Newcastle-on-Tyne. He taught himself the guitar as a child and developed an interest in jazz at the age of 14. After three years at teacher training college, he became art teacher in a village school and formed a band in Newcastle called Last Exit. In 1977 he moved to London to join The Police. He has written all The Police's hit singles, and plays bass and a variety of other instruments.

Janice Turner was born and educated in Lancashire where she played in various bands while still at school. She toured the USA and Europe as a bassoon player with the Lancashire Schools' Symphony Orchestra. She now lives in London where she works both as a journalist and a musician.

Gary Twigg, who was born in Portsmouth in 1954, turned professional at 16 and has recorded with such artists as Barbara Dixon, Graham Bonnet, Marshal Hain and Gerry Rafferty. He currently plays bass for Sheena Easton and recorded her recent video album. He also writes with Brian Chatterton.

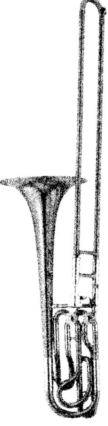

Midge Ure combines his front role for Ultravox with record production for Modern Man, Snips, and Ronny and Phil Lynott. He was born in a poor area of Glasgow where the only ways out were to become either a footballer or a musician. After spells with

Scottish bands Salvation and Slik he moved to London and eventually joined The Rich Kids, which was when he bought his first synthesizer.

Geraint Watkins was born in South Wales and played in bands there before moving to London where he joined various groups, including Juice on the Loose, on the pub circuit. In 1978 he recorded a solo album produced by Andy Fairweather Low. From 1979-1981 he toured and played with Shakin' Stevens; since then he has been working with Dave Edmunds.

Jimmy Webb started songwriting at 13; he developed from transcribing other people's music for $50 a week into one of the top writers of the 1960s with hits like *By the Time I Get to Phoenix, Up, Up and Away,* and *MacArthur Park.* In 1969 he dropped out for a year to concentrate upon becoming a performer and since then has made a new career for himself recording, producing, performing and arranging.

John Williams, born in Australia in 1941, studied with Segovia and received a classical training in London and Siena. After a decade of recording and touring success with the classical guitar, he expanded into contemporary music with a number of well received albums. In 1979 he helped to form the band Sky, which allows him to develop

his interest in contemporary music as well as pursuing his solo classical career.

Simon Woodroffe trained in theatre in London and began lighting for rock shows in the early 1970s. He started and ran a European lighting company before deciding to concentrate on stage and lighting design. He now designs and produces shows for many major touring acts.

Chris Wright took a post-graduate course at Manchester Business School and became an artists' manager helping to break new acts. He later joined forces with his main rival, Terry Ellis, to form Chrysalis which, with groups like Jethro Tull, Blondie, Ultravox and Spandau Ballet, has become one of the world's biggest independent record companies inside ten years. He is chairman of the British Phono-graphic Industry (BPI).

Hans Zimmer was born in West Germany and encouraged to play music by his mother, a concert pianist, and his father, an inventor. He designed synthesizers after leaving school and was among the first specialist synthesizer players. In 1979 his collaboration with Trevor Horne and Geoff Downes produced the worldwide hit *Video Killed The Radio Star.* As well as producing bands like The Damned, he has co-written the filmscores for "Moonlighting" and the forthcoming Nicholas Roeg film.

Historical Introduction

*"... the underlying impulse for all
pop musicians in all pop genres
is simply the pleasure of making music..."*
SIMON FRITH

Popular Music 1950-1980

These days pop music is plagued by adjectives. As a rock critic I get 20 to 30 LP's to listen to each week and the only way through the ever growing pile is a process of instant classification. Using whatever I already know about the performers – looking at their pictures on the sleeves, working out their instrumental line-ups – I sort them into genres even before listening to them. Rock, pop, rock 'n' roll, soul, reggae, punk, disco, middle-of-the-road, teenybop, electronic, singer/songwriter, country, heavy metal, and so on – after twenty-five years of listening to pop music I no longer think much about these distinctions. They come naturally, just as in the recording studio every session musician knows what's meant when the producer asks for, say, a funk bass. To more casual listeners and players, though, it's this multiplication of terms that has

made so much music-writing and music-making so mysterious. In this chapter I will explain where the most important idioms came from and what they stand for historically.

The paradox of pop is that while the making of music becomes ever more complex, both technically and commercially (I have no idea how a synthesizer works; I'm constantly baffled by the complicated division of labour in the music business), it remains, nevertheless, a central part of daily life. Men and women have always used song as the most direct and intense way to express their feelings; music has always been rooted in rituals of both public and private celebration and display, and it still is. It remains a crucial part of religious worship and political parade; it still lies at the heart of our experiences of community, friendship and struggle, of our definitions of love and happiness, of our enjoyment of party and dance. We still remember and turn to pop songs in times of joy and grief.

Commentators of all sorts have suggested that

Elvis Presley

when popular music became pop – a commodity to be sold in the market place – then the folk use of music came to an end. The argument is that over the last hundred years people have stopped making music for themselves and have become dependent on strangers doing it for them. Even live musical performances have become, it seems, such huge shows of noise and glamour that for the audience the experience is like pressing one's nose against a shop window: the music is on public display but it is not really "ours".

I don't agree with this argument but it is an influential one, even within the pop world. Elvis Presley fans in the 1950s, Beatles fans in the 1960s and Sex Pistols fans in the 1970s all talked in terms of reclaiming "their" music from the distant super-stars and money makers. The fact was, of course, that Presley, The Beatles and the Pistols were as dependent as the stars they replaced on the technology of pop and on its commercial machinery, and there is an important lesson to be learnt from this: the history of popular music this century is, indeed, the history of an increasing division between music-makers

and music-consumers, between musicians and audiences, but this *hasn't* sapped people's urge to make music for themselves, to use music to mark their lives. All that's changed is what it means to "make music". And my guess is that there are now more people making music than ever before. Throughout the twentieth century, every time there has been a boom in record sales there has also been a boom in the sales of musical instruments.

Technological and commercial developments have changed the processes of music-making, but have not changed people's reasons for playing and listening or the nature of musical experience. For example, the musical importance of the early recording devices was that, by capturing on shellac the uniqueness of specific performances, they made much more widely accessible the *emotional* qualities of live music: the unique sound of a singer or instrumentalist could be widely heard, their performances endlessly repeated, without reference to sheet music or written notes. The blues, the most intense and moving of modern musical forms, was only able to make its remarkable mark on

The Beatles

The Sex Pistols

twentieth-century western culture because it was recorded and could be heard and studied outside its usual context. Similarly, the development of the electric microphone and amplification in the 1930s, and of tape recording and hi fi in the 1950s, opened up new possibilities of intimacy in performance. The boundary between speech and song became blurred, and popular musicians were able to explore emotional complexity in musically accessible ways, without needing the knowledge or skills of classical performers and audiences.

Why do popular musicians in the 1980s make the sounds they do? This can be answered in three ways: by reference to what's possible, to the technology of music making, to pop instruments and their players' technical skills; by reference to what sells, to commercial calculations of what an audience will buy, what market a musician can reach; and by reference to an aesthetic, to conventions of what sounds good. The differences between pop genres are differences along all these dimensions: different genres use different sounds, instruments and techniques; they are aimed at different listeners; they refer to different ideas of what is musical and what sounds good. Hence the differences between, say, Genesis and Motorhead, Paul McCartney and John Lydon, Barry Manilow and The Gang of Four. They are all popular musicians, but they make different sorts of noise with different sorts of instrument for different sorts of audience with different ideas of art.

Two more things need to be said about this. First, in pop all genres are open; they are sources of sound and attitude available to anyone. Pop is a constant process of theft and imitation. Musicians, writers and producers steal each other's ideas and phrases, mix up conventions, rush to use the latest technological toy. Pop develops not just by shifting idioms but also by keeping them swirling around together. Second, the underlying impulse for all pop musicians in all pop genres is simply the pleasure of making music, just as pop listeners of all sorts draw on their chosen sounds for similar bursts of energy and community and feeling. The history of pop in the last thirty years, then, has not been a neat linear progress, one sound leading to another. There has, rather, been a multiplication of sounds, and a permanent tension between the need to stay still – to build stars and exploit hit formulas – and the recurrent demand for change, for new musics for new times.

The 1950s

In *After The Ball,* his excellent history of pop, Ian Whitcomb describes how the technological developments of the early decades of the twentieth century – records and recording, the radio, the cinema – transformed popular music. He points to the emergence of the national – and

Frank Sinatra

Bing Crosby

20

Johnny Ray

then international – singing star, the increasing distance between these highly paid performers and the mass audience, the new reliance on music professionals and the subsequent decline of home-made music which led to the fall of the sheet music and piano empires and to the rise of "the bland, universal well-made song."

This is the background to the state of pop in 1950. Pop music between the wars had been dominated by dance music, by big bands and swing orchestras adapting ideas and sounds from jazz and blues, and by theatre music, by songs taken from Broadway and West End musicals and revues. In the 1950s both big band music and theatre song went into decline. The most important reason for this was the new sales demand for vocal records. Radio programming was increasingly organized round these records – rather than round live dance broadcasts – and big bands became uneconomic to run.

The shift of attention from the band to the singer and from the tune to the song, had begun with the 1930s development of the electric microphone and recording techniques (in both the broadcasting and recording studio) which enabled singers like Bing Crosby to "croon", to become more "knowable" to their fans, to perform with greater intimacy and sexiness and personality. The star of the 1940s was Frank Sinatra, but the sign of what was to come was the 1950s success of Johnny Ray, an over-the-top emotional singer who appeared to weep as he sang. The impact of this sort of personal style was reinforced by the development of television, which could bring singers into people's homes in close-up.

As singers became the dominant pop stars, so the meaning of the pop song changed. The song remained central to how pop was organized – round a catchy tune and a sentimental lyric – but it was now a vehicle to display a singer's personality rather than being the object of music making in itself. Tin Pan Alley professionals still churned out melodies for money, but songs were increasingly written as forms of direct expression, rather than as attempts to construct moods and feelings through their scored lyrical and melodic arrangements. Frank Sinatra's hits, for example, depended for their emotional meaning on his work rather than the songwriters', and this shift marked too the declining chart importance of songs from the musical theatre. Theatre songs had always been the most sophisticated Tin Pan Alley productions – they had to carry a story, give a character definition (as they still did in the great 1950s musicals, *West Side Story* and *My Fair Lady*), but the new singing personalities

Jerry Lee Lewis

Don't Be Cruel

Goodnight Irene

Put Me Down

It All Depends

Music

1. PUT ME DOWN
(R. Jones)
2. IT ALL DEPENDS
JERRY LEE LEWIS
EPA 108
MEMPHIS, TENNESSEE

Sun EPA-108

Muddy Waters

Chuck Berry

1950s independent labels: several independent record companies, such as Sun and Chess, emerged in the United States in the 1950s. Their output was directed at black and minority white audiences.

Pioneers of R & B: Muddy Waters expressed the blues with amplified instruments as well as the voice. Chuck Berry adapted R & B to appeal to whites as well as blacks, and, with Fats Domino, Bill Haley and others, created rock 'n' roll.

Fats Domino

needed simpler material, more rawly expressive songs, which were taken from country music and the blues.

The record sales boom of the 1940s consolidated the hold on popular music of the major record companies (Victor and Columbia in the USA, EMI and Decca in Britain), which had survived the 1930s slump by taking over the small companies collapsing all around them. Hence Whitcomb's model of popular music as a big business of star professionals singing songs and displaying personalities, both of which had to be "bland" in order to appeal to as many different people as possible. This development contained, by its very nature, the seeds of a converse process. In the 1950s an increasing number of independent record companies – such as the Ertegun Brothers' Atlantic, the Chess Brothers' Chess, Sam Phillips's Sun – and radio deejays like Alan Freed emerged to service the music markets ignored by the major companies as too small. These companies produced music that was primarily black styles but which also included the folk-based country and hillbilly sounds of the white south. Such music, black and white, originated in the rural experience of church and work, dance and celebration, but there had been important musical changes in the previous decade as rural workers moved away from home into the armed services during World War II and into northern towns to take advantage of the war and post-war economic upswing. Black and white rural music became, in Charlie Gillett's words, "the sound of the city."

Rhythm and blues

In so doing music became, necessarily, louder, cruder and more aggressive. Musicians took advantage of the development of the electric guitar in particular to create a sound capable of competing with the noise of traffic and urban crowds, that could ripple off a club stage with enough edge and off-beat to cut through any amount of drunken din. This music had to have city rhythms and city sounds, which are quite different from country rhythms and sounds.

Rural blues became urban blues, urban blues became rhythm and blues and the small combo dance music of bands such as Muddy Waters' kept the blues emphasis on the voice and vocal expression but now applied this emphasis to amplified instruments as well. The guitar, bass and miked harmonica took over from jazz's brass and wind as the "voices" of black music while the piano and saxophone became rhythm instruments, their effect swamped unless played in bursts, on the beat, to support the drums.

23

Country dance bands, emerging from the pre-war sound of "Western Swing", made similar changes, bringing the electric and steel guitars to the fore, wiring up the bass, using the piano for a boogie style beat and making the singer the central personality. The Grand Old Opry purists might have argued the correctness of country bands using drums and amplifiers, but they were necessary for white musicians, just as they were for black musicians – to make themselves heard.

Rhythm and blues and electrified honky-tonk were functional forms of music, moulded by the experience of travelling musicians performing for a living; they developed styles which appealed to dancers and which could hold their own as immediate entertainment. But such music was also recorded by the new independent companies, and its live power – its energy, sense of fun, sexual expressiveness and its ability to drive through distracting backgrounds and use sound as a physical barrier – reached white teenagers who had never seen this music performed, but could certainly sense its appeal.

The independent record companies and the R & B radio programmers began to notice that they had a new market: white teenagers partying along the South Carolina coast or listening

Alan Freed

under the bedclothes to Alan Freed in Cleveland and New York. More significantly, club owners and studio engineers began to be pestered by young whites wanting to make such music for themselves. Southern boys such as Elvis Presley, Jerry Lee Lewis and Buddy Holly – who, a generation before, would have become hillbilly singers – developed rockabilly, country music with the sound, voice and rhythm of urban R & B.

24

Rock 'n' roll

Rock 'n' roll was, in musical terms, the product of blues and country music, but its huge impact on the music industry and on popular culture generally was more dependent on sociological than musical factors; the musical hunt for the first rock 'n' roll record long ago reached the 1930s. What mattered about rock 'n' roll in the 1950s was its youth; its expression of a community of interest between performer and audience; and its account of a generation bound by age and taste in a gesture of self-celebration, in defiance against the nagging, adult routines of home and work and school.

This youth movement was made possible by two non-musical developments: full employment and television. The relative affluence of the 1950s gave working class teenagers a disposable income they had never had before, while the rise of television as the medium of family leisure meant that previous forms of entertainment – radio, pop music, the cinema and dance halls – had to find new and more specialist markets. They turned to youth, and so the emergence of the teenage consumer meant the institutionalization of teenage places, teenage tastes, teenage habits and teenage styles. At the centre of it all was the sound of rock 'n' roll.

Rock 'n' roll, then, described a new market, a new set of attitudes, and a particular sound. In terms of its musical origins rock 'n' roll was not explicitly youthful – early rock 'n' roll hit-makers such as Fats Domino and Bill Haley were hardly teenagers – but rock 'n' roll stardom soon became a matter of the youth voice and the youth song, so that Elvis Presley became rock 'n' roll's superstar because he so clearly *represented* his listeners and Chuck Berry became the most successful R & B performer to adapt its loose limbed lyrics to the interests of the white, teenage record-buyer.

The major record companies and established musical professionals, initially jolted by and contemptuous of the rock 'n' roll explosion, were quick to apply their methods to the teenage market. Their task was to discover acceptable teenage stars – hence the procession of pretty Italian boys on the American TV programme *American Bandstand* and the show-biz moulding of Cliff Richard and Tommy Steele in Britain – and to make sure they sang songs with teenage themes; love songs, for example, had to focus on the problems of first love, courtship and interfering parents.

By the end of the 1950s the idea that rock 'n' roll was a do-it-yourself music seemed to have been forgotten. Elvis Presley had moved from the

Rock 'n' roll derived from R & B and country music. The Crickets, *above left,* Little Richard, *above right*, Roy Orbison, *right,* Carl Perkins, *far right,* and Bill Haley and the Comets, *below,* produced wild, exciting music which appealed to the rebellious and newly affluent youth of the United States. In 1959 Buddy Holly, The Big Bopper and Ritchie Valens were mourned by fans the world over.

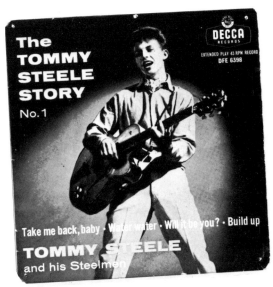

The
TOMMY
STEELE
STORY
No. 1

DECCA
RECORDS

EXTENDED PLAY 45 RPM RECORD
DFE 6398

Take me back, baby · Water water · Will it be you? · Build up

TOMMY STEELE
and his Steelmen

British rock 'n' roll stars Cliff Richard, *above*, and Tommy Steele were imitations of American rock 'n' rollers, moulded by their record companies.

Melody Maker

FEBRUARY 7, 1959   EVERY FRIDAY 6d.

PLANE CRASH KILLS STARS

Harriott is back

Tour all set for Woody Herman

PLANS for Woody Herman to lead an Anglo-American big band in Britain have been settled. His tour will open on April 4.

The famous American leader will bring six musicians from the States and the group will be built up to a 16-piece by British jazzmen.

A spokesman for the National Jazz Federation, which is organising the tour, told the MM: "We can't pick the British musicians until we know who Herman is bringing with him. Several top names have been mentioned but Woody has not settled his line-up yet.

The band will play 19 concerts in 16 days, ending the tour on April 19.

The American sextet will be featured on the first part of each concert, with the Anglo-American big band playing the second half.

BRITAIN TO SEE CARMEN McRAE

NEW YORK, Wednesday.— Singing star Carmen McRae will kick off her first European tour with a visit to Britain in April.

Being lined up for her are a TV show, a concert tour and, possibly, night club dates.

At the end of her British tour she will go to the Continent for further engagements.

REDHEAD AT THE LYCEUM

NEW YORK, Wednesday.—The world's pop fans were shattered this week by the tragic deaths of three top disc stars—Buddy Holly, Big Bopper (J. P. Richardson) and Ritchie Valens.

Holly had been set to fly to Britain for a TV show on March 8.

The three singers died when their chartered, single-engine plane crashed near Mason City, Iowa, at 1 a.m. on Tuesday.

They were appearing in a package show "The Biggest Show Of Stars For 1959" and had hired a plane to take them from a date at the Surf Ball-room, Clear Lake, Iowa. The pilot of the plane was also killed.

Top vocal group, the Platters, and the rest of the show had travelled by coach.

'A lesson'

Tim Gale of General Artists Corporation, which was booking the show, told the MM: "We have fought against artists chartering their own planes. Maybe this is a lesson to all of us. It is a real tragedy."

Buddy Holly was married only a few months ago. His disc career had cooled off recently after he severed connections with his manager, Norman Petty, and with the Crickets, with whom he toured Britain last year. His latest disc, called ironically enough, "It Doesn't Matter Anymore," showed signs of bringing him back into the charts.

The Big Bopper, 27-year-old J. P. Richardson, sold a million copies of his Mercury disc of "Chantilly Lace" and he was to have received a Golden Disc at the end of the tour. A Texas disc-jockey for eight years, he was an active songwriter. He leaves a widow and five-year-old daughter.

Ritchie Valens, 17-year-old star of Del Fi Records, was making his first in-person tour. His "Donna" is currently fourth in the Hit Parade.

The Marquee Club Gala Night on to welcome back alto

Berry Gordy

Martha Reeves and the Vandellas

Tamla Motown: at his base in Detroit, Tamla Motown's founder, Berry Gordy, assembled a collection of unknown but highly talented producers, writers and artists. Following his discovery of singer/songwriter Smokey Robinson, Gordy put together the songwriting team Holland-Dozier-Holland, which wrote a string of hits for Martha Reeves and the Vandellas, The Supremes, The Four Tops and others.

Smokey Robinson and the Miracles

independent Sun label to a major corporation, RCA; he took his songs from established music publishers and established song writers, and was making Hollywood films. Black and white dance bands continued to tour the South, fill urban clubs and make juke box music, but teenage pop itself had become a new idiom, referring vaguely to rock 'n' roll's beat and electric instrumentation, but subjecting them to traditional pop arrangements (think of the strings on Cliff Richard's records) and subordinating them to the logic of traditionally well-made songs.

Vocal groups

Creative attention swung from the performers to the record makers – to the songwriters, arrangers and producers for whom the singers were simply a teenage front. The decline of chart rock 'n' roll as a live dance form meant the rise of new sorts of pop sound, emerging from hit-making factories like New York's Brill Building. In Phil

Phil Spector

Phil Spector in 1958, aged 17, with his first protégés, The Teddy Bears.

Carole King, perhaps the most prominent member of the team of songwriters assembled in the Brill Building at 1619 Broadway by Don Kirshner. Other members included Gerry Goffin, Bobby Darin, Neil Sedaka, and Neil Diamond.

Spector's "little symphonies for kids" what mattered was the "artificial" process of studio music making. Spector and his fellow producers built up layers of noise that could never have been reproduced live but did cut through the tinny radio sound of the bedroom transistor and car speaker with the impact of early rock 'n' roll.

The early 1960s was the era of the vocal group, the girl group in particular. Individual voices were defined by the effects of harmony and cross-talk, their very anonymity making the songs speak for everyone. The Spector sound of The Crystals and The Ronettes was matched by the surf sound of The Beach Boys and by the vocally and rhythmically more complex Motown sound of The Supremes, The Miracles, The Marvelettes and The Four Tops. Spector derived his vocal group sounds from the street corner, acapella doo-wop singers of New York R & B; The Beach Boys reorganized Chuck Berry according to the close harmonies of Barbershop quartets; and Tamla Motown took its voices straight from the church, from the pleading and response of gospel music. But in all these records the key people weren't the singers but the producers. Phil Spector, Brian Wilson, Holland/Dozier/Holland, Smokey Robinson and the rest were the first musicians to set out to use the

The Beach Boys with guiding light Brian Wilson, *second left.*

recording studio as their creative instrument, to equate making music with making records and to see the challenge of pop as the creation of new sounds rather than simply the transmission or reproduction of old ones. For them, the commercial and the aesthetic objects of pop music making were inseparable: to make records to sell meant making music that sounded good in specific contexts – on AM radio, in the car and on cheap record players – and this was the artistic challenge in itself.

The 1960s

To read about the New York pop scene of the early 1960s is to read about a commercial jungle. Hundreds of young songwriters, singers, session men, engineers and producers were involved in a desperate competition for a break, a hit or a sound. But, if this was exciting behind the scenes, the equation of music-making with record- and money-making didn't satisfy the original rock 'n' roll urge to make music directly, and in the early years of the 1960s this urge was better expressed in Britain than in the United States. This was partly due to the surprising chart success of traditional jazz bands and their skiffle-playing offshoots – such straightforward acoustic sounds inspired thousands of young people to bang a box or strum a guitar – but what mattered in Britain more was the lack of a teen pop industry. Ambitious young songwriters and record producers couldn't parallel Phil Spector's or Brian Wilson's careers; despite rock 'n' roll, the British entertainment industry, British record companies and British broadcasting, were still dominated by London-based, show biz values.

British beat

Teenagers still wanted their own music and so, particularly in the provinces, do-it-yourself skiffle experiments rapidly became a commitment to do-it-yourself rock 'n' roll. It was The Shadows' classic line-up (drums, bass, lead and rhythm guitars) that inspired musicians round the country, not Cliff Richard's success as a balladeer. These British rock 'n' roll bands were, though, equally eager to imitate the sounds of American teenage pop, to get the Spector effect live, to use voices in the Motown style. The sound of British beat was the result of combining *all* the elements of American pop – not just rock 'n' roll and rhythm and blues, but girl groups and Motown too. The Beatles, for example, had half a dozen girl group covers on their first two LPs; the Mersey Sound of fellow performers like The Hollies and The Searchers depended on the American pop use of vocal harmonies.

British beat: The Shadows' four-piece instrumental line-up, *above*, inspired British groups who added vocals and other instruments to create a totally new sound.

The Rolling Stones

The Dave Clark Five

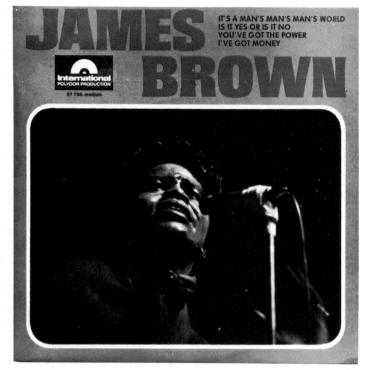

Black's influence on white: black singers like Sam Cooke, *above,* Aretha Franklin, *top,* and James Brown, *left,* influenced white vocal style, while the blues guitar of B.B. King, *right,* did much to bring about the guitar's dominance of white rock music.

British beat emerged from musicians' attempts to solve two problems at once: on the one hand, they wanted to sound like their favourite American records; on the other hand, they had to make a living playing in clubs which meant they had to play dance music with enough loud energy and local familiarity to bring the crowds back. Their starting point was a 1950s rocking sound, but in developing this guitar-based music the groups found that their most significant instruments were, in fact, their voices. British singers began to take on a new, raw quality as they shouted to be heard; vocals were individualized – to distinguish one local group from another; British beat developed a style of blues-derived singing that was both more expressive and more personal than anything previously heard in British rock 'n' roll (thus The Beatles sang in obvious Liverpool accents). Just as importantly, voices became central to the groups' musical arrangements – vocal harmonies and back-up chorus sounds had to do the job of the strings and echoes and studio tricks of the teen pop records.

The success of British beat, first in Britain itself, then with its "invasion" of the United States and the rest of the world, had two immediate effects. First, white ears grew accustomed to expres-

sive, personalized singing styles and the pop charts began to open up to black singers too. The appeal of black music to whites ceased to derive from its raucous instrumental textures and beat – well enough copied by white groups – and became attached to its singers, whose unique sounds could not be imitated so easily. In soul music, vocal conventions taken from the church, from testifying, were applied to secular love songs and dance music. Singers like Ray Charles and Sam Cooke were the models for British beat vocalists, and the pop-marketed soul sound of Motown was joined in the charts by more intense voices – Otis Redding, Aretha Franklin, James Brown. At the same time, the expressive, voice-like instrumental approach of black musicians also began to inspire white pop players and, because the guitar was the basic tool of rock 'n' roll, so the electric blues guitar (as played, for example, by BB King) became the basic tool of rock.

Secondly, the success of British beat groups vindicated the 1950s promise of rock 'n' roll as do-it-yourself music. By the mid 1960s there was a boom in music-making as never before, and this time the musicians wrote their own songs and began to control the sounds of their own records. In adapting sophisticated studio tracks

BILL GRAHAM PRESENTS IN SAN FRANCISCO

JEFFERSON GRATEFUL
AIRPLANE DEAD
MONGO SANTAMARIA
FRI & SAT ONLY

MONGO SANTAMARIA
COLD BLOOD · ELVIN BISHOP GROUP
THURS & SUN ONLY

FRIDAY & SAT AT WINTERLAND · FILLMORE ON THURS & SUN
GLENN McKAY'S HEADLIGHTS   MAY 2-3 MAY 1-4   BROTHERHOOD OF LIGHT

to the rough music of cheap local gigs, British groups had had to learn how arrangements and songs worked, and it soon became easier to write songs that sounded right than to work on other people's. Again, The Beatles' practice became the model for everyone else. They wrote teenage songs which didn't follow Denmark Street's rules, but were funny, ironic, quirky and personal. (One of The Beatles' advantages over previous British rock 'n' rollers was that they learnt their pop skills away from the centre of the music business.) What started as a pop revival, a new burst of teenage rock 'n' roll, ended up, then, suggesting quite new possibilities for popular music as a form of artistic expression: rock 'n' roll became rock.

Rock

The beat boom in Britain drew in musicians, like The Rolling Stones, who had previously despised pop and worked deliberately in jazz and blues. In Europe too, where the 1950s impact of rock 'n' roll had been simply a number of unimpressive imitation Americans, musicians now heard in British beat implications for new sorts of national music. But the effect of the British invasion was most dramatic in the United States. The Beatles' generation of musicians across the Atlantic had, like them, grown up on rock 'n' roll, but they had also grown out of teenage pop in the 1960s and drifted into more "serious" musical forms – urban folk, for example. The Beatles' records reminded them of the power of rock 'n' roll – not just the power of its sound, but also its cultural power, its ability to move audiences and to dominate people's lives. The Beatles' success suggested that it was possible to have a mass cultural impact while preserving one's status as a "real" musician. There were two consequences.

First, folk rock. Folk musicians, led by Bob Dylan, began to go electric, to sing to a rock 'n' roll beat and to follow the conventions of dance party music. In doing so they brought to popular music a new account of the pop song as, on the one hand, a means of social commentary – the folk protest tradition became part of pop with the protest song – and, on the other hand, a form of self expression, something like poetry in its creative use of language and its reflection of a unique sensibility. Folk rock, Bob Dylan's work for example, suggested that pop could be both publicly responsible and privately revealing.

Second, bohemian rock. The Beatles found fans among folk singers and they found fans in the overlapping artistic and bohemian communities of New York and San Francisco, among the old beatniks and the new hippies, in the pop art

Bob Dylan was inspired to go electric by the success of The Beatles and thereby did much to initiate folk rock. Later, The Beatles were to be inspired by Dylan.

galleries and studios. The people there, too, realized that this revised rock and roll could be both a form of personal vision and a means of media shock. On the West Coast folk musicians and bohemians worked together (in groups like Jefferson Airplane and The Grateful Dead) to make acid rock – music as psychedelic experience, pop opened up into rambling, improvised instrumentals. On the East Coast the Velvet Underground, pushed by Andy Warhol, developed a harsher, more discordant and challenging art rock sound, more self-conscious in its image and effects, less comfortable in subject matter (drugs as destruction), less concerned with musical technique, more concerned to develop expressive electric sounds – noise and distortion and feedback.

As such knowing artists and singers began to use rock, so rock itself began to be influenced by their approach – The Beatles were inspired by Bob Dylan as he had once been by The Beatles. British beat groups too began to make music that was determined not by the immediate demands of a dancing crowd or by the market calculations of the major record companies, but only by the constraints of technology and technique. By 1967 the dominant pop attitude was that everything was possible. The Beatles made the move from pop to rock most dramatically as they ceased live performance and focused on the creative possibilities of the studio, beginning to explore (with producer George Martin) the implications of multi-track recording. *Sergeant Pepper's Lonely Hearts Club Band* became the symbol of rock as a recording art.

Popular music making, even for performing bands, was now pushing hard against the boundaries of technology. The emphasis in groups like Cream and Pink Floyd was on musicianship and experiment. Jimi Hendrix, in particular, brought to rock the improvising skill and imagination of a jazz player and applied them to all aspects of electric guitar playing, with his amplifier a crucial part of his instrument. Hendrix not only inspired all subsequent rock guitarists but also drew the attention of jazz musicians like Miles Davis to the expressive power of electric improvisation around a steady rock beat and on from there to the possibility of jazz rock.

Rock was something more than pop, more than rock 'n' roll. Rock musicians combined an

Miles Davis

emphasis on skill and technique with the romantic concept of art as individual expression, original and sincere. They claimed to be non-commercial – the organizing logic of their music wasn't to make money or to meet a market demand; they were, indeed, contemptuous of "commercial pop". In fact, though, the music made on these apparently non-commercial principles turned out to have its own mass audience. Pop music fans were changing too, preferring albums to singles, investing in hi fi,

The Beatles' *Sergeant Pepper* album

using music as a source of personal instruction and experience as well as for dancing and fun. Rock fed into (and fed off) the rebel stance of late 1960s youth: the anti-Vietnam war movement – both in and out of the army – the campus revolts, the hedonistic celebrations of drugs and sex. The new rock musicians and the new rock audience celebrated each other at the Woodstock Festival, but even there it was easy to see that the strands of pop that had come together to make rock were unravelling again.

By the end of the 1960s there were three distinct rock idioms. Progressive rock was music made with an emphasis on complexity, originality, musicianship and a pushing for effects which inspired musical instrument makers, studio designers and electronic inventors to meet the need for new machines, new sounds and new perfection. Heavy metal musicians refined the improvised high-volume blues of Cream and Jimi Hendrix into the Led Zeppelin formula of dominant bass lines, tour-de-force guitar solos, earth-shaking drums, shrill singing.

Progressive rock was created by talented musicians who were prepared to explore the full potential of the ever-developing technology. New sounds were created by Jimi Hendrix, *left*, The Pink Floyd, *above*, and Jack Bruce, Eric Clapton and Ginger Baker who formed The Cream.

They were in pursuit of the overwhelming live noise that became the mainstream sound of American stadium rock. Singer/songwriters, like Paul Simon, James Taylor and Joni Mitchell, sought, by contrast, to use every possible studio device to enhance the meanings of their songs and to reveal themselves. Such intimacy was also dependent on the technical progress of amplification and recording.

These rock forms were clearly different from the continuing pop traditions – the middle-of-the-road music of entertainers like the Carpenters and the young pop sound of the teenybop idols – and by the end of the 1960s they were also more profitable. Rock had become a big business, with its own booming support system – radio (the FM network), magazines (like *Rolling Stone*), promoters and producers, specialized record companies (the rise of Warner Brothers, for example, depended on rock, and in Britain too new rock labels, like Island, flourished).

The 1970s
The 1970s began as the age of the superstar. Rock musicians commanded huge record company advances and concert fees, employed armies of lawyers, accountants and roadies, and invested fortunes in their own studios and record companies. Solo artists like Paul McCartney and Paul Simon, and groups like Emerson, Lake and Palmer and The Who could determine their own

recording budgets, justifying all expenses, all advances, all self-indulgences, by reference to the final sales figures. The more money that was spent on making a record, it seemed, the more money was made on it. 1960s' affluent youth were becoming 1970s' affluent adults, with ever more spending power.

The success of the superstars (superstars because they crossed all taste barriers) masked the fragmentation of the music market that was going on around them. The 1970s saw, for example, a new separation between black and white musics. The chart success of 1960s soul (and the appearance of Otis Redding at the Monterey Festival, and Sly and the Family Stone and Jimi Hendrix at Woodstock) had suggested that the concept of "race" music was dead; and black musicians, certainly, borrowed techniques from rock. Producer Norman Whitfield, for example, drew on rock's studio ambition to develop a more elaborate, more tricky, more argumentative version of the Motown sound. This movement coincided with the aggressive political articulation of black consciousness, and early 1970s soul music was consequently "blacker" than it had been before – commenting

Singer songwriters like Paul Simon, *opposite above left*, James Taylor, *opposite above right*, and Joni Mitchell, *right*, used sophisticated new studio techniques to project their songs and themselves to the full.

on black American experience, aiming at black markets and using those elements of R & B that had not been appropriated by white musicians (funk, for example, with its complex bass rhythms, its use of horns and its ghetto-coded vocals). These developments were most obvious in the soundtracks written for the parallel black films (like Isaac Hayes's *Shaft* and Curtis Mayfield's *Superfly*).

The white rock audience, with its own styles and stars now, was simultaneously losing interest in black music; only Stevie Wonder was heard as comfortably experimental enough to count as an honorary rock star. And so black producers' recording skills and black film writers' elaborations of funk, became for white youth an aspect, once more, of the dance floor; while black consciousness music went underground, to emerge at the end of the decade as rap, the street talk of young blacks over a studio-clever beat. There was a parallel movement in Jamaica. The dance music of the 1960s, ska, became the more self-consciously black sound of reggae, and while Bob Marley could be sold to the rock audience because he had performing charisma, good songs and familiar, guitar-based arrangements, reggae itself remained a black music, popular among whites only as a cult.

Both "disco" and "reggae" became, like "Motown" too now, terms of rock abuse, describing music that rock fans heard as boring, monotonous or simple. In fact, it was disco's producers and deejays, Jamaica's dub mixers, who pioneered a new approach to recording, taking a new interest in the effects of re-mixing studio sounds and varying beat speeds, and in playing tricks with the record itself – speeding it up and slowing it down, adding echo and repeat and electronic noise. All these games were, eventually, played by rock musicians too (who took over the 12″ single and the idea of different mixes for different occasions), but they had made their first impression on the white market on the dance floor – and it was the dance floor to which rock musicians finally returned.

Within rock itself the rise of the superstars meant a new concern with glamour, which became the object of rock irony and rock fantasy. Glitter-rockers played games with it, like children with a dressing-up box; performers like Elton John and Rod Stewart lived more like Hollywood film stars than rock 'n' rollers; pop

Stevie Wonder and Bob Marley (inset), *left*, were, for different reasons, the only black artists acceptable to white rock audiences of the mid-1970s.

Glitter rockers like David Bowie, *above*, and The New York Dolls, *below*, took the new found glamour of the rock star out of the private jet on to the concert platform.

artists like David Bowie and Roxy Music in Britain and the New York Dolls in the United States, explored the star making process itself, its artificiality, its illusions of wealth and ease. The *image* of the rock star – previously taken to be quite natural (rock was sincere) or entirely false (a cynical sales device) now became part of musicians' creative effort. Music and image became integrated in the articulation of rock personality (and thus the way was prepared for the use of rock video).

For other musicians, though, such as Graham Parker in Britain and Bruce Springsteen in the United States, who were less arty and more committed to traditional rock 'n' roll values, there was an increasing sense that show biz rock lacked vital ingredients. Spontaneous energy, a direct tone of voice, the sense of community between performer and audience were denied by the musicians' money, equipment and fame. Rock music itself seemed to be increasingly clichéd, concerned obsessively with the difficulties of fame and wealth, irrelevant to day-to-day leisure needs. The roots of rock as a participatory culture, an immediate response to circumstances, were being neglected as the music became, instead, something that had to be mediated through an elaborate show-biz set-up.

Punk

This feeling was reflected too in the growing grass roots musical activities of semi-professionals (old and new) playing live rock 'n' roll and R & B locally, recording themselves in front room studios and putting out their own records. Out of this movement – pub rock in Britain, garage rock in the United States – emerged the explicitly anti-rock approach of punk. The immediate impact of a group like The Sex Pistols was shock – what was on display was a particular kind of nihilism, a gesture of refusal. But what was important about punk as popular music was its account of musical realism. Pitched against the rock artifice of expensive studio productions, elaborate stage shows, refined musical technique, well-crafted words and melody, was the raw punk sound of bashed guitars and battered drums, minimally competent musicians, four track recordings, crude club PAs. Punk songs were bursts of rage and boredom, immediate rough shouts. Such music was, in fact, as carefully thought out as progressive rock – its effect was a matter of artistic calculation – but its social meaning was different: this was music that anyone could make anywhere.

The new burst of local music making, the critique of rock superstardom and big business,

Sex Pistols poster

coincided with the end of the record sales boom. The industry, which expanded so remarkably from the mid-1960s to the mid-1970s, had reached its sales limit and even began to decline. There were various reasons for this. The recession in Europe and the United States affected all expenditure, and unemployment hit young people in Britain particularly hard, just as the 1970s rises in petrol prices cut into mobile young American pockets. At the same time, the youth bulge of the 1960s – on which rock prosperity had been built – was moving into middle age and, inevitably, cutting back on music buying, while the new rock generation was, in demographic terms, considerably smaller. Changes in leisure technology also affected musical consumption. The video tape recorder transformed home habits (more watching, less listening); hi-fi cassettes and home taping cut into record sales.

The rejigging of the multi-national entertainment corporations, as they eyed the leisure openings of the 1980s, had particularly dramatic effects in Britain: EMI and Decca, which had dominated British record production for forty years, were both taken over. Since the rise of The Beatles, British pop musicians have had an unprecedented international influence, but this influence has declined in the last ten years. Punk

was, by its nature, a nationalist movement; American and European disco were the 1970s world sound. In sales terms Britain is no longer the world's second major market – Japan and Germany are, after the United States, the best record selling territories, and it is their audiences who are likely to determine the international sound of popular music in the 1980s.

The 1970s ended in sharp contrast to the way they had begun: the booming business and the carefully consolidated different market tastes had become a worried business and a volley of musical experiment. The major record companies, concerned about their prospects, campaigned for a levy on blank cassette tapes and became more cautious than ever in their signing policies, while at the local level there were more musicians than ever playing more different kinds of music for more labels, more studios, more producers, more entrepreneurs. Punk itself rapidly became just another idiom, to be used or not at will, but its effects were lasting. In challenging 1970s record company conventions it had also challenged consumer assumptions. Music made without reference to commercial criteria could be much more quirky in its idea of what sounded good. The punks themselves were influenced by reggae, as well as pub and garage rock, and post-punk groups like The Human League used all sorts of sounds that had previously been kept apart – funk and glitter, rock and disco, avant-garde electronics (the German legacy of Can and Kraftwerk) and teenybop.

This reflected a second punk legacy: a

Electropop: the electronic music of German bands, such as Kraftwerk, *above*, influenced electropop bands like The Human League.

thoughtfulness about what popular music was for. Post-punk musicians have been determined to keep control of their sounds, to become part of the star-making machinery only on their own terms. The most important musical result of this has been the increased interest in the recording process, in production effects and in electronics. While rock was becoming an expensive business in the 1970s, its infra-structure was becoming cheaper and more accessible. Better and better sounds could be coaxed out of cheaper and cheaper equipment – whether electronic instruments like the synthesizer and its surrounding gadgetry, or electronic studio and recording devices. By the end of the decade popular musicians could make more noise and more noises, than ever before.

The late 1970s saw the continuation of several trends. In both the United States and Britain adult-oriented rock (AOR) – music slickly manufactured in the studio – continued to sell; *Rumours* became the best-selling album of all time for Fleetwood Mac, *below*. Others, like Bruce Springsteen, *below opposite*, have remained successful while committed to the rawness and spontaneity which mark rock 'n' roll's roots. Disco music, exemplified by the work of Chic, *above opposite*, retains its popularity. Blondie, *below centre*, helped to pioneer the video boom, now a growing industry marketing LP-length video cassettes as well as video promos for every potential hit single. The sustained success achieved by The Police, *right*, on both sides of the Atlantic marks them out as the latest in the line of great rock bands.

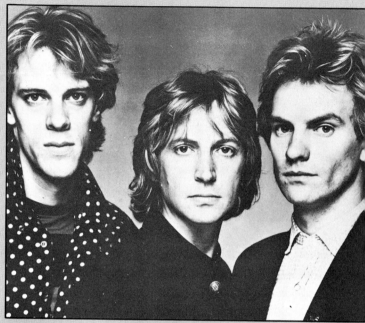

Pop and history

The problem of pop history is that it has to have a beginning and an end. It's impossible not to treat pop as news and change of fashion, not to describe styles in terms of progress – one sound leading to another. But this is only to skate over the surface of music's popular use and meaning. Pop is unchanging too: Frank Sinatra was as big a star in 1980 as in 1950, and numerous performers (like the country star Ernest Tubb and the R & B star Muddy Waters) made a living throughout these thirty years by not changing their basic style. Types of music may go out of chart fashion, except for the occasional "revival", but they don't stop being played and heard – there are still working trad jazz bands and rock 'n' roll singers and Mersey-beat groups, and there will doubtless still be punk and disco performers in the 1990s.

There are other ways, then, of writing the pop story – by tracing the continuities that run across the genre divisions. The history of dance music, for example, cuts across black and white styles, involves its own fads and follies (the jive and the twist, the shake and the hustle, the pogo), its own institutions (British Northern Soul, American Beach Music, gay discos and teenage ballrooms), its own mixtures of rhythm (from Jamaica and Nigeria, from Cuba and Brazil) and texture (from talking drums to syn drums). The history of lyrics, similarly, involves not just the 1960s development of folk-poetry, but also the preservation of word play, the legacy of pun and metaphor and fun with common speech that has passed down from Cole Porter to Smokey Robinson to Elvis Costello. And at the heart of all pop idioms is a catchy tune, a hook, a principle of melody that hasn't changed for fifty years.

From the musicians' point of view the history of pop looks different than from the fan's or critic's standpoint. The key change in the last thirty years hasn't been the multiplication of pop styles, but the reorganization of the division of music-making labour. In 1950 there were obviously different roles: the performer, the songwriter, the musical arranger, the session musicians and band members, the record producer, the recording engineer. By 1980 this division had broken down from both ends. Performers now wrote their own material, were involved in its production and arrangement, and were concerned about their recorded sound. To be a pop musician meant to be familiar with electronics, with amplification and recording techniques, with the sound mixing process in performance and studio alike. At the same time, the producer's and engineer's role had become in-creasingly creative. Their growing musical importance was reflected by the rise of inde-pendent studios offering unique, personal sounds and skills, and by new royalty arrange-ments – producers had as much creative claim on a record as its writers and performers.

These developments reflected changing musical ambitions and changing claims to musi-cal control, but they had been made possible, and necessary, by technological changes, by the ways in which new instruments and new methods of recording had transformed what it meant to make music in the first place. The story of pop can't be understood without reference, in particular, to the electric guitar, tape recording and the synthesizer.

The guitar

The most striking aspect of modern western pop is the dominant sound of the electric guitar. Country music and the blues, the American folk roots of pop, were both guitar-based forms of music, and the guitar's importance for them lay in its value as an instrument accompanying the voice. The guitar has a number of advantages over other instruments in this respect: it's flexible – strummed chords have simultaneous rhythmic and harmonic weight while individual strings can be plucked to play a tune; it's convenient – a performer can sing and play it at the same time, and can move with it easily round the stage and from show to show; and it's relatively easy to use effectively – efficient accompaniment doesn't need great musical virtuosity, which is why teenagers have picked up guitars so eagerly over the last twenty-five years.

The guitar already had a central place in grass roots American music by the 1920s, so it's not surprising that developments in guitar techno-logy have had such a startling effect on pop – and, indeed, guitar makers have always been concerned to solve pop guitarists' problems. The crucial development before the war was a result of the sudden popularity in the southern United States of Hawaiian guitarists. Hawaiian musicians got their unique sound by playing with a metal slide (an idea taken up by both the bottle-neck blues players and the country steel guitarists) and the resulting wailing effect suggested that the guitar could be vocalized – made expressive like the voice and voice-played instruments and able to sustain notes and vary tone and pitch in a vocal manner. Guitar manufacturers responded to this idea by developing ways of amplifying the guitar's notes electrically rather than with a sound box. Rickenbacker developed an electric "Hawaiian" guitar as early as 1931, but the solid body electric guitar emerged after the war (the Fender Telecaster came onto the market in 1948, the Gibson Les Paul in 1952) and it was this instrument that was important for country stylists like Merle Travis and blues stylists like BB King.

The immediate appeal of the electrically amplified guitar was its volume: guitarists could

Les Paul with his singing partner, Mary Ford.

now play loud enough to compete with any other noise. But what mattered more in the long term were the opportunities for new sounds. Guitarists were no longer dependent just on what their fingers were doing and on the sound quality of the guitar itself: electrical amplification was also a creative tool and, over the years, numerous effects devices have been invented – wah-wah pedals, fuzz boxes, tremolo arms. By the end of the 1960s the electric guitar in the hands of a virtuoso like Jimi Hendrix was an even more flexible, more personal instrument than the voice: it could be sweet and sour, bullying and pleading; it could make a unique, individual sound – rock fans can instantly identify the electric voices of, say, Chuck Berry, Bo Diddley, Eric Clapton, Frank Zappa, Mark Knopfler or Ry Cooder.

The bass guitar

The bass guitar shared in this development. The original electric bass, the Fender, was designed to allow players to play not just louder but more clearly and more precisely; the result was that the bass could also now carry a lead melodic line – hence its use as a riffing instrument in heavy metal and could be rhythmically fluid and personally expressive – hence its use in jazz, disco, reggae. The electric bass and the electric guitar became, then, synonymous with rock power – an easy finger movement could blast out a room – and rock guitarists were the easiest musicians for fans to identify with. The

recurring sight of audiences miming to the guitar – head back, eyes shut, face grimaced, fingers clutching – was a sign of how directly now these notes were heard to flow from personal feeling.

Recording

Recording was, in its early days, simply that: the direct recording of a performance onto a cylinder or disc. What record buyers heard was the sound of the original performance. The 1930s development of electrical microphones and amplification meant more accurate recordings – subtler, softer sounds could be captured and a greater range of tones preserved – but recording still meant recording a particular event, and this didn't change until after the war, with the use of tape.

Tape was an intermediary in the recording process: the performance was recorded on tape; the tape was used to make the master disc. And it was what could be done during this intermediate stage, to the tape itself, that transformed pop music making. First, producers no longer had to take performances in their entirety. They could cut and splice, edit the best bits of different performances together, cut out the mistakes, make records of ideal not real events. Secondly, on tape sounds could be added together artificially. Instruments could be recorded separately; a singer could be taped, sing over the tape, and be taped again. Such techniques gave producers a new flexibility – musicians no longer had to crowd in the same room, with all the problems of mike position, relative volume, etc – and enabled them to make records of performances, like a double tracked vocal, that were impossible live (though musicians and equipment manufacturers were soon looking for ways to get the same effects on stage).

In the early 1960s, then, distinctions began to be drawn between studio and live music, though, generally this was seen in terms of the studio improving the performance, compensating for the lack of live atmosphere. The next development, in the mid-1960s, was a system of multi-track recording which enabled sounds to be stored separately on the same tape and altered in relationship to each other at the final mixing stage, rather than through the continuous process of sound addition. This sort of multi-tracking gave record producers complete freedom to work on the tape itself, to produce a recorded "performance" that was actually put together from numerous, quite separate events. The judgements, choices and skills of the producers and engineers became just as significant

47

musically as those of the musicians and, indeed, this distinction – engineer/musician – became increasingly meaningless as the definition of music changed. Studio-made music need no longer bear any relationship to anything that can be performed live; records use sounds – the effects of tape tricks – that no-one has ever even heard before as musical.

Synthesizers

The growing importance of synthesizers has partly been the result of the emergence of electric guitars and tape recording. Pianists needed an instrument with the acoustic piano's rhythmic, melodic and harmonic qualities but with pop volume and power and pop mobility, so electric keyboards were invented, electrically amplified pianos like the Wurlitzer, the Fender Rhodes and the Clavinet. Other musicians were concerned to get studio effects live, to devise instruments that could use taped sounds, on-the-spot mixing – hence the Mellotron. Synthesizers too have answered both these demands, but the synthesizer also, crucially, creates completely new sounds. The pitch, tone and volume of electronically produced notes can be separated; they are variable elements, which is why electronic music sounds so different from amplified acoustic music and why such words as "cold" and "mechanical" are used to describe it.

Dr Robert Moog, inventor of the Moog synthesizer.

The Moog synthesizer was publicly unveiled in 1964; the nearest equivalent previous instruments in terms of producing sound electronically were, oddly enough, the electric organs – the Hammonds, Voxes and Farsifas so common in

early Sixties pop. Synthesizers were soon developed that could be worked vocally and percussively, though in pop they have mostly been played as keyboard instruments. They are, in technological terms, highly sophisticated — the banks of wires and knobs and lights even look daunting – but one joy of the synthesizer is that it allows people to achieve dramatic effects with minimal technique in traditional musical terms. By the end of the 1970s synthesizers had become sufficiently cheap to be accessible to many would-be pop stars; the resulting spread of synth-pop challenged the place of the guitar as the dominant pop instrument and threatened the traditional rock group line-up – drummers, for example, might appear to be unnecessary if musicians can plug into drum machines. The usual distinction between live and studio music makes no sense when tape-recorders become a stage instrument, when live performers work with pre-recorded sounds. The electric guitar became pop's most personal instrument and made rock a particularly aggressive form of self-expression, but the synthesizer remains obstinately impersonal – it is hard to hear its sounds as spontaneous, as an overflow of human feeling – and it is this effect that synthesizer musicians, particularly in Germany and Japan, have been concerned to explore.

Conclusion

I began this chapter by arguing that for all its commercial and technological trappings pop music is still the result of people's urge to make music for themselves, to turn experience and feeling into song and song into experience and feeling. In this story of pop I stressed the continuing importance of the voice, pop's personal touch. I have ended by noting the emergence of the impersonal sound of the synthesizer, the breakdown of the distinction between engineer and musician, and the collapse of any idea that a record or performance can ever, now, be a matter of *individual* expression – pop music making has become, by its nature, a collective process.

However, these two positions are not as contradictory as they look. Pop music has always been the result of tensions – between musicians and record companies, fans and businessmen, technology and art, expression and routine – and it's inevitable that, as the meaning of music making changes, so do such tensions. I'll go on listening to pop for the same reason as I have always listened – for the moments when the tensions seem resolved and out of endless curiosity about what will happen next.●

Writing and Arranging Music

*". . . it is the stuff that comes from
the heart, and not the clever
things, that works best."*
PAUL SIMON

The Popular Song Analyzed

A popular song is something kids sing in the playground, bus drivers whistle as they sell tickets and waiters hum as they carry trays back to the kitchen. It is a melody from a Broadway musical as much as it is *Ten Green Bottles* sung by cub scouts. Professionals sometimes call it the three-minute art form.

However good or bad a song is, it will have an emotive quality resulting from a combination of rhythm, melody, harmony and lyrics which creates a mood. Words give a song meaning, and so a song will affect many people in a similar way. Instrumental music, on the other hand, may strike each individual differently because what they make of the music will be more determined by their knowledge of music as a whole.

Film music, when heard in conjunction with images on a screen, will appear to sound different if removed from the visual stimulus. If the film has been seen by the listener, the music may conjure up scenes from the film; if the music is heard "cold", the musical experience of the listener will determine how they accept or interpret the music. For example, the unaccompanied mixed choir used in Ligeti's 'dawn of man' sequence in the film *2001 – A Space Odyssey*, created a perfect background, but heard out of context it can sound dissonant, weird and frightening, reflecting a lack of understanding of the composer's intent. In fact, the music was not written for the film but composed to be performed in concert before the film was even made. Thus, instrumental music is often experienced as a background to something else, although this may not have been the intention of the composer.

Instrumental works with strong melodies, such as those of The Shadows and Booker T. & the MGs, in fact follow the structural and harmonic standards of a lyrical song, which is why they have much appeal.

Rhythm

If you cannot dance easily to a song but find it good nonetheless, the chances are that the melody, harmony and lyrics are exceptional, because rhythm – if sufficiently infectious – is often the only element needed to sell a song. Remember, for example, the thunderous rhythms of Bo Diddley that captured the R&B

Bo Diddley rhythm

bands of the late 1950s and early 1960s. Buddy Holly's *Not Fade Away*, which appeared originally as the B-side of a single and became a hit for The Rolling Stones, used the same rhythm. The song has only two chords – E and A – but the rhythm thumped out by Charlie Watts and Bill Wyman against Mick Jagger's insistent maracas, topped off with Brian Jones' wailing harmonica created an animalistic sound that strengthened the Stones' image as the wild men of pop.

In direct contrast is Paul McCartney's *Yesterday*, wistfully sung to guitar and string quartet and achieving its emotional thrust through a sparcity of sound and quasi-classical arrangement. Having heard *Yesterday* cajoled, beefed-up and many times murdered in a thousand clubs and bars, I believe that McCartney's original version is the simplest and most successful, supporting my philosophy that the original of a song is usually the best.

Structure

The structure of today's songs varies considerably, but the classical *da capo* aria is still the most widely used form. This consists of:

verse one (with or without refrain)
verse two (with or without refrain)
bridge (or middle eight)
verse three
repeat bridge
repeat first or third verse
end

A hit that fits this structure perfectly is Elvis Presley's *His Latest Flame* in which, instead of a chorus, the refrain is the last line of each verse: "and Marie's the name, of his latest flame". In fact, the rhythm of the guitar and drums is a variation on Bo Diddley's:

Rather than finishing the song abruptly, as the writers of jazz, early blues and folk like to, pop songwriters try to "leave them with the melody still in their ears" because this adds to commercial appeal. Presley's song illustrates this perfectly: the hook – the catchy part of the tune – is left going around in the listener's head.

The *da capo* aria structure is fundamental to

Valerie Simpson and Nick Ashford

the balance of *His Latest Flame*. This structure can be varied in several ways: for example, an instrumental solo can follow the third verse prior to a return to the bridge, or such a solo can even replace the third verse. If the song needs to be short, there may be only one bridge.

Short songs and long songs

Three minutes is still the length of most pop songs because that used to be the official time allowed for a song on the radio. Diana Ross' superb *Ain't No Mountain High Enough*, by the two Tamla-Motown writers Nick Ashford and Valerie Simpson, is considerably longer than this, but fails in the truncated version as a single. The song's chorus runs as follows:

Ain't no mountain high enough,
Ain't no valley low enough
Ain't no river wide enough
to keep me from you.

The melody of the chorus opens the song with the singers singing "ah-ah-ah-ah-ah" instead of words. This is followed by the first verse, a repeat of the chorus sung to "ah", the second verse, and again the chorus to "ah". The bridge then follows, but is 16 bars long, twice the length one would expect from a middle eight. Approximately three-quarters of the way through the song the climax arrives, just where it should in a well-constructed piece of dramatic music. The chorus bursts in with "ain't no mountain high enough" while the band stops momentarily, punctuating the beginning of each measure.

The song then goes into a short, eight-bar instrumental with the chorus returning, the longer melody of the "ahs" now being sung with the words and interspersed with shorter snatches of "ain't no mountain high enough" alongside the chorus, creating a contrapuntal form. If the chorus of the song is A, the verse B, the bridge C and the instrumental D, the structure looks like this:

A	B	A	B	A	C	C	A	A	D	A fade
Ch.	V.	Ch.	V.	Ch.	Bridge	Ch.	Ch.	Coda	Ch.	
10	16	10	16	10	8	8	8	8	8	8

The verses are 16 measures each and the chorus 10 measures until it becomes a recurring series of 8 measure lengths at the end.

Contrapuntal form

This is a wonderful song, with a brilliant arrangement lasting about six and a half minutes. Unfortunately, before the advent of the 12-inch single, Motown released a three and a half minute version which gives only one chorus/verse/chorus before going into the second half of the bridge and then on to the rest of the song. This is akin to taking a chunk out of the middle of a classical symphony before the audience has become used to the main theme.

Another example of excellent writing for a long song is Jimmy Webb's *McArthur Park*. An entirely new section with a different melody suddenly appears in the middle of the song, followed by an up-tempo instrumental section – again different from anything that came previously – and the song culminates with a magnificent, operatic rendering of the main chorus. Such songs are exceptions to the rule and are successful only when handled by excellent writers and masterful arrangers. The development of a song into a suite of different sections is a speciality of Webb's; there have been other successful attempts at this, such as the amazing *Aja* by Steely Dan, a rock-jazz flirtation with the avant-garde.

Blues patterns

Our discussion of structure has so far dealt with a fundamentally western approach, but pop music, more than any other except perhaps jazz, relies on a mixture of African, Eastern, folk and country influences. Traditional European harmony pervades early pop to the extent that the blues generally use the three primary chords of a key. For example, the standard blues pattern in the key of C is: four bars of C, two bars of F, two bars of C, one bar of G, one bar of F and either two bars of C or one of C and one of G7 – 12 bars in all. Thousands of songs have been written using this basic structure: *Long Tall Sally*, *Blue Suede Shoes*, *Rock Around The Clock* and most of Chuck Berry's songs are just a few.

Notable exceptions to this are *Heartbreak Hotel*, an eight-bar blues (C,C,C,C7,F,F,G,CG7) that leaves out the return to C in the middle of the standard 12 bars and goes straight from F to G, which works because the eight bars are balanced. *You Keep A' Knockin'* by Little Richard has a similar structure (C,C,C,C,G,G,C, C), but is harmonically different from *Heartbreak Hotel*.

African and gospel influences

African influence, and to a certain extent folk, can be seen in songs like Stevie Wonder's *Uptight* where the chords oscillate a tone apart, and have nothing to do with the primary chord structure of I, IV, and V (tonic, subdominant, dominant). Here the basic structure (C,C,B-flat, B-flat, C,C,B-flat, B-flat) continues through the song with "uptight" coming in every four bars from the back-up singers, punctuating a four-bar call-and-response motif.

Many gospel-influenced songs such as the Isley Brothers' *Shout* and *Twist And Shout* derive their excitement from the simple device of audience participation: the audience is asked to respond by repeating or voicing the group emotion ("shout"), while the lead singer ad-libs or hammers out the lyric lines against the beat.

Single chord songs

Condensing this effect produces songs built on one chord. Breaking the chord into a series of riffs, or rhythmic figures, adds interest, but there is still only one chord lying behind them. The Knack's *My Sharona* is a powerful number whose main riff consists of a rhythmic punching of one note in octaves, although the flat third and fifth chords emerge briefly within it (see below).

Heavy metal groups, from Uriah Heep and Black Sabbath to Grand Funk Railroad and MCS, have all used the single chord technique with riffs as a basis for outrageous guitar solos, because it is easy to go overboard when you have no harmonic structure to worry about. All that remains is rhythmic interest from the drums and bass and as many different sounds from the guitar as you can create; within this realm Jimi Hendrix was king. Ry Cooder's *Hollywood*, completely in the chord of C, combines interesting half-spoken lyrics with a soul chorus ("down in Hollywood"), interspersed with great vocal displays from Chaka-Khan and Ry himself. The song never lacks interest, because the mood is well established by the band's solid groove.

Building on a riff

The riff, and later the electronic sequencer bass line, have always been building material for the pop song. In *Paperback Writer* and *Day-Tripper* by The Beatles, for example, it is the guitar riffs that grab the listener's attention and keep it to the end. This use of the riff is an extension of the

rock 'n' roll bass lines of the 1950s, themselves derived from the "walking" left hand of the early boogie-woogie piano players. Today, the riff has become a major element in jazz/funk and modern soul songs. Listen to any disco record – it is the bass or guitar riff that gets feet tapping. Master of the art is the group Chic, whose biggest hit, *Le Freak,* is simply a guitar riff with incidental vocals and an instrumental section that is actually a development of rhythmic intensity without melody. The riff is so solid it can easily stand alone, irrespective of who is singing or the lyrics of the song.

As long as it works musically, pop music has room for every kind of idea. It is not true, however, that the musician needs no more than a single harmony to make a song work. For a song to be something one person can play and sing, using a piano or guitar, usually some form of harmonic variation is required. Good examples of this include *Yesterday, Something* and *My Way.*

There are different forms of pop song construction, but all rely upon a memorable hook, interesting harmony and exciting rhythmic or emotional content. Most successful songs tend to include a simple and easily recognized element, and a musical feature that is original or surprising. Haircut 100's hit *Love Plus One* is one such example: the soprano sax leads into the fade-out with a catchy phrase and is joined by tenor saxes with a contrapuntal, big-band riff that melts perfectly with the sopranos and cuts across to accent the odd beats. By remaining "immobile", the recurring Gs in the second bar allow the notes B, C, D and C to create a bouncy, be-bop accent:

Shifting the accent on to an even beat is a favourite rhythmic device. For example the lead-in to the chorus of ABBA's *Money, Money, Money* contains a strong accent on the last quaver of the first measure, and this shifts the beat forward, creating what feels like the start of a new riff, but a quaver too soon. The last crotchet of the second measure is accented, throwing everything back into 4/4 time. This is syncopation, a trick used by many composers from Beethoven through Stravinsky to Frank Zappa.

Lyrics

Lyrics can have almost as much influence on a song's structure as harmonic progressions and riffs because they often determine phrase length and the type of melody. Bob Dylan's *A Hard Rain Is Gonna Fall,* for example, varies considerably in the number of lines per verse. The first verse, which begins with, "Where have you been my blue-eyed son, where have you been my darling young one" is reminiscent of earlier traditional folk ballads, and is followed by a resumé of strange places and imagery, all beginning with "I've been . . .". The number of "I've seen"s or "I've heard"s varies from verse to verse, so that instead of a regular four or eight lines, one verse will have five, another nine, and so on.

Another example, again from Dylan, of how the number of words can alter musical line length and enrich the over regular character of most lyrics, is *Sad-Eyed Lady Of The Lowlands.* Initially, the song rolls along in a steady 6/8 beat, but in the chorus – "where a sad-eyed prophet says no man comes" – instead of eight measures we suddenly find nine due to an extra measure that follows the word "comes". This structural change was made to allow the extra words of the second line to make their point, a very useful technque for avoiding rhythmic monotony.

Conversely, Stevie Wonder's *Happy Birthday* is a terrific example of the shortened phrase. The beginning verses of the song move merrily along in four-bar phrases until the chorus, at which point Stevie appears to have wanted to

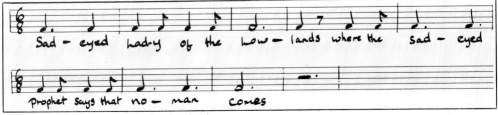

Bob Dylan's *Sad-Eyed Lady Of The Lowlands.*

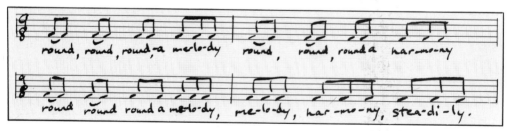

sing "happy birthday to you" without leaving the measure after each line silent, which would have kept the phrases to four bar lengths. Instead, he sings the lines one after the other, creating a six-beat instead of an eight-beat pattern (see above).

The last "happy birthday" does not have "to you" in it and so lasts only four beats. There are 16 beats to a line but instead of being divided up as 8-8, they come out as 6-6-4. A parallel in jazz would be the way in which Dave Brubeck divides up 9/8 time in *Blue Rondo à la Turk* into 2-2-2-3 instead of 3-3-3.

This brings me happily to the suitable use of lyrics for the subject matter of songs. There is such a variety of subjects covered in popular music that listing them all would take a very long time indeed. Suffice to say that love (returned or unrequited), death, politics, places and personal situations are probably the most widely-covered areas.

Sometimes music is extolled simply for its own sake. Al Jarreau has written words to Brubeck's *Blue Rondo à la Turk* which describes music as it is constructed. The words are admirably suited to the music, because the strange accents of the 9/8 time in four beats would make a personal subject difficult to imagine after the Brubeck Quartet's excellent recording. The opening states simply:

Ronettes, Crystals, Righteous Brothers and Ike and Tina Turner), The Beatles, Burt Bacharach and Hal David (all those great songs for Dionne Warwick, among others), Bacharach's work with Carole Bayer Sager, Holland-Dozier-Holland (the wealth of material from the Tamla Motown stable), Crosby, Stills and Nash, Stevie Wonder, The Eagles, The Bee Gees and a host of modern groups from Squeeze and Madness in England to the New York groups, Kraftwerk in Europe, Yellow Magic Orchestra in Japan; and Air Supply and Rick Springfield in Australia.

The pop song today

Never has there been a time when more sources of inspiration are available to the writer and more variety of music to the listener. In some areas, a "local" record or song will be a refreshing alternative to an otherwise pervasive middle-of-the-road sound. Since Small Faces' Steve Marriott delivered *Lazy Sunday Afternoon*, a number of English groups have proved that the right accent can give local flavour to a song, which, in Marriott's case, harks back to music hall but sells because it is about real life. *Cardiac Arrest*, by Madness, is a warning to the workaholic; Charlie Daniels' *Devil Went Down To Georgia* appeals directly to American southern rock audiences; Elvis Costello's *Good Year For The Roses* merges Nashville's finest with

and it continues throughout as a kind of jazz/soul homage to music.

In this book many artists, writers, arrangers and performers have used examples to illuminate musical points and references. In order to understand the popular song fully, it is necessary to listen to a lot of different songs. In my view the great songwriters – those who have led pop in new directions – are the following in chronological rather than merit, order: Cole Porter and Irving Berlin, Buddy Holly, Phil Spector (The

English irony: and the comic impressionists the Heebee Geebees have many audiences, including the subjects of their parodies, rolling in the aisles.

Pop music is a fast and furious business, but more than anything else it is disposable; it is music for *now*. Some songs, great songs, live on years after as milestones, but most importantly, they reflect people's thinking, their hopes and dreams and the social values of their time. Most of all, though, pop music should be fun.●

How to Write Songs

When I was thirteen I saw my sweetheart sipping slurpies at the Dairy Queen with a rival and I went home and wrote my first song: five years later I was astounded to discover I had become a professional songwriter. The decisions I made then were instinctive; I wrote songs in a certain way because they felt right and, until I began to think about writing this piece, I have probably never given a single moment's thought to the logical process I use every time I write a song.

Types of song

One of the first decisions I must make when I begin to work on a song is what kind of song I wish to create. The following is an abbreviated list of the basic song types that might constitute an ambitious songwriter's repertoire.

The ballad was originally a musical narrative. Nowadays the term refers to a love song with a moderate to slow tempo.

The country ballad is probably descended from folk music of the British Isles. It usually has a slow tempo – commonly in 3/4 time – and inevitably deals with the pangs of unrequited love. It utilizes simple chords, melodies and traditional American instruments, such as the steel guitar, harmonica and acoustic guitar.

Rhythm and blues (R & B), a forerunner of rock, is the logical evolution of 12-bar blues into complex rhythms, chord progressions and orchestrations. Traditionally Black music, it frequently utilizes brass and reed sections, electronic organs and electric guitars and basses.

The R & B ballad developed from R & B, and found its own unique expression in Motown (short for "motortown", the city of Detroit). These are love songs in moderate tempo; a favourite way of performing them is with a string section and a straight four in the bar feel.

Rock 'n' roll, or rock, was up-tempo party music, spawned by the advent of electric guitars. It was traditionally small combo music utilizing blues motifs from the American South and strongly syncopated. It developed with groups such as The Beatles and The Rolling Stones who incorporated sophisticated chord progressions and subject matter. Mick Jagger once said that "true rock 'n' roll must be about sex."

The rock ballad is a love song with a heavy back beat. Instrumentation, motifs and vocal style are derived from traditional rock 'n' roll, but are presented in a moderate or slow tempo.

Special material is found in musical comedy, television and films, where many unique song types have evolved to serve a specific purpose. These may be based on traditional folk themes or on styles that are intrinsic to the subject matter.

It is essential to study all song types and as a serious songwriter to learn to imitate them, both because they are proven commodities, and because a songwriter's chances of success are greatly increased by his or her versatility. There are, of course, many variations – hybrids and cross-breeds – on these basic song types.

Choosing a title

Once you have decided the type of song you wish to write, the title is the next most important thing. It almost invariably generates the thrust or theme of the song's lyrics and often appears rather conspicuously at the beginning or end of a verse or chorus. I choose a title before I begin to write the lyric or melody. I am at liberty to change the title at any time, but by choosing it first I have anchored the entire process to something stable.

An obvious shortcoming of most songs submitted to me by aspiring songwriters is lack of continuity. Even extremely talented and creative songwriters experience frustration over deciding how to continue a line of thought, and it is therefore helpful, when you set out, to have a destination in mind. A clever or touching phrase is extremely valuable as a target for a lyric line, and it follows that in most cases this should be the song's title. While experience may provide other solutions to the problem of continuity, choosing a title is certainly not a bad way to begin.

Where do song titles come from? They need not be complicated or artificial; many of the greatest consist of a single evocative word, such as Paul McCartney's *Yesterday* and Bill Anderson's *Still*. I often look to everyday speech for simple phrases whose very familiarity increases the possibility of writing a hit. A songwriter should always listen for interesting turns of phrase at the dinner table or to a friend's unique insight into a common problem or feeling.

A song's title often comes from intense emotions that the songwriter needs to express; deeply felt convictions about people, places or things have been at the heart of some of the most successful songs. A simple word or phrase that can be applied uniquely or obliquely to a subject is ideal: a perfect example of this is Paul Simon's *Still Crazy After All These Years*.

Choosing a form

Having chosen a title that reflects the subject, style and intent of my poetry-to-be, I next confront the more difficult task of choosing the form of the song. Much of what has been written to explain song form is cliché-ridden and outdated, and I am therefore presenting my own system of classification. (I have dispensed with the amorphous As, Bs and Cs normally used to refer to a song's parts, because I feel more specific terminology is needed.)

The verse In poetry, one line is called a verse and a sequence of lines is called a stanza; in songwriting, however, a sequence of lines is called a verse. For our purposes, a verse may be any number of lines in any meter or combination of meters.

A verse can fulfil two functions in the form of a song: it can stand alone or it can precede a chorus. When a verse stands alone it comprises a complete thought. Such verses almost always end with the title of the song, for example, *Walk On By* by David and Bacharach. When a verse precedes a chorus, on the other hand, the last line will not usually be the song title. Instead, it will be used to provide a lead-in, or set-up, for the chorus, as heard in *You've Lost That Lovin' Feeling* by Spector, Mann and Weil.

The chorus always follows a verse or bridge and, by its very nature, is a repetition of the central theme; think of *The Night They Drove Old Dixie Down* by J. R. Robertson, for example. Sung choruses probably originated in religious and church music; they were intended to be catchy, repetitive lyrics and melodies which the con-

Jimmy Webb's 1982 album

gregation could easily remember. We do not use the word so differently today; the chorus of most popular songs is augmented with additional instrumentation or voices. A tuneful, easily sung chorus is often called a hook because it is intended to lodge itself in the listener's mind, for example, *Baby, Baby Don't Get Hooked On Me*, by M. Davis.

Sometimes it is advisable to modulate the end of a verse to a different key – often higher – to "set-up" the chorus, and, whether this is done or not, the chorus should always have a different melodic and chordal character than its verse.

The last line of the chorus is often the song's title, but, almost as often, the title will be the first and main statement of the chorus, in which case it is often repeated for effect before a secondary title, or contributing phrase, ends the chorus. An example of this is *Going Out Of My Head*, by David and Bacharach.

The bridge is used to cleanse the palate, to eliminate the boredom of too many identical verses or choruses; this is why the bridge is often referred to as a release or breakstrain. Its melodic and chordal character must be essentially different from the verse and chorus, and it may occasionally provide other relief in the form of modulation to a different key, often higher.

Here then, are some examples of combinations of these component parts, as found in some of my songs.

The Worst That Could Happen: verse / chorus / verse / chorus / bridge / chorus.
The Moon's A Harsh Mistress: verse / verse / instrumental bridge / (modulation) / verse.
In *Up, Up, And Away*, although the chorus consists of only one line, the form is still similar: verse / chorus / verse / chorus / bridge / verse / chorus.
Didn't We: verse / verse.

These simple parameters are rarely exceeded, but experimentation is enjoyable, and often, as in the case of *MacArthur Park*, advisable: verse / chorus / verse / chorus / verse / verse / instrumental bridge / (modulation) / chorus.

I caution against over-planning when creating a song form; songs often have aspirations of their own.

Writing the song

Whether the words or the music come first in the songwriting process is the question most frequently asked of professional songwriters. Frankly, this question is about as sensible as the paradoxical "chicken or the egg" riddle. The words and music for *Didn't We* came into my

head simultaneously; but usually I first get the title and some idea of the story or feeling I wish to convey, and then devote serious energy to the music.

The second most serious failing of aspiring songwriters is a tendency to lapse into musical cliché. It is simply not true that all tunes have already been written; sometimes the hardest task is to avoid copying yourself. I try to select an unusual combination of intervals to form a melody and a reasonably unique chord structure to accompany this, because it is often the chord structure that makes the difference between a commonplace, overly familiar melody and one that, at least, creates an illusion of originality.

Short of plagiarism, all forms of existing music should be studied and emulated for their unique qualities, especially the classics. I believe strongly, for example, in the classical technique of substitution – using an unexpected chord – and in what I call "alternate basses", bass notes that are not the tonic of the chords sounded.

Words on to music

With a song title, a form and at least a working model of the melody and chord structure, I am ready for the hardest work of all: superimposing the lyric over the melody.

The rhythmic patterns of a melody often naturally suggest the number of syllables in a given phrase. Often, the first words that come to mind – nonsensical or unrelated to the song's title as they may be – provide the best clue to the eventual construction of a phrase, and substitution may be made immediately to point the line more directly at the target – the song title – which will usually be at the end of a verse or the beginning of a chorus. At any point in this superimposition process the melody may, and should be, changed to accommodate the obvious suitability of certain words and phrases to each other. Conversely, the writer may wish to change the lyrics to preserve a particularly exciting musical passage.

Writing lyrics

One music encyclopaedia defines a song as "the musical setting of a poem". The great majority of songs deal with highly emotional material – they are either happy or sad, with few songs falling in between. It would seem proper therefore to refer to lyrics as poetry, because poetry, as defined by Clement Wood, is "the expression of thoughts which awake the higher and nobler emotions, or their opposites, in words arranged according to some accepted convention." However, the regular meter of most lyrics makes them technically *verse*. Nonetheless, these two definitions of lyrics do coexist peacefully: verse representing rhythm and poetry representing emotional content.

Sadly, the lyrics written by most beginning songwriters are rarely great, and are often poor enough to prevent the song from being recorded. I believe this is because the writers have not spent enough time reading the great poets and absorbing their techniques of writing and expressing imagery. Someone might say, "Surely, this is not the path to originality." I would reply that without studying the great poets, most would-be songwriters will not possess the tools with which to create originality. A study of Dylan Thomas will indicate immediately some of the possible and desirable uses of words, and point the way towards an understanding of imagery. Imagery might be defined as "describing the obvious by comparing it to the unobvious."

Sherlock Holmes – or at least his creator, Conan Doyle – believed in the science of observation, that one might deduce facts from a series of seemingly unrelated clues. It is the poet's task, since he already knows the solution – the song's title – to provide the listener with isolated and seemingly unrelated clues. This is best accomplished by observing the behaviour of people and nature, patterns of speech and physical responses, and describing these with unique similes and metaphors or in "unobvious" ways – Paul McCartney's *Eleanor Rigby* is an excellent example of such a lyric. Only the songwriter will know if he has succeeded in this difficult task, but the listener will certainly know if he has not.

It is fortunate that a poet is often forced to seek an unusual way of expressing a thought in order to complete a rhyme. In fact, rhyming dictionary in hand, it is advisable to explore all possible solutions to a rhyme scheme, including changing the original word selected for rhyming against to one that is more rhythmical, clever and to the point.

Although many songwriters scorn its use, a rhyming dictionary contains rhymes that most of us cannot possibly remember and catalogues them for easy access. Its one drawback is that, if used fanatically, it may produce stilted or strained rhymes (rhymes for rhymes' sake). It should be used only to find natural-sounding language which still manages to avoid cliché.

A thesaurus also deserves a place on top of the piano; it enables the poet to find alternative words that mean essentially the same thing. If a rhyme scheme is stubborn and difficult to complete, a thesaurus may suggest another word that is more easily and naturally rhymed; and when a word of a certain syllable length refuses to complement or fuse with the melody, a thesaurus may furnish another word of different syllable length that fits neatly and suggests even more unique imagery.

The words of all songs need not be rhymed; some of the most evocative language of the last two decades is found in John Lennon's *I Am The Walrus* in which he clashed words together with a great natural ferocity to produce a series of fascinating, surreal images. Nor need the songwriter always construct patterns of imagery that can be understood by a five year-old. When Bob Dylan speaks of "a chrome horse diplomat who carried on his shoulder a Siamese cat", we picture an individual, although he has not been described in great detail; Dylan has made us feel disdain for him and has said in a more succinct way: "This man is hard and pompous, he is cold and powerful, he waits, he watches and he plots."

It is not my purpose to try to explain the complete lexicon of the serious poet – there are innumerable books which explain the mathematical science of constructing the many forms of verse. However, some study of the classical technique is invaluable in mating lyric to melody. I have often found, for instance, that the rhythm of a certain musical phrase may run counter to the natural accents of its accompanying lyric line, even though the number of syllables may fit the notes precisely. It is necessary, in such an instance, to adjust the lyric, using some of the basic rules of meter, to slide it forward or backward until its natural accents become synchronous with the melody.

A well-written poem, possessing original imagery and expression, perfectly measured and rhymed, once melded with a unique melody will create a near flawless, albeit sometimes sterile, song; the traditional methods should not be completely disregarded.

Evaluating a finished song

The final part of the songwriting process is often the most painful: self-evaluation. When I have completed a song, I ask myself the following questions:

Is this the kind of song I wanted to write? (If the song is good, this question can be omitted.)

Have I created an inventive melody and chord structure?

Have I used original imagery in seeking out my target – the song title? If there are any negative responses, I must go back and rewrite the song – a tiresome fate, but endured with grim stoicism by many who are successful. ●

Songwriting

Songwriting is not as easy as it used to be. Browsing through sheet music of the past, one is struck by the fortunes made from simple songs such as *Goodnight Irene* and *The Man Who Broke The Bank At Monte Carlo*. In those days music publishers printed music regularly, few singers wrote their own material and hits were somehow easier to pick. The successful songwriters of today, however, frequently wear more than one hat, doubling as singers, musicians, record producers or even managers. Most artists write their own material, and solo singers are conspicuous by their absence. The top pop groups either collaborate among themselves or contain a songwriter of the standard of Sting, Mike Barson or Phil Oakey. Many of today's hit records reveal that the song itself is not the key selling factor but is more a coat-hanger on which the record producer can hang some saleable sounds.

Listen to and analyze today's hits for their style, lyrics and chord changes, because these are the songs people want. If there is a shortage of songs in any one style today, it is probably the tuneful, fast rock opuses such as *Bad Moon Rising, I Will Survive* and *Proud Mary*. Aim to write something equivalent to *River Deep, Mountain High* or *Reach Out, I'll Be There*. If you want to write ballads, try to make them as brilliant as *You've Lost That Loving Feeling* or *Ain't No Mountain High Enough*.

Starting a song

How does a tune come into being? Rarely when it is consciously sought; perhaps when driving through the night something comes into your head; or, more likely, when sitting with your guitar and moving through a chord sequence a melody is suggested. Sometimes an interesting title will provide a hook and jumping-off point. A memorable, totally original title will attract attention, and having a good title to begin with is better than skimming through the lyrics to find something that will just suffice.

It is useful to keep a list of titles and ideas for possible songs – something you hear in conversation, a newspaper headline, an everyday phrase (*How Do You Do*) or a play on words (*I Second That Emotion*). A good hook can sometimes lead to a good tune and the lyrics will then

flow without effort.

Collaboration with a friend who is on the same musical wavelength can be an advantage, especially if you are in a rut or find your inspiration running dry. Few hits today are written by just one person; collaborating can spark off ideas and provide constructive criticism. There are many useful organizations such as American Guild of Authors and Composers (AGAC) in the United States and The British Academy of Songwriters, Composers and Authors (BASCA) in Britain which provide free and friendly advice.

Building up a song

Study chord formation and make yourself aware of the differences between as many chords as possible. Note the different effects created, for example, by G2 and G9; how a good bass line gives a solid foundation to a chord progression and thus the tune; how a "pedalled" bass note with changing chords in the right hand can create a modern effect; how occasional dissonant harmony suits some songs – consider the subtle differences between B-major7 with a flattened fifth, B diminished and C-sharp7 with a flattened ninth – note that in all these chords F natural plays a prominent part, but its importance varies.

The emotional effect of chord changes can be spine-chilling, so try experimenting with inversions (where the bass note is not the root of the chord). First inversion (E on G-sharp, for example) is wonderfully churchy; second inversion (E

Bob Barratt's notes of ideas for songs

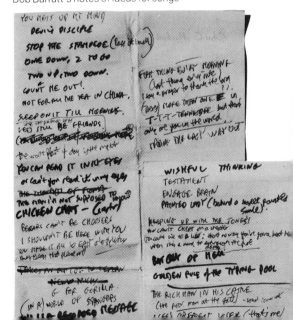

Successful songwriters, *above left*, Conway Twitty, composer of *It's Only Make Believe*, Claude Francois (*My Way*); *above*, Carole Bayer Sager (*You're Moving Out Today*); *left*, Bob Dylan; *below*, Phil Oakey of The Human League.

on B) is similar but different; and third inversion (E7 with the seventh in the bass) is always interesting.

Discover how changes from one section of a song to the next can be effective. Try, for example, going from a relative minor key, such as G minor to B-flat major; or a sudden change of a minor sixth, say, starting in C and cutting abruptly to A-flat as a bridge or middle-eight.

Do not be afraid to stay on one basic chord if it works. *Proud Mary* is an example of this; when the chord eventually changes the effect is dramatic. A bright guitar-based song like *Gentle On My Mind*, however, may be strengthened by changing the inner harmonies while keeping the bass on the root note of the chord – in this song the inner harmonies change as follows: E to E-major7 to E6 and back to E.

In a ballad, a repeated pattern of phrasing – incorporating rhythm and melody – can help to ingrain the tune in the listener's mind. Good examples of this are *Strangers In The Night, It's Impossible* and *My Way*.

Versatility is a great asset; avoid writing everything in mid-tempo, 4/4 time, and in the key of C-major. Tension can be built in many ways – transferring an accent forward by a quaver, holding it back by a crotchet, writing the odd phrase entirely across the beat – but the best way is to start your melody in a low register and build, as in *It's Only Make Believe, River Deep, Mountain High* and other successful songs.

Aim to write a record rather than a song and, even if you are not an experienced arranger, think in terms of orchestration. The interweaving of vocal lines within a vocal group interpretation, or between solo singer and back-up vocalists, gives a professional polish exemplified in the classic Tamla-Motown releases.

Trends change fast and songwriters like Neil Sedaka who have moved with the times for 25 years or more cannot but be admired. In the 1930s most songs had an 8- or 16-bar verse, followed by a 2-bar refrain in A,A,B,A formation. Song structure has steadily become more free, so that nowadays anything goes, although a certain amount of light and shade and recurrent chorus are usual.

Lyrics

Trends in lyric writing change quickly also, so watch your use of words. The genius and wit of Cole Porter and Oscar Hammerstein found a home in musicals, but the best outlet for witty or complex lyrics today is in country music, although "idea" pieces such as *You're So Vain, You're Moving Out Today,* or *Where Do You Go*

To My Lovely? are always welcomed in the pop market. Thirty years ago 90 per cent of lyrics were straightforward love songs and 10 per cent were novelties. Today a novelty can still break through – *Coward Of The Country*, for example – but it is a tough world for the ordinary love song; the lyrics have to be painstakingly contemporary to be successful.

Half of the songs in the charts are not about love. The near-biblical imagery of Paul Simon, Bob Dylan and Leonard Cohen has spawned descendants such as Bob Geldorf's *I Don't Like Mondays* and Ultravox's *Vienna*.

Although there are few rules about lyric-writing nowadays, words still need to sound good. Nothing sounds worse than a misplaced accent or a forced rhyme, and no word should be used simply because it is the only one you can think of. Use a rhyming dictionary with caution; the best words, like the best tunes, flow naturally.

The lyrics must also fit the character of the melody. "You can lift me high, you can bring me down," for example, will sound odd if "high" is sung on a low note and "down" on a high note. A bright melody normally signals a happy song unless it is tongue in cheek, such as *How Could You Believe Me When I Said I Loved You When You Know I've Been A Liar All My Life*. A minor key is often best suited to sad lyrics; a straight waltz (3/4 time) with harsh snarling lyrics is probably better changed to 12/8 or even 9/8.

Rather than fill every bar with a gabble of words, leave space. Four- or eight-bar links can be effective, perhaps reiterating a catchy phrase stated in the introduction.

Advice for beginners

A Bachelor of Music degree is not essential, although Harvard School of Music did Cole Porter no harm. It is a shame that more music graduates do not turn to pop music, because such people have a formidable armoury of musical weapons at their disposal. The more musical theory you know, the more tools you have at your fingertips which will greatly facilitate the process of songwriting.

If youth is on your side – if you can stay in touch with the top 100 – your chances of breaking into songwriting will be greatly improved. If you can actually break new ground and at the same time interest those people who have an ear for the commercial – in other words, if you can write a song as original as, in their time, were *Norwegian Wood, Up, Up And Away, Winner Takes It All* or *Purple Haze* – you should be on your way to a successful songwriting career.●

Songwriting

Paul McCartney in conversation with George Martin.

George *I'd like to take one of your songs and then talk about the way it started.*

Paul Shall we pick one that you know a lot about as well so that you can fill in? . . . *Ebony and Ivory?*

George *Now how did that start? What was the thought process – did you think of the tune and then start to think about words – how did you begin?*

Paul I was in Scotland and, as can sometimes happen, one good time to write songs is when you're not in a very good mood. It's like a kind of psychiatrist's couch in a way, and often what you do is take your guitar or piano, your musical "crutch", and go off in a room and sort of sulk almost; you sulk to the song. It makes you feel better because you're getting it out. And as I recall, I wasn't feeling that brilliant, so I thought, "oh hell, go and get away," and so I went into a little studio I've got there and I sat at the piano – the Rhodes. With me it's always piano or guitar: that's the only two ways I write; I rarely write in my head, although I do a little bit.

I'd had this title lying around for a while. the whole thing goes back quite a few years, when on TV, or on the radio, I heard Spike Milligan make this analogy with black and white notes on the piano; he'd said, "you know it's a funny kind of thing – black notes, white notes, and you need to play the two to make harmony folks!" He just made a little joke out of it. I thought: "yes, this is a good analogy for harmony between people because if you've just got the black notes you're limited, and if you've just got the whites you're limited; eventually you've got to go into them both. So I was thinking, "if I was going to write a song about that, what might it be called?" And I came up with the idea of ebony and ivory by thinking what are those actual things made of? I don't know if they're actually made of ebony.

George *They used to be; they're not any more, just painted wood. They're not ivory either – plastic now; that's why they don't go yellow!*

Paul So I thought ebony and ivory sounds nice. Black is easily associated with ebony; there's a magazine called *Ebony.* Ivory I wasn't too keen on us coming from elephant's tusks but I thought, well still . . . it symbolizes it. So I had this little thing, ebony and ivory, so when I sat down in this

not particularly good mood, I thought, "O.K., let's see what can we do with it." I then tried to paraphrase Spike's thought. I sat down at the piano, selected a key, and it's the sort of a key you feel like; I felt a bit like E Major that day. I hit the chord E and the tune just came on hearing the chord and messing around a bit; the next chord, F sharp minor, being a natural thing in the E sequence. *Ebony and Ivory*, and I thought, "well that's quite nice, a little bit of tune started off" and then, *"sit together, go together, live together, in perfect harmony – ivory –* good that's a nice little rhyme." *Side by side on my piano keyboard,* I thought, "Yes that's O.K. because it explains the whole thing about this analogy on the keyboard." *Oh Lord why can't we?* – I think that got a little bit changed later on. *Why won't we? why don't we?* It wasn't very exact when I first got it, and that was all I had that day; that's all that came up.

I really liked that, so I stuck it down on a bit of tape and thought that's a good basis for a song. It's a nice chorus and I liked the tune. I liked that little jump of a fourth in the opening phrase. Then, *We all know that people are the same wherever we go;* that came later. I knew I couldn't just do it with the chorus; I needed a verse and it is often quite hard when you've got this little inspirational thing. Often I find I've said it in those first four lines, and I don't actually want to say any more. If I was being artistically true to myself, I'd make the rest of it instrumental; but you know songwriting – you've got to do better than that. That's where the job set in on that one. Often the second verse has to say it again in a different way and still retain the interest. In fact eventually, you remember, I was going to try and write another verse. *We all know that people are the same wherever we go, There is good and bad in everyone* etc. In fact I did try, but it wasn't good. It was a repeat, and it wasn't poetic – the words didn't scan nicely. I thought, "no, that's the only verse that really fits with the chorus," so that's why we started to get into modulations and repeated it that second time.

The original idea was that I could sing this with somebody black to further symbolize the whole thing, by having a black man and a white man singing side by side on their piano, because for me it was a message song. My favourite first choice was Stevie Wonder. I'd sing it all through once and he'd sing it all through once, hopefully giving his own interpretation, giving another meaning to the lyrics almost. You remember we did the demo; that was the way I envisaged it.

Paul McCartney and George Martin. (Photograph by Linda McCartney.)

The problem I was talking about before, I had felt with the chorus: I'd almost said it *all*. Then, when I'd got that verse, I thought well I've *really* said it all now; there's no way forward unless I try and try and try. I really couldn't get anything I was happy with, so then your modulation became another part of the song.

George *Now, I remember how it developed from there: at the studio in Montserrat it was just the two of you – you and Stevie Wonder – really building it from nothing. The interesting thing to me is that both of you were multi-talented people and, for me, it was unique to have these two people starting alongside each other and going parallel – you on the real piano and Stevie on the Fender – and gradually we built up from there.*

Paul Stevie on drums and me on bass, and I remember it was your idea to keep it just the two of us, because at a certain point we were thinking we might get somebody else in to help with the harmonies or whatever. But we decided no, let's just make it a McCartney-Wonder job.

George *And when we came away from Montserrat it was virtually finished except for the backing vocals.*

Paul Yes, we'd done it all.

George *You put on basic piano, bass, and guitar, and Stevie had done Fender Rhodes, CS80 and Moog synthesizers and drums, and you did the drums on the other one.*

Paul We did backing vocals with Stevie and we did our technique of both singing the same line. It was very much a co-thing. It was one of the nice things about talking about the song; the original inspiration being a black fellow and a white fellow. Another very interesting thing I thought about the song at the time is that, when I played the melody on the piano, ebony happened to be two black notes and ivory happened to be all white notes which is something I kept meaning to bring out in video clips. I tried it, but they didn't get it to look right; but that's always very encouraging when you get a bit of magic like that: it's like, ooh He's on our side, it's working for us. And eventually – when you said let's keep it two people, I think it's nicer, it's a better idea, it's more complete that way – I was happy to do that.

So this theme that started just in the writing carried right through to the recording and even crazily enough right through to the video itself. We had those big hang-ups when Stevie couldn't come for the video and it was *almost* going to be a big wash-out, the whole thing. I rang him and said we're all waiting, and he said he couldn't make it for five days (which was all we had in the schedule), so we did all our video bit in London and he did his bit in L.A. Not the song though: some people have since said to me, "Is it true that you recorded your bit of the song in London, and his bit miles away?" The song itself wasn't done like that; it was a "live" performance.

George *Would you say that* Ebony and Ivory *is fairly typical of the way you write. There isn't a standard way is there?*

Paul No, not really. Talking very generally, originally John and I always used to write on guitars, because there wasn't a pianist in The Beatles. There wasn't a piano thing; in fact you used to do nearly all the piano stuff, especially anything that needed fingering – we had to call in the "experts"! So it was nearly all done on guitar and, when we got into piano and stuff, I wrote things like *When I'm Sixty-Four.* That was possibly the first song I ever wrote on the piano.

George *And generally, did the melody come without the words? Or did they come together?*

Paul That's where there's no formula.

George *A lot of people, even to this day, think that John wrote music and you wrote words or vice versa.*

Paul No way.

George *Or that you collaborated on songs. I think it is worthwhile to put on record that you used to write your songs individually quite a long way back.*

Paul Before we started writing together, we were separate writers. The first thing I ever wrote was a song called *I Lost My Little Girl.* I was fourteen. It was the guitar chords, G G7 C, and against those falling chords I sang that going up thing, *"I woke up late this morning"* (see below).

That is quite a nice sort of little early rock 'n' roll tune. John, I don't think, had written anything at that time. I first saw him when he was at a Woolton Village Fete; he was on the side show. He was in a checked shirt and had this skiffle group, and he'd got this Del Viking song *Come Go With Me* which was a big hit then. They obviously hadn't got the record because he didn't have the words; he'd just heard it, picked it up and liked it and he'd written all his own words, "Come go with me to the penitentiary" – kind of skiffley words, folksy words – so he had virtually re-written the song. I think it was one of his first songwriting efforts. But then, once we'd found this interest in common and thought we'd like to write songs, our major aim was: what will be the next new beat, will it be calypso? This would be the year that Butlin's brought in rock and calypso ballrooms! I was fifteen.

George *That must have been about 1957.*

Paul And we were taking things like *New Musical Express,* just as punters – not in a group yet – just on the edges. All the Lonnie Donegan and skiffle and stuff was coming in and getting everyone interested in guitars; and Elvis, Buddy Holly, Chuck Berry records were around. So we sagged off from school (we were both at school still I think), although John must have just been near to leaving; he was at Quarry Bank School, and I was at another local grammar school, Liverpool Institute High School. We used to sag off to my house nearly always, because my dad went to work and we'd started to look for this new beat. We were trying to think what's it going to be: Latin hasn't been done for a while – Edmundo Ros revisited!, maybe we could get away with this, it's beat-y. (It's funny because now Latin's coming back: Kid Creole, a lot of the Soul Sister stuff. A lot of the young groups think it's the really hip thing.) So we were looking around for this new beat. Was it going to be rock? For the life of us we couldn't find it, so we were just kicking away four-in-the-bar just to make a good old row and keep everyone on the beat for dancing. The ironic thing was, of course, that the minute we stopped trying, we managed to find the new beat which was crazy because that's what we'd spent all our early days trying to do. So John and I wrote a bunch of songs.

George *Individually?*

Paul No, from then on, I think, we wrote stuff together. I don't think John really wrote much individually. I only had this one song *I Lost My Little Girl* in which the lyrics were a bit diabolical:

I woke up late this morning
My head was in a whirl
And only then I realized
I lost my little girl
Uh huh, uh huh uh
Her clothes were not expensive

And this is the line that used to make John cringe:

Her hair wouldn't always curl
I don't know why I loved her
But I lost my little girl
Uh huh, uh huh uh

At the time I'm talking about we managed to get

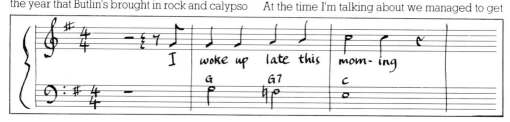

written about ten or twenty songs, but none of them were really very good. The nearest any of them came to anything was the start of *Love Me Do,* which was a little bit later, but that was about the nearest I think. There was a song called *Just Fun:*

We said our love was just fun
The day that our friendship begun
There's no blue moon that I can see
There's never been in history
Because our love was just fun

another line we weren't too keen on! We could tell what wasn't good, but we couldn't put the good one in its place.

It was very early days, when we were getting pipes full of Typhoo tea, smoking tea just to be groovy and do something. Anyway, we wrote this bunch of first songs which somehow reached the magic mythical figure of 100. We used to write to people, "We have written approximately

John Lennon, George Martin and Paul McCartney

100 songs but we feel we're getting better now", but it was only about twenty, if that! We had all these little songs: *Too Bad About Sorrows, Just Fun* (with little stage directions of oohs and aahs like angels); and on every page it had "A Lennon-McCartney Original", "Another Lennon-McCartney Original", "Yet Another Lennon-McCartney Original"!

Actually, you've only just reminded me that we obviously thought of ourselves as a writing team; from the word go we kind of liked this Lennon-McCartney thing. I might have been holding out for McCartney-Lennon, I'm not sure. John was holding out for Lennon-McCartney. I think it was decided it sounded better, so I eventually gave in – yes, Lennon-McCartney rolls off the tongue better. So in this early partnership we were trying to get something done and mainly it was a Buddy Holly kind of influence. For one reason: we knew three chords, A D and E, and all his stuff

Paul McCartney during the *Tug of War* sessions. *Photograph by Linda McCartney.*

was in A D and E, so no wonder we were influenced. Eventually I think *Love Me Do* was probably about the best thing we'd got, and that was when we met you and after that we started *Please Please Me*. That was a John song really. *Please Please Me* John had written on his own.

George *That was a Roy Orbison-type thing.*

Paul And he'd written it real slow, and in fact Roy Orbison should do it that way – slow. It'd be a hit for him. Get him on the phone right now! So that was one of our first good songs, and then *From Me To You* I remember as our second, and I think by then we were really into it. I wouldn't have said there was any looking back after that.

George *I remember you then, because it was like a hothouse plant being forced out and suddenly emerging with flowers all over it!*

Paul With middle eights even!

George *It came from being rough and ready people. I mean, songwriting-wise you were getting real classy, you were getting everything*

tidy and getting really efficient by this time.

Paul We were really interested in the idea of being real musicians, and in a way when you think of Lennon and McCartney it's Rodgers and Hammerstein because that's who we were emulating. All our heroes were just Chuck Berry, Little Richard and the rest. There might have been a little Goffin and King in there, because we were very keen on their stuff. So we were starting to be really good then. I think for me one of the great clinches was one morning hearing the milkman whistle, *"Is there anything that you want?"* I said that's it, I'm in; that was it really, I think that was the best compliment I've ever been paid to this day. I'd got home late from a club and me and the milkman were on the same wavelength; I was just getting into bed and I could hear him rattling his bottles outside and whistling *From Me To You.* I wrote that! That was a fabulous feeling, I must say: I could obviously go on and on for ever.●

Songwriting

The way I wrote songs ten years ago was very different from my current method of working. After years of writing, I have only in the last two years developed a system. I used to work in bursts rather than slowly and steadily, but now I find that by putting in time every day – if I am in a writing period – I can get more done than if I just sit around and wait for a song to happen. One of the benefits of working like this is that one can see the entire germ of a song develop from start to finish. Working steadily, it generally takes me about four to six weeks to complete a song, but if I am not working steadily it can take from four to six months.

The writing process

I work with my guitar and a legal pad and use about 50 pages to develop a song. I get going fairly early in the morning, because my mind is sharp, and start by dating the pad and putting down personal comments, such as how I am feeling that day, so that it becomes a diary of sorts. Slowly, a song will begin to emerge although sometimes it will stagger along, day after day, making no progress at all. The first page might have all sorts of lines that will never be used, but as I turn the pages, a little thought might come forward and suggest potential for development.

These notebooks are the clearest record I have of how my songs developed lyrically. I don't keep musical records, although I wish I had for the earlier material, but because they were written on scraps of paper, there isn't much left of them today.

I try and put as much information as possible into a song at the very beginning, and my first step is to write out the lyrical structure. If, for example, the song is a simple A, A, B, A – verse, verse, bridge, verse – and the first verse has eight lines, I will write down one, two, three, etc., and put in the title of the song as the eighth line, if that is where I want it to fall.

I already know that the next verse is going to have the same structure, but the title probably won't go at the eight spot because that would be predictable. Instead, the song might end with the title, so I will put it in as the last line and maybe put it in the second verse as well, knowing that it will be thrown out later on.

If the title is interesting and evocative, I will use it as inspiration or include it within the song's structure by pencilling it in in certain places. For example, there's a song I am working on at the moment called *Train In The Distance* in which one line repeats – "everybody loves the sound of the train in the distance, everybody thinks it's true". Because a train in the distance is an interesting metaphor for hopes and expectations, it will be used throughout the song. Sometimes however, the title is simply a title, as was the case with *Late In The Evening*. If I could have found another title, I would have: I would have done anything not to have a song called "Late in the Evening", but that was just the way it fell and I didn't try to fight it.

If a theme appears in the first verse, I will make a note of it. I don't notate or write on music paper, but I am always thinking about the structure of the song. For example, I might take a phrase that was in the opening, or the title, and use a part of it later on, or invert it, or use it in the bridge. It might also be used in an unexpected way, because the listener is usually so familiar with song structures that most of the time he or she knows, consciously or subconsciously, that a certain verse will be repeated. This works both for and against the songwriter; there is pleasure in receiving what you expect but the weakness is that it can be boring. However, in general my aim is to deliver what people expect because, if a familiar structure is set up and then changed to something unfamiliar, it can be disturbing or annoying to the listener. If a writer arbitrarily sets up a structure and then breaks it without cause, the song tends to ramble and become incoherent; it is also more difficult to write a song like that.

One of the most satisfying achievements – if you can make it work – is when a song follows a circular route and ends up back where it should have been at the beginning, but one plane higher, like a spiral. You cover ground and when you return home it's familiar, but you should have covered enough ground so that when you return to the beginning it's not the same in feel, title or melody.

Bridge Over Troubled Water

The way *Bridge Over Troubled Water* developed reflects my old style of writing. It was written in 1969; I had been listening to a lot of gospel music which had a great influence on me, especially the gospel quartets. A lot of pop singers grew out of these quartets which were actually the precursors of "doo-wap" rock 'n' roll. They had their heyday in the late 1940s and early 1950s with groups like The Dixie Hummingbirds, The Swan Silvertones, and Sam Cooke and The Soul Stirrers.

One song that particularly impressed me was *Oh Mary, Don't You Weep* by The Swan Silvertones. There's a brief moment in the song when the guy sings a scat line and says something to the effect that he will be someone's bridge over deep water, so I'd have to say that *Bridge Over Troubled Water* actually came from that.

While working on the song, I was fooling around with two different approaches. One was sort of folkish and, although I knew it was not going to be kept in the song, it filled up some space. The other approach had to do with diminished chords. I wrote the song on guitar, but knew I was going to use some kind of gospel piano and, similarly, although I wrote it in the key of G, I knew it was going to end up in the key of D or E-flat.

I don't remember much about actually writing the song – it just seemed to happen suddenly. The lyrics and melody grew simultaneously and the first two verses were written pretty quickly for me, because I'm generally a slow writer. *Bridge Over Troubled Water* was a very simple melody, although harmonically it wasn't straight-ahead.

Song About The Moon

A song which is not put out yet, called *Song About The Moon*, is typical of my present method of writing. Musically, it began with the old Sam Cooke song, *If You Ever Change Your Mind*. I was playing along with the record one day and started making chord substitutions, changing the harmony and then the melody. At a certain point I stopped and said, well, this is no longer a Sam Cooke song; it's different, and I like it.

I kept singing the title of my song, and hated it. I kept thinking: I wish that phrase would get out of my head, it means nothing to me and it's leading me nowhere. It must have stayed around for months, and I would sit and scratch on my pad "Song About The Moon" and nothing would happen. Then, one day, it just began to flow and finished itself.

I was sitting in my apartment, looking out over the park and I wrote, "If you want to write a song about the moon, walk along the craters of the afternoon." That was good because it superimposed the topography of the moon on to the topography of New York City. I saw the craters

in my mind's eye as if they were right there in the middle of the streets and buildings. So I wrote, "If you want to write a song about the moon walk along the craters *in* the afternoon." "*Of* the afternoon" implied that the afternoon had craters, which was too arty.

Having used the word "moon", there was the most typical rhyme going – "moon", "tune" – so I had to be very careful. Next came, "when the shadows are deep and the light is alien". Now, because you rarely hear the word "alien" in a song, your ears have to tune in, which is good, and there were the two elements – the moon and the streets – linked as well.

Then came "and gravity leaps like a knife off the pavement"; the two things were still linked, but the violence of the city was also implied. Next came, "and you want to write a song about the moon, you want to write a spiritual tune", and then I did some humming and "presto, song about the moon". In other words, what I am saying in the song is that, if you want to write, make a magical leap: you don't have to work on it; I'll show you how easy it is – just say "presto, song about the moon"; and there it is.

In the second verse I decided to use the same form of "if you want to write a song about . . ."; but what did I want to write? I always use the same subject, my favourite, and the only one which is really important in my view: the heart. So I wrote, "if you want to write a song about the heart". Because of the structure of the first verse, this beginning to the second implied that a long involved thing about the heart was coming up. Rather than do that, and create what I call the "if ever I should leave you" syndrome – the type of song, which makes you think "oh god, we have to wade through all the seasons now to find out what's going to happen" – I jumped back and wrote, "if you want to write a song about the heart, think about the moon before you start". In other words, I came back to the first verse to imply the danger of writing about the heart.

Next came, "because the heart howls like a dog in the moonlight and the heart can explode like a pistol on a June night". I was thinking about Jean Harris who had killed her lover, which was a big news story at the time. By following this with, "so if you want to write a song about the heart, and it's ever longing for a counterpart, write a song about the moon", the song was tied up because the title had been used for the last line of the verse, making the whole thing symmetrical. Because I was invoking the moon in relation to the heart, it now had the potential for being something more. I still didn't know where I was going, but I had established that the moon was more than just a cliché.

I was beginning to think that the idea of the song was becoming too complex and inaccessible; that you had to know too much to like it. I kept asking myself, what was I actually talking about? What was the point of the song? Although I was enjoying it, I figured that I should be able to say what I had to say simply; it couldn't take this much to say what I had to say. Musically, I was keeping the song simple, without any flat nines or jazz chords.

Next came a little bit in the middle – "laughing boy, he laughed so hard he fell down from his place; laughing girl, she laughed so hard tears roll down her face" – but I don't know why I wrote it. When I referred back to the structure I realized I had a new element – the middle part – but I still had the moon and heart to think about and somehow they had to be tied together.

For the last verse, I wrote, "if you want to write a song about a face (tears rolling down her face), that you really can't remember but you can't erase, wash your hands in dreams and lightning." Then I started to use imagery that wasn't simile or metaphor; I just went straight into it: "Toss your hair at whatever is frightening. If you want to write a song about a face, if you want to write a song about the human race, write a song about the moon." And that's how it ended.

The song is about love, which is what I set out after, and so love, which is one of the most clichéd things around, became an acceptable subject for a song.

Words

When I first began writing, I was really just doing college literary stuff and hadn't yet discovered my own voice or set of symbols. I now see that I tend to use a certain group of words and ideas, mostly related to the body – the heart, bones, hands. I was very critical of my work in the beginning, but not sophisticated enough to know that what I was doing was naive. I hadn't lived enough or been exposed to enough to realize that what I was saying wasn't new. It was new to me because I hadn't said it before, but it wasn't new to the world.

I write almost exclusively from personal experience. With other songwriters I can sometimes see where a thought came from, but why a writer will choose a particular phrase, why it struck him in such a way that he knew there was a song there, is inexplicable.

I think most songs should be written in the vernacular. There is, however, some good news and some bad news about this: the good news is that it's simply the way we all speak; and the bad

news is that it's . . . simply the way we all speak! So there is a problem that has to be dealt with. To get around it, I will sometimes break the vernacular by using a word that wouldn't normally appear in a song, as I did with "alien" in *Song About The Moon*.

Odd as it may sound, I don't think poetry lends itself to song. We are all so accustomed to hearing popular songs sung the way we speak that poetry simply doesn't sound natural to our ears.

Editing your own words is a significant part of writing songs: the writer must edit all of the time. On the other hand, I'm more interested in hearing what people feel and in their mistakes than in their editing ability.

I had a title of *The Late Great Johnny Ace* going around in my head while I was still working on the *Still Crazy* album. At one time I was going to write a play about Johnny Ace and John Kennedy; then when John Lennon was murdered he became the third Johnny Ace. I decided I still wanted to write a play, but would try first to edit it down, to write it as a song and put all the thoughts into the song. When I had finished, I said, well, I guess it's all been done in the song, so I don't have to write the play.

Music

The music I love is the music of my early adolescence: guitar and vocal, four-part harmony groups on the corner and Southern rock 'n' roll which I used to listen to on the radio.

If you play five melody lines for someone with a certain amount of taste and musical sophistication, they will probably pick the most musical. What I'm interested in, however, is what comes out of someone's heart when they sit down at their instrument or use their voice to pour it out.

With my own music I have discovered that it is the stuff that comes from the heart and not the clever things that works best. If I listen to my old songs, I can see the intellectual choices that I imposed on the music, which is the trap of using technique as the chisel to create the piece. You chisel into your creative impulse with a technique and you might, for example, decide that the chisel will be 10/8 time becoming 6/8, as I did in *How The Heart Approaches What It Yearns*. I did it because the melody and the chords were so simple that I thought I'd better make them tricky, but trickiness can get in the way, which is why I don't think computer thinking is a substitute for creativity.

In developing the musical side of a song, I pay attention to the song's essence: whether, for example, it's a rhythm pattern or a melody. *Late In The Evening* is a rhythm song and has to do with words and rhythm rather than the melody, which is essentially the blues. If the rhythm pattern is the essential piece of information, then my first reaction is that the rhythm must be varied for interest. My second response is that, if the rhythm pattern is the thing I want to vary, it might be varied with the melody.

So there are these three elements I must deal with – melody, rhythm, harmony: the natural inclination of a song decides which I put first. The natural inclination of a song, however, implies a deviation from it. For example, I have a rhythm song and I am looking for some direction. I might look towards harmony or melody, or I could look for another rhythm direction, but my first instinct is to look in one of the other two areas. If I have a simple harmonic structure and a particular rhythm that I like, I would rather keep that rhythm going and vary the harmonic structure, by changing key or something similar. Likewise, if I have an unusual, unpredictable harmonic structure, I might find relief by changing the time signature, or using a simpler harmonic structure in the bridge, but in another key.

All of these elements have lyrical implications. The lyrics and the music have to work synergistically for the song to be good; if the song makes a radical change harmonically, there has to be a change lyrically as well. It can be, ironically, opposed to the initial change, but there has to be some recognition that something else is happening; it's a marriage, not just two elements wandering off any which way they like.

Sometimes I will write a song that feels natural from a guitar point of view but in a key that I can't sing in, so I'll transpose it or tune the guitar down a tone, as I did with *The Late Great Johnny Ace*.

I have gone through different phases in my music writing. There was a time when I used a little exercise – incorporating all of the 12 notes in the chromatic scale – to get me going. In serial, or 12-tone, writing the writer had to use all of the notes before he could repeat a note, so the centre key was blown away, but what I was doing was more for the fun of it. I got the idea from Carlos Jobim. I used to analyze his music, and one day I realized that he was using every note in the scale. He came into the studio once and I said I admired his music and asked how he had decided to use every note in the scale; he had no idea what I was talking about: it had somehow happened naturally with him. However, I used my exercise as a means of getting the song going, and it can be a great help as long as it isn't the motivating force.

I used this technique for a while, but I don't any longer because I am going back to simpler melodies. Originally I moved away from the simple songs because I thought they were *too* simple. Now that I am going back to them, I have to keep reminding myself that it's all right to write a simple song.

The most beautiful tunes are the simplest, but they have all been written, at least that's how it feels when you're writing one cliché melody after another. Before, I was trying to write melodies that never previously existed, and within the context of popular music that's almost impossible because we are talking about vocal music to be sung by untrained voices, so the range isn't that great; you can't make really big leaps in the singing.

There are piano clichés as well as guitar clichés, and I don't advocate one instrument over the other for popular music. The guitar dictates a certain kind of melody, and pianistic songwriters are different from guitar writers. Even though I use a guitar, the way I compose is closer to piano because I am working with bass lines and leading tones a lot, and I know where I am going harmonically; I am not just strumming. My hand always wants to go to certain chords that I love, and certain hand positions just lay themselves out perfectly on the guitar. For example, if I can get an open E string on the bottom, I will be happy, so I try to get into the key of E if I can, or A, or something similar.

Songwriting today

A little while ago I was watching a music show on television. A lot of the ideas seemed silly, but then I thought, they might be silly now, but in a few years these ideas are going to be much more clever and sophisticated. It's like any artist's early work: in the beginning it is usually naive, and slowly it becomes more sophisticated. Today, someone with some talent might be involved in video, which might strike many people as unusual. But in the future, people won't find it remarkable at all.

An interesting problem for many songwriters is what happens to them when they become too good for commercial taste. The age of the average listener – the record buyer – tends to remain the same, or perhaps drift up a bit and so the writer finds himself in a situation where, as he grows older, he is dealing with a much younger audience. I once read an interview with Hoagie Carmichael a year or so before he died, in which he was asked what he would write today if he were still writing. He answered that he *was* still writing, but nobody wanted to hear his music: in fact, those were some of his best songs.

Each new group of 16 or 17 year-olds that

Paul Simon

wants to listen to, or make, music has to start at the beginning, and I guess that's the fun of it. But this also means that people who are more mature are not going to be able to speak to them because they're not interested in the pain of growing up as a 16 year-old. For example, I am just interested in the pain of growing up at *my* time in life, so there inevitably comes a point at which the record market ceases to exist for certain artists, something that has already happened to a lot of people from the 1960s and 1970s; they are simply not around any more.

The pity of this is that in the popular arts we tend to discard people and ideas very easily. The public doesn't expect a popular artist to mature, and consequently they never become anything other than aging popular artists. I read a review of the work of a famous songwriter from the 1970s a little while ago and the critic was basically saying that the writer was a leftover and it was time for him to move on and make way for the next guy. I thought this was terrible, because there usually comes a time when the public stops paying attention, and it is usually at that point that the songwriter has just learned how to say what he or she wants to say.

The songwriters who tell us what they are thinking and feeling give us all a way of knowing what our generation thinks. It's very important that they keep saying it; it's not very important that it should be in the charts. I find that the more popular I become, the more difficulty I have in getting people to look at my work seriously. I feel like saying, look, there's so much that's inhuman on this planet, and I'm saying something, so listen and tell me what you think. That, in my view, is what writing songs is all about; and that is the response that a song should generate.●

Songwriting

Like most writers, I have no pre-set ways of composing a song. Original ideas begin in the unconscious. I believe there are billions of processes going on in the brain and only a tiny proportion is apparent. The rest are unconscious. Our logical minds are in compartmented boxes and when those boxes are disturbed, when one is asleep for instance and not being logical, an idea can flow from one rigid box into another and that's where you get a spark.

If you take a basic idea out of its environment and put it into another frame of reference, that's when you get magic. And when you "wake up" and cement the ideas together with hard work and graft, clocking on in the morning and doing the job, the process is completed.

Synchronicity

I never write to order, only because I enjoy writing. I love the feeling of finishing a good song. But without that initial spark – one line – perhaps a melodic phrase, it would not begin. Anything can be the trigger for a song; it can be a riff that my fingers have found on the guitar, or a lyrical ideal. For example, when I was in Scotland I had the idea of taking the Loch Ness monster and putting it into another environment. I call the song *Synchronicity,* which is a theory propounded by Jung. It's about things being connected without being logically together; for example, there are a lot of parallels in the lives of Abraham Lincoln and John Kennedy – nothing that makes any sense logically, but it is synchronistic, there's a meaning to it.

So in my song I have the interplay of a man in an ordinary domestic situation who is depressed with his life and I have the monster in the chorus. Many miles away something crawls from the slime – the man goes to work and it's awful – many miles away something crawls to the surface of the dark Scottish lake – he comes home and it's the rush hour and everything is terrible and he's going to kill himself – many miles away a shadow – he sees the house in his headlights – many miles away there's a shadow on the door of the cottage by the shore of the dark, Scottish lake. So you have two separate ideas linked together in a song going back and forward, and they both mean something separately, but together they are much more interesting.

A demo to convince the band

Having finished a song, the most difficult thing in the world is to sell it to your colleagues. I make the best demo I can, singing and playing guitar, bass, piano and drum machine. I get a good version so that people will see its potential. Also I feel that you need something solid to kick against before you go into the studio with the band. On occasions I have gone along when someone says, "Let's go into the studio and see if we can do something." Perhaps one time in a hundred something fantastic happens in that way, but ninety-nine times out of a hundred it's hard going.

Most of my demos survive intact as far as arrangements go, but if someone comes up with an alternative idea that's fine. There are occasional times when the band rehearse a song and their ideas just explode, put it onto an extra rung, which is great. But in the main, my original demo is very similar to the finished track and I find that satisfying.

Ideas from the piano

I have been experimenting with the piano recently, finding that it triggers a different set of ideas from the guitar. Keys are very important. If you play D flat on the piano it gives a wholly different emotional tenor to the same key on the guitar. I'm learning to play the oboe now. It has a lovely sound and again it has put me in touch with different areas. I find that being at home with many different instruments gives me a wider source of inspiration. I love discovery; once you have learned something it becomes mundane, but the excitement of exploring new fields is a wonderful inspiration.

The Beatles were a blueprint for my musical interest. They showed that boys from an ordinary background could do anything with music if they dared. And they set an example for adventure that is very much a part of British music; they began the idea of groups, or members of groups, writing their own music and since then groups have been expected to do just that, which is a wonderful sign of creativity in our country. We do try to be original. We may not always be successful, but a lot is always happening here. And some of it is very good indeed.●

Sting, *right,* on stage playing a pogo stick bass. Much of his songwriting inspiration comes from his ability to play a wide variety of instruments, each one opening up new areas of expression.

Theatre Lyrics

Ten years ago Stephen Sondheim gave an informal talk in New York as part of a series of lectures called "Lyrics and Lyricists". It was a significant contribution to the understanding of a writer's craft and his words are timeless. The following is an extract.

I'm going to talk only about theatre lyrics, lyrics in a dramatic situation on a stage in terms of character – not pop lyrics . . .

I first got into lyric writing because when I was a child of 11 my parents were divorced and we moved to Pennsylvania. I moved there with my mother, and among her friends were the Hammerstein family. They had a son my age and we became very close. Oscar Hammerstein gradually got me interested in the theatre, and I suppose most of it happened one fateful or memorable afternoon. He had urged me to write a musical for my school (George School, a Friends school in Bucks County). With two classmates I wrote a musical called *By George*, a thinly disguised version of campus life with the teachers' names changed by one vowel or consonant. I thought it was pretty terrific, so I asked Oscar to read it – and I was arrogant enough to say to him, "Will you read it as if it were just a musical that crossed your desk as a producer? Pretend you don't know me." He said "O.K.," and I went home that night with visions of being the first 15-year-old to have a show on Broadway. I knew he was going to love it.

Oscar called me in the next day and said, "Now you really want me to treat this as if it were by somebody I don't know?" and I said, "Yes, please," and he said, "Well, in that case it's the worst thing I ever read in my life." He must have seen my lower lip tremble, and he followed up with, "I didn't say it wasn't talented, I said it was terrible, and if you want to know why it's terrible I'll tell you." He started with the first stage direction and went all the way through the show for a whole afternoon, really treating it seriously. It was a seminar on the piece as though it were *Long Day's Journey Into Night*. Detail by detail, he told me how to structure songs, how to build them with a beginning and a development and an ending, according to his principles. I found out many years later there are other ways to write songs, but he taught me, according to his own principles, how to introduce character,

what relates a song to character, etc., etc. It was four hours of the most *packed* information. I dare say, at the risk of hyperbole, that I learned in that afternoon more than most people learn about song writing in a lifetime.

Two principles

It's hard to talk about lyrics independently of music, but I will try. Obviously, all the principles of writing apply to lyrics: grace, affinity for words, a feeling for the weight of words, resonances, tone, all of that. But there are two basic differences between lyric writing and all other forms, and they dictate what you have to do as a lyric writer. They are not even rules, they are just principles. First, lyrics exist in time – as opposed to poetry, for example. You can read a poem at your own speed. I find most poetry very difficult, and there are a few poets I like very much. Wallace Stevens is one, but it takes me a good 20 minutes to get through a medium-length Wallace Stevens poem, and even then I don't understand a lot of it, yet I enjoy it and can read it at my own speed. That's the point. On the stage, the lyrics come at you and you hear them once. If there's a reprise you hear them twice, if there are two reprises you hear them three times, but that's all. Quite often you've had the experience, or you've heard friends say, "Gee, I didn't get the lyric until I heard the record." Well that's the problem, you only get it once. The music is a relentless engine and keeps the lyrics going.

This leads to the second principle. Lyrics go with music, and music is very rich, in my opinion the richest form of art. It's also abstract and does very strange things to your emotions. So not only do you have that going, but you also have lights, costumes, scenery, characters, performers. There's a great deal to hear and get. Lyrics therefore have to be underwritten. They have to be very simple in essence. That doesn't mean you can't do convoluted lyrics, but essentially the thought is what counts and you have to stretch the thought out enough so that the listener has a fair chance to get it. Many lyrics suffer from being much too packed.

I'll give you some samples of my own later, but my favorite example is "Oh, what a beautiful mornin'/Oh, what a beautiful day." I would be ashamed to put it down on paper, it would look silly. What Hammerstein knew was that set to music it was going to have an enormous richness. It did, it's a *beautiful* lyric – but not on paper.

I have a book of Hammerstein's lyrics and one

of Cole Porter's. Hammerstein's you fall asleep reading, while Porter's is an absolute delight, like reading light verse. "Oh, what a beautiful mornin'" is not anywhere near as much fun to read as to hear. An imitation Hammerstein lyric that I did is "Maria" in *West Side Story*, a lyric I am not terribly fond of except for one good line: "Maria, I've just kissed a girl named Maria." I remember when I wrote that I thought, "I can't do anything that bland and banal but I'll fix it later." Of course when it went with the music it just soared, it was perfect. The fancier part of the lyric "Say it loud and there's music playing/Say it soft . . ." etc., etc. (I'm too embarrassed to quote it) is a very fruity lyric, too much, overripe.

I've always thought of lyric writing as a craft rather than an art. It's so small. There are how many words in an average lyric? I'm tending to write long songs these days, but the average lyric has maybe 60 to 80 words, so each word counts for a great deal. Now, any novelist or short story writer takes as much pains as he can over each individual word, but they are not as important as in a lyric, not even as important to a playwright because each lyric line is practically a scene in itself. If there are 12 lines in a song, this is like 12 scenes in a play, and if one word is off it's like an entire section of the scene.

The opening line of *Porgy and Bess* by DuBose Heyward, who wrote all the lyrics for the first act, is "Summertime and the livin' is easy" – and that "and" is worth a great deal of attention. I would write "Summertime when" but that "and" sets up a tone, a whole poetic tone, not to mention a whole kind of diction that is going to be used in the play; an informal, uneducated diction and a stream of consciousness, as in many of the songs like "My Man's Gone Now." It's the exact right word and that word is worth its weight in gold. "Summertime *when* the livin' is easy" is a boring line compared to "Summertime *and*." The choices of "ands" and "buts" become almost traumatic as you are writing a lyric – or should, anyway – because each one weighs so much.

Oscar Hammerstein once told me how astonished he was to learn that the sculptor of the Statue of Liberty had carved the top of the head as carefully as the rest of the statue, even though he couldn't possibly have known that one day there would be airplanes. That's what you have to do in a lyric, too – every word counts, whether the audience hears it specifically or not. In "Everything's Coming Up Roses" there was very little to say in the lyric after the title was over, so I decided that I would give it its feeling by restricting myself to images of travelling, children and show business, because the scene was in a rail-

road station and was about a mother pushing her child into show business. Now that may be of no interest except to somebody doing a doctorate in 200 years on the use of travelling images in *Gypsy*. But the point is, it's there, and it informs the whole song.

On one level, I suppose, lyric writing is an elegant form of puzzle, and I am a great puzzle fan. There's a great deal of joy for me in the sweat involved in the working out of lyrics, but it can lead to bloodlessness, and I've often been capable of writing bloodless lyrics (there are a number of them in *West Side Story*).

Anyway, all the principles extend from this one, which is lyrics existing in time.

I would like to talk next about influences. Oscar I have told you about. The main thing he taught me was that it's content that counts. It's what you say rather than how you say it, and clarity of thought, making the thought clear to the listener (that has to do with the lyrics existing in time again). Oscar also said, "Say what you feel, not what other song writers feel." When I started out writing love songs I would write about stars and trees and dreams and moonlight, the usual song writer's vocabulary. That's fine if you believe it, but I didn't.

The next major influence in my lyric-writing life was Burt Shevelove. Burt advised me, "Never sacrifice smoothness for cleverness. Better dull than clumsy." I agree. An awful lot of lyrics suffer from the lyric writer having a really clever, sharp idea which he can't quite fit into the music, so it sits there clumsily and the singer is stuck with singing it. The net result always is that it doesn't land with the audience. It has to be smooth if you are going to make the point.

Arthur Laurents is the collaborator with whom I've worked the closest. He's taught me a great deal about matching diction with ideas and continuity of content. He also is terrific on titles as any good book writer-collaborator had better be if he works with me, because I steal from them all the time. "I Feel Pretty" is a title of Arthur's and "Some People" and "Something's Coming." Anyway, Oscar, Burt and Arthur have been my three major influences.

The genesis of songs

I go about starting a song first with the collaborators, sometimes just with the book writer, sometimes with the director. We have long discussions and I take notes, just general notes, and then we decide what the song should be about, and I try to make a title. If I am writing the music as well as the lyric I sometimes try to get a vamp first, a musical atmosphere, an accompaniment, a pulse, a melodic idea, but usually the tone comes from the accompaniment figure, and I find that the more specific the task, the easier. If somebody says write a song about a lady in a red dress crying at the end of a bar, that's a lot easier than somebody saying write a song about a fellow who's sorry. I would like to quote Oscar on this subject, in a marvellous introduction to a book of his called *Lyrics*: "There is in all art a fine balance between the benefits of confinement and the benefits of freedom. An artist who is too fond of freedom is likely to be obscure in his expression." So what you want is something specific, but not too specific.

Then I usually make a list of useful rhymes related to the song's topic, sometimes useful phrases, a list of ideas that pop into my head. Then I try to make a prose statement to the point, so that it won't get lost. I find it useful to write at the top of the page a couple of sentences of what the song is to be about, no matter how flimsy.

Here are some of the first notes I put down when writing *Company*. "Everybody loves Robert (Bob, Bobby) . . ." the idea of nicknames had already occurred to me. Then I had Robert say, "I've got the best friends in the world," and then the line occurred to me, "You I love and you I love and you I love," and then, talking about marriage, "A country I've never been to," and "Who wants vine-covered cottages, marriage is for children." It's all Bob's attitude: "Companion for life, who wants that?" And then he says, "I've got company, love is company, three is company, friends are company," and I started a list of what's company. Then I started to expand the lines: "Love is what you need is company. What I've got as friends is company. Good friends, weird friends, married friends, days go, years go, full of company." I started to spin free associations, and I got to "Phones ring, bells buzz, door clicks, company, call back, get a bite," and the whole notion of short phrases, staccato phrases, occurred to me. By the time I got through just listing general thoughts, I had a smell of the rhythm of the vocal line, so that when I was able to turn to the next page and start expanding it I got into whole lists of things: "No ties, small lies. So much, too much. Easy, comfy, hearts pour, the nets descend, private jokes," all short phrases – but what came out of it eventually was the form of that song, which worked out better than I had expected.

Clarity

Words have to sit on music in order to become clear to the audience. I am talking about clarity, remember, and clarity has to do with that thing I

talked about, time. You don't get a chance to hear the lyric twice or to read it, and if the lyric doesn't sit and bounce when the music bounces and rise when the music rises, it isn't just a question of mis-accents, which are bad enough, but if it is too crowded and doesn't rise and fall with the music, the audience becomes confused. There's a song in *West Side Story* called "America" and thank God it's a spectacular dance because it wouldn't get a hand otherwise. It has 27 words to the square inch. I had this "wonderful" quatrain that went "I like to be in American/O.K. by me in America/Everything free in America/For a small fee in America." The "For a small fee" was my little zinger – except that the "for" is accented and the "sm" is impossible to say that fast, so it went "For a smafee in America." Nobody knew what it meant, and I learned my lesson: you have to consider a singer's tongue and teeth.

I find it useful to write backwards, and I think most lyric writers probably do too when they

"America" dance sequence from *West Side Story*

have a climax, a twist, a punch, a joke. You start at the bottom of the page, you preserve your best joke to the last, the ideas should be placed in ascending order of punch. And another thing, the last word ought to be singable. It always bothered Oscar that the last line of "What's the Use of Wond'rin'?" is "And all the rest is talk," and he always claimed that the number never became as popular as it should have because "talk" is not a word that is graceful for a singer to hold. The "k" cuts it off, closes the sound. It's best to end with an "ow" or "ah", open sounds that the singer can go with. Two of the most useful words in the language are "me" and "be", but unfortunately they have pinched sounds.

Rhyme

Many lyric writers don't understand the difference between rhymes and identities. In a rhyme, the vowel sound is the same but the initial consonant is different, as in "way" and "day". In identity, both the vowel and the consonant that precedes the vowel sound are exactly alike, as in "consternation" and "procrastination". That is not a rhyme, it is an identity. It's not that identities are outlawed, it's just that they don't prick the ear the way rhymes do. They don't point up the words, so if you are going to use an identity you have to use it carefully.

You try to make your rhyming seem fresh but inevitable, you try for surprise but not so wrenching that the listener loses the sense of the line. The hardest kind of word to rhyme is "day" because it makes you concentrate on the content. "Day" is when I use my rhyming dictionary, going down the list of all the "a" rhymes to find something that will express the vague thought in my head; whereas if you are going to rhyme a word like "orange" it restricts your thought about content greatly. In a way, it makes it easier for you.

The function of a rhyme is to point up the word that rhymes – if you don't want that word to be the most important in the line, don't rhyme it. Also, rhymes helps shape the music, it helps the listener hear what the shape of the music is. Inner rhymes, which are fun to work out if you have a puzzle mind, have one essential function, which is to speed the line along. Examples are to be found in Cole Porter's "Where Is the Life That Late I Led?" Porter is a master of inner rhymes which make the line not only funnier but also speed it up, as "Where is Venetia who loved to chat so?/Could still she be drinking in her stinking pink palazzo?" The inner rhyme speeds it, makes it funnier, gives it a shine. "And lovely Lisa, where are you, Lisa?/You gave a new meaning to the leaning tow'r of Pisa" – the inner rhyme makes this a superb joke with the "leaning" and the "meaning". Inner rhyme can also be used for strength. "Our love was too hot *not* to cool down" – the "not" makes that rock solid.

As for alliteration, my counterpoint teacher had a phrase "the refuge of the destitute". That's my attitude toward alliteration. Any time you hear alliteration in a lyric, get suspicious. For example, when you hear "I Feel Pretty" and she sings "I feel fizzy and funny and fine", somebody doesn't have something to say.

Humour

It's always better to be funny than clever, and a lot harder. One laugh per score is a lot for me, anyway, and I think most of my shows have one

laugh. In *West Side Story* there's the section in "Gee Officer Krupke" which uses a favourite technique of mine, parallel lines where you just make a list:

> *My father is a bastard,*
> *My ma's an S.O.B.*
> *My grandpa's always plastered,*
> *My grandma pushes tea.*
> *My sister wears a moustache,*
> *My brother wears a dress.*
> *Goodness gracious, that's why I'm a mess!*

That's not exceptionally funny on its own, but it brought down the house every night because the form helps make it funny. It was a genuine piece of humour because it depended not on cleverness but on the kids' attitudes, and that is what humour is about: character, not cleverness.

Writing habits

I write lying down so I can go to sleep easily. That's true. I write about ten minutes and sleep for two, on the average. I write on legal pads in very small writing, partly for frugality – I used to write on both sides of the page, and Leonard Bernstein got annoyed because he would be constantly try to find lyrics and turning the pages over and over, so I don't do that any more. I find it very useful to use a separate pad for each section of the song.

I do lots of recopying – that's like pencil-sharpening. I get a quatrain that's *almost* right, so I tear off the sheet and start at the top on a clean one with my nice little quatrain which I know isn't right – but this makes me feel I've accomplished something. I use a rhyming dictionary, the Clement Wood, which is the only one I would recommend because it's the only one with lists of words where the eye goes up and down the columns. You don't use a dictionary for trick rhymes, of course, you won't find them in there. I also use a thesaurus, and I find "The Dictionary of American Slang" very useful in writing contemporary stuff.

I use soft lead pencils, very soft. Supposedly that makes the writing easier on your wrist, but what it really does is allow you to sharpen it every five minutes. I am very undisciplined, though most of the writers I've worked with have been disciplined. Arthur Laurents, James Goldman, George Furth – they always meet deadlines. They work steady hours; they get up at a certain time in the morning and they knock off at five. I have to have somebody pushing me constantly to get it in by Tuesday, and then Monday night I start to work on it.●

77

Arranging Music

Arranging is precisely what the word suggests – the presentation of an original piece of music in a way that enhances the subject and pleases the listener. The success of an arrangement depends not only on the skill of the arranger, but more importantly, his taste. It ranges from the simplest of instruments to a full blown symphony orchestra, and the specific art of arranging for an orchestra is, of course, orchestration.

So a boy vamping away a favourite piece on a mouth organ is in effect arranging that music. The very limitation of the chords on his instrument can change the harmonies of the original, and the "arrangement" may not improve the original, but that is where the delicate matter of taste comes in. At the other end of the scale we can listen to Stokowski's arrangement of Bach's *Toccata and Fugue in D Minor.* Originally designed to be played by one person on a pipe organ, the arrangement involves anything up to one hundred players, and is very grand indeed.

Quite often arranging involves composition – the adding of fresh material to the work. An obvious example is the well known version of *Singing In The Rain* performed by Gene Kelly. The introduction to this song, impeccably scored by Lennie Hayton, now seems to be an integral part of the song; indeed one can hardly think of the song without it, but it did not exist until the film was made in 1952 although the song was written many years before.

So how do we go about writing an arrangement? If we are starting with a pop song, all we usually have is a top line – the tune – and the chords that make up its harmonies. If you can read and write music, so much the better, but a lack of formal music need not stop you from making a good arrangement for a small group of, say, bass guitar, electric guitar, keyboard and drums. The chords can be learned by the guitar and keyboard players, and the bass part has to be designed to anchor the whole sound. In devising a part for the bass it is important to find an interesting line that sings in partnership with the voice. It is not enough merely to fill in the basic notes of the chords, although that will do to start with. Try to write a new tune on the bass – not too clever or complicated, but one that walks hand in hand with the voice. Listen to the way other people do it.

The trick of devising little snatches of counter melody is very useful in sustaining interest in the song, and the keyboard or the electric guitar may be used for this – provided it does not get in the way of the song. Such ideas should be used as a frame for the picture, unobtrusively supporting the main theme. The drums will then lock the whole into the basic rhythm, but again a good drummer will look for opportunities to support the song with the right flourish without being too obtrusive. I always like to hear the bass drum and the bass guitar locked into a solid unified sound.

There are four basic elements to consider in arranging – melody, harmony, rhythm and form.

Form

Every piece of music has some sort of shape, and the arranger's responsibility (as well as the producer's) is to ensure that the shape from beginning to end is satisfying, creating interest at the beginning, bringing out the best elements of the song and building the interest right up to the end.

The early records I produced with The Beatles show arranging at its most basic. When I first heard *Can't Buy Me Love,* for example, the song was the straightforward verse and chorus. I thought an introduction was needed, so I took the first line of the chorus, repeated the last word twice and changed the harmonies, and started with that, before letting rip on the verse. The length was dictated by the average time that the ever powerful disc jockeys liked their records to be – between 2½ and 3 minutes. After the first statement of the song a change was desirable – hence George's guitar solo, then back to the chorus once more and exit the way we began, with a restatement of the introduction. One could hardly have a simpler arrangement. This is a far cry from the complexities of classical sonata form or even later works in the rock 'n' roll idiom, but it serves to illustrate the importance of the shape of the piece.

Melody

No amount of arranging is going to turn a sow's ear into a silk purse, and the basic tune of a piece is obviously the most important, together with the lyrical content if it is a song. The arranger must never forget that, and all other parts of the arrangement must serve as a frame. There is often room, however, for other lines, and the clever arranger will look to the effective use of counter melodies either on voice or instruments, using the basic melody as a springboard. But again, simplicity is the keynote. I do not believe that the human ear is capable of enjoying more than two – possibly three at a stretch – lines of melody at the same time. It used to be fashionable in Bach's time to have four or five tunes all weaving around in a fugue, but frankly it makes listening hard work. Make a rule to concentrate on creating just one counter melody, a really good design to run along with the tune. It is surprising how it fills up the sound. Listen to the two lines of strings on *Diamond Dust* from Jeff Beck's *Blow by Blow* album and you will see what I mean. There are just two tunes running together, with a slight interval in time and it is obvious that any more sound would be overkill. Quite often it is not necessary to compose a new tune to fit the original, as a part of the original will sometimes serve as a counterpoint to another part of the tune. *Eleanor Rigby* contains an example. At the end of the song, to add interest, I was able to use as a counterpoint a line from the bridge – "Oh, look at all the lonely people" – running parallel to the sung line "All the lonely people, where do they all come from". Another useful idea from Mr. Bach is to take a piece of the tune and turn it back to front, or upside down, or use it in half or double time. When it came to devising a solo for *Nowhere Man* the line was conceived by turning the basic tune upside down, going down where the original went up and so on, but obviously choosing intervals that matched the harmonies. And sometimes a complete reversal of a tune works. At the end of *Rain,* John's voice track was lifted off and turned back to front. Apart from the shock novelty of the backward words it did make a very good new tune.

Harmony

Behind the clearly defined line of the melody we have the background wash of the harmony. In picture terms I think of this as a colour wash filling out the sharp outline of a drawing. In a small combination the harmony is provided by the keyboards or the guitars or of course backing voices, and in large ensembles anything goes from woodwinds, brass, horns or strings to choral and synthesizer sounds. If more than one instrument or voice is providing the harmony, it is important to make sure the register of the chord is right and varied between the instruments. If the guitar is playing chords in a low register, make sure the piano is *not* doing the same (unless you are aiming for a thick and turgid sound) and, of course, do vary the texture throughout the work. Give the players something interesting to do. Most chords in popular music consist of only three notes, with added sixths or sevenths or diminished chords requiring one more, but a lot of beginners forget how important is the inversion of those notes – which note is to be the lowest. Sometimes the original chords in a song can be changed, updated to give a new slant but arrangers are warned they stick their neck out every time they tamper with the original harmonic structure. Nine times out of ten the original chords are best, although of course, there have been brilliant examples of inventive changes. Listen to Klaus Nomi's version of *Falling In Love Again.*

Rhythm

Rhythm is the punctuation of the song. Rhythm and tempo set the mood of music more tellingly than anything else, and if you get it wrong all the other rights won't make up for it. In the days before rock 'n' roll, the rhythm instruments in a band were felt rather than heard, and it wasn't until the 1950s that the heavy back beat laid a strong emphasis on rhythm. Fashions come and go, from the syncopated Latin beat of bossa nova to the four in the bar bass drum of disco, and there is still a great deal of room for inventiveness in rhythms. The British band The Police have shown how compelling is the use of West Indian rhythms, giving great contrast to the regular rock 'n' roll on-beat off-beat pattern. Nor is it necessary to have drums to provide the rhythm. Combinations of instruments can be used to give a pulse to the music most effectively. But this is where we begin to merge arranging with orchestration.

Orchestration

Once an arranger aims at using instruments that are not part of his normal group, which he cannot control or rehearse, it is almost essential for him to be able to read and write music. Obviously, the more he knows about instruments the better he will be at writing for them, and I advise any would-be arranger to be as inquisitive as possible with other instrumentalists. Most musicians are pleased to talk about their instrument and suggest on the way it should be scored.

Strings

It is well known that a piano part is written on two staves with a bass clef for the left hand and a treble clef for the right. Writing for strings introduces a new clef, which indicates the position for the viola part. The clef sits on Middle C, which is the middle line of the stave, so effectively it is a "halfway house" between the bass and treble clefs. By tradition a string orchestra is divided into parts – first violin, second violin, violas, cellos and basses (although quite often the bass part is a duplicate of the cello). I believe that if you can write well for a string quartet you will write well for an orchestra, for working with a quartet teaches you to space the instruments properly and to use their sounds economically. If I am adding a string "blanket" to an existing rhythm track or writing a string score to carry the voice, the principles are just the same. Thinking of the string quartet, I try to give each section only one line to play – no "divisi" writing unless it is absolutely necessary, and I like to place the parts with a good distance between them – particularly in the lower sections. It is risky to put a bunched chord, such as one would play on the piano with one's left hand, on to the cello and viola lines. It would usually sound very thick and ugly.

The ranges of all the string instruments overlap considerably. In the middle register it is difficult to distinguish between cello and viola, for example, but the viola has a huskier tone. The violin, of course, can reach very high notes, but personally I find them screechy and thin unless played superbly.

An arranger should always bear in mind the number of players available for the score, and

Tug of War: *above,* part of the full score of George Martin's overdub arrangement. *Right,* details of the score showing parts for voice, woodwind (contrabassoon), brass (horns) and strings (first and second violins, violas, cellos and double-basses).

even the acoustics of the studio. After a string quartet I do not think there is a satisfactory sound for strings until one has at least three players on each line, so my minimum orchestra is generally 8 violins, 3 violas and 3 cellos. Having said that, I have to confess that when I scored *Eleanor Rigby* I doubled the string quartet exactly, using 4 violins, 2 violas and 2 cellos. But as a rule, two stringed instruments together create a slight "beat" which does not give a smooth sound. There is nothing quite like the sound of many strings playing beautifully in unison. All the slight discrepancies in pitch, vibrato and harmonies melt into one unmistakeable liquid sound that is a delight to the ear. On the score of Paul McCartney's *Tug Of War* I wanted a rich ambient sound, so he agreed we should record the strings at Abbey Road, Studio One. This is an enormous room, and consequently has a long period of reverberation. But it needs filling. No point in having a handful of strings, and fortunately we were able to afford the luxury of a large section. It was recorded using 20 violins, 8 violas, 6 cellos and 3 basses. Very satisfying! No synthesizer can get anywhere near that sound.

Brass

In the classical orchestra most of the brass work is done by a section of trumpets and a section of trombones, with the occasional use of a tuba to fatten the bass. Treated quite separately, and often regarded more as an adjunct to the woodwind section are the French horns. Saxophones are rarely used in the classical orchestra, but their brother instruments are to be found in the woodwind section.

Trumpets

Unlike the members of the string family which sound exactly as their notes are written, the trumpet is a transposing instrument. The B flat trumpet is the regular one, and to hear a Middle C on this instrument the player has to sound the D above. I remember once giving instructions to some players in John Lennon's earshot. He worked out on his guitar the notes I had been calling out and gently told me I was mistaken and was giving the wrong notes. When I explained the reason for the difference he scratched his head and said "Bloody silly instruments!" I had to agree with him; there is not much logic in transposing instruments, but it is something we have to live with.

Triads of trumpets at intervals of thirds and fifths make a fine sound, and unison passages with saxophones at the same level in octaves below make strident effective passages if the

writing works well. The trombone section provides the bottom end of the brass, although a solo tenor trombone can sing well into the trumpet range, and the bass trombone gives a specially low and fat sound to beef up the bottom end of the section. This was the basis of the big band sound of the 1930s, and one can learn a lot about the use of these instruments from records of that period. Unlike the trumpet, the trombone is a non-transposing instrument using the bass clef, so anyone with a knowledge of the piano left hand will be familiar with its notation.

Saxophones

The other half of the big band was the large saxophone section. This instrument family is all transposing, each one in a different key to its brother. It makes life difficult for the reader of a score or the arranger, but the logic is that the fingering is virtually identical for all saxophones, merely sounding higher or lower according to the type. The standard section consisted of two alto saxes, two tenors and a baritone, but the complete range includes a bass sax and a soprano sax. The size of range, technique and notation of all these instruments is practically identical.

The written compass is

but one has to remember that the soprano saxophone will sound a whole tone lower, being in B flat, the alto will sound a sixth lower, being in E flat, and so on, so that the bass saxophone will sound two octaves and one note lower than it is written! Somehow I can never get used to the absurdity of indicating a note such as

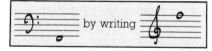

but that is the way it has to be, and it does help saxophone players who can use almost the same fingering on any saxophone in the range.

Contemporary popular music sees the use of various mixed combinations of trumpets, trombones and saxes, quite often speaking in unison in highly rhythmic punctuated parts. Maurice White uses them most effectively with Earth Wind and Fire, conducting dialogues with the lead vocal and guitars. On McCartney's track *Take It Away* I used 2 trumpets, 2 saxes (alto and tenor) and a trombone, and for the most part had them playing in unison or octaves, only rarely splitting in chords.

Woodwind

The woodwind equivalent of the string quartet consists of bassoon, clarinet, oboe and flute, and two of each forms the standard orchestral woodwind section. However, unlike strings, these instruments do not merge completely into each other, and although they blend well, one still feels each one is a soloist longing to shine. The B flat clarinet, the only transposing instrument in the group, was the main one to break out of the classical mould, and there are many fine recordings of the use of the clarinet in jazz. To a lesser degree has the flute let its hair down, and the oboe and bassoon scarcely ever at all. They are all useful colours in the palette of the orchestrator, but they need to be used with care.

Bridging the gap with the brass section are the French horns. This is a difficult instrument to play really well as a great many of its notes have to be found by "lipping" rather than with the keys. In Mozart's time horns without keys were the thing, and like bugles, all the notes had to be found by adjusting the embouchure or lip pressure. The French horn is an instrument capable of frightening intensity or equally soulful gentle sounds. It can merge well and support the cello line, fill in harmonies in the middle register, or play fine solos in the low range of a trumpet. It has a vast span of over three octaves sounding from

and good players can reach beyond this range. Being in the Key of F, all its notes are written a fifth higher. Consequently the treble clef is commonly used. On the Beatle track *For No-one* – really a Paul McCartney track – I engaged Alan Civil to play the horn solo, and he reached his high D with apparent beautiful ease, so much so, that it sounds effortless. In truth it was most difficult to play really well. The listener to this record may hear him play an apparent E flat – sounding A flat – as his top note. I have to confess we sped the tape up by a semitone to get the desired effect!

Percussion

There is a great arsenal of weapons in the percussion armoury, and an orchestrator can use them with great effect. The range is mentioned elsewhere in this book, from the huge grand cassa or symphonic bass drum, through the tuned pedal tympani (whose note can be varied even after they are struck) to the upper regions of hand cymbals and tambourines. In the world of popular music anything that makes a good sound when struck is useful, and many is the time I have put to effective use a leather covered piano stool which gives a very satisfactory sound when struck with the palm of the hand. South America and Africa are a great source of unusual percussion instruments, the conga drums and bongos giving colourful sounds. An orchestrator will find many percussion sounds useful in combination with other instruments, for they can give a harder edge to the sound. Particularly effective is the mixture of loud staccato brass and xylophone, the chippy sound of the percussion adding a biting clarity to the attack of the brass.

There are so many percussion instruments to play with that the orchestrator must experiment for himself, and note the most attractive sounds that he hears on records.

Keyboard instruments

The range of keyboard instruments has developed tremendously in recent years. While only a few years ago one was limited to the conventional piano, electric piano, Hammond organ and celeste, nowadays there is a vast range of synthesizers and hybrid pianos (such as the Yamaha electric piano) which give an unlimited tonal range. Indeed, a would-be orchestrator could profitably study the range of keyboard instruments for a long time and still not cover the full range.

One should, however, learn the possibilities of the basic keyboards thoroughly before venturing into the jungle of synthetic sounds. A conventional piano is capable of amazing tonal differences according to how it is played and recorded, and the versatile Fender Rhodes electric piano is useful for providing anything from a bright chippy sound to a dreamy stereo wash of sound.

Advice for beginners

The essence of arranging and orchestrating is first having the necessary vivid imagination to know what kind of sound you want to achieve, and then having the ingenuity and experience to know how to achieve it.

If you use conventional classical instruments, you must learn how to write for them, and when using more unusual sounds you must either know how to obtain these sounds yourself or else be able to communicate clearly with the performer.

Never have we had such a vast range of colours in our musical palette. All the more important to be able to paint with taste! ●

Arranging

A lot of young people ask me how to get started as an arranger. It's a difficult question to answer because everybody I know did it in a different way. To become a good arranger you have to practise and you have to write an awful lot of music, that much is obvious. One of the most difficult things – for me as a piano player – when I started arranging was to keep in mind how each instrument actually sounds. We all take it for granted that we can recognize, say a trumpet or an oboe when we hear one. But try to sit in your room and *imagine* that sound until it dictates what you write for a particular instrument. It's an exercise I still do and recommend. Even today I sometimes wish I were a drummer rather than a pianist, because I could probably communicate more easily what I want rhythmically.

Apart from learning about instruments and how they sound, the most worthwhile experience for aspiring arrangers is to exploit whatever access they have to musicians. Use friends or groups and write for them, whatever the combination, because the theory of arranging is meaningless unless you know how it sounds in practice. Just to hear it played back can be marvellous. Also try and maintain flexibility because an arranger doesn't always end up with a balanced orchestra.

Early experience

I went through four years of college where I learnt to play jazz and graduated with a degree in classical piano. I dabbled in arranging and composing at that time but did nothing like the amount of work I should have done to become a proper arranger and composer. Although I intended to continue studying I had a family by then, so took any job I could get.

My basic experience was gained around 20 years ago working with Andy Williams as a conductor/arranger on his television show. It wasn't particularly creative, nevertheless the training was invaluable because of the sheer speed at which you had to work. Everything had to be done between Wednesday night and Thursday afternoon, week in, week out. It certainly sharpens your ability to get through an arrangement.

It was around then I started to do more arranging than playing. I used to stay up on the road

writing for Andy Williams, and a road band then used to play the songs. While it was good to hear them so soon after writing, they were seldom properly played. It was a very enervating process because I wasn't sure in those days whether the fault lay with the bands or with my arrangements. When a good band finally does get hold of your arrangement there's such a surge of excitement and hope, if it sounds like you'd always imagined.

One thing that bands with less ability taught me was the virtue of simplicity. My main problem was using chords that were too hip. I was trying to put too many extensions on the chord when a much simpler inversion would have done.

Arranging and orchestration

Arranging is closer to composing than orchestration; it's a form of recomposing or restructuring. If a singer wants to do an old standard, the arranger's instinct is to find another way to do it. When Quincy Jones came to me with *Lush Life* he wanted to tailor it to Donna Summer's style rather than doing just another be-bop version of what is traditionally a jazz singer's ballad. In fact, it was a difficult song to adapt although most of the chord changes aren't really much altered from the original. Those I made were to find a rhythmic impulse that would be comfortable for Donna rather than to alter the harmonic structure. Often this kind of work can be done as a simple sketch. You don't have to become totally involved in orchestration. I know arrangers who never orchestrate.

Orchestration can be as creative or uncreative as you wish. Orchestrators for film composers often receive a complete sketch which is a simple copy job: you expand the G as played by a flute and the first violins, and put it on the score.

This approach of doing a sketch and giving it to the orchestrator never works for me, so I usually do the full score myself. I change a lot as I work, which is nobody's fault but my own. My rationale is if you have a sketch that's complete enough to include all those little things you're so choosy about, you might as well put it on a score yourself.

When the film *On Golden Pond* was being edited some of my recordings, including some solo piano pieces, were used for temporary fill-in music. The director, Mark Rydell, didn't tell me that he necessarily wanted a rearrangement, but he liked the idea of the piano as a featured instrument. I didn't argue because it was a very comfortable approach. Nevertheless, rearranging your own music often takes longer because it involves the separation of orchestration, arranging and composing. For me, the notes and their harmonic structure are inseparable. Having done it one way, it's very hard to do it another.

Arranging and recording

I truly enjoy arranging. I don't mind the empty page. However, I do resent the calligraphy, which is a personal chore. Someone like Al Ferguson loves it. He enjoys the physical act of writing out the music. Some arrangers, like Richard Rodney Bennett and Billy Byres, are confident enough to write in ink, which is something I can never bring myself to do.

The job of an arranger is to provide a blueprint. There's a tendency nowadays, with current recording techniques, to leave everything until the studio and not to work out arrangements in advance. A lot of people actually like going into the studio without any concept and building from there. It's not very efficient and can be shamefully wasteful. You shouldn't go into the studio without the kernel of an idea. That doesn't mean you can't change anything later, just that you need some kind of initial direction. I don't have the patience to start from nothing and I get very bored if groups take days and days to achieve something that should have been done quite simply. That said, I could probably stay quite happily in the studio for a year enhancing what I've done on one record.●

Dave Grusin, *above,* at work. A "blueprint", *right,* unlike a printed score, indicates what notes the various instruments should play and when; it omits any unnecessary musical notation.

Arranging

Before starting an arrangement of a song, I like first to work with the singer to select the right key, which is tremendously important, because it can define the whole of any subsequent arrangement. Cleo Laine and I sometimes take three or four hours just finding the key to a tune, and, as often as not, we end up with one that neither of us could have anticipated.

Cleo, because of her extraordinary voice, can select a very low key outside the normal female range, which is usually a fourth or fifth higher than the male key. *Tea For Two*, which we did many years ago, is traditionally A-flat, but Cleo recorded it in G, which took her to the lowest extremes of her range – D below middle C. The original was a rather bright and cooing young newlyweds' ditty from the musical *No, No, Nanette*. Cleo, because she saw it as the song of an older woman, turned the whole thing on its head by making it very slow and low-key in both note and mood.

Having decided the approach, it required all my skills to devise an original arrangement. Cleo wanted the song to start from nothing, then gradually add the instruments before returning to nothing. So I began the arrangement with just a piano accompanying her voice. Then a flute comes in unobtrusively and is followed by a bass. The rhythm section doesn't come in until halfway through the piece. Over the next eight bars the rest of a 20-piece band is introduced very softly before the accompaniment fades away and the song ends, as it began, with the solitary piano.

Arranging for Cleo is unusual because her voice, unlike a lot of singers', benefits from the simplest arrangements. Overdoing the background with too intricate or complex details detracts from her quality. However, many singers, perhaps with their stage performances in mind, like their arrangements to include a theatrical element. Nat King Cole used to do that a lot. Being such a fine musician he probably contributed to the original sketch of an arrangement. He certainly had a unique ability to dovetail his performance to the accented notes of the orchestration. Sammy Davis Jr is another example, although in his case it's the dancer in him that needs something rhythmic to pick up from the

arrangement. This is all the more reason for working with singers first rather than arranging something on speculation, then expecting them to grasp your ideas. It can be disappointing. I've even turned down offers from singers as great as Ella Fitzgerald and Lena Horne, simply because it wasn't possible for us to get together before I started the arrangement.

Arranging is rather like tailoring: you can either make something to fit the singer personally or you can produce something off-the-peg. I know which I prefer.

Arranging for films

Film arranging, like working with a singer, is best as a collaboration. When I was doing *Darling*, which John Schlesinger directed, I couldn't come up with a successful arrangement for a scene that John felt was particularly important. Finally, we went through the scene shot by shot with John groaning and moaning, in an approximate musical fashion, in time to the shots. I then had to translate everything he felt about the scene, not to mention his imperfect vocal efforts, into some kind of arrangement. In fact, it was enormously helpful because it wasn't until we sat down together that the arrangement took shape, and in the end we created a successful scene.

Supporting the vocalist

Traditional techniques that band arrangers use to help instrumental soloists, like riffing, can also serve for a singer, particularly an ad-libbing vocalist. These provide a background for inspiration without being too obtrusive. Devices such as sudden soft passages created by tremolos from strings or keyboards, the rhythm section starting quietly and crescendoing over six or eight bars, work very well for singer and instrumentalist alike.

An introduction can also help set the right mood for accompanists and singer. Modulations, although sometimes tricky for singers, can work wonders when they make a singer hear a song in a totally different way, even though it may be only a semi-tone away from the original.

The musician/arranger

Arrangers who play instruments write in a slightly different way from what I call desk arrangers. Musician arrangers are invariably most aware of the capabilities and limitations of their own instruments. A common error made by inex-

John Dankworth performing with his big band in 1961.

perienced piano playing arrangers, for instance, is to overwrite for the brass. The poor brass players, who have to use their lips rather than their less sensitive fingertips, really suffer and can't give their best. An effective, and more considerate, solution is to rest the brass for eight bars, give that space to another instrument, then bring back the brass with a wham.

I once used to think that players would be insulted unless given something technically difficult to perform. This isn't always the case. String players tend to be an exception. Many of them can stand up and play an entire concerto with a symphony orchestra and they understandably resent being forced to play simplistic accompaniments all evening for some light entertainer. Nevertheless, I do believe that every good arranger comes of age when he realizes that the way to get the best from musicians is to give them the simplest means to an end. There's nothing clever about writing something technically difficult. If you have the choice between using 15 notes in quick succession or one note with a glissando, use that one note every time.

Performing

I believe, and many musicians don't agree, that one must share one's enjoyment with the audience: tell them what's happening, explain the motivation of a piece, introduce the other musicians, and make sure that my own music doesn't outstay its welcome because I'm not a great soloist. I keep my solos short and, I hope, to the point. Generally, I simply try to give the audience the best performance possible.

If anything goes wrong, you have to learn not to panic and to pick yourself up as fast as possible. I remember conducting the Scottish National Symphony Orchestra in my early days when Cleo Laine was singing and she either missed or repeated a bar. For a combo this wouldn't have been any problem. They automatically would have waited two bars and caught up. With a symphony orchestra, reading the music for the first time, everything fell to pieces. I managed to stop half of them and somehow communicated that they should pick up at a certain point. Afterwards I crawled off the stage with my head hanging very, very low. It turned out the audience hadn't noticed a thing. Even the concert master didn't know what I was talking about and reassured me that many worse things can go wrong.

You have to learn to cope with mistakes and to make sure they don't affect your performance. Even if you've just fallen flat on your face, it

is very important in the next five seconds to continue trying to give the best performance of your life.

Starting out

If you have ambitions to arrange, find out what thrills you about a piece and then analyze the arrangement. With classical symphonies it's easy enough to get the scores. You often discover that the most terrific effects, where you wonder how on earth anyone could achieve such amazing complexities, turn out to be very simple musical devices. When you reduce the 40-odd lines of a symphony to a simple piano score, you'll realize that the secrets are very elementary. It's only a knowledge of instruments, but what a knowledge, that enabled Tchaikovsky to know exactly which register to employ to suit the qualities of each instrument; an instrument playing outside its most effective range will weaken the overall impact.

For aspiring jazz arrangers the task is much harder because many jazz scores are either lost or difficult to find. Most of Duke Ellington's scores no longer exist because the band books were lost, and since then only one or two people, like Gerry Mulligan and Bob Bruckmeyer, have ever come close to capturing the Ellington sound. Without a score you have to resort to the old stand-by of playing a record or tape over and over until you think you've discovered the heart of the piece.

Learning through imitation

If your imitations sound nothing like the originals, don't worry unduly. The most unique players and writers are often the worst imitators. I used to listen to Charlie Parker a lot in his heyday. I'm convinced he would play what he thought were the sincerest imitations of Benny Carter or Johnny Hodges. He never sounded like either one of them! He simply sounded like Charlie Parker the whole time. An English tenor sax player I know idolized Lester Young and refused to listen to anyone else in his younger days. He played beautifully and utterly believed he was playing just like Young. To me he didn't sound the slightest bit like Young. He did sound exactly like Don Randall.

We all start out by modelling ourselves on someone, so it's encouraging to think that if Charlie Parker or Don Randall had been better imitators they wouldn't have been such great originals. In striving after the sounds of your particular idol you may not discover how they did it, but you might well find something unique and original of your own.●

Film Music

The process of writing music for films is the same, whether the end-product is for the cinema or for television, and nowadays, of course, you are very likely to be working on something which is intended for both.

If the film is based on a novel or a play, the first thing I will do is to read it. If there is no source, I will begin by viewing the film without any pre-conceived ideas. Sometimes I see the film at an early stage in its editing process, which frankly can be confusing – it may be too long and its sequences may not be in their final order. Sometimes one has the luxury of being brought in while the film is being shot, and sometimes even before. An advantage of being involved while the film is being shot is that you can be brought out to a location, which is helpful in forming your ideas.

There is a great difference between the music that was written for the silent films and the music produced for films with synchronized sound, and it is important for composers of film music to understand this. When film was first put together in such a way that it could be screened for a public, it was always meant to have music with it. Before 1927, the year that synchronized sound was first commercially used, music was always provided by "live" musicians, and because the film was silent throughout, there had to be music throughout. This could be provided by anything from a single musician – maybe a pianist, or an organist – to a symphony orchestra in the larger cinemas in London, New York, Chicago, Paris and other major cities. Recently in London I was involved in reviving this practice: the five-hour silent film *Napoleon* was shown with a "live" orchestra. This was a unique experience, not like anything else: it wasn't like opera, or ballet and it wasn't like synchronized film. It was somehow a mix of the two, and the audience got a terrific emotional charge out of the film by having the live music there.

The role of film music

In 1927 *The Jazz Singer* hit the public, and with this new technique of being able to put all the sound on film and the possibility of hearing the actors speak, and hearing sound effects and music as well, the role of music in film slipped to perhaps a third of its former importance, be-cause it had to share the soundtrack with speech and sound effects. So, when I am called in to play my part as composer, I look at the film before the music is put on, and perhaps before sound effects are put on. The director and I then decide what role the music is going to play in the film. It cannot blanket the film from beginning to end, and it cannot provide all the drama as it did in silent films. It has to play a specific role.

In a film like *The French Lieutenant's Woman*, which I scored for Karel Reisz, what you are doing is elaborating the interior life of the characters and their experience of Lyme Regis, or Victorian London, or a love affair or whatever: something they are not saying in the dialogue that may be appearing on their faces as they, for example, open a window and look out to sea. I try to convey what they are feeling, but I don't actually have to describe the physical location. This is a very important distinction which reflects the new thinking in cinema music. Music for epic films like *Star Wars* or for thrillers, where the music must provide tension, is different: there the composer must hark back almost to a silent film technique where the pictures must be described a great deal of the time.

The French Lieutenant's Woman is greatly concerned with the thoughts of the characters, so the music comes in to try to project their emotions whenever the director and I feel there's a gap for it. It is programmed through the film so that the audience receives music in regular doses – not continuously and not too close together. The music should be placed so that it is heard to the best possible advantage, so that it's actually right for the film. Karel Reisz made a very important statement about film music. He said music for him is part of the script. Just as a costume can be right or wrong or a set can be right or wrong, so the music can actually be telling the audience the wrong thing or the right thing. The key is to discover what the music should be telling the audience.

Choosing the sound

Technically what happens is that the composer views the movie and has a discussion with the director about what he is trying to achieve. Some directors are very explicit about this: others have difficulty in expressing what they need; they have to find their way. The composer may start to view the film at an early stage in the editing, and he may think – I certainly have – Oh God it's awful, it's boring, and what have I gotten into, and can I get out of it! But there is the fascinating process of seeing the film through the editing process in which it is fined down, shortened, tightened, sound effects added, dialogue is post-synched, and it all begins to look very much better and to make more sense.

When you are assimilating the material, reading the book, seeing the play, or seeing the film, you're beginning to have ideas as to what sort of sound will complement the material. Before you compose a note you try to get very clearly in your mind what sort of orchestra is going to be there on the day, several months hence perhaps, so that, if as you compose you think of a viola solo, an oboe solo or a flute solo, you know that that instrument is going to be there because it fits into the overall sound which you have already determined. It is really wise and professional to try as far as you are able to choose your line-up *before* you actually begin to compose.

You arrive at your basic sound because this music is part of the script. Just as a costume designer may decide that that character is going to wear red in that scene, and black in that scene, so I too will choose the sound. Perhaps it is a subject that calls for romantic string music as in *The French Lieutenant's Woman*. The director, Karel Reisz, actually evoked the score from me. He had a struggle. I got some parts of it right, but I couldn't immediately solve the opening theme. In my view, the opening theme of the film, which plays usually with the title and opening credits, should sum up what the whole film is going to be about. To get this right I try to talk to the director and ask him what emotion he wants to sum up, what he wants to say at the start, what he wants the audience to know.

In *The French Lieutenant's Woman* John Fowles, the author, deliberately created an enigmatic character. You don't really know much about her until the very end. I started by looking at the picture and thinking that it was rather sad, so I wrote a sad theme. But Karel said he didn't want a sad theme, so I tried a melodramatic one, but that gave the impression that there was going to be a murder in the film or that the character was going to throw herself off the end of The Cob!

I was completely stuck. Karel and I were together, improvising music, sweating and straining. I eventually got up from the piano and said to him, "Now what is it you want the audience to know about this woman at the start of this film? The first shot is enigmatic: a woman walks down a quay in wild, wind-swept weather and looks out to sea, and that's all we have and that's not enough to inform a piece of music." Karel said,

"It's about someone who is trying to express emotion, unfulfilled yearning," and I said, "That's fine, you've said it to me. Go away, I can do it now." And that is how the opening music of the film was evolved, and then, of course, the theme was reprised through the entire film, and represented Sarah's story; someone who was trying to fulfil her own destiny, trying to find the right love, in the right time, trying to do something with her talent, do something about her position in society, and overcome all this in Victorian times.

"Unfulfilled yearning", that was marvellous. Every project and character has their little secret which must be ferreted out, and it's a good idea to make the director try and express it to you verbally. Sometimes it will be crystal clear. In the TV series, *Churchill – The Wilderness Years*, it was clear very early on. Ferdy Fairfax, the director, said he was going to treat Churchill as a "Godfather" figure; he would shoot the film with very hard lighting and stark contrast; and that it was about someone who was trying for power, with a carrot dangling in front of his nose which gets further and further away until suddenly in the end he has it. That was one aspect of it. The other was a time bomb, the year 1939; the audience knows that after eight episodes there will be war. Knowing these ideas, I could put together elements that would convey them.

Assembling the cues

When the film is fairly complete and close to the final cut, the second stage in the making of the score occurs: the editor, the director and myself will sit down in front of an editing machine called the Steinbeck. Instead of sitting upright as it does in a projector, the film lies flat in front of you like recording tape, and there is a little screen above the reels; you can stop the film, go forwards, backwards, and view it in whatever way you wish, reel by reel. This trio will decide where the music is to be placed, where each individual cue is to start and where it is to end. This may take several days, depending on the length of the film, and it is exhausting because it's so concentrated.

Once it has been decided where the music is to be placed, the editor draws up a shot list, describing each music cue shot by shot. A sequence may last as little as a few seconds or it may be one and a half minutes, or even three and a half minutes, and so on, and a sequence can be made up of anything from one to an infinite number of individual shots. The editor provides a single sheet of paper for each sequence, listing the shots chronologically, timing them exactly and describing them minutely: in fact all the

Carl Davis in the film studio cutting room, *left*.

Shot list, the music cues for the opening credit sequence of *The French Lieutenant's Woman* span one minute, thirty and one half seconds. Scribbled at the top are Karel Reisz's words which inspired Davis' music: "strong, unfulfilled yearnings."

[strong, unfulfilled yearnings / feelings]

11-2-81

"THE FRENCH LIEUTENANT'S WOMAN": MUSIC CUES

1M1:

    'MAIN TITLES' (now with titles' timings)

1. Music starts at:

	Mins.	Secs
Karel credit starts fade on		
Karel credit full on		
Karel credit starts fade off		
Karel credit faded out ALSO	0	00
Meryl's credit starts fade on		1
Meryl credit full on		1½
Meryl credit starts fade off		3½
Meryl credit faded out ALSO		4½
Meryl starts upstairs and cam. starts pan up ALSO		4½
Jeremy's credit starts fade on		5½
Jeremy's credit full on		8
Jeremy's credit starts fade off		9
Jeremy's credit faded out ALSO		9
"French Lieutenant's Woman" credit starts fade on		9
"French Lieutenant's Woman" credit full on		10
Meryl steps from top of stairs over onto Cobb. Sea revealed		12½
"French Lieutenant's Woman" credit starts fade off		13½
"French Lieutenant's Woman" credit faded out		13½
Sarah past camera		14½
End of Cobb revealed AND		15½
Leo McKern etc. credits start fade on		20
Leo McKern, etc. credits full on		21
Leo McKern, etc. credits st..		28
Leo McKern		28

91

composer needs for writing the music to the precise length required.

Composition

Up until about two years ago, I went home with these sheets of paper and I worked on what I thought were the appropriate pieces of music for each of those cues; if it was a love scene, or a battle, or a tense moment or whatever it was, I would compose music to fit the mood and fit the length of the cue. Now, I have been thinking for years about why film and music go together so well, and I suddenly realized that it has to do with time. A film lasts for an hour-and-a-half and it moves forward during that time. Music also exists in time and moves forward, and I think this is why the two complement each other so well. Since I realized this, I have paid more attention to the development of the music in the time allowed, both within the individual cues and within the film as a whole.

Some composers work and compose without playing any music at all; they hear the composition in their minds. I can do this, but usually for film music I like to play. It is a source of inspiration and I frequently start to compose by improvising and playing. Then I take my time sheet and my piece of manuscript paper and work out whether the piece is slow or fast or medium, and it is then possible to measure it because the way to write out music is to work in bars: you can measure how many seconds there will be in a bar and then you just multiply so that you know how many bars are going to get you to the end of the cue. This may seem very primitive, but I can think of no better method.

You have to take care that the tempo you imagine with a piano will work well with other instruments. Fingers tend to move rather glibly over the keys of a piano, but strings or brass take more time to articulate a tone.

The great recent development which has vastly improved the lot of the film composer is home video. Before this it was impossible to work with the film at home; home projection was almost useless because you could not turn the film backwards and forwards. Now I can play the music on the piano while watching the film at home on my television, and this has, of course, been marvellous. Also I can brief the director and work with him on the film at home, and I no longer have the traumatic experience of everyone first hearing the music in the studio.

Imagine arriving in the studio; you've got a big orchestra in front of you; you've got a set amount of time to complete the recording; the film goes up; you record your music; and the director says.

Carl Davis conducting the Wren Orchestra of London

"Weeell, I know I said it ought to be slow, but really it ought to be fast." This is a nightmare for the film composer, but it is something that we all have to cope with and the real nightmare is that we have limited time. When the musicians are in the studio they cost an enormous amount of money. Their time is very set and when you get involved in extensive revision on the spot, when in fact you have made a wholesale mistake, you are really in trouble. Hopefully, preparation with the director at home circumvents this: you can agree at least about the basic quality, whether he likes the melody and the emphases, so that when you get to the studio you only have to deal with details which can be amended quickly.

Orchestration

Once the director and I are agreed on all the music, and this may involve a lot of toing and froing and revision on my part, I then have to realize the music into an orchestration. This involves me in scoring. Some composers do this entirely by themselves, some have assistants. Some short-score, or sketch their ideas briefly, and bring in an assistant who works up the finished orchestration, because this work is very time-consuming. On the other hand it is vital that the composer be very much involved because that orchestration is what people will hear.

precisely the right moment in terms of the action which I can see on the screen.

Another composer's aid is the click track, which is the equivalent of a metronome. Each musician and the conductor wears a set of headphones and hears a click which will be in a tempo set by the composer. This means that everyone will remain exactly "in sync" to the film. In my view this is sometimes over-used, especially when every piece of music in a film is recorded to a click. It can be useful when a piece must be played strictly in rhythm and you want to synchronize and hit various points in the action; then it cuts down on the number of takes, but for a cue which is slow and romantic, you don't want to have "click click click" going on in your ear, because that militates against the players playing expressively. The click track is a very useful tool, but it must never be regarded as anything other than that.

On the first day in the studio you are showing everybody the music for the first time. People will be saying they like that part – they don't like that part – can that be slower – can that be faster. In other words, you will be working on the score as well as recording it. You are still part of the team; you cannot regard film composing *ever* as something you do without any regard to what other people think. You are participating in a team of people and the production of the music is viewed, not from the point of view of your ego, but from the point of view of its effectiveness and how they see it in the film. And of course no-one has heard the music before, except perhaps on the piano. When you lift your baton for that first cue, it's terrifying but very, very exciting.

I used to do it all myself, but recently my workload has grown so I now short-score in as detailed a form as I can, bring in an assistant to expand the short score, and then review it with him. I wish I had the time to do it all myself because I feel that delegating the orchestration ends my involvement as a composer too soon. After all, when you expand your music from a sketch in one, two, three or four staves to eight, ten, twelve, fourteen, up to thirty-six staves, you are still composing, still thinking of details. However, I now work with people who understand the effects I want, and I keep looking at it.

Once you have the score it is handed over to a copyist who extracts the individual parts from it so that each player has his own part to play from.

Recording film music

So the day of the recording session arrives, and the editor has extracted all the individual cues from the film and has made a reel of just the sections that you are going to put the music over. A recording studio that is equipped to record film music has projection facilities, as well as the usual recording equipment. Normally the film will be projected on a full size screen, which the conductor faces with the orchestra seated between him and the screen.

The film is projected onto the screen with a counter which tells me in seconds exactly where I am in my cue. I will annotate my score accordingly so that, for example, the crescendi occur at

The final dub

The final step in the film process is, of course, the dub of the film. Some composers call it "the battle of the dub", because it's there that the three sound elements – speech, effects and music are put together on a single track. Final decisions about the music are made; where it is to be put; sometimes cues can be reversed or swapped around; frequently cues may be dropped. It is not uncommon for entire scores to be discarded at this stage and there is also the decisive factor of what *level* it is going to be played at: that is extremely important, and there a composer can lose out. The single sound of a rock falling, or a footstep, or a door closing, or tanks, machine guns, bird calls, can obliterate your entire score unless the dub is very carefully and tastefully done. The dub is the final step, and in a way it is the most crucial one, because it determines, at last, what the public is going to hear.●

Songwriting for Advertising

Songwriters usually get involved in writing jingles and music for screen commercials because someone approaches them. The work comes through agencies, and it is possible to get onto an agency's books by sending them cassettes of your work: if they like it, they will keep you in mind for the future. My involvement in commercial music started in 1965. At the time, McCann-Erickson were producing commercials for Coca-Cola and using current pop groups like The Supremes. Roger Cook and I had just written the hit *You've Got Your Troubles* for The Fortunes, and Coca-Cola wanted to use The Fortunes and the writers of that particular song. The Fortunes had a sound that seemed to work with our type of writing, and although at the time they became better known in the United States for their Coca-Cola commercials, their real success came with *I'd Like To Teach The World To Sing,* which we wrote for them.

The briefing
At present I work mostly through the music production company Air-Edel who liaise between the client and myself. They might receive a call from an advertising agency requesting that I do a

Roger Greenaway in the eight-track demo studio at his home. Most of the musical ideas for a jingle are played on synthesizers at the demo stage. Using different synths, it is possible to indicate the feel of the finished background for the "voice over". Demos often sound better and more enthusiastic than the final master because they are recorded in a more relaxed atmosphere.

commercial for one of their clients. Air-Edel will say if they think I am right for the job, or they might suggest me if I had not been requested. If they feel I am not right for the job, they will try to persuade the advertiser to use someone else.

Once a job has been offered and accepted, I go to the agency for a briefing and am given what is known as copy – a brief description of the product being sold. The copy does not normally constitute lyrics, because it has been written by advertising copy writers, rather than by a songwriter. If the copywriter has made an attempt at poetry, the lyrics are usually humpty-dumptyish and not very good. If the copywriters are unable to produce any key words or phrases for me, they will give me a general idea of the type of music they have in mind for the piece, for example, hit parade pop.

I can change the wording of the copy, with the exception of the logo lines – the words or phrases that the advertiser has included in the piece. I am happy that a scan – a specific rhythmic pattern – is rarely demanded because it gives me more freedom to play with the words and allows me to move in different musical directions.

Sometimes I am given copy that consists only of logo lines, the bulk of the commercial being instrumental. In this case we use what is known as a voice over (VO) whereby the logo lines are either spoken or sung in front, behind, or between the melody. This means that the music I am creating is, in effect, background sound and must on the one hand not interfere with the VO, but on the other hand be sufficiently interesting for the listener to remember and recognize.

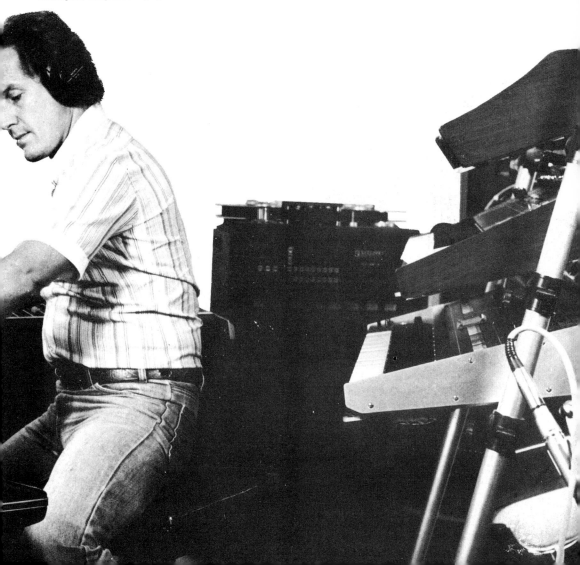

The songwriting process

The creative aspect of songwriting is intangible and therefore difficult to describe. Personally, I find it difficult to pluck a melody out of the air and add the words as an afterthought. For an instrumental piece, the title is the springboard that gets my musical ideas flowing. For example, if I am given a title like *You've Got Your Troubles, I've Got Mine,* these words suggest a melody, and I will mull over the copy until a melodic sequence comes to me. I may produce a line or two, and then it can be anywhere from a few minutes to a few hours before a basic melody is established.

In the early stages of writing I do not use any instruments, although I might sing into a tape recorder. Only after I have something fairly solid will I try the piece out on a piano or guitar and if I am not happy with what I have written, the chords will sometimes introduce a different melodic structure to the same words. In general, songwriting is a trial and error process of adding and eliminating until something solid emerges.

If I am working on a commercial that is purely melodic – without words – and it is for television, the copy will include information such as what the film will show and what should be expressed about the product. From reading the copy, specific words will come to mind and from these I then proceed as if I had words. This type of assignment is more difficult because I must act as both copy and music writer. I need the words – even if I have to write them myself – to be able to create the music.

Making a demo tape

Once the words and music are in reasonable shape, I make a demo tape at home where I have an eight-track studio, using a drum machine and a Moog, or perhaps a Jupiter 8 – one of the new machines that can do everything from bass to keyboards. The demo usually contains some suggestion of the particular instruments that will be used in the finished piece, and I will sing the lyrics to illustrate the phrasing of the song, because this can be the most difficult aspect to convey.

The demo is presented to the client for approval; it will include only one or two basic ideas, because I prefer to keep it uncluttered. If the agency and the client like it, the demo then goes to a proper recording studio where we use session musicians who play specifically for commercials. If the piece is complicated an arranger will be brought in, but if it is just a rhythm section with a Moog overdub for the melody, I will write out the chords for the musicians myself.

Singing for commercials

Sung and spoken words for commercials must be clearly enunciated, but it is equally important that the singers convey the feel of a piece and do not just read and sing the music and words in front of them in an uninspired way. Few people today write an arrangement for singers, and it seems that some of the best singers do not read music very well, if at all. To establish the mood, I will sing the piece to the singers who usually pick it up after one or two trials – they have to be quick to work in commercials. When I feel they have grasped the basic feel of the piece, I will let them develop and interpret it as they wish.

Precision timing

Time is money in the advertising business. For a television commercial I am usually limited to 28 seconds and for radio 30, but either can be up to 60 seconds long. The timings now being used are based on the metric system, which means that pieces will be 10, 20, 30, 40, 50 or 60 seconds long; 20, 30 and 40 seconds are the most commonly used.

The synchronization of words, music and images is essential in a commercial, so I often use a click track monitor (see page 93) to facilitate precise timing. This saves a lot of time, and therefore money, in the studio; and, if the music is being recorded before the film is made, it helps the film editor. In any kind of film music there are specific points where music or percussion enter to signify what is happening in the film, and this requires perfect timing. The film editor's job is much simpler if a click track has been used because all of my "call signs", or special effects, will be on the right frame and match the film exactly.

The finished product

A client often prefers the demo to the finished product, which is probably due to the psychology of recording. Making a demo is fun because there is no pressure and it does not matter if the final product is not quite right. Most people today do demos with just a rhythm section and a few Moog overdubs and, for some reason, the feel of the basic rhythm section on a demo is often better than the end result. Frequently the vocals on a demo are also freer and more relaxed. After the demo stage, musicians are brought in and the piece is orchestrated; the entire operation becomes complex and pressurized. Once you are in the studio, you know you have to get it right. When the red light goes on it is impossible to relax, because you know this is it, this is the real thing.●

Performing Music

*". . . feeling is what marks out a
true performer."*
JEFF BECK

Vocals

A natural talent for singing is a precious gift, but to have talent is one thing and to know how to use it another. Young singers are sometimes told they have natural talent and do not need training, and some popular singers do indeed become successful without any training at all. The majority of successful singers, however, have had some kind of coaching and there is no doubt that with training every singer will improve and find it easier and more rewarding to perform.

To assume that one has a good or a poor voice is often a mistake because it is impossible to hear oneself as others do; a good teacher will recognize talent immediately, even if his pupil is unaware of having such a gift. A coach is also invaluable for helping a singer become conscious of what is naturally unconscious. Breathing and producing sound, for example, are natural, "unconscious" functions, yet the singer must learn to discipline and control these if he is to make the most of his talents. If taught correctly, a singer is always in control of his voice and will know not only how to produce notes, but also how they will sound even before he sings them. A talented singer without training will probably have difficulty with breathing and voice production, especially the high notes, but a singer who has been trained will produce these with comparative ease.

Voice range

Notes that are sung, like words that are spoken, are created by air forced through the vocal chords causing them to vibrate. The sound waves created by the vibrating vocal chords are passed into the mouth and nasal cavity which acts as a resonating chamber. Tight vocal chords produce high notes and slack chords low notes; it goes without saying that women have tighter vocal chords than men.

While voice ranges of individual singers vary, the standard range is as follows: bass – middle C to C two octaves below; tenor – G above middle C to G two octaves below; alto – C above middle C to C below middle C; soprano – G one and a half octaves above middle C to G below middle C. There are many variations within these ranges; for example bass singers may reach as high as tenor G above middle C, and a soprano's range may be to C two octaves above middle C. Between these four ranges exist the contralto (deep alto); baritone (midway between tenor and bass) and mezzo-soprano (between soprano and alto).

Most singers can sing in two registers: the lower, or chest, voice; and the upper, or second or head, voice. In male singers the latter produces the sound known as falsetto. Singers such as Smokey Robinson and groups such as The Stylistics use falsetto as a distinctive feature of their style, while a singer such as Rod Stewart prefers a husky tone obtained by pushing the upper extremities of his lower voice. Those who wish to preserve a conventionally good singing voice will do better to use their second voice, which is thinner and softer in tone, than to strain at the upper end of their lower voice.

It is important that a vocalist sings in his or her most comfortable range and a good teacher will attempt to establish this. It is unwise, for example, to encourage a baritone to strive for a tenor range because a relaxed, even tone will prove impossible; the smooth, refined phrasing of a singer such as Frank Sinatra appears effortless because he exploits only the range in which he is comfortable.

Use and abuse of the voice

Some people feel that the shouting, screaming and straining that produces the husky quality heard in the voices of singers such as Paul Rogers, Robert Plant and Mick Jagger is a misuse of ability. For a Mozart aria this would certainly be true, but then a *coloratura* soprano, breathtaking though her performance may be, does not produce the gut-reaction that Tina Turner can create in the listener with her sensuous rasp.

The relaxed, easy pace of old-fashioned singing would be incongruous for a song such as *Roxann* by the Police, and in the world of rock a high tenor voice such as Sting's can add a sense of urgency to the excitement of the music. Sting uses the top range of his chest voice almost exclusively to produce a strident, anguished tone that is perfectly suited to rock. One of the most fascinating voices today is that of Donald Fagan of the now defunct Steely Dan. Listen to the last verse of *Haitian Divorce* or *Gaucho* to hear how Fagan uses whines, admonitions and lyrical melody lines, spitting out words and crooning long notes, as if his voice were an instrument.

Phrasing

The art of using a line of music to convey the meaning and mood of a song is known as phrasing, and the truly great singers are those whose phrasing is near-perfect. Lingering over a long note, adding a small flourish, changing inflection on certain words – all are devices capable of turning a simple melody into a memorable performance. It is possible for singers without superb voices to be successful through the use of good phrasing, and many unexceptional singers perform admirably because they have acquired the art.

The great singers have all developed their own distinct styles of phrasing: Shirley Bassey has a great sense of the dramatic which is expressed through her ability to hold long notes for exactly the right amount of time; the precise staccato interjections and grunts of Otis Redding and James Brown express soul singing at its best; and Aretha Franklin is unparalleled, not only for her immense vocal range, but for her ability to sing high or low, loud or soft, with equal proficiency.

The ever-popular Barry Manilow belongs to the Sinatra/Bennett school of singers and uses the type of phrasing found in the Cole Porter and Irving Berlin songs, but with modern overtones. David Bowie, on the other hand, by employing a mixture of heavy vibrato, whispers, falsetto and screams can, in one song, create a kaleidoscope of emotions, as heard in *Wild Is The Wind* with its throw-away, spoken lines intermingled with throaty, rock choruses. Al Green is yet another singer with a highly developed sense of phrasing. By using a device learned from Otis Redding, Green splits a word on a long note into a number of short staccato syllables; in *Let's Stay Together,* for example, he sings "I" as 'I-hi-hi-hi" with each "hi" becoming progressively softer as though he is caressing the word.

Interpretation

A natural talent for singing is more than the ability to move people by the quality of a voice. The ability to inject emotion and excitement into a song, for example, is something that cannot be taught, and in some cases an unexceptional singing voice may actually suit a particular style of music. Interpretation should not involve vocal pyrotechnics to show what a singer is capable of; rather it should express his individuality. A singer should not force himself to sing a song he does not like because it will inevitably sound stilted; the most successful interpretations are those sung by singers who truly believe and feel the words they are communicating.

Shirley Bassey

David Bowie

James Brown

Sarah Vaughan

The way in which a singer interprets a song is closely linked to phrasing, and the two jazz singers Ella Fitzgerald and Sarah Vaughan exemplify this. Fitzgerald has an effortless style that makes jazz singing appear easy – which it is not – and performs stunning flourishes and cross-timings with equal ease. Vaughan has mastered the art of improvised "scat" singing (using sounds such as "be-doo-be-da-da" instead of words) to use her voice as a lead instrument, with an overall effect of sparkling energy.

Many people react negatively to the long drawn-out words and threatening upswings of early Sex Pistols' music, but Johnny Rotten gave a new dimension to the word "Sprechgesang" (speak-sing) coined by Arnold Schoenberg in the early 1900s. Speak-sing is used by many folk and country singers, but never with the intensity of the Pistols.

An excellent example of different ways of interpreting the same song can be heard in Madness' single *It Must Be Love*. Madness have retained the flashy swing of the original Labi Siffre version but execute the song in an apologetic, cockney tone without vibrato or heavy phrasing. The line "I need to be with you every night, every day, I couldn't be happy any other way" verges on deadpan, yet through a simplicity of interpretation the song achieves a unique, straight-to-the-heart pathos.

The voice as instrument
The human voice is capable of greater flexibility and expressiveness than any instrument yet created by man. Traditional folk-singing is usually sung *a cappella* (unaccompanied) or, if accompanied, a single guitar, violin or accordion

usually suffice. Work songs from the American South were often accompanied by the clapping of hands or by work tools struck in time, and the theme might be shared antiphonally by a lead singer and ensemble, as heard in the well-known traditional *Pick A Bale O' Cotton*:

Lead singer	Ensemble (refrain)
Me an' my wife gonna . . .	*Pick a bale o' cotton*
Me an' my wife gonna . . .	*Pick a bale a day*
Oh, Lordy . . .	*Pick a bale o' cotton*
Oh, Lordy . . .	*Pick a bale a day*

From the simple to the complex, this device has permeated all forms of popular music. Part of the chorus of Kenny Loggins' hit *This Is It*, for example, runs in a similar fashion with singer answering the chorus:

Chorus	Lead singer
This is it . . .	*Make no mistake where you are . . .*
This is it . . .	*You're going no further . . .*

In The Beach Boys' hit *Good Vibrations*, Mike

The Beach Boys

Love sings "I'm picking up good vibrations" in a low register accompanied by "good . . . good . . . good . . . good vibrations" in a high register, interspersed with simple skat, "baap . . . baap". Skat is one of pop's most original devices which, like many innovations, was born of necessity: in the 1940s the recording industry was faced with a great loss of revenue due to a musicians' strike and to avoid potential disaster, a few companies came up with the ingenious idea of using voices to provide accompaniment rather than instruments. Thus phrases such as "baap-shu-wap", "dum-dum-dum" and "ramalamadingdong" replaced the rhythmic and melodic phrases normally created by instruments and percussion. While barber shop quartets and close-harmony groups had existed for decades, the use of vocals for an entire rhythm section was a totally new idea and long after the strike ended the style became an indispensable ingredient of rock 'n' roll that is still in use today.

Harmony

Vocal harmonies can give polish and presentation to an otherwise ordinary song. The Everly Brothers sang in two-part harmony giving each part equal importance, and early Beatles' singles were executed in the same vein. The Beach Boys made four- and five-part harmonies a strong feature of the so-called "surfing" music originating in the West Coast in the 1960s and Brian Wilson, the group's principal innovator, was a great admirer of the close-harmony group The Four Freshmen, to whom he owes a great deal.

The use of harmony grew to operatic proportions with Queens' hit *Bohemian Rhapsody*. The problem with this kind of super-production, however, is that unless a complete choir is taken on stage when performing live, it is impossible to reproduce the recorded sound without the use of tape. In their rock opera *Tommy*, The Who resolved this problem by using a taped recording to create a fairly good live reproduction on stage. The music was then re-recorded for the film version using a large cast of singers plus a symphony orchestra. Performers such as Diana Ross and Stevie Wonder use a small group of vocalists on stage as well as background vocals from members of the band.

Singing in harmony is more difficult than most people realize and the complex vocal arrangements of a Beach Boys' or Queen song in fact require countless hours of practice. A singer who reads music will find it easier to sing harmony than one who does not, because he has only to read and sing the notes written. The

non-reading singer, even with natural talent, has to depend solely upon his ears and memory and learn his part of the harmony by heart. Learning a part, however, is only one half of the battle – singing with the rest of the group is the other.

Harmony parts usually fit around a solo melody singer, yet it is not enough for a harmony singer simply to sing the correct harmony because tone and feeling must also be present. It is easy for a singer to go out of tune and/or timing when singing in a group, especially a singer whose ear for harmony is undeveloped, and so some singers

Diana Ross and Stevie Wonder.

will block out the sound of the other members' voices; hearing the other members, however, is the only way to be sure that everyone is in tempo.

The smaller the group, the easier it is to sing in harmony. In a duo, for example, the harmony singer has considerable latitude because he has only to blend his notes with one other voice; thus duos such as The Everly Brothers and Simon and Garfunkel produced excellent harmony lines partly because they had great scope within which to work.

Three-part harmony is more difficult because the two harmony singers must not cross each other's notes since balance and sound will be affected. Four-part harmony is still more complex and the upper, middle and lower parts must stay in their own registers, which is why vocal groups with three or more singers often use specific people for specific registers. The Four Freshmen and The Temptations, for example, both use a high tenor, bass, tenor and baritone. Some all-male groups, such as The Stylistics, use a specialist falsetto. The Pointer Sisters use a contralto and two sopranos.

Counterpoint

Counterpoint is a complex feature of harmony, consisting of two or more lines of music that are separate but which create a harmonic whole. One excellent example is the chorus of The Beatles' song *Eleanor Rigby* in which Paul sings, "All the lonely people, where do they all come from?" while the backing vocals sing, "Aah, look at all the lonely people" in a different rhythm and with different notes. Although everything is happening simultaneously, the individual parts do not coincide note for note. See example below.

Similarly, in Earth, Wind and Fire's *Boogie Wonderland* the middle choruses have two sets of vocals going on at the same time singing different but complementary lines: the female group, The Emotions, sing the main line while the male vocalists sing a counter melody:

Female vocals *"Dance . . . . . . boogie wonderland"*

Male vocals *"Dance – ooh, ooh, ooh! Dance – ooh, ooh, ooh! Daa-ance."*

Counterpoint is a traditional musical device which reached its greatest heights in the works of J. S. Bach. Two vocal groups who specialize in this exciting form of harmony are The Swingle Singers – who do excellent vocal renditions of some of Bach's instrumental works – and the King Singers.

Vocal spread

The Swedish group ABBA have made harmony and counterpoint a major feature of their work and have learned to subtly juxtapose female and male voices for greater variety. In *Does Your Mother Know* the high-pitched female voices sing, "take it easy, take it easy", while the male lead remains one octave below. Interesting combinations also come from bands such as Steely Dan where the same parts are doubled by a man and woman. Thus, instead of a female or male back-up, there is tight vocal support for the lead singer that blends perfectly without one tone overriding the others.

To achieve the widest possible spread of harmonies, a mixed choir such as that used in the Stones' *You Can't Always Get What You Want* is an approach worth following, because by using a mixture of male and female voices the entire vocal range can be employed. Other bands base their sound on one or more groups of voices. The Eagles, for example, have a beautiful spread of harmonies, which incorporates the full vocal range, providing a backdrop for the lead singer, as heard in *New Kid In Town* from the album *Hotel California*.

Style

It is important for singers to develop a unique style for the simple reason that an impersonation is never as good as the original. From Frank Sinatra to David Bowie and from Bessie Smith to Kate Bush, the successful singers are as easily identified by their voices as they are by their faces. Simon and Garfunkel have a style totally distinct from other duos due to Garfunkel's ballading which blends in neatly with Simon's wistful exhortations; Al Jarreau, a jazz-based,

modern soul vocalist uses his voice to create sounds similar to a guitar, percussion and violin, making his vocals part of the band's sound.

The many fine cabaret-style vocalists, who can do well-phrased impersonations of famous singers singing famous songs such as *My Way* point up the fact that individuality is more recognizable in the use of the voice than in its quality. No one could accuse Mick Jagger of having a great singing voice, but he is always recognizable for his urgent, energetic R & B-style vocals. Nor is the wealth of control and flexibility of Aretha Franklin or the late, great Minnie Ripperton available to every singer. The singer must cultivate those aspects of his singing which are unique to him. Mark Knopfler of Dire Straits, for example, half-talks his lyrics which suits his introspective writing as well as his voice.

Korg Vocoder: a vocal synthesizer which translates words, fed via the microphone, into musical sounds.

Vocal aids

For most professional work microphones are used to project a singer's voice, and so it is essential that a singer develop a good microphone technique. If a singer is too near the microphone, distortion is produced; if he is too far away, there may be loss of tone due to the microphone not picking up all of the harmonics. There are so many high-quality microphones now available that even a nondescript voice can be given depth and sibilance. There are also echo and reverb devices, compressors, limiters and graphic equalizers and a host of other effects, all used to enhance the human voice. The vocoder is the culmination of these being a vocal synthesizer with keyboard; the singer need only speak words into a microphone and the keyboard will produce the notes.●

Singing

My father was a singer, and so singing was in my family, and I can't remember ever not singing or not wanting to sing. I wouldn't say my mother was a "stage mum", but I was given all the things that would hopefully put me on stage one day, such as singing, piano and dancing lessons. Although most of this early training soon left me, it gave me a foundation because when I started to sing later on I tried not to abuse my voice by becoming a voice "basher", something many untrained singers are liable to become.

Training

Training isn't so much a matter of acquiring tricks as it is of practising. When I started singing professionally and began to listen to a lot of singers, I became aware that they were doing things I could hear in my head but couldn't express with my voice, and so I decided to have further training to improve my range and breathing, both of which are important in jazz singing and improvisation.

While I was singing with John Dankworth's jazz orchestra I went to a teacher in England and, because she was a classical instructor, I told her I didn't want to change my sound – which was contemporary – but did want to improve my range and protect my voice. She helped me more by instructing me in the psychology of singing than by giving me theory: if I was trying to reach a high note, for example, she would say, now you're going to sing a note that you don't believe you have in your body and to do this you're going to imagine you have strings on your ears and will rise forward on your toes, and it will come. Eventually I didn't have to do these exercises, and now I don't even think about a note, although I still need to hear it in my head.

To be able to sing what is in your head, you must acquire a certain amount of technique which you can't achieve without a range of an octave; and if you sing continuously within the same range, you will find it difficult to improve or advance. When I joined John Dankworth I felt he preferred to work in the higher registers rather than the lower. Without my being aware, John would write an arrangement for me a semi-tone or tone higher than I would normally sing, and so I began slowly to expand my range.

Health

I don't agree with the idea that throughout his working life a singer can ride on personality, emotional know-how or the fact that he was once a famous singer and so people will still come to hear him. Many singers could still be singing today if they had looked after themselves physically and, while it might be all right for a singer to abuse his health when he's very young, at a certain stage, if he wants to continue singing as he did when he was 20, he must consider his health.

Although I have done some opera, I wouldn't be accepted today as an opera singer because of a slight cloud over my voice caused by smoking cigarettes early in my career. This caused permanent damage because I'm susceptible to bronchitis and the combination is obviously not good for a singer. There are exceptions to the rule and I know many fine singers who do smoke, but there are just as many, such as myself, who can't sing if they smoke or drink heavily. Whether a singer does or doesn't, his first concern should always be for his health; a musician can blow an instrument or play piano if he is physically unwell, but a singer won't be able to sing.

Listening

Listening is an important aspect of learning to sing and many singers don't listen closely enough. If you sing out of tune and can hear it, you can always correct yourself; if you sing out of tune and you can't hear it, that's trouble. Learning to listen means listening with concentration and practising this every day; listening to complicated solos and then singing them is probably one of the best ways for a singer to improve.

If a singer trains his ears by listening, or through ear-training if he doesn't have natural ability, many exciting things can start to happen. For me however, this has been a double-edged sword: having a good ear has made me lazy about learning to read quickly because a good ear is an advantage to a slow reader.

Styles

When I hear classical singers producing beautiful sounds I sometimes wish I had gone in that direction. I know how to use classical singing techniques, such as bringing the sound forward into the palate and up to the top and using the diaphragm, but these things don't suit my style of music. However, it's a great help today for a singer to be versatile because of the wide range of classical and popular music being performed. Ideally, a classical singer should know how to sing in a popular vein, and vice versa, but classical singers are likely to find this difficult because they are often afraid of hurting a pure sound. Sometimes I distort my sound because of the music I'm singing, and at other times I'll sing with only pure sound, but I know that no matter how pure my voice may become, it will never be pure enough for opera or *lieder*.

Influences

When I was very young I would cry if I heard violins playing, I have always been emotionally involved in music, seeking out and being affected by all the music going on around me. When I started singing professionally, it was primarily the music and film singers who impressed me – a decidedly mixed bag which is perhaps why I have such an eclectic style and attitude and like classical as well as popular music. As I grew older and began to think for myself, I discovered I liked singers such as Billie Holiday, Ella Fitzgerald and the jazz band singers, who at the time were not popular with the public, although they eventually became big stars.

I would listen for many different elements from these singers: from Billie Holiday it was the dramatic content of her singing and the way she treated each word as meaning something special; even the tritest of songs acquired weight when Billie sang it. With Ella Fitzgerald it was her improvisational ability that amazed me; the vocal agility that enabled her to move around like an instrument, the way a musician improvises. When I was living in England I listened to British, rather than American, groups such as John Dankworth, Ronnie Scott and the jazz musicians, but I continued with the classical singers as well. Although I used to listen to entire solos and try to work out where or how they came about, I was always more of an intuitive than a technical singer; I always did things that I felt worked best for me.

When listening to instruments, I didn't pay much attention to technique but was aware if a player was very adroit because phrases done at great speed always excited me, as well as odd notes that I hadn't heard before. Occasionally an instrumentalist would use notes I didn't expect and I would want to imitate them, and I eventually incorporated this into my own style of singing.

Instruments and voices

Good sound from an instrument is similar to good sound from a voice, and I'm fortunate to be able to recognize both. As a rule I don't differentiate between instrumental musicians and singers,

John Dankworth and Cleo Laine

but a voice has a kind of magic because you are never sure if it's going to come out or not. When I go for a high note, for example, even if it's in my head, I'm not always sure that the equipment in my throat and lungs – or whatever makes it all happen – is going to work. An instrumentalist might have difficulty because of a mechanical problem with his instrument, which he can fix, but that can't be done with the voice.

Jazz

I don't know why I'm known as a jazz singer – I don't consider myself one and I prefer to simply sing a song and get the most out of it as a dramatic piece. I can bend a note, do the odd thing that a straight singer can't and I don't sing strictly on the beat as a classical singer would, but I can't do chorus after chorus off the top of my head. To me, if you're a jazz singer you should be able to do what a jazz instrumentalist does, and I can't.

Performing

If we're going to do a new programme, we try to find new material which is always difficult because we have to wade through tapes and records of old songs or current songs – if we're going to do current songs – and eliminate. If it's original material, the lyrics must be written and learned, which can take months. At one time I used to change my programme every year, but now I don't change it so often.

I always rehearse until half an hour before a concert or, if it's a completely new programme, right to the start of the concert. I never go straight into a theatre and perform without first spending at least an hour or more rehearsing, getting the amplification right and working with the band, which is my warming-up time. I don't go for every high note when I'm rehearsing; instead I'll try one, and if it's there I don't strain in case I wear my voice out.

By the time a singer steps out on stage he should have practised enough so that he doesn't have to worry about the music, and what happens should come naturally. I don't go out on stage knowing I'm going to do this or that because then it all becomes too automatic. Each audience is different and when I first walk out I weigh them to see whether they are my kind of people or not. I like to see the faces in the first few rows so that I can sing to a person and sense how they're relating to me and whether they're enjoying themselves; I don't like it if the spotlight is too bright and there's just a black void. Occasionally I see someone with an angry expression and go off stage thinking the person must have

hated me, but they're usually the first ones back stage to tell me they loved every minute, so you can't always judge from a face. I try to do my best and try not to be affected by anything like that, but I also try to get some kind of current going between myself and the audience.

I pay attention to what is happening, but not in a self-conscious way. For example, I assume I'm singing in tune but, if I'm not, I'm aware of it; but if something is wrong and I *am* in tune, then it must be someone else. In this situation a singer can adjust unless he has perfect pitch, and then it can be painful. Relative pitch allows the singer to move back and forth with the instruments, but if he has perfect pitch and has to work with whatever instrument is put before him, it can be exceedingly frustrating. If a singer goes out of tune or time and is not paying attention to the band, a disaster can occur and everything will crunch to a halt; however, unless you are singing with a symphony orchestra, such disasters can usually be averted.

I automatically adjust my style to the kind of back-up band I'm working with. I wouldn't sing with a single instrument the way I would with a symphony orchestra; that would be like singing *sotto voce* with one and coming on like a power-house with the other. Although I would need intensity with the single instrument, I would adjust my voice as far as volume was concerned. If the amplification isn't good with a symphony orchestra, I tend to over-sing because I feel I must give much more than I actually need to. It's difficult for me to put the brakes on; I have to tell myself to pull back, I'm never going to beat this orchestra and won't have any voice left by the end of the evening – but I still tend to sing louder than I would with a small group.

There's a special exhilaration that comes from working in front of wonderful bands, such as Basie's or Ellington's, which is another reason why I tend to over-sing; I love it so much I want to go full blast. At a certain point they will give me all the power I want and I have to consider how far I can go without busting my voice. I have this sorted out now, but early in my career I did everything I shouldn't have done from the point of view of preserving my voice. Still, it's terribly exciting when the band is together, the rhythm and arrangement are right and you are in good voice – there's nothing like it in the world.

Recording

There are singers who are recording animals, who record beautifully and get what they want, yet fall to pieces in front of an audience. I'm essentially a performing animal; while I don't fall

Cleo Laine

to pieces in a recording studio, there's usually something I don't hear in my recordings that I can only hear when I'm on stage.

Advice for beginners

Whenever young singers talk to me, I tell them that their voice is like a thumbprint – if they have mistakes or faults in their voice – nobody else can acquire those faults. A singer can listen to other singers and take on bits and nuances of their style, but young people generally take the thumbprint and become impressionists. If you take a thumbprint of a singer, you will always be second best, so you must take what is *not* part of their thumbprint and add it to yours. In that way you will eventually become an original sound.●

Keyboards

Keyboard instruments fall into two basic groups: those that are responsive to the strength of the musician's touch on the keys; and those that simply trigger or pluck a note in the same way however the key is pressed. The piano, clavinet and clavichord are touch-sensitive; harpsichord and organ are not. There are synthesizers of both kinds.

Acoustic keyboards

In my view the piano is growing in popularity again as a musical instrument for the home. The guitar has been the main instrument of popular music – and in the home – since the 1950s; but the piano was the established instrument – almost part of the furniture – in the 1800s and the early decades of this century.

The nineteenth century was the great era of the piano; it was then that Liszt and others produced their great works for it; but the instrument has its roots considerably earlier, during the 1700s, in the time of Bach. He used three main keyboard instruments: the organ, which of course was a woodwind instrument; the harpsichord, which had strings that were plucked when the keys were pressed; and the clavichord, which was the closest to the piano. It had hammers for striking the strings; but instead of

retiring to let the strings vibrate freely, it lifted the string and held it in that position, so muffling the sound. It was very much quieter than a piano, and that is why the piano was called a *pianoforte*, meaning soft-loud.

My favourite type of piano is the Bösendorfer, in fact the best piano I've ever played was a Bösendorfer at Linz, in Austria. It was nine foot, but it went down to a C; Bösendorfers often have a little envelope that opens you down to an F, but this went down to a C below the F.

There is a type of Bösendorfer, the largest size of all, which isn't over strung. All the strings run vertically up and down, so the bass strings are well separated from the treble – marvellous for stereo recording.

My own piano is an Ibach. It has a beautiful tone and a little bit of brightness which I like. It's only six foot nine, but like most people I have a space problem.

Upright pianos

Upright pianos are really grand pianos turned on their ends so that they can fit into small spaces. There are usually two pedals: the sustain pedal which keeps the sound ringing on even after the hands have been raised from the notes; and the soft pedal, sometimes known as the *"una corda"* pedal, a term which describes the mechanism exactly. Each note of the middle range of the instrument has three strings assigned to it which are struck simultaneously by the hammer. A shift

The king of pianos: the Imperial manufactured by the Austrian firm Bösendorfer who have been making pianos for over 150 years. This model is nine foot six inches in length with a keyboard that encompasses 8 octaves. Opening the flap at the lower end of the keyboard provides extra notes down to an F.

Gary Brooker

Geyer upright piano

mechanism, activated by the soft pedal, moves all the hammers laterally so that only one string (*una corda*) is struck, creating a softer sound. The honky-tonk piano has an extra pedal which causes the hammers to strike the strings in a way which gives the jangling, cowboy piano effect exemplified in Paul McCartney's *Rocky Raccoon*.

Touch-sensitive electric keyboards

There are a number of electric pianos available and, like acoustic pianos, they are touch-sensitive; the most widely used are the Rhodes, the Wurlitzer and the Yamaha electric grand.

The Yamaha sounds most like an acoustic piano; it is in fact a baby grand with strings, hammers and the same action as a normal acoustic piano, but with the additional benefits of phase, chorus, treble, bass and volume controls. It is made to the overstrung design – as is Helpinstill's electric piano – which characterizes most good acoustic pianos. The longer a piano's

strings, the better its sound; to gain maximum length, bass strings are strung diagonally across the frame, above and at an angle to the treble strings. The Yamaha is very useful for touring bands, because the body splits into two sections; the harp, or frame holding the strings, comes away from the keyboard, hammers and electronic controls, enabling two people to carry the piano.

A gigging, freelance keyboard player usually requires an instrument which he can move and set up by himself. Whether he uses ancillary keyboards and synthesizers or not, he will need a basic piano sound from a keyboard that reacts to touch and pressure. The most popular electric portable is the Rhodes, of which there are several models. Most common are the 73 Stage, which requires an external amplifier, and the 73 Suitcase, which has its own amp and speaker system; 73 refers to the number of notes available. There are also 88 and 54 models, although the latter does not come in suitcase form.

On all models of Rhodes pianos the sound is produced by a hammer striking a metal tine, the vibrations from which induce a signal in the pick-up which is amplified by an amplifier. The Rhodes is easy to tune; each tine has a spring which can be moved up and down.

Rhodes pianos have a distinctive bell-like quality coupled with a warm tone, excellent for creating moods with a sustained lingering quality. It is used to great effect on innumerable recordings, including Elton John's *Daniel* and Steely Dan's *Babylon Sisters*.

The great rival of the Rhodes piano is the Wurlitzer EP200. This uses a simplified piano action, a hammer striking a metal reed, the resulting vibrations being received by pick-up

The Yamaha CP70 electric grand, *below and right,* is very popular with touring musicians due to its easy manoeuvrability. Each string has its own pick-up and, in addition, there are controls for chorus, treble and bass voices, and phasing facilities.

plates. Individual reeds are tuned by adding or removing pieces of solder which are stuck on the end of each reed. This is fiddley and requires patience coupled with a good ear or an electronic tuning device. The Wurlitzer's tone is harder and brighter than that of the Rhodes, but it doesn't have the sustain of the latter and is therefore best used in staccato passages. Supertramp's *Dreamer* features a Wurlitzer piano.

Hohner D6 clavinet

The clavinet, especially Hohner's model D6, is capable of very exciting rhythmic work. It is an electric instrument, strung like an acoustic piano, but the hammer-action strikes the strings like a bass-player banging a string against his fingerboard. It is not very effective in slow passages, but for up tempo music (Stevie Wonder's *Superstition*, Andy Kim's *Rock Me Gently*) it beats rhythm guitar every time, having a bright, cutting tone.

All these instruments react to the speed and pressure of the player's touch, so that a musician can really colour his playing with sensitivity in the hands. With non-touch-sensitive keyboards – organ, harpsichord and most synthesizers – volume pedals and vibrato/tremolo effects have to replace those nuances normally achieved by the fingers.

Non-touch-sensitive keyboards

Until the invention of the tone-wheel organ, which was patented by Laurens Hammond in 1934, all organs were reed or wind instruments, activated by keys and bellows-driven. Hammond revolutionized the instrument by using a synchronous motor, powered by an alternating current. The motor turned 95 tone-wheels, each producing fundamental pitches with no harmonic overtones. A system of drawbars, which could bring in other notes and frequencies at different volumes, enabled a sound to be built up from various separate constituents (rather like additive synthesizers, *see Synthesizers*).

The Leslie tone cabinet was developed for use with the Hammond organ; it comprised a speaker with two horns mounted on a revolving spindle. The spindle was driven by a motor and had two speeds. The slower speed produces the characteristic, haunting Hammond sound with the tone apparently changing constantly. This is achieved by the movement of the horns – first

facing the listener, then pointing away, then turning back and so on – so the effect on tone is bright, dull, bright, dull. The higher speed provides a lovely rippling tremolo. Good examples are all Booker T & the M.G.s albums, Billy Preston's work on The Rolling Stones' *Sticky Fingers* album and The Beatles' *She's So Heavy*.

The harpsichord is strung but, instead of a hammer action, little quills pluck the strings. Because the plucking action is always the same, the amount of pressure applied to the keys does

Morley harpsichord

not affect the volume or tone of the sound. By using pedals or stops, similar to those of a church organ, different effects are obtained. You can play in octaves, only striking one key at a time: quills pluck the required note plus the octave above or below. The "lute" stop produces a sound like a lute by causing the quills to pluck the strings very close to the nut. Little soft pads can be brought into contact with the strings, producing a "harp" sound. And there are many other possibilities.

The harpsichord has a bright, delicate tone, which is exemplified in pop music in songs like *In My Life* from The Beatles' *Rubber Soul* album and The Stranglers' hit single *Golden Brown*.

Combining keyboard instruments
Along with my piano, my other main instrument is a Yamaha CS80, a synthesizer which I play as if it were a piano (*see Synthesizers*). For effects I use an ARP synthesizer. I haven't experimented with synthesizers as much as some keyboard players, mainly because my energies are taken up with the three things I do best: writing, singing and accompanying myself.

I have never been very interested in the organ, in spite of the fact that it played such a big part in my major hits with Procol Harum. I started Procol with the idea of using a piano and organ together – something unusual then because it was considered a luxury to have two keyboard players. But I thought they sounded great together.

Our line-up in Procol Harum was myself on the piano, Matthew Fisher on the organ, Robin Trower on guitar, B. J. Wilson on drums and Dave Knights on bass – a five-piece. This allowed us to have particularly strong backing to any solo. If the guitar was playing alone, he could have the piano and organ behind him; the same applied to the piano solo, when he had a guitar and organ backing. It is not a combination that has been much used, but I think it could come back.

Composing on piano
I nearly always write my songs by sitting down at the piano and experimenting. I've sat on trains countless times and had ideas, known what the chords were, written them down along with the melody, and then gone home to find it's all rubbish when tried out on the piano.

Ray Charles, *left,* incorporates a blues-influenced style in his playing.
Jerry Lee Lewis and **Elton John,** *insets,* have used country and western tempos for some of their rock 'n' roll and ballad compositions.

I find the piano right for composing, because it reacts to how I feel and how I'm playing at the time. And of course, it gives chords, fill-ins, rhythms, bass lines and melodies all in one shot.

I don't find composing on the piano restrictive; my fingers don't automatically run in grooves, and I don't just reproduce material I've played before. If I play a chord I've used before, I scrap it immediately.

Until recently, I wrote only the music – not the lyrics – for songs, but for my most recent album, *Lead Me To The Water*, I did both. This did not alter my approach of always thinking of the music first. At the creative stage I use dummy lyrics – real words rather than just *la da da* – but with no particular sense. The advantage of writing the lyrics myself is that I can make them match the sound as I think they should. Some words aren't nice to sing; they don't lend themselves to carrying on a note – you can't, for example, sing plaaaank or swaaank. There are all too many words like that, and if I write the lyrics, I can easily find substitutes. All the same, it can be difficult to produce lyrics which both suit the notes and make enough sense to preserve the story line.

Styles of piano playing
In my view my style of playing piano – and most other people's – is an assimilation of styles. I don't think there is such a thing as basic rock 'n' roll piano style. Some early players, like Jerry Lee Lewis for example, had a style which was basically boogie – good left hand rhythm and diddley work on top, but with plenty of major chords. Others, like Ray Charles, had a more rhythmic, rhythm and blues type style, using plenty of sevenths and what I call minor type playing, when you play individual notes and get minor thirds even though you're actually playing a major chord. This style actually stems from straight blues; you can see it in the work of Muddy Waters and similar guitar players.

Early rock 'n' roll piano was mainly up tempo, but Jerry Lee Lewis also used a pumping, country and western tempo, and Ray Charles played some slow numbers. Generally speaking, piano playing was quite "busy". People like myself who came later learnt, and used, all these styles.

Another important style, which I use for a certain type of song, is best described as ballad style. Carole King, Elton John and even Carly Simon often play this way. We may have derived it to some extent from country and western, but actually I suspect it owes more to Floyd Cramer – a major influence on many of us.

Modern recording and sound techniques have had a major effect on piano style. Today you can play one chord on the piano that can be made to last electronically for, say, four whole bars. Provided it is good sound, in itself it is effective. People like Gary Numan have made much of this.

Among my favourite styles these days is that of Dr John (Mac Rebenneck), although his is a direct copy of Professor Longhair's, the New Orleans pianist who had a kind of "rolling" style. The New Orleans style – not Dixieland, but New Orleans rock – has been a major influence.

I think the growth in popularity of albums has also affected style: the album gives musicians the opportunity to mix material, to vary the pace. For a varied album, you need up tempo material along with solid songs and some dreamy stuff – perhaps a ballad starting with piano only.

Jazz piano has had an enormous influence, though to assimilate the style of greats such as Count Basie you have to be technically superb. I suspect that many people achieve this to a great extent by relying on a repertoire of "licks" which they insert in their playing. Dudley Moore is an example; he is an excellent jazz pianist, and he introduces a selection of licks into his playing. A lot of top guitarists are like that; they have six or eight licks and they play them in different keys – sometimes major, sometimes minor – and because of what is going on behind them – because it is a different song – they sound different. People pinch licks all the time and modify them a little. I've got a few licks which I use from time to time and they're ones I've had since the early days.

When it comes down to it, the sort of playing that young pianists should try to emulate is Count Basie's. The older he gets, the fewer notes he plays, yet each one tells beautifully. It seems terribly simple – as if anyone could do it – but of course, it's not so simple; and you have to have thought of it in the first place.

To understand how that kind of playing is achieved you have to go back to the question of technique. Count Basie has a very mature approach to technical ability. He made a decision that he would prefer to go for telling simplicity, rather than dazzling, busy playing.

In order to have this choice at all, you must be a master of technique; at the same time, I believe you have to be able to put technique second to your desire to create your own music. There is no substitute for a way of playing that will reach across to people; but technique is the springboard for achieving that goal.

I learnt the piano by getting my knuckles rapped when I played a wrong note. I often had to learn pieces I didn't like. It wasn't an enjoyable way to learn; and even at the age of seven or eight I knew I could be taught better.

I went to the lessons because my father sent me – just like many others of my generation. We had no guitars, or records – except "78s" – or any popular music to speak of. We played little classical pieces like *Humoresque* or *To A Wild Rose*; the business of learning just wasn't much fun, or particularly interesting. It is vital that teachers encourage pupils, especially children, to like music by getting them to play pieces they enjoy.

My only enjoyment of music at that stage was playing duets with my father, who was a professional musician. Maybe this kept my general interest in music alive – I never thought about much else – even though I didn't enjoy the lessons.

In retrospect, though, I believe musical discipline is important for young people. The right approach is to practise every day, and learn to read music. I'm not a good reader, but I could have been if I had practised every day for an hour. Even the mundane routines, like scales, arpeggios and consecutive thirds are important. If the fingering is automatic, later on it will be easier to concentrate on musical ideas when composing, or to have a greater range when playing.

Some people think that the greater a musician's technical proficiency, the more difficult it is for him to be creative. I think this is evading the issue, which is that if creative talent is there it usually comes out somehow, whether the person is technically skilled or not. But I do think I might have ended up in a different field of music if I had been a better technician. As it is, I make up for not being a particularly technical pianist by versatility – by being able to sing, accompany myself on the piano and write songs. It is also true that I found my creative niche precisely because I went into popular music, where it is usual to have to play it by ear, to try to produce what people want to hear at the time.

Possibly the most serious drawback of great technical ability is a tendency to write songs that are over-complex. This can be disastrous. There is definitely a right and wrong use of sophisticated technical ability. These days I practise mostly in order to get ideas, rather than to improve my playing ability, although I will practise when there is an important recording session or tour coming up. My advice is to become as technically accomplished as you can, but to play only music that you enjoy.●

Playing Piano

The characteristics that differentiate one piano from another include factors such as whether it was made in a factory or carefully hand-crafted; whether the keys are ivory or plastic (ivory absorbs sweat from your hands better); and where the wood came from and whether it was aged naturally or synthetically. My main criterion for judging a piano however, is simply how it sounds but the piano is such a unique and wonderful instrument that even a poor one will give a musician the opportunity to make incredible music.

Pianos

There are many different makes of grand piano ranging from Bösendorfer, Steinway and Yamaha to Baldwin, Kawai, Chickering, Bechstein and Blüthner. The makes most often found in the studios are Steinway. Bösendorfer and Yamaha, but the huge Steinway B is without doubt the work horse of the industry; there have been more hits recorded on this piano than on any other, including Ray Charles' recording of *I Can't Stop Loving You* and Elton John's *Don't Let The Sun Go Down.*

I prefer the German-made Steinway known as the Hamburg because the wood is from Africa and dried at a lower temperature than those made in the United States. German wire also makes for an extremely sensitive instrument and the Hamburg is widely acclaimed by session players and classical pianists alike.

Bösendorfer's Imperial concert grand has nine extra keys at the bottom and a purity and roundness of tone that is unique – it also has a price tag that is unique. I used a Bösendorfer when I did Boz Scaggs' *Silk Degrees* album and found it to be both a remarkable ballad instrument, as heard in *All Alone,* and a powerful rock 'n' roll tool, as in *Jump Street.* The Bösendorfer was also used extensively by Michael Omartian for Steely Dan's *Katie Lied* album.

The electric piano

Some of my earliest memories of the electric piano include Ray Charles playing a Wurlitzer on a recording of *What'd I Say* and later on Jo Zawinul's *Mercy, Mercy.* Larry Knechtel can be heard playing the Hohner electric on The Association's version of *Never My Love,* and I played one on Steely Dan's *Black Friday* album opposite Michael Omartian.

The Fender Rhodes was the first electric piano I ever owned and its touch-sensitivity and sound made it a refreshing improvement over the out-of-tune pianos I had used previously. The most significant feature of the Rhodes is its ability to record cleanly and effectively, for example, Richard Tee's performance on Paul Simon's *Still Crazy* album and the classic Elton John version of *Daniel.*

When Yamaha came out with their CP70 electric grand, it often replaced the acoustic grand in live performances, and their most recent hybrid – the GSI digital synthesizer – has become an essential part of my recording set-up. The GSI includes most of the electric piano sounds and a wide range of complex synthesizer sounds as well, all with 88-note touch-sensitivity. A few examples include my own recordings on the *Toto IV* album, specifically *The Soul In Africa,* and Elton John's *Empty Garden* album; I also used a GSI recently in a duet for Michael Jackson.

Reading music

Reading music is simply a language by which musicians communicate with one another, be it a simple chord sheet or a full piano concerto. A player either has soul or he does not, and the road to being a good, funky rock 'n' roll player is not going to be made more difficult by an ability to read music, as is sometimes claimed. Billy Preston, Leon Russell, Richard Tee, Nicky Hopkins, Elton John and Keith Emerson all read music, just to name a few. On the other hand, many notable musicians have not been able to read music and I do not believe that an inability to read has ever hindered a person's ability to play.

Reading music does not necessarily mean being able to sight-read a concerto, merely the ability to understand a double-staved part with a bass line, a melody line and the inversion of the chord written out. This is essential if a group of musicians is to record a piece reasonably quickly. The sessions I've done with Steely Dan are written out in intricate detail allowing a player to memorize a part much more quickly for the actual take.

Classical music

Classical music provides an endless well of harmonic possibilities for the musician to draw

The Steinway Grand B-211, *left and inset,* has probably been featured on more hit records than any other piano.

The Rhodes electric piano, *above,* features in the line-up of many contemporary groups. Its characteristic bell-like tone is produced by very simple mechanics.

The Yamaha GS1 digital synthesizer, *right,* produces both electric piano and synthesizer sounds with touch-sensitivity.

upon, and my own classical background has not only given me the tools and techniques needed to express myself, but has also increased my harmonic scope enabling me to draw upon ideas I once thought impossible. The idea that a classical background will somehow prove detrimental to a musician's expressiveness and inventiveness is a myth; after talking with the likes of Oscar Peterson and Jo Zawinul I would hate to try and convince them that studying classical music has prevented them from expressing their souls. It is inevitable that, once the point of becoming a hot lick expert has been reached, a musician will want to expand into unknown territory – and this is where a classical education often comes to the rescue.

Influences

My father was a session pianist for a long time and showed me many things I could not have learned from listening to records. When I was 12 my father was doing a Sammy Davis Jr. album in the Olympic Studios in London. About the time the session was ending, Procol Harum were also finishing their first album at Olympic and I had the chance to meet Matthew Fisher, the organist,

who proved to be a great influence and introduced me to my first Mellotron. Other organists who have impressed me include Billy Preston, Keith Emerson and Booker T, of whom I did my best imitation on The Pointer Sisters' version of *Fire.*

The other main influences on my musical career were Larry Knechtel, Jimmy Webb and Mike Laing. Larry Knechtel played on Paul Simon's *Bridge Over Trouble Water,* The Association's *Never My Love* and Jimmy Webb's *McArthur Park.* Webb has been a great influence on me as a songwriter and pianist. Mike Laing, who played piano on Herb Alpert's hit *Rise* and who can sight read or improvise any style, taught me a great deal about different playing styles.

I would love to mention all the pianists who have ever influenced me, but there are simply too many. I am just proud to be a part of the history of rock 'n' roll keyboards that began with people such as Jerry Lee Lewis, Little Richard and Ray Charles.

As for the new electronic equipment around today, I say; let there be new music for the new instruments.●

Synthesizers

Synthesizers recreate the ingredients of sound – pitch, tone, volume and articulation – electronically. All sounds travel in waves, which, in a synthesizer, are created by an oscillator. The more frequently the wave vibrates, the higher the pitch (or frequency).

As well as its fundamental pitch, a sound contains harmonics. To see how these shape the tone (or timbre) of a sound, try this experiment: almost close your mouth and make a humming noise on one note feeling it vibrating in your head. Holding the same note, open your mouth slowly until you hear a second note a fifth higher sounding with your original note. By opening your mouth still wider, you will hear other higher notes. The overall effect is to change the tone of the note from a mellow to a bright sound. In the same way all sounds are given their quality by the number of harmonics present, and this is determined by the shape of the wave. Four waveforms which vary in width and height are shown below with their respective harmonic content. The sound of a flute is very close to a sinewave, hence its sweet round tone. A violin's tone is very brilliant because many harmonics are present; the waveshape is a mixture of ramp and square waves. In a synthesizer, filters are used to add or eliminate harmonic frequencies from the oscillator in order to shape the timbre.

A sound rarely remains at a fixed volume throughout its duration. A note played on the piano starts with a fast attack (the sound rises to its full volume, or amplitude, rapidly) and then slowly decays. A note played on a cello might start with a slow attack, then be sustained for the duration of the bowing, and stop abruptly as soon as the bowing stops. In a synthesizer these

Waveforms: the colour, or timbre, of a sound depends on the number of harmonics present. This is determined by the shape of the soundwave. A sine wave (top) contains no harmonics and is the purest of all wave-forms, with a sweet sound not unlike that of a flute. The sawtooth (or ramp) wave has all harmonics, odd and even, present and gives a hard, "edgy" sound. The smooth, muted tonal quality of the triangle wave, which contains some odd harmonics, is similar to a sine wave but less pure. The square (or pulse) wave, including all the odd harmonics, has a clear, hollow sound.

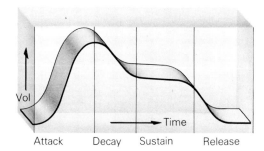

ADSR: the volume level of any sound varies over time and can be divided into the four categories above.

factors – attack, decay, sustain and release – are known as ADSR and are regulated by the envelope generator.

Theoretically it is possible to synthesize any sound which lasts just a fraction of a second. However, elements such as breathing, bowing and variation in vibrato, make the precise reproduction of musical sound very difficult. The first synthesizers were hopelessly unstable; composers spent most of their time replacing blown valves and tuning drifting oscillators.

Voltage controlled synthesizers

The real synthesizer revolution took place in the 1960s, when valves were replaced by transistors – cutting the equipment size by half – and voltage control was developed by Dr Robert Moog and Don Buchla. Voltage applied to an oscillator can vary the pitch produced. The standard method is an increase of one octave in pitch per volt; hence a C raised by two octaves would have two volts applied to it. Voltage control of filters and amplifiers is also possible.

Although in theory, the parameters of sound (pitch, tone and volume) can be controlled on a synthesizer by a number of devices, the piano-

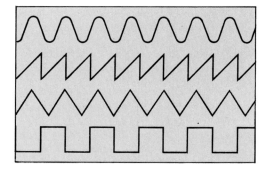

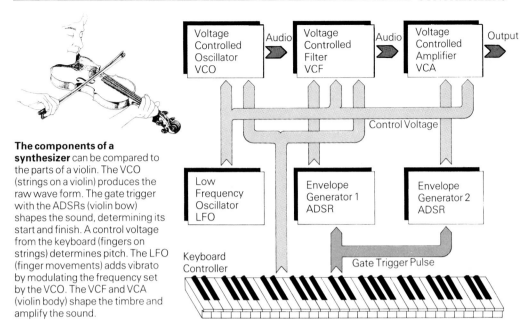

| Voltage Controlled Oscillator VCO | Audio | Voltage Controlled Filter VCF | Audio | Voltage Controlled Amplifier VCA | Output |

Control Voltage

| Low Frequency Oscillator LFO | Envelope Generator 1 ADSR | Envelope Generator 2 ADSR |

Keyboard Controller

Gate Trigger Pulse

The components of a synthesizer can be compared to the parts of a violin. The VCO (strings on a violin) produces the raw wave form. The gate trigger with the ADSRs (violin bow) shapes the sound, determining its start and finish. A control voltage from the keyboard (fingers on strings) determines pitch. The LFO (finger movements) adds vibrato by modulating the frequency set by the VCO. The VCF and VCA (violin body) shape the timbre and amplify the sound.

type keyboard is easiest and most popular. The keys can determine fixed pitches as well as acting as a "trigger" for the envelope generator. Therefore, the ADSR of a note can be achieved by one finger movement and, because all sounds are produced by a voltage and controlled by a voltage, the interrelationship of sounds can be achieved with absolute precision.

The components, or modules, making up such a system are as follows: the VCO (voltage-controlled oscillator) generates either audible or controlling (modulating) waveforms; the VCF (voltage controlled filter) shapes the raw waveforms by adding or removing harmonics so giving tone or timbre; the VCA (voltage controlled amplifier) controls the amplitude (volume) of audio signals or controlled voltages; the ADSR (attack, decay, sustain, release) or envelope generator, controls the shape of a sound. Other modules are incorporated in many synthesizers; these include noise-generators (sources of random voltage fluctuations), switches, mixers (for combining 2 or more sources) and sequencers (for producing pre-set rhythmic or melodic sequences).

Such synthesizers are known as voltage controlled modular synthesizers. In the first of these the various modules were external, connected (patched) with leads instead of being wired internally (hardwired) into a set configuration; this was intended to give maximum flexibility. All the inputs and outputs of each module were connected to jack sockets on the front panel which could be patched with jack leads from one

module to any other. However, any moderately complicated patch soon turned into a jumble of wires, which made the system look like some crazy telephone exchange. Certain manufacturers tried different patching techniques: the ARP 2500 had numerous coloured sliding switches, a very expensive method of patching and not really any better than using leads; EMS in London tried a "patch-matrix" board on which little pins were pushed into crosspoints.

Modular synthesizers then are made up of several modules, each with one designated function; the modules can be connected externally in any configuration and can be controlled by voltages. They are produced by Moog, Buchla, Polyfusion, Emu Systems, Roland and PPG.

Patching a synthesizer with leads was very time-consuming and therefore impractical for

Moog System 55 modular synthesizer

Minimoog

stage use. Since most sounds were produced by a relatively standard method of programming, manufacturers began to incorporate certain commonly-used configurations of modules into their instruments' designs. Connections were hardwired, no leads were required and such synthesizers came to be known as performance synthesizers.

Sequencers

Most of the early synthesizers were played with a 12-tone keyboard. However, other forms of control for use alongside the keyboard quickly developed, the most important of which was the sequencer. This is basically a voltage store unit, capable of memorizing whole musical lines: in effect giving the musician another hand. Once programmed, it can replay the stored sequence at any speed and, unlike a tape recorder, it will stay in pitch regardless of speed since it simply replays controlled voltages while the VCO generates the sound. The other sound parameters (tone, volume and ADSR) can also be controlled through the sequencer.

Two types of sequencer are used nowadays; the most basic is the analogue sequencer, such as the Moog Sequential Controller. This consists of rows of knobs on which control voltages are pre-set; a trigger, or "clock", moves the sequencer on from one knob to the next setting off the pre-set voltages. The system is limited by the number of knobs available, which is usually no more than 24. Consequently, a pre-set

Roland Microcomposer MC-4

melody cannot contain more than 24 notes.

Digital sequencers are more sophisticated: they use computers, or microprocessors, to generate the voltage. One of the most advanced is the Roland Micro composer MC-4 which can control four different voices, or synthesizers, at the same time. Its greatest advantage is its memory capacity which can store up to 12,000 different notes (the equivalent of 12,000 knobs on an analogue sequencer). Entire compositions can be written into its memory, and it is considerably easier to programme than its analogue counterpart. A tune can be played straight into the memory from a synthesizer keyboard at any speed, and a calculator-type keyboard can be used to enter pitch and timing values.

Sequencers enable anybody to play a composition; it is not necessary to be a keyboard virtuoso. A melody can be programmed and the machine will play it; although, of course, if you put rubbish in, you will get rubbish out.

Polyphonic synthesizers

Advances in technology – especially the invention of integrated circuits and microprocessors – started to influence synthesizer development towards the end of the 1970s. Simpler ways of controlling the sound, and another major reduction in component size and price, helped to make synthesizers more and more accessible. Voltage-controlled oscillators and filters could now be made as small as a single micro-chip and it became possible to build polyphonic synthesizers which could play more than one note simultaneously. A true polyphonic synthesizer should have a voice for each key on the keyboard. Korg attempted this with their semi-modular FS-3100, which had 48 voltage-controlled filters and amplifiers. Twelve VCOs (one for each semitone in the scale) were subdivided to give a four-octave, 48-note polyphony across the keyboard. Moog attempted a similar system with their Polymoog.

There was another approach, developed by EMU Systems, Sequential Circuits, Oberheim and Yamaha. They limited the polyphony to anything from four to eight voices by using a microprocessor to scan up and down the keyboard detecting what keys were being depressed and assigning these to any free voices available. Cost and components were kept down while a very satisfactory polyphony was obtained. As well as using a microprocessor in assigning the voices, Oberheim and Sequential Circuits used it to programme these settings into a memory for instant recall at the touch of a button. The "performance-oriented" synthesizer had arrived.

Yamaha CS80, *right:* one of the first polyphonic synthesizers. It is a very expressive instrument, incorporating a totally touch-sensitive keyboard, and demanding a great amount of control and dexterity from the musician. Vangelis, Stevie Wonder and Andy Clark are among the best players of the CS 80.

Prophet 5, *left,* from Sequential Circuits: the workhorse of the synthesizer world. Its inventor, Dave Smith, included a microprocessor in the design that controls and stores all parameters of sound for instant recall. Joe Zawinul, Herbie Hancock and Chris Franke use Prophet 5s.

The Roland Jupiter 8, *left,* another sophisticated synthesizer, is able to "split" the keyboard, meaning that different sounds can be produced in the left and right hands. These sounds can then be "layered" on top of each other.

121

The control room at Snake Ranch
Studio, London. Hans Zimmer and
engineer, Steve Rance, are
working with several synthesizers,
drum machines and computers on
a movie soundtrack. This control
room is considerably larger than in
most other studios since most of
the recording takes place here
rather than on the studio floor
(which would be necessary for
acoustic instruments). The video
equipment, tape machines,
sequencers and synthesizers all
run in synchronization with each
other and are controlled by
computers. The control room, in
effect, becomes a musical
instrument. The equipment
shown here includes (around the
room, beginning top left):
Apple II computer
Roland SH2 synthesizer
Roland System 100M synthesizer
Roland TR808 drum machine
Korg 3300 synthesizer
Roland microcomposer
Prophet 5 synthesizer
Large modular Moog synthesizer
Moog analogue sequencers
Roland vocoder
Yamaha CP70 piano
Roland Juno 6 synthesizer
Roland Jupiter 8 synthesizer
Minimoog
Roland Jupiter 4 synthesizer
JVC U-matic video recorder
Lexicon 224 echo/reverb
Soundcraft 1624 mixing desk
Numerous effects
. . . and one large fan.

A lot of manufacturers started building programmable polyphonic synthesizers: Roland with their Jupiter four and eight-voice; the Prophet five and 10-voice from Sequential Circuits; the Korg 3200; and the Oberheim OBX. Only Moog's Polymoog remained "unprogrammable". Yamaha duplicated the front panel of their CS80s and CS60s so that a memory could be activated by switching from panel to panel. Their equipment features velocity and pressure-sensitive keyboards, so that the sound can be altered by the different speeds and pressures with which a key is struck.

Digital synthesizers

The microprocessor has certainly made synthesizer control much easier. Until recently, commercially available synthesizers were still using the old concept of VCO, VCF and VCA to generate sound. The idea of creating sound purely by computer (digitally) has been around for a long time, but the prohibitive cost of a large system has meant that only the big universities and similar institutions have been able to afford computer synthesis. Now, with the advances in microprocessors and integrated circuits technology, it is possible to build digital synthesizers cost effectively.

Digital synthesizers, such as the CMI Fairlight, use typewriter keyboards and light pens that can draw waveforms straight on to a television screen. The basic concept of the digital synthesizer is more abstract than that of an analogue system. Rather than using fixed "building blocks", such as oscillators and filters, to create a sound, a digital synthesizer is like a blank sheet of paper on which the musician "designs" his sound. Since a computer is very much more precise than the best analogue system, the qualities of sound can be much better defined.

The choice of digital systems is overwhelming. At the top of the range are the NED Synclavier and CMI Fairlight, while at the bottom are the different types of Casiotone. A useful feature of the Fairlight, Synclavier and Emulator systems is their capacity to "sample" (record) an acoustic sound like, for instance, a milk bottle being struck, and to incorporate it into their bank of sounds. These sampled sounds can be modified in a variety of ways – for example, a complete scale can be built from one note – and then they can be played with the keyboard.

Digital synthesizers are part of a very new world and digital technology is advancing rapidly, but they have not made the analogue synthesizers obsolete. Each synthesizer has its own potential, and can create original sounds.●

Digital synthesizers range from the advanced Synclavier II, *above*, to the modest Casio tone, *below*.

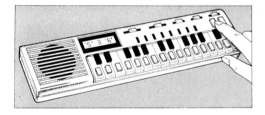

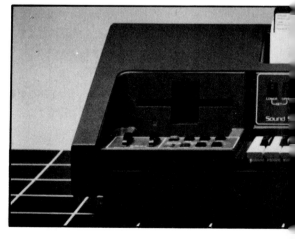

The Fairlight CMI, *above,* is able to sample acoustic sounds which can be played in pitch on the touch-sensitive keyboard. Sounds can be synthesized by drawing waveforms with a light-pen on the VDU, and sequences of up to 50,000 notes can be stored in its memory. All sounds are created digitally.

The Emulator, *below,* samples acoustic sounds which can be performed on its keyboard or sequencer.

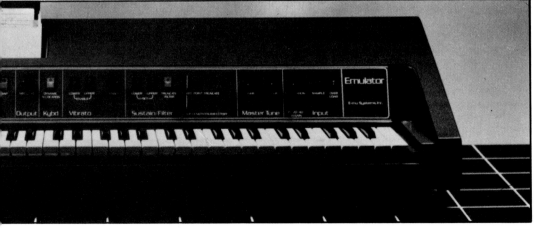

Electronic Music

We have also sound-houses, where we practise and demonstrate all sounds, and their generations. We have harmonies which you have not, of quarter-sounds, and lesser slides of sounds. Divers instruments of music likewise to you unknown, some sweeter than any you have; together with bells and rings that are dainty and sweet. We represent small sounds as great and deep; likewise great sounds extenuate and sharp; we make divers tremblings and warblings of sounds, which in their original are entire. We represent and imitate all articulate sounds and letters, and the voices and notes of beasts and birds. We have certain helps which set to the ear do further the hearing greatly. We have also divers strange and artificial echoes, reflecting the voice many times . . . and some that give back the voice louder than it came . . . We have also means to convey sounds in trunks and pipes, in strange lines and distances.

Today we tend to think that we of the twentieth century are responsible for the creation of electronic music, and yet the quotation above is taken from Sir Francis Bacon's *New Atlantis*, published in 1624, illustrating both how much music has developed over the past 350 years and, perhaps more interestingly, how little.

The foundations of electronic music

The physical and mathematical principles of instrument design and composition can be traced back to Ancient Greece, and these same principles reappear continuously throughout the history of Western music. Pythagoras' observations on vibrating strings, for example, dominated the evolution of music theory until the seventeenth century.

A new view of music did not appear until 1863 when Herman von Helmholz published his revolutionary book *The Sensations of Tone,* explaining that characteristics of sound are determined by a complex relationship of fundamental tones and harmonic overtones. This breakthrough, along with Bell's electronic transmission of sound in 1876, Edison's 1877 phonograph and the appearance of Thadeus Cahill's sound staves, or telharmonium, in 1897 – an instrument large enough to fill six box cars – set the

stage for major developments in twentieth-century music.

When the Danish scientist Waldemar Poulsen presented his telegraphone, or wire recorder, in 1898 he paved the way for the storage, manipulation and study of sonic information. However, working with wire recordings presented many problems, not least of which was the need to tie knots in the wires in order to edit.

In 1923 Leon Teremin invented an instrument that could produce sound electronically. Called the theremin, it consisted of a rectangular box with two vertical poles on either end. The proximity of a player's hands to one of the poles determined pitch, while the distance of the other hand from the other pole determined loudness.

Twenty-five years passed before magnetic tape recording had advanced enough to introduce John Mullin's 1948 version of the German magnetaphone – a precursor of the Ampex 300 Series tape machine.

The first commercial application of the magnetic tape recorder was made in the United States in 1948 for the Bing Crosby radio show. Because the show was always running overtime, Mullin told Crosby that the problem could be resolved by recording the show and then Mullin, scissors in hand, would edit the tape to time. Problems arose, however, when it was discovered that there were only six reels of tape available in the entire country and no new reels were being manufactured in Germany. Thus the original tapes, with thousands of edits, had to be used over and over again, and in fact lasted until 1950.

Composers, such as Pierre Schaffer and Pierre Henri in Paris and Vladimir Ussachevsky and Otto Luening in the United States, were quick to see the potential of the recorder to manipulate sound, and in the late 1940s and early 1950s Schaffer and Henri experimented with *musique concrète*, the manipulation of recorded sound, in the ORTF Studios in Paris. Like Ussachevsky and Luening, they used studio oscillators and the sounds of voices and instruments pre-recorded on to tape. The tape was then cut and re-assembled, and/or re-recorded at different speeds both forwards and backwards, and the sounds altered with filters, compressors and the like.

In the 1950s a key figure in the development of electronic music emerged: Les Paul, a great innovator who is often overlooked in these days of microtechnology. As early as 1954 Paul was using techniques such as overdubbing, tape speed manipulation and feedback to create such hits as *How High The Moon.* Similarly, little credit is given to Lennie Tristano, the jazz pianist, who released *East Thirty-Second Street,* using Paul's recording process.

The synthesizer

In the 1920s, Maurice Martinot, a Parisian instrument designer, assembled a keyboard instrument that contained electronically controlled sources of sound. Both the Ondes Martinot of 1928 and the Hammond organ of 1929 are today considered precursors of the synthesizer, and in 1929 there appeared an instrument that contained four oscillators controlled by paper rolls, anticipating by more than 30 years the computerized synthesizer.

It took those 30 years to create an instrument that was compact, playable in real time (the duration of the music as intended by the composer) and capable of exercising control over all the parameters of sound – loudness, pitch, timbre, duration and varieties of attack and decay. Except for size, these conditions were nearly met in 1960 by the RCA Mark II Columbia-Princeton synthesizer. The Mark II however, filled several rooms and access was limited to a few composers; it accordingly remained available solely to members of the academic world.

It was not until Donald Buchla and Robert Moog produced the modular synthesizer with integrated circuitry that electronic music leapt beyond the bounds of academia into the mainstream of modern music. The modern synthesizer owes a great deal to Moog, who, in 1964, produced the first practical keyboard synthesizer.

Popular applications

Much of The Beach Boys' work was inspired by innovators such as Van Dyke Parks, Paul Beaver, Stephen Despar and even a little by myself. Few people have missed the electronic music used in The Beatles' songs and yet *Rain* and *Tomorrow Never Knows* were created before synthesizers were available in England. Due to experience gained at the sound laboratories of the BBC Radiophonics Workshops in the late 1950s and early 1960s, George Martin was able to help The Beatles create the effects they desired.

In their first album, *The Notorious Byrd Brothers,* The Byrds processed voices with a synthesizer, and a similar technique was used by the Doors in *Strange Days.* When groups such as Emerson, Lake and Palmer began to perform live with a vast array of synthesizers, feedback

and echo equipment, the entire world of performing began to change.

Such groups were the predecessors of today's modern, sophisticated synthesizer groups such as Human League, Ultravox, Kraftwerk and Yellow Magic Orchestra. The path was well laid by a host of individuals as well: Karlheinz Stockhausen, Frank Zappa, Keith Emerson, Herbie Hancock, Brian Eno, Rick Wakeman, Jean-Michel Jarre, Mike Oldfield and, in the classical pop field, Wendy Carlos and Tomita.

The potential of the synthesizer

Historically – and its history is comparatively short – the synthesizer has been viewed with suspicion by many traditionalists who believed that the instrument had the potential to replace legions of musicians, not to mention entire orchestras. In 1967 Paul Beaver and I were asked to synthesize a string section for a film being produced by Twentieth Century-Fox because all of the premium players were engaged. Shortly after finishing the job, we were told by a large and powerful union that we would no longer be able to use the synthesizer to "replace other musicians", and word was circulated among contractors that we were not to be hired to play the synthesizer again. The union, however, made the mistake of putting this in writing and Paul and I threatened a lawsuit for restraint of trade. Our argument rested on the fact that the union had tried to impose similar restrictions on the use of the Hammond organ in 1938, was consequently sued and defeated.

In much the same way that a painter mixes colours on his palette or canvas, a synthesizer has the potential to reproduce nearly any audible sound by combining different sonic elements. The simple fact is that the synthesizer does not replace anything; no amount of elaborate programming and technique can approach the delicate articulation of a fine string player, the subtle timbral changes of a well-trained flautist or the *embouchure* of a trumpet player such as Roger Voisin. The synthesizer can "sound like" another instrument, but this is only a thin representation or caricature of the original sound. Replication of sounds or instruments is the most academic feature of the synthesizer and the safest and most boring ground for the artist; the instrument holds far greater fascination for those who see it as a means for departing from the traditional, into new and unexplored areas of sound.

In most art forms the artist imposes order upon the chaos of his medium – order imposed on words defines literature; order upon stone defines sculpture – and so it is with electronic music. Early in the history of the synthesizer, the acknowledged process for creating music electronically was to combine the rational and the intuitive. For the electronic music conceptualist, the synthesizer has the potential for creating thousands of timbres and orchestral combinations never before heard. Most of these have not yet been explored and, in fact, the most productive period in the history of electronic music was during the five or six years following the introduction of the Moog, Buchla and ARP instruments in the mid-1960s. Much of the electronic music of the past decade has been but a pale replica of the sounds discovered during this period.

The synthesizer can achieve results which conventional instruments cannot; for example, it can play fast, repetitive lines of music with great accuracy for extended periods of time, allowing for continuous or changing rhythm patterns. The instrument can produce a vast range of sounds, or can pre-programme a complex array of sounds that can be varied and/or instantaneously recalled. Digital technology enables the synthesizer to store sounds and entire sequences or combinations of voices, just like an analogue multi-track recorder. As a generic group, synthesizers – digital or analogue – have the most extensive range of pitches possible, and can reproduce the many colours of sound.

Electronic music and film

The use of electronic music in films is not new, yet its extensive use in the Francis Ford Coppola epic, *Apocalypse Now*, in 1979 represented a milestone in the industry. The entire soundtrack of the film was electronically generated with the theme song emerging and receding from sounds of jungle warfare, jets, gunshots, crickets, tanks, missiles, boats, animals – even silence.

Other breakthroughs in the film world include Wendy Carlos' unique interpretation of Beethoven's Ninth Symphony for the film *A Clockwork Orange*; Paul Beaver's work on *The Illustrated Man*; and Beaver's and my own joint efforts on *Rosemary's Baby* and *Performance*. More recently, the enormously popular sound track from *Chariots of Fire* was achieved by Vangelis' imaginative use of synthesizer and conventional instruments.

The new age

With the new digital technology offered by instruments such as the Fairlight CMI, Touche and Synclavier, the subtleties of individual sounds can be expressed by audio technicians

VDU screen on a Fairlight CMI, *above:* waveforms – generated by any sound, not just by musical instruments – can be altered or completely rewritten using a light pen. The Fairlight will produce print-outs showing waveforms such as that for a note blown on a saxophone, *right*. Once the desired sound has been created, a scale derived from it can be played on the keyboard. The Fairlight will also generate printed music and rhythm sequences, *below right*.

knowledgeable in acoustics and sensitive to the construction of sound. The Fairlight CMI, for example, can record the sounds of a violin, trumpet or even a whale. With the sound waveforms represented on a video screen, any aspect of the tracing can be changed with a light pen to alter the sonic results. The original sound or the altered version can be stored in a digital memory and then "played" on a keyboard and instantaneously realized as a musical line. Other instruments currently on the market offer both similar and different capabilities.

Using tape and/or digital technology, sonic artists are now composing symphonies for live performance and are able to sample their work long before the first musician brings bow to string or horn to lips. To the extent that the artist is able and willing to risk quantum leaps into the unknown, the continuing development of the artistic imagination and creativity are insured.

Electronic music is beginning to creep back into traditional symphonic orchestration and live acoustic performances. The work of Terry Riley, Laura Dean's *Night*, commissioned for the Joffrey Ballet, and the opera *Lear* by Riemann are all examples of this paradox. Thus the contemporary music that many orchestras now play emulates the sound produced by the synthesizer and so, perhaps, the evolution of electronic music has come full circle.●

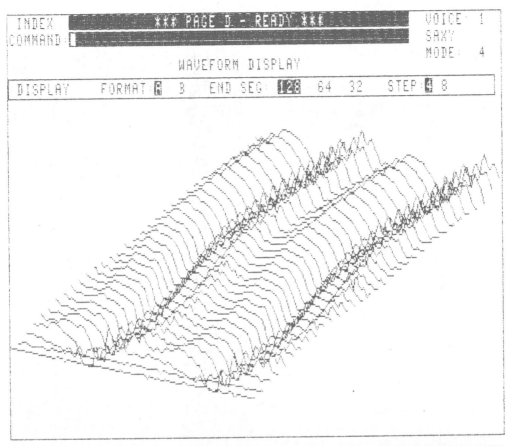

```
INDEX            *** PAGE D - READY ***          VOICE  1
COMMAND:                                         SAXY
                                                 MODE:  4
              WAVEFORM DISPLAY

DISPLAY    FORMAT A  B   END SEG: 128  64  32   STEP:4 8
```

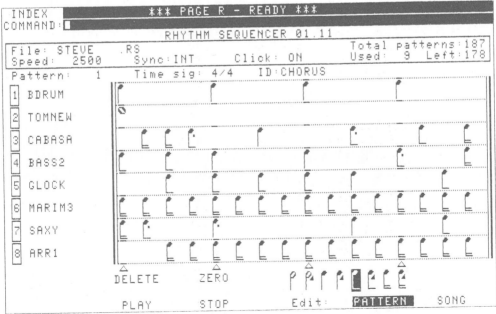

```
INDEX            *** PAGE R - READY ***
COMMAND:
                RHYTHM SEQUENCER 01.11
File: STEVE    .RS                     Total patterns:187
Speed:  2500      Sync:INT    Click: ON  Used:  9 Left:178
Pattern:   1      Time sig: 4/4    ID:CHORUS
1 BDRUM
2 TOMNEW
3 CABASA
4 BASS2
5 GLOCK
6 MARIM3
7 SAXY
8 ARR1
      DELETE       ZERO

      PLAY         STOP        Edit: PATTERN    SONG
```

Playing Synthesizers

I have many different synthesizers: an ARP 2600, an Odyssey, two Mini-Moogs and a Moog Source which is monophonic and holds 16 programmes. On stage I usually use a Prophet 5, an Oberheim 8-voice, a Mini-Moog, a Moog Source and an Emu – a digital keyboard with a 16-voice polyphonic sequencer.

The Emu acts primarily as a keyboard controller for creating polyphonic sequences. Up to 16 voices can be plugged in and they can come from several synthesizers, for example, the Oberheim 8-voice and the Prophet 5 together produce 13 voices; add two Mini-Moogs and perhaps another Moog or the Odyssey, giving a voice each, and I have 16 voices. Each synthesizer can be programmed for a different sound: say, bass on one, strings on another, brass on another, and so on. The Emu remembers the keys I play and, when put in playback mode, will play the synthesizers exactly the way I played them, mistakes and all; this helps me to integrate my various keyboards. Theoretically I could create an entire song, if I had enough memory, and then overdub using the Emu almost like a tape recorder.

At the moment I'd like to do something more elaborate, to synch up my Linn drum computer, all my keyboard synthesizers and my Apple computer, so that I can, theoretically, have an entire orchestra at my disposal. The system would then have enough memory to store all of the different manipulations and modulations that I might make. One keyboard could control the

Herbie Hancock

Apple II computer: used with synthesizers and keyboards this can act as a sequencer, taking care of all switching and programme changes.

lot and the Apple could take care of all of the switching and programme changing, so that I wouldn't be stuck with just one programme.

Emu also make a digital synthesizer called the Emulator. The great thing about this is that it can digitalize sound: you can take a microphone, make some sound and the Emulator will then show you the waveform on its video screen; then you can manipulate the wave and therefore the sound using a light pen. Fairlight, the Australian company, make a digital synthesizer called the Fairlight CM1. This will do what the Emulator does, but it does a lot more besides and is therefore extremely expensive.

I began in music as a pianist, so playing the synthesizer is difficult for me because I am used to a touch-sensitive instrument. The latest concept in synthesizers is an instrument called a Crumar, which is said to be touch-sensitive; Yamaha also make some synthesizers with touch-sensitivity. I haven't tried either yet but, if they approximate to the feel of a piano, synthesizers will become yet more popular and an even bigger element in contemporary music.●

Computer Music

Listeners to popular music are becoming acclimatized to the concept of what a computer-minded musician would term "programming" as opposed to "composing". Computers now offer the musician/composer complete control over every facet of recording, including the mixdown stage; this brings the musician into much closer contact with the aesthetic and practical processes of committing music to tape. Because of this a cross-fertilization of ideas and techniques is taking place between the studio and the live performance.

An orchestra's performance of a classical piece is judged upon such criteria as quality of technique and faithfulness and sensitivity to the composer's intent, whereas excitement and immediacy are usually the prime goals of the pop music composer, who is also very often the performer of the work as well. Thus a schism has existed for some time between the faithful performance of classical work written out in great detail, and the on-the-spot performance of popular work by musicians who may take a number of liberties in their live performance of a recorded song and jam their way through arrangements set up merely as guide lines. Of course, blends of the two approaches exist in profusion, but a new clear-cut category is now emerging due to the use of music-dedicated computers: the performer/composer who presents his audience with both modes at the same time.

The new musician

The extensive memory capabilities of computer instruments, such as the Fairlight, enable a composer to experiment wildly with any form of sound and to take as long as he likes to create arrangements of any level of complexity. Couple this with the new ability to shape and modify sound with digital synthesizers, and you find there is enormous scope for a type of musician who could not have existed before. This new musician spends many hours composing, rearranging and polishing his music in order to present the entire work live to an audience. He dictates how the music is to be played to an almost infinite degree using his computers, while remaining free to play essential parts himself; in essence, he accompanies himself many times over. Performances thus ebb and flow

Warren Cann operating a Linn drum computer (see Drums). Nowadays it is possible to perform entire compositions, including both pre-programmed and improvised music using computer instruments.

depending on how much the musician utilizes sounds from a pre-programmed bank of music, and this is dependent only upon his whim and mood of the moment. Thus, the precision of composed music, faithfully interpreted, is combined with the excitement of live improvisation.

Live music, outside of "real time"

Given time, audiences will become accustomed and attuned to this type of spontaneous performance, and will be able to evaluate the skill of those who practise the new art of programming and their success or failure in using the new technology to realize their artistic aims.

The introduction of musical computer technology, which is happening right now, will broaden and enrich music immeasurably. For the first time audiences will be able to experience a live performance, made outside of "real time".●

Guitar

The guitar was in use in the middle east long before the birth of Christ; the Spanish form became common in Europe about 400 years ago and at the time no one could have foreseen the number of modifications the instrument was to undergo nor how immensely popular it was to become. To trace the guitar's development to the present day is to see not only the birth of many unique playing styles, but the growth of the popular music industry as well.

The acoustic guitar

No significant changes were made in the construction of the guitar until the early 1900s when American companies such as Gibson and Martin began to produce steel-strung – as opposed to the usual gut-strung – guitars. There were two distinct types: the round-hole guitar and the "cello" guitar, the latter so-named because its contoured top and f-holes were similar to those of a cello. These guitars were larger than the classical Spanish type and, because they were played with a flat pick instead of the fingers, produced greater volume and attack (the speed with which a note reaches its maximum volume).

As guitars became easier to handle and their volume level improved they were used increasingly for singing and dancing, and by the 1920s the acoustic guitar had begun to replace the banjo in the rhythm section of many dance orchestras. Although the volume of the guitar was adequate for accompanying singing, in a band the guitar was still "felt" rather than heard because it did not have the penetrating quality of a saxophone, for example. Players such as Eddie Lang, Dick McDonough and Karl Cress developed the melodic potential of the acoustic guitar, but in this guise it was best used as a solo or duo instrument.

Today, following a number of technical refinements, there are many manufacturers of fine, nylon-strung acoustic guitars, such as Ramirez, Contreras and Rubio. Their guitars are widely used by classical musicians, but they are also often used for folk and film music because of their distinctive timbre. The leading manufacturers of steel-strung acoustic guitars are Martin, Guild and Gibson while others, such as Yamaha and Ibanez, command their own share of the market at a lower price range.

12-string   Nylon-strung

The Martin D45, *above,* is one of the finest examples of a steel-strung, acoustic guitar. It is also one of the most expensive, containing pearl abalone inlay. *Left,* a 12-string acoustic and a nylon-strung classical guitar.

The 12-string acoustic guitar has two sets of six strings each; the top two pairs (E and B) are tuned in unison, and the rest in octaves from G to low E. When strummed a 12-string guitar has a sparkling, ethereal quality, and when used melodically it produces a solo line with a distinct glitter, as heard in the introduction to The Byrds' recording of *Hey, Mr. Tambourine Man*. The sound produced by a 12-string is very different from that produced by a six-string: compare *Tambourine Man* with, for example, Paul Simon's *Frank Lloyd Wright*.

The Balladeer, *right,* made by Ovation. Like all their instruments, it has rounded back and sides, a design which gives the guitar its distinctive tone. It is available in both acoustic and acoustic-electric versions; the latter has pick-ups inside the body of the guitar and a battery-operated pre-amp: this amplifies the acoustic sound, making a microphone unnecessary.

The Gibson 335, *right,* combines the warm tone of an acoustic guitar with the sustain qualities of a solid-body electric. It first appeared in the late 1950s and is still a very popular instrument.

The acoustic-electric guitar
In the early 1930s it was discovered that by fitting a ceramic pick-up (electric poles that pick up sound waves) under the guitar's strings and connecting this through a lead to an amplifier, the problem of volume was eliminated. This discovery led to the creation of the acoustic-electric guitar: a steel-strung acoustic guitar with a pick-up mounted on the end of the neck, where it joins the body, to produce a warm, mellow tone. The acoustic-electric guitar became a fully fledged solo instrument able to hold its own with other band instruments, and players such as Charlie Christian were quick to recognize its potenital, with many jazz and country players following close behind.

The "cello" type acoustic guitar with one or two pick-ups continued to rate highly with both jazz and R & B musicians, and Gibson therefore produced a hybrid instrument which resulted in one of their most popular models: the 335. The body of the 335 is much slimmer than a standard, full-bodied acoustic; it has a solid block centre supporting the pick-ups and hollow cut-aways beneath the f-holes to create an acoustic sound.

By removing the central solid block and slimming some of their acoustic-electric models, Gibson created the Byrdland and L5 slim-line models, but the 335 remains the most popular acoustic-electric guitar and has been imitated many times over by a host of manufacturers. One such was the production of a collaboration between Ibanez and George Benson: the GB10, an acoustic-electric model with a very small body.

The electric guitar
A turning point in the history of popular music occurred in the mid-1940s when innovators such as Leo Fender and Les Paul realized that, because the sound transmitted to an amplifier

133

did not rely so much upon the acoustic properties of the guitar as on the vibration of the strings over the pick-up, an electric guitar did not need an acoustic body. As a consequence, Fender and Paul began to experiment with guitars constructed from solid pieces of wood and discovered that, by placing the pick-ups in various positions on the guitar's body, considerable variations of sound and tonal colour were possible. As a result for the first time in the history of popular music, a purely electrical instrument became available to the guitarist.

One major disadvantage of the amplified acoustic guitar was that howling, or feedback, was often produced at high volume levels by sounds in the hollow body interacting with sounds from the pick-up. Because the solid body guitar did not suffer from this problem and was easy to mass-produce, it soon became immensely popular. Almost overnight the adoption of the electric guitar by the first rock 'n' roll bands made it a symbol of the new youth culture, and manufacturers began to produce different makes and models offering features such as tremolo arms, various pick-up configurations, shaped bodies and fingerboard scales.

The Stratocaster and the Les Paul

Throughout the early and middle years of rock, Fender and Gibson led the field in innovatory design and sound quality; two guitars in particular have been heard on more records than any others and stand out as consummate examples of their expertise: the Fender Stratocaster and the Gibson Les Paul. Other companies have testified to the importance of these two guitars by using the model names for their own designs and thus one can buy, for example, a Schecter Stratocaster or a Japanese copy of a Les Paul.

The Stratocaster has three single-coil pick-ups that can be used in combination, separately or simultaneously and it thus offers the maximum range of tonal variety. While custom-builders such as Schecter, Mighty-Mite, DiMarzio, Boogie and a host of Japanese craftsmen have created their own distinct designs, the Stratocaster is still the most widely imitated.

The Les Paul retains the original cut-away shape but features two double-coil pick-ups to eliminate hum. One pick-up is mounted near the bridge to create a cutting, treble sound and the other, positioned near the fingerboard, produces a warm, mellow tone.

Special electric guitars

Solid guitars have been designed with two necks that enable the player to utilize, for example, 12

Eric Clapton playing a Stratocaster, an instrument designed by Fender and copied by a number of other companies. It incorporates three pick-ups which can be used separately or together.

or six strings on the same instrument. Attempts have also been made to incorporate a bass and lead guitar on to the same body, but these do not compete with the individual instruments because they do not have the optimum qualities of either one. In an attempt to duplicate the sound of the sitar, sympathetic strings (strings that ring in sympathy, but are not actually struck) have been added to the electric guitar and, although the sound is not terribly close to that of a sitar, the effect can add an unusual flavour if used sparingly, as in Steely Dan's *Do It Again*.

Tuning

Standard guitar tuning is, from top to bottom, E, B, G, D, A and E. There are also a great many "open", or "altered" tunings used in country and blues-based music; two popular ones are the G tuning – D, B, G, D, G and D – and the E tuning – E, B, G-sharp, E, B, and E – which give an extremely useful open chord for playing slide guitar or certain folk progressions. However, because of the strain placed upon the guitar neck by the E tuning – G raised to G-sharp, D to F and A to B – it is often better to use the G tuning.

The Fender Telecaster, *below,* originally named the ''Broadcaster'', was the first commercially produced solid electric guitar.

Gibson Les Paul Standard, *left:* original versions of this instrument, made between 1958 and 1960, are highly-prized collector's items. Two pick-ups are used, as opposed to three in the Les Paul Custom, *above,* played by Pete Townshend.

The Yamaha SG2000, *below,* is a high-quality competitor to American-manufactured instruments. Many leading guitarists, including Carlos Santana, favour this model.

Styles of playing

The guitar has been played with more individual styles than any other instrument. Basic right hand techniques include strumming, finger-picking, flat-picking, finger-picking with thumb and finger-picks and a host of new techniques such as imitating a pedal steel guitar by manipulating the volume control knob with the little finger to swell the notes. One need only compare the playing of Larry Carlton, Nile Rogers and Jerry Reed to hear how different and varied the approach can be.

For left-hand techniques, apart from the usual run-type passages and chord shapes, bending notes – without the use of a tremolo arm – has become standard fare for today's player. Bending two strings simultaneously creates an expressive, slightly out-of-tune effect which Carlos Santana often uses; listen to his *Samba Pa Ti*.

From BB King through Eric Clapton, Jimi Hendrix, Van Halen and Steven Lukather, the technique of playing rock and blues, as vast and varied as it may be, always comes partly from the player's psyche. The guitarist should bear in mind that, no matter how proficient his technique, without a good feeling for his instrument and the music – and the essential elements of instinct and emotion – the resulting sound will be dry and mechanical.

Effects devices and accessories

Rock music is enriched not only by playing technique; a vast range of electronic devices are now available enabling the guitarist to manipulate sound as he never could in the past. The echo chamber helped produce the unique sound of The Shadows and Duane Eddy; the fuzz box first appeared on Spencer Davis' *Keep On Running* and immediately afterwards on the Stones' hit *Satisfaction*; Cream and Jimi Hendrix added the wah-wah pedal; and the amplifier has become such an integral part of popular music that it might be said that many guitarists now "play" the amplifier as well as the guitar. In recent years analogue and digital delay units have joined chorus pedals as part of the range of accessories used by most professional players, and when playing live some musicians use as many as ten different effect units linked together.

The most recent innovation – still being perfected – is the guitar synthesizer which enables

Midge Ure of Ultravox, *left,* experimenting with some effect units. Electronic devices can expand the sound capabilities of the guitar enormously and range from echo chambers, fuzz boxes, wah-wah pedals to analogue and digital delay units and chorus pedals.

Korg guitar synthesizer

the guitarist to trigger a synthesizer through a pitch-to-voltage connector. Roland have produced the most successful model to date, although many other systems have been tried with varying degrees of success.

In terms of research, the guitar is probably served better than any other instrument. There is more modifying equipment available today than ever before and, with sophisticated recording and video techniques, it is now possible to learn to play the guitar with comparative ease.

Advice for beginners

There was a time when guitar teachers would tell their pupils to go out and buy the best guitars they could, even if it meant spending a lot of money. There were some grounds for this approach, principally the fact that many cheap guitars had a high and difficult action as well as being inaccurate in the tuning. Nowadays however, there are many fine and accurate reproductions of famous makes available – both in the acoustic and electric ranges – which are reasonably inexpensive. Before you buy your first guitar try to learn some chord shapes from a friend; by being able to play a little you will be able to judge for yourself the action, the tuning and the overall feel of the guitars on offer. Nevertheless, take someone who knows guitars with you if you possibly can.

There are so many different styles of guitar playing and so many successful players with personal, idiosyncratic techniques that the beginner must decide on his own approach to learning. A teacher is more important for would-be classical and jazz players, than for rock, blues or soul players. Any expert tuition is obviously going to be invaluable, but remember that a great many of the foremost guitarists are 75 per cent self taught; the 25 per cent has often been learned in the early days from a friend who has shown them some chords and right hand techniques. But the onus will always be on the learner; time and effort are the two essentials.●

Playing Guitar

A conversation between exponents of two very different styles of guitar-playing.

EC *What do you think are the main differences between our respective music?*

JW Classical music more obviously draws on past tradition and concentrates on interpretation. Popular music, as a creative part of contemporary culture, deals with individual expression of ideas and feelings.

EC *I'd agree that I differ from most classical musicians in my dislike of repeating anything. I prefer to have something there, and then to be gone. Even with licks I can never do them the way I think of them: when I actually play them they emerge as a form of hybrid. And yet I place very little emphasis on creating something new. I'm more concerned with just playing the notes as well as I can. The most important thing is to be able to do the simplest things with the greatest amount of feeling.*

JW That's what I like about a great classical player like Itzhak Perlman. There are things he finds in the notes, and in the relationships between the notes, which evoke feelings that have nothing to do with formal interpretation. Even for the general public there's a difference between two great violinists like Perlman and Pinchas Zuckerman. Perlman senses the sublimity and the agony of the music – nothing technically complicated – by discovering the key feeling in a slight turn of a note. It's the equivalent to a bluesy note in popular music. A lot of classical composers allude to that kind of feeling which all but the very greatest musicians fail to approach. So there is an area in the interpretation of classical music which is creative.

EC *That rigorous approach towards technical interpretation is developing in my kind of music with musicians making a strict culture out of interpreting original blues and ragtime styles. There are now quite rigid ways of playing these things.*

JW Which presumably is not necessarily a good thing.

EC *It's probably necessary as an academic form*

of study for people who regard the music as an art form. It isn't the way it was meant to be. I remember rather unsuccessfully transcribing country blues records when I was learning. It took years to realize that someone was using a dropped sixth or God knows what. Nobody really knows. Even authorities in the field, who say something was Spanish tuning or an open A or G, don't really know, unless they were actually there which they probably weren't.

JW So you think young musicians should rely more on spontaneity?

EC *There's an irony in that because I couldn't pick up a guitar right now and start entertaining whereas you could. That's the real difference between us. Being electric rather than acoustic my music is at one remove from yours because it has to go through an amplifier first. Apart from the early days playing in bars I've never played in close proximity to people.*

JW Do you miss that?

EC *Yes, because people ask me to play socially.*

JW Don't you feel you could play like that on an acoustic?

EC *I could probably busk it. But I feel I wouldn't be giving people what they wanted. I remember in a hotel in Ireland once there was an acoustic guitar which I was invited to play. I cried off, partly because I go to pieces if I make a mistake and partly because Albert Lee, the guitarist in the band, is so much better at entertaining people. He played* The Deer Hunter *for about an hour and had everyone moved to tears. I could never do that.*

JW Stanley Myers certainly hit a spot of genius with that piece of music.

EC *You've worked with him on films?*

JW Quite a bit. I love doing film music. The guitar works especially well. I would have thought there are lots of movies where they should use you.

EC *I don't much like the film world and have never had much to do with it. My recorded music has been used occasionally. Anyway, there are a lot of people who can do what I do on a much more professional basis.*

JW What about up on stage, do you feel you seek a sense of isolation in front of the audience?

EC *I don't seek it because it's already there. I remember seeing Segovia once and felt privileged knowing that a lot of what he was doing wasn't reaching the audience. I wasn't hearing any more than the others but I had an extra awareness from having been up there myself.*

JW Would you describe yourself as a perfectionist?

EC *Perfection is a necessary aim. Without it you're lost. There are lots of musicians who can play something off pat without being conscious of the rattles they're making. They don't seem to possess the ambition to get it right.*

JW In classical music perfection is inherent in the idea of interpretation. If you're playing a Bach Prelude and you want to get the piece across as you think it should be then any distraction is an impediment. You should not aim at perfection at the expense of the music itself, but the ambition is important because, in a way, the interpretation is the message.

EC *In my early twenties I thought it was a matter of getting it as perfect as you could, which I suppose was a symptom of youth. I always wanted to do one more take. Now I've gone in completely the opposite direction: one take and that's it.*

JW That takes an enormously skilful combination of feeling and control which takes years to acquire. You need that control to express the whispers in music – those three little notes or the quiet harmonics – just as much as the more extrovert sections. To make every note sound as though it's essential needs as much technique as feeling.

EC *The guitarists I admire most had that same kind of special touch rather than any great facility of style. Guitarists like B.B. and Freddie King, Robert Johnson, Blind Blake and a lot of slide players like Elmore James.*

JW What about jazz guitarists? Like Joe Pass, for instance?

EC *I can't understand why the first thing Joe Pass does is put on a neck pick-up and stay there. The first time I heard that style broken by a jazz guitarist was when Gabor Szabo, who used to play with Chico Hamilton, just flipped to another pick-up in the middle of a solo; he also bent a few strings.*

JW I find a lot of jazz guitarists lack any real dynamics or, rather, the blend of dynamics that reveals the soul of the guitar. From my classical standpoint, popular music has a wonderful range of dynamics that could be better exploited if more musicians would risk being as idiosyncratic as someone like Django Reinhardt.

EC *I especially appreciate the crossover between the acoustic and the electric in Reinhardt. I love the roundness beneath the bite of the amplification. At first electric guitars were really just an extension of acoustic ones. It was the most exciting sound: people like Charlie Christian or Lonnie Johnson, or, suddenly, in the middle of Louis Armstrong's* Hot Five *there's an amazing amplified guitar solo that's actually acoustic.*

JW I feel you use the electric guitar as though it were acoustic.

EC *I suppose I do. I avoid fuzz tone or anything that detracts from the wooden sound of the guitar.*

JW I'm never particularly aware of the specific limitations of the electric guitar, but one great advantage it has over the acoustic is its ability to sustain a note.

EC *I don't agree. A well made acoustic can do it just as well.*

JW The danger of saying that is to forget that the whole attraction of the acoustic sound is in the dying note, its fall and renewal. And it has a stillness, which is something that I think distinguishes your work.

EC *The Stratocaster gets closest to that. It has that wooden sound and an almost banjo effect in that it goes dead unless you really force it. If you place the pick-up selector between the bridge and the middle pick up it makes a unique sound. Now it's even possible to use five pick-ups instead of three, so they're in between each combination, which produces an amazing mix of sounds.*

JW What do you use apart from the Stratocaster?

EC *An old semi-acoustic Gibson ES335 for the electric-acoustic tone we discussed. I use Music Man amps, a wah-wah occasionally and an MXR mixer.*

JW I played a Gretsch when working with Patrick Gowers. I was terrible. You should've been standing over me with a whip telling me to do it properly or not at all. I was trying to use classical technique and fingering to produce sounds which technically you wouldn't get except with the fingers.

EC *The most difficult thing would be sustaining a note, getting vibrato by playing laterally instead of horizontally and vertically as you do with a classical guitar.*

JW I do that on a classical guitar too. I think I was conspicuously muddled at the beginning because I had the wrong guitar. I've since settled down with a Les Paul that I used occasionally with Sky. I feel comfortable with it personally although not necessarily in relation to the culture to which it belongs.

EC *People were quite shocked when you picked up an electric guitar. It was very brave of you.*

JW If you call making an idiot of yourself brave. While other musicians realized I was trying to do something new, lots of people didn't appreciate

it. However, I do think there's an important place for the electric guitar in classical music. Michael Tippett has used one in two of his operas.

EC *What acoustic instruments do you use?*

JW Until a few years ago I had only a Fleta, a Spanish guitar, which is hard to play, a little percussive and difficult to record. But when it's warmed up it's the king of instruments. Like a Maserati it needs a lot of driving. Now I have an English guitar by Martin Fleeson that I use occasionally on records. And I've recently discovered an Australian called Greg Smallman working out in the bush who uses traditional methods to produce some of the best guitars in the world. By taking the best of a lot of guitars – like an extra bit of *sostenuto* from one or the power of the Fleta – he has managed to improve the overall performance of his instruments. For instance, the top of the Spanish guitar is always fan stringing, which he has replaced with grid stringing. Such guitars have a wonderful sound with fuller volume and an expressive middle feeling without the tubbiness you often get with guitars that are made to be easy and middly.

EC *What about the new technology? Does that affect you much?*

JW I think once technology has been assimilated into a culture – like the electric guitar – it's for the general good. But at the moment a lot of musicians are too susceptible to electronic and computerized gimmicks to the point where any real instinctive feeling, and therefore the whole culture of music, is threatened.

EC *It's so simple now to buy some piece of technical equipment and within a week sound like something you hear on the radio simply by pushing a few buttons and playing a few notes. You don't have to go further than that; you've achieved what you set out to achieve. There's no exploration to be done because it's already been*

John Williams

done in the factory.

JW Popular music is so ephemeral nowadays. Everyone seeks newer and newer sensations. Once it was the flavour of the month, now it's flavour of the week. It worries me that music is such a slave to fashion.

EC *I'm in two minds. When I'm watching someone good with a synthesizer I'm envious because it requires a great amount of technical knowledge which I don't have, and, in the end, lack the inclination to acquire. On the other hand, an electric guitar is still a guitar even when it's unplugged; practice is still possible. Unplug a synthesizer and there's nothing. I also feel it cuts in half the number of potential musicians because not only do you have to be a very good keyboard player, you've got to be a scientist too. I can't imagine Ray Charles being a great synthesizer player.*

JW What about Stevie Wonder?

EC *At least Stevie Wonder plays the synthesizer as though it's an instrument. Most people use it for economy as an acceptable substitute for the original, which really annoys me. Synthesize the string section and people'll take it for the real thing, even better perhaps. There's always a little hiss at the back which gives it away, but people don't care any more. I don't like things that are supposed to sound like other things. I remember years ago, when I was working out an approach to a solo, I often used to go for the sound of a harmonica or a saxophone. I'd ask myself how would King Curtis or Little Walter play this? That kind of thinking can be very helpful, but I never wanted it to come out sounding like a sax or harmonica solo. Indeed, I would have been very upset if people thought it had.*

JW It's that physical action of making the sound that's central to the whole experience of music as a form of communication. There's neither experience or resonant body in a synthesizer sound: once the programme's set every note has the same value, unless counter-programmed in which case everything is random. That said, we used synthesizers with Sky and I think they can add a very pleasing colour in conjunction with instruments like a piano or an acoustic steel guitar. But it is aggravating the way synthesizers are used in general. There's a depressing sameness about them that's rather like having the same brand of marmalade every morning for six years.

EC *I agree they've been done to death except by a few masters like Stevie Wonder who can still get that little bit more out of them. Perhaps we're being a bit unfair. It's rather like saying the piano's only got 88 notes and you can't go any further – except you can, you can play it better.*

JW Because each of the 88 notes is different.

EC *They all sound the same except for the way they're struck.*

JW Only in the most general way. They're not as similar as they would be programmed on a synthesizer. The harmonic content is entirely different.

EC *Although I'm told that you could have a synthesizer that'd give you that feeling.*

JW It'd cost a lot more than a piano. Another aspect of the new technology that worries me is the way it separates the consumer from the people who are making the music. The daughter of some friends, involved with a group at her school, made a recording with another friend of mine who is a composer/arranger. They came up with a kind of cheeky version of a Eurovision Contest song, not at all bad for 16 year-olds. There's a whole choir singing with great enthusiasm and the production is fantastic, all synthesizers, which the kids think is great because it's so up to the minute and they might get on television with it. Yet it would've sounded a hundred times better using just a couple of guitars and a piano. If that's an example of the effect of technology on ordinary music making, I think it's very depressing.

EC *A friend gave me a cassette the other day of something he had done. It was perfect, except for his voice which was the only thing not synthesized. If he'd used ordinary instruments they would have sounded just as swappy as him and the whole thing would have blended much better.*

JW What would your advice be to a young musician starting out?

EC *Quite simply, to take the instrument whose sound you like best and learn to play it without ever taking the easy way.*

JW How did you learn?

EC *I taught myself to harmonize each string with the next to make up a chord, starting with the top E, then hitting the next string, which would be the B, so that the two were in harmony without being fingered at all, then finding somewhere on the third string that was in tune with those two, and so on down the strings. At the time I thought I was making up my own chords until I discovered they had names like A and E and so on.*

JW Did you find that your fingering was the same as other people's?

EC *Pretty much, except for the barré chords like F and G for which I use my thumb across the bottom of the neck. What about you? What would you advise young musicians?*

JW To enjoy making music with others without any thought of ambition or where it might lead you, that's the most important thing. All the great musical cultures have been social cultures. You can still see this today with the blues or any other kind of ethnic music like flamenco.

EC *The best session musicians are the backwoods types, people whose names you never know. They're very simple and to the point in their style.*

JW Those kinds of people aren't obsessed with individual success or ambition. Chinese potters didn't sign their work, it formed part of a community culture. Ours is surviving by the skin of its teeth because it is divided between the five per cent who make it to the top and the 95 per cent who are left to consume. I think at last there is a rejection of that, and I hope the kids – especially those with no jobs or prospects – are learning to enjoy the music they make for its own sake.

EC *But the average kid starting out today still wants to begin at the top. Even if he's unemployed he wants a Gibson guitar and forgets that you can make very good sounds with a cheap guitar.*

JW After a year at school he could make a guitar for himself. But this isn't encouraged. Really it's like being in a lunatic asylum: kids are made to conform to what their doctors think is sane. They're told they should aspire to what their bosses have, a Les Paul or whatever.

EC *My favourite guitar was one I bought for a couple of pounds in an arcade. Eventually someone sat on it and broke my heart. I wouldn't be upset if one of my electric guitars was stolen because they don't really mean that much to me. Because I'd discovered this one and found out its true worth it meant so much more to me because of that. And it wasn't something I'd seen someone else using.*●

Playing Guitar

Some see me as a guru of the electric guitar; I'm not sure about that. My aim is comparatively simple: getting wonderful sounds out of the instrument. I may be good at doing this, but I don't regard my playing as magical. If you want real guitar magic, listen to Jimi Hendrix. He was a natural; once I put my palm against his, and discovered his fingers were much longer and thinner than mine and incredibly powerful.

Maybe one reason why I sound original is that I'm on the look-out for ways of playing that don't hurt the fingers. Bending the strings can be painful, even on a top class guitar. Another factor could be pure laziness: I like getting good sounds with the minimum of effort.

Getting the very best from a guitar

Most people have never heard me get the best out of a guitar. Recording puts a barrier between the artist and the audience. The producer can never get really close to the player or the music because of the mechanics that have to come between them; and the recording artist is too busy to be his real self, because he's trying to be on top form for that moment when the record button is pressed.

I only get the feeling I'm putting my true self across when performing live. Even then it may only be for a single number, or just a single phrase. You get the same problems when you make films as you do with recording. I have this dream about being filmed in some rotten old dungeon – a sort of club where there's all kinds of wickedness going on. I would have completely forgotten about being filmed; I'd be just lying there on a sofa, slumped back with a cigar and a pint, just playing the guitar and not caring a damn about anybody. That's when you would really hear me. Records never have, never will, show my real potential.

To do my absolute best, I have to go into a trance. That sounds corny, but it is true. If it's a good night on the road, with perfect sound and good monitors, and if the audience is dynamite, there's a real chance of my "going off" into a state of altered consciouness – it might be in the blues or the middle of a furious bass drum pulsation rock 'n' roll number. Achieving that intensity as often as possible is the problem a performer just has to face.

Putting the guitar before the gadgets

My main preoccupation as a musician these days is flying the flag for the electric guitar. My total concern is for the instrument itself, rather than gadgets that go with it. It is quite alarming what can be got out of a synthesizer, for example; you can't deny they produce fascinating effects. But to my mind the gadgets should never take over from the guitar.

The only concession I've made recently to modern developments is to buy a nice, new polished guitar to replace my battered old one; and I only did that because I saw a friend of mine, a keyboard player, with millions of dollars worth of keyboards round him and drums up to the ceiling. That shamed me into it. The new guitar is an exact copy of the old one. One producer described my old guitar as a battered piece of wood with strings on it; and perhaps that is how it should be: guitars are, after all, for playing, not for looking at.

Most of the interesting things I'm doing at the moment are concerned with coaxing more out of the guitar without using heavy special effects; a little bit of echo perhaps, and a slight form of wave modulation in the delay; that's the sort of thing that will keep me going for a long time.

The new technology is a real threat to the guitar. I showed a 12-year-old girl a digital sequencer the other day; she was extremely impressed with the incredible things it did. A little later she heard me playing the electric guitar. I did a fast lick, and she said "Why do you have to make all that effort? Why can't you just press one of the strings?"

That shocked me. In a few short months this girl had come to grips with rock and roll – or anyway what she thought it was all about – and now she was moving on to something new. It didn't say much for the lifetime of work and dedication the best artists put into playing. Thinking it over, I realized that she didn't truly understand what good playing was about, because when it comes down to it, there are things a machine cannot do.

At a concert the other day a drummer got up and moved away from his drums, pressing a switch on a battery of instruments. Then he stood rocking and rolling in front of the drums while the machine belted out a perfect mechanical beat. The audience loved it, but the truth was that sound was totally soulless – a mindless, metronomic beat with no elasticity, no give in it. Only humans can produce the sort of sound I'm talking about; it's a question of feeling, transmitted through varied tone, good use of sustain and many other things. Many young fans just don't have the ear for the real thing any more; too many bands are just producing flat sheets of sound.

Guitar techniques

I steer clear of most synthetic effects, and achieve my tonal range manually. The guitar has the potential for great tonal variation: you've got a long stretch of string, it makes a great deal of difference where you hit it, how hard you press, whether you're on the fret or slightly behind it, or whether you are damping it with the palm of your hand. There's an infinite variety of tones that can be got even from a ten cent guitar from a joke shop. Provided an instrument has got the frets in the right place and the harmonics are right, and you are fussy about such things, you can make good sounds even with a joke amplifier.

I didn't realize until recently that I'd stopped using the plectrum. I must have phased it out gradually. Possibly it happened because of my tendency to drop the pick when I hit a chord really loud. In order to cover up my embarrassment, I would try to play better without it, and gradually the habit stuck. There's a technique I learned from Chet Atkins that gets me out of a lot of trouble sometimes: you pick triplets with three different strings, but instead of picking each one separately, with the piece of plastic, you have three fingers going at once. It's almost a classical technique, but because of the electric guitar's close action and response, you can't really compare the two. I think both are equally difficult: pulling five separate strings as you have to sometimes on a nylon string guitar is quite a feat.

The plectrum still has its role for picking out rhythms when I'm recording, also for playing close to the bridge, and for stroking the strings in a "feathering" action: there's no way you can produce similar sounds with your fingers. I also like using a pick for low rhythms on the low strings; that produces a different sound again.

Some people have the idea that there is a special, unorthodox Jeff Beck grip. If there is, I'm not aware of it. I don't watch myself play on film: in case it looks awful.

Guitar styles

With regard to style, I don't like messy sound. People like Barney Kessel, who use plenty of chords, are what I call messy. I admire Mark Knopfler of Dire Straits: a beautiful player. He sounds as I would like to sound if I was doing a relaxed, country style number – actually some-

thing I've never had a chance to do.

One of the greatest dangers for a guitarist is learning material parrot-fashion. I really think this is the kiss of death for a performer. It makes you go on stage so confident that you end up not worrying about your playing. That's why there are so many ordinary guitarists around. They are not prepared to make a mistake, or on the other hand, to worry if they do. I don't agonize if I make a mistake, as long as it isn't too ghastly, but I do worry if the number as a whole is not getting to people, or if I cannot make up for some bad bit with a climax.

Guitars and amplifiers

My feelings about guitars must go back to my early fascination with the instrument. I was interested in the electric guitar even before I knew the difference between electric and acoustic. The electric guitar seemed to be a totally fascinating plank of wood with knobs and switches on it; I just had to have one.

I fell in love with the Fender early on, and the affair has lasted, with a short gap in the middle for Les Paul guitars. I own a ridiculous number of guitars, mainly because I designed one for El Ibanez – a Japanese company. I was popular there at the time. They went through about 40 prototypes before coming up with the satisfactory version, and I kept them all. The final guitar was well made, but still not up to the battered old Fender. In spite of the amazing Japanese technology and craftsmanship, that guitar still doesn't make me feel at home. Putting it on, I feel as if I'm wrestling with something rather than getting into a favourite suit.

I owe a good deal to Leo Fender. I used to collect Fender catalogues and leave them on the table so people would think I was going to buy a guitar; in fact I couldn't afford one. The catalogue listed names of players who used Fenders. I used to dream about being one of those names – a dream which has recently come true.

Amplifiers were quite a concern to me in the early days when most were completely crude and lacking in power. Mine were home made: I had a bigger set-up than anyone else, and it produced the type of completely clear sound I wanted. Incidentally, the power and clarity of my amplifiers must have made a contribution to my style. Wah-wah pedals and that type of equipment never meant much to me, although there was a time when it seemed you couldn't do without one.

Accompaniment for electric guitar

The perfect foil for the electric guitar is a good

bass guitar and a wonderfully huge fat drum sound. If you want to knit the sound together, then the Prophet 5 keyboard is tremendous. But you need a keyboard player sensitive enough to know what the tune needs, and who is prepared to alter it if the guitar is to be the lead instrument, but isn't matching the keyboard sound.

Although I am basically wary of gadgets, or anything that interferes with real playing, I do experiment with a synthesizer for effects, and I'm currently working with some interesting digital echoes. But fuzz, overloaded amps, flanging and the like are not for me.

Early influences
My devotion to the electric guitar goes back to when I was very young. I can remember just being very impressed with the sound of the thing. Les Paul was the first player I singled out; I think because he played the signature tune on some radio programme. My elder sister also influenced me. She listened to Radio Luxemburg; she would never say, "Oh, I *love* this guy," or, "Elvis is great"; she would point out a guitar solo.

After Les Paul, the next important influence – and it was some time later – was *Hound Dog*. Not so much Elvis, the guitar solos; they put me on the floor for several months. Then I started to take in what rock 'n' roll was about: the outrage of it – hips wriggling, greased back hair.

In the early days the guitar was just a prop that groups used. People are so used to advanced guitar playing that they forget that. People like The Searchers and The Dave Clark Five were mainly vocal, and I was most interested in bands that used the guitar to great effect – people like Scotty Moore, Cliff Gallup and Gene Vincent – all of them in the States, which is where my musical roots are.

Gene Vincent and the Blue Caps were "my" band for quite a time. Their guitar playing was staggering, and I discovered that it developed in the most unexpected way. They hired some guys for a session to do *Bebopalula*. No one knew what would happen; the session musicians were real country boys. They said they couldn't very well play Hank Williams type music as a backing, so they just turned up the treble on the guitar, hammered hell out of the drums and it sounded right. That's how The Blue Caps got their style.

Many of my early ideas came from that group, learnt parrot-fashion. One could hear everything that was going on in the background behind the vocal. There was one electric guitar, and the rest was rhythm guitar, an upright bass, a bass drum

Jeff Beck

and one snare; it was easy to tell which was the electric guitar, and I thought it was the ultimate.

The ideas I got from them never saw the light of day because the guys available for forming bands in England weren't into that kind of thing. So my style developed on its own.

Learning the guitar
I was never taught to play the guitar. Or rather, I went for one lesson and discovered the teacher was decades out of date. Anyway, I was happy with the way I was playing. My ear was good enough to pick up tunes from the radio, and, most important, I knew when I was going wrong. If you're learning that way, you have to have enough natural musical ability to know when you are making mistakes. Another reason I was put off having lessons was the unpopularity of the

guitar at that time; if my friends had seen me with a guitar case, they would have thought it a joke.

You could more or less do without chords when I started playing. Early fifties rock records had rhythm guitar, but it was almost buried. It was obvious what key the stuff was in, and with a powerful focal and back beat, you could sail along playing almost anything over it, as long as it was in the right key.

My first lick was *That'll be the Day* by Buddy Holly. He had three notes running into each other where most players had trouble getting one out clearly. It made a bell-like sound. I thought it was quite something, and once I'd picked it up, kids at school said, "Hey, Jeff can play the guitar". I couldn't really.

Mind you, George was let into The Beatles on the basis of one good lick that he could play. That sums up how things were then. There wasn't a potential rock band on every street corner like there is now.

Developing a style

I started performing in pubs and clubs when I was 13 – often having difficulty making myself look old enough to be let in where there was a bar. My style developed piecemeal at that stage; I played in band after band, probably as many as ten of them, hoping to find one in which I could play without copying somebody and without overkilling the main feature. It was quite normal to go from band to band in those days. Money was non-existent, and unless one of the players had a father with a car, you didn't travel outside your own locality.

Looking back, it's probably true to say that my style had emerged when people began ringing me up and asking me to play. But I wasn't conscious of having anything individual at the time. That only came when I joined the Yardbirds. By then I reckoned I had been through everything. I'd studied blues as well as rock 'n' roll; but I never seriously considered classical guitar. Which is not to say that I objected to it; I'd simply have to have been a different person to play acoustically.

Joining The Yardbirds was an unbelievable thrill. Not having to go out to work any more, doing all day the things one fought to get home for – it all seemed too good to be true. At that time, playing didn't seem like work, and being young, handling the pressure was no great problem.

The future

Every guitarist worries where he is going. There was a time when my mind was literally crumbl-ing with uncertainty about what I wanted to do. It was when John McLaughlin was in his heyday with Billy Cobham, and he may well have contributed to my confusion. I got to know their music well because I worked with Michael Walden, who took over from Cobham on drums. I came to realize they didn't have much in common with rock 'n' roll; at the same time, one had to be impressed with their sheer musical ability. It made me realize I wasn't as interested in music for its own sake as they were. They seemed to be more involved in the music than in the playing; McLaughlin is a great guitar player, but he's unemotional, and I think feeling is what marks out a true performer. McLaughlin would express himself by hanging on to a note a fraction longer – not something most people would notice. I need to pour it out, like a singer, and that comes across to most audiences with much greater impact.

I'm thinking about my future as a player again now. I've always hoped that I was slightly ahead of guitar rock, the heavy metal type stuff and the west coast rock scene – my aim has been to be a little more outward-thinking about the music. But this could mean that I'm out on a limb, losing touch. But I still have fans from the Yardbird days, and I can fill 3,000-4,000 seaters in the States. I owe a lot to that group – like I do to Leo Fender – it was where I went crazy, did everything you could possibly do to a guitar, smashed it up, jumped on it, bent all the rules. Perhaps something radical like that will happen to me again.

Advice for beginners

My advice to anyone interested in the guitar is to concentrate on it as an instrument for playing in its own right. Anything that prevents you playing naturally should be avoided. Make practising a habit; and if you want to be creative, be ruthless with yourself. Cut out anything which sounds like someone else's playing. Forget about what you did the day before. Some of my best ideas come when I'm crashed out on the floor, watching TV with the sound off.

All I think about is the notes I'm playing at the time; if they make up a good idea, I may spend a week developing it. But most of the time I'll just be looking for three or four notes no one played before.

If you find – and we all do – that you're getting sloppy, maybe harping on a particular idea too much, stop immediately and start doing exercises. But there again, there's no substitute for real inspiration: the best exercise is the challenge of being on stage playing a good tune.●

Pedal Steel Guitar

The development of the steel guitar began about one hundred years ago when the standard, small-bodied, gut-strung European guitar was introduced to Hawaii. The islanders soon adapted the instrument to suit their own musical tradition. They found that by running a hard object, such as a knife or bottle, along the strings, a singing sound could be produced, and they discovered that the instrument was easier to play in this mode if it was supported horizontally in the lap.

As the Hawaiian style of playing became established, the guitar underwent alterations, such as the addition of steel strings to produce greater volume. These were raised above the fretboard at the nut end of the instrument to avoid the clash of the slide on the frets, and for better resonance. Other developments included an enlarged sound chamber incorporating a hollow neck, and the use of open chord tunings, allowing the player to either strum with his thumb or pick single-string melodies.

The dobro: the design of this resonator guitar has hardly changed since it was invented in the 1920s. A round, metal dish below the bridge amplifies the vibrations of the strings creating the distinctive "jangly" sound.

The Hawaiian guitar had its first impact on American music in the 1900s when Hawaiian music, singers and dancers became popular on the west coast. This led to the incorporation of Hawaiian musical elements into American popular music.

The dobro

The dobro, or resonator guitar, was invented by the Dopera brothers of California in the early 1920s to provide dance band guitarists with an instrument which could match the volume of the growing numbers of front-line brass instruments. The loud, nasal tone of the wooden-bodied instrument appealed to the Hawaiians and became a favourite with steel guitarists who were trying to integrate the Hawaiian guitar into country music. Today the dobro is still used in traditional country music and is designed in much the same way as it was 60 years ago. Dobros were also manufactured with metal bodies; these were played by early Delta blues musicians who used it to develop the bottleneck style of playing. Although this technique resembles that of the steel guitar, the roots of each style are different.

Electronic amplification

A significant innovation for the steel guitar was the introduction of electronic amplification. The steel guitar was the first instrument to which it was applied and players discovered that they had what they had always wanted: unlimited volume, tonal range and sustain, literally at their fingertips. In the 1920s Rickenbacker and Vega were among the first companies to develop electric lap steel guitars; these were made of solid wood, cast aluminium or both. (It was to be some years before pick-ups were added to standard acoustic guitars.)

In the 1930s the lap steel guitar enjoyed a boom in the United States when Sears Roebuck and other national mail order companies devised the idea of packaging and marketing the instrument, including with it a small amplifier, picks, bar and instruction material. While the concept of using the instrument as a revolutionary means of teaching failed, the project succeeded in exposing the steel guitar to the entire country.

The pedal steel guitar

Both Gibson and Rickenbacker began to experiment with complex tunings by increasing

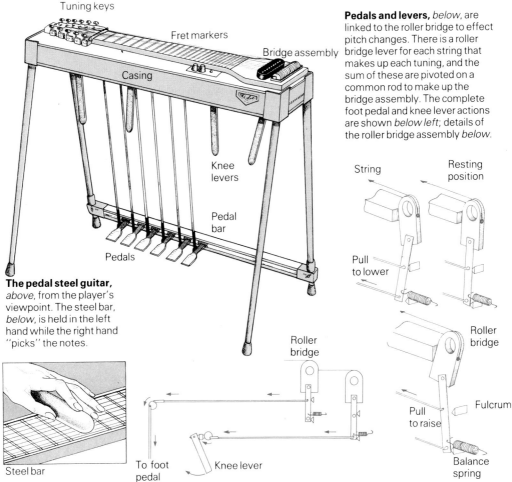

Tuning keys

Fret markers

Bridge assembly

Casing

Knee levers

Pedal bar

Pedals

The pedal steel guitar, *above,* from the player's viewpoint. The steel bar, *below,* is held in the left hand while the right hand "picks" the notes.

Steel bar

Pedals and levers, *below,* are linked to the roller bridge to effect pitch changes. There is a roller bridge lever for each string that makes up each tuning, and the sum of these are pivoted on a common rod to make up the bridge assembly. The complete foot pedal and knee lever actions are shown *below left;* details of the roller bridge assembly *below.*

String

Resting position

Pull to lower

Roller bridge

Roller bridge

Pull to raise

Fulcrum

To foot pedal

Knee lever

Balance spring

the number of strings on the steel guitar from six to seven or eight. Two or three necks were soon built into one instrument resulting in complementary tunings with a wide range of chord possibilities. Bigsby, Gibson and Fender were the first to devise a mechanical method of raising and lowering the pitch of the instrument by the use of pedals, and the first manufactured pedal steel guitars appeared in the late 1940s.

The original concept of the pedal steel guitar was to enable the player to change a complete tuning by using one pedal, for example E-ninth to A-sixth by shifting the G-sharps to As and the Bs to C-sharps. Later, the split pedal was introduced enabling, for example, G-sharp raised to A with one pedal, and B to C-sharp with the second pedal.

The three manufacturers developed their own systems of pedal changes, but Paul Bigsby's company – despite being the smallest – created the prototype for the modern pedal steel guitar.

The only major innovation introduced since Bigsby's prototype is the knee lever which was incorporated in the early 1960s.

Technique

The pedal steel guitar "lies on its back" supported by a leg at each corner, and the musician sits to play it. As with the electric guitar, the strings are stretched between the bridge and nut, but are raised higher off the neck. More than one neck can be incorporated on both pedal and non-pedal steel guitars; the most common is the double-neck, ten-string type with two sets of strings, each tuned to an open chord.

The foot pedals of the guitar are the "fingers" of the instrument and determine, like the fingers of an electric guitarist, the nature and extent of the chord shapes. The mechanism allows for the lowering and raising of each string independently. The instrument may be pre-set to raise or lower strings by different amounts according to

B.J. Cole

Pedal steel tuning, *right,* using two foot pedals and one knee lever. By activating the changes, either singly or in combination, the following chords can be obtained at the open position: pedal 1 – C sharp minor; pedal 2 – E sus 4; pedals 1 and 2 – A6; pedal 2 and knee lever – B7; knee lever – G sharp min7.

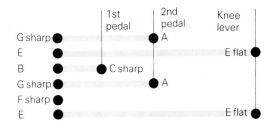

Open chord inversions, *below,* using pedal changes with the left hand holding the bar on the fret indicated.

Open E tuning		E6 with lever engaged	E6 with pedals 1 & 2 engaged	Octave
G sharp ●		● C sharp	● E	
E ●		● G sharp	● B	
B ●		● E	● G sharp	
G sharp ●		● C sharp	● E	
F sharp ●		● B	● C sharp	
E ●		● G sharp	● B	
		5th fret A6 open	7th fret B6 open	12th fret

which movement is activated. The pedal bar is fixed between the two front legs of the instrument, just above the floor; pedals should nearly touch the floor when they are fully depressed.

With his right thumb and at least two finger picks, the player plucks the strings using a technique similar to that used on a classical guitar. In his left hand, the player holds a cylindrical steel bar with his thumb and first two fingers parallel to the frets; when the bar is slid up and down the strings, it acts as a moveable fret, producing the characteristic singing sound.

Range of expression

While the pedal steel guitar has overcome acoustic and harmonic limitations, it is still looked upon as a novelty instrument and somewhat esoteric; its potential is hugely underestimated by most composers and arrangers. Its musical scope is in fact vast, since it is capable of a wide pitch range as well as full chords to which can be added a melody line to provide complete harmonic voicings.

Arranging for the pedal steel guitar should be approached as if the instrument were positioned in the orchestra directly between the strings and guitars, but not far from the piano. Chord symbols should always be indicated and written melody lines should specify whether extra harmony notes are to be added to the main line; dynamic indications should also be used.

Performers

Buddy Emmons, who was involved in the forma-

tion of two pedal steel manufacturing companies, has been a leading performer since the mid-1950s. He made a revolutionary jazz album in 1962 using Sonny Rollins' rhythm section; he introduced the instrument into soul music with Ray Charles, and into film music with Henry Mancini. Jimmy Day featured on many of the early Everly Brothers hits and worked with Elvis Presley, Willie Nelson and many others. Sneaky Pete Kleinlow was responsible for integrating pedal steel guitar into rock 'n' roll as co-founder and leader of The Flying Burrito Brothers; he has also worked with Little Feat, Stevie Wonder, Joni Mitchell and John Lennon. Speedy West originated a gutsy, aggressive style of pedal steel playing in the 1950s, working with Tennessee Ernie Ford, Merrill Moore and Jimmy Bryant; his style has inspired many electric guitarists. Pete Drake was the steel guitarist on Bob Dylan's *Nashville Skyline* and *John Wesley Harding* albums. He went on to work with George Harrison and Ringo Starr.

Advice for beginners

Although the pedal steel can be mastered through determination and practice in much the same way as other instruments, it can be very intimidating for the beginner due to its complicated mechanics. Try to obtain a simple 6- or 8-string lap steel first – which are relatively inexpensive (£50-£200/$100-$400) – and concentrate on the hand techniques. Then, if you become "hooked", the cost of a pedal steel (£500-£1500/$1000-$3000) will not be wasted.●

151

Bass Guitar

The bass guitar evolved out of a need to improve the sound of the double-bass in terms of amplification and tonal range. Originally an orchestral instrument that had been utilised by jazz bands, the double-bass began to present problems for bands in the 1950s who required something louder, more portable and more adaptable to the kinds of bass lines that rock 'n' roll demanded. Although Bill Haley's Comets, The Crickets and Elvis Presley's backing musicians used double-bass at first, many people welcomed the electric solid bass guitar which was developed in the late 1940s by Leo Fender.

The Fender Bass

Since its development, the Fender Bass has become one of the most widely imitated designs. Where guitars have gone through many alterations in basic shape, as well as in pick-up development (to say nothing of "gimmicks"), the bass that has been most used, admired and relied upon has been the Fender. Some other companies, such as Gibson, Rickenbacker and Mosrite, developed distinctive designs of their own and for a while during the 1960s these challenged the Fender, because they were used by such bands and players as The Who, the Ventures, Chris Squire of Yes and later Paul McCartney.

The Fender was really a guitar, fretted and tuned like the bottom four strings of a guitar (but an octave lower) and therefore easily playable by a reasonably competent guitarist (this perhaps explains why so many non-flamboyant guitar players liked to play the bass in the early days of band formation). The startling design of the Fender (like a kind of super space gun with its double cut-away and contoured body) was well suited to the rock image and, because the body was solid, it was devoid of the feedback problems to which the semi-acoustic basses such as the Höfner violin bass (which McCartney used for years with The Beatles) were prone.

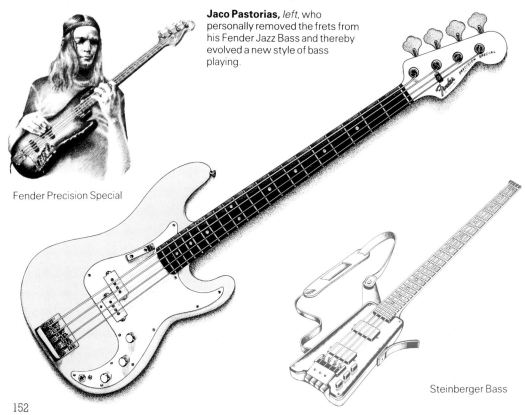

Jaco Pastorias, *left,* who personally removed the frets from his Fender Jazz Bass and thereby evolved a new style of bass playing.

Fender Precision Special

Steinberger Bass

152

Stanley Clarke playing an Alembic.

The Fender Precision Bass – originally shaped like today's Telecaster Bass – had one pick-up mounted in the middle of the body plus a tone and volume control. Fender continued to experiment with new ideas; the Jazz Bass was a major advancement in that it had two pick-ups, one near the bridge and one in the middle of the body: these could be used separately or together. The Precision Special, introduced in 1980, has two central pick-ups.

When Jaco Pastorias came to prominence, through his playing with Weather Report, he took the state of the art further still. He removed the frets from his Jazz Bass and, using only the back pick-up (thereby creating a harder sound), evolved a whole new style of playing which took slurs, harmonics and subtle nuances only possible on a fretless instrument into account. Fretless basses had been on the market for some time, but no-one had done much to exploit their characteristic sound. Nowadays, through the music of Weather Report, Alphonso Johnson and Jaco Pastorias' impressive work with Joni Mitchell, the sound of the fretless bass is well established. With many imitators, but few competitors, Leo Fender has moved on to produce the Music Man range, with its active circuitry (an additional power supply within the guitar itself) and most recently – with one of his original designers, George Fullerton – the new G and L range. Fender Basses are heard on thousands of hit records, from the great agitated bass lines of James Jameson on the early and middle Motown repertoire, to today's Rock, Funk and New Wave.

The custom builders

Having put the Fender in perspective, a number of custom builders, who have achieved remarkable results, must be mentioned. The most significant of these is probably Alembic: the first company to use active circuitry in the controls of the bass. This, combined with the use of hardwoods and quality brass fittings, made it the Rolls-Royce of basses. This in turn has resulted in a whole new industry: replacement spares. Companies like Mighty Mite, Schecter, and Di Marzio began to produce high-quality replacement pick-ups, machine heads and fittings which were the same specification as the originals but with much improved materials. Because Fender used a bolt-on neck, it is now possible to replace a whole guitar body and neck with alternative woods. You can even buy a guitar which is a carbon copy of a Fender design but with Schecter parts. Customised basses of this kind tend to be expensive but the quality of the

materials pays dividends in performance and appearance.

New developments

The first really important design change occurred in the mid-1970s, when companies like B.C. Rich manufactured basses carved from a single piece of wood. This was a departure from the conventional bolt-on, or glue-on, necks. It provided more sustained and improved tonal qualities, although if the neck was damaged the whole fingerboard had to be removed.

The Steinberger is the most significant recent development in bass design. This not only does away with the conventional guitar-shaped body, but the neck and body are moulded from one very rigid piece of graphite, glass fibre and epoxy resin. The ball-end of the string is held in place at the nut and the instrument is tuned at the bridge-end with small knuckled screws similar to the fine-tuning screws on violins and cellos. The advantage is that a musician can continue to articulate notes on the fingerboard while adjusting his tuning with his free hand. The manufacturers claim increased harmonic content and sustain, as well as near-indestructibility. However, as the instrument is such a recent innovation, these claims have not been fully tested.

The role of the bass player has changed dramatically over the years. From being solely an element within the rhythm section, it has, through the works of Jack Bruce, Jaco Pastorias, Stanley Clarke and Louis Johnston, come into its own both as a solo voice and as an exciting individual ingredient in popular music.

Advice to beginners

Most of the time the bass guitar does not play solo and the primary objective is always to provide a good, solid, reliable foundation to a song or rhythm line. A lot more variety can be achieved by playing the first and second inversions (*i.e.* the third and fifth notes) of a chord rather than staying in root (the first note) position (a good example of using the second position can be found in *God Only Knows* by The Beach Boys).

It is also an advantage to know the main styles of plucking the strings. The pick is used extensively in rock music while most Motown records use a finger style of playing. One of the most distinctive bass sounds can be heard in funk and disco music where the strings are pulled outwards and allowed to slap back against the body of the instrument. Quincy Jones and James Jameson provide some of the best examples of this technique.●

Playing Bass

I use Fender Jazz Basses and Fender Precisions. My white Jazz Bass is my favourite; I have had it for 12 years. I use the Precisions for the heavier music, where the rhythm is more to the front and you have to bash it out of the guitar. A fretless bass is ideal when a sweet, cello-like, more melodic part is required – say for a ballad – but it is more difficult to play. Intonation is really critical when you are recording in the studio. You can't afford even the tiniest mistake, and this is why I have maple inlays on the fingerboard of my fretless – taking the place of frets – so that when I'm up the octave I can see where I am and get the tuning spot on.

A lot of people fall down because they don't recognize that fretted and fretless basses are two different instruments – you can't approach them in the same way. Jaco Pastorias is remarkable in that he can play either with complete confidence and play exactly the same things and at great speed.

I don't usually use an amp in the studio because I know my guitar and I find that I can get a very good sound with direct injection (DI). But I take an amp to the studio if a producer asks me to, perhaps because he wants some extra weight or a different sound through the amp. I normally take a small combo, a speaker and amplifier in one unit. I also like the Ampeg Portaflex speaker because it's on a low level.

Sometimes I record using DI and amplifier together. For a loud rock recording, for example, I have to have plenty of wind moving in the speaker – lots of sound at the bottom end – which the amp can give, and then I can get an edge which will cut through this texture with the DI unit. To get this sort of sound you play over two tracks or more.

Playing techniques

The most varied aspect of bass playing is the right-hand technique. Basically the left hand finds the notes, but right-hand techniques have come a long way since the days when almost everyone used a pick.

For a medium tempo pop tune, it is best to play in the middle – halfway between the bridge and the bottom of the fingerboard. The nearer you get to the bottom of the neck, the more open and full the sound becomes. My own preference is to play right on the bridge with my thumb on the back of the pick-up, and I use my fingers to pluck the strings. This is the style perfected by Bernard Edwards of Chic; he gets a very tight, staccato sound. If I play this way in the studio, the sound may be too hard, so I am sometimes asked to play a bit more *legato*, more smoothly.

Most sounds can be produced with the fingers. I have never seen players I admire using a pick, and I rarely use one myself. Occasionally I am asked to play with one at a session – perhaps to play fast semi-quavers (sixteenth notes).

Larry Graham's thumb technique

Disco music or something up tempo may require a thumb technique, which is best played at the bottom of the fingerboard where you can really strike the strings with your thumb.

Now, with this technique you don't just pluck the strings with your thumb. The method was developed by Larry Graham. He was in a trio which became a duo because the drummer left, so he used his thumb as the bass drum and the snap – or some people call it the pop – where you pull the string away from the fingerboard and it snaps back on to it, was his snare drum. You must hit the string really hard with the thumb and then pull it away with the first finger and let it snap back. It was once described to me as like opening a door; you twist your wrist as if you were opening a door handle: slap with the thumb and pull with the finger.

There's a lot of wear on the strings with the slap technique. If you use the thumb a lot, the strings go very dull after a week or so. If I'm working on that sort of gig or recording, I change them once a week. Many people change them every week, or even every session, if they want a clean, bright sound; some players change them every three months, and there are people I know who have had the same strings for years. It depends on the sound you want.

Great bass players

I grew up in The Beatles era, and the first bass player I really listened to was Paul McCartney. Then I was impressed by Andy Fraser from Free and Jack Bruce with Cream, both British bass players. Soon after that I started listening to American music and the band that really turned me on was Sly and the Family Stone; when I heard Larry Graham playing with them, I couldn't believe it. Stevie Wonder also: I'd never heard anyone play like that.●

Playing Bass

Paul McCartney in conversation with George Martin.

George *How did you come to be a bass player?*

Paul It's a bit of a story. Actually, some book came out recently which had me as a rather callous character, and one of the things that annoyed me was that this idea of me grew out of the story about Stuart Sutcliffe who was our first bass player. Stuart became our bass player because we didn't have one. In fact, the original Beatles line-up was three guitars, and we'd turn up for a date and the fellow would say, "Where's your drummer?" We'd say, "No drummer man, the rhythm's in the guitars!" That was how we used to sell it! We had to have a "line" because they all expected drummers. "So, the rhythm's in the guitars! Oh yeah!" And we'd get on with it.

Stuart who was a friend of John's from art school won a painting prize which got him £75. That was a fortune in those days and suddenly one of your friends had a roll of £75, so we persuaded him to spend it on a bass! He wasn't too keen, although he loved the whole thing really.

George *He was a musician anyway, though?*

Paul No! No question of it; but it was a question, like, "You can learn Stu, you really want a bass don't you." It was like, "Do I? O.K." Eventually after plying him with a few drinks we persuaded him this had to be, this was his future. So he bought a lovely big Hofner bass. At that time bass was the instrument you got lumbered on; it was very unglamorous.

George *It was a kind of back seat thing?*

Paul Fat boys played bass, if you remember. It was like you grow like your dog – you grow like your instrument. I didn't fancy it at all. I had a guitar; I was one of the three rhythms in the guitars.

We went to Hamburg. My guitar broke because it was ridiculously cheap. My dad has always instilled in me not to get in debt, so I paid about £7 for this guitar which immediately broke. Everyone else didn't care – their dads hadn't told them – so they were into £50, an arm and a leg, but they got good guitars. So, when my guitar broke, they stuck me on piano. We'd had a piano at home so I could vaguely pick out C and E, and as long as I just vamped I was learning chords; I started to pick up quite a bit during that time.

Then Stu was going to stay in Hamburg with Astrid; they'd fallen in love. So I persuaded him to lend me his bass, but he wasn't too keen on me turning the strings round so I had to learn it upside down with these piano strings because we couldn't afford bass strings! We used to cut them out of the pianos. All these clubs would wonder what had gone wrong with their pianos! We had these pliers and it was, "All right lads quick it's an A – which is the A? – dong, dong!" and we'd just nick an A string. You'd be surprised how well they work.

George *Wasn't it hard on the fingers though, because they're pretty hard things.*

Paul It was murder! But it was better than nothing. Stu used to have bleeding fingers from those strings – horrific big ruts in them. So I eventually persuaded Stu to lend me his bass.

George *Why were you lumbered rather than George?*

Paul I don't know. I think it was a question of, "I'm not ****!**!** playing bass – I'm not going to do it!" We used to have arguments about stuff like that. Another key argument in those days was who'd drive the van. Anyway I got lumbered. I was the one. Well, I was the one whose guitar had broken and they'd shifted me to piano, so they figured they could shift me to bass. Stu was leaving; they'd kept their guitars in tune and intact and still had them. In fact they'd bought new ones. They'd gone into hire purchase in Hamburg.

Then I looked around for a bass of my own and, being left-handed, one of the big factors was symmetry, because if you turn most guitars upside down they look stupid because they've got a cutaway. The violin shape is very symmetrical. If you turn that upside down, you've only got to move your scratch plate and you've really got a pukka looking thing. Actually all the controls stay the wrong way but no one noticed that!

George *Is that why you started on the Hofner?*

Paul That plus the price. I couldn't dream of getting a Fender, which everyone else had, because they cost about a hundred quid and no way could I get into that kind of money then. We were on fifteen quid a week in Hamburg! The Hofner was more like thirty quid.

From then on I was serious because I'd got a bass and that was committing myself. Until then I'd been a bit dubious. So, I wasn't ruthlessly ambitious and trying to get rid of the bass player; I was lumbered really.

I think in all our early recordings the bass isn't

very interesting; in fact, in the mixes bass and drums are quite low. It starts to become prominent in *Sergeant Pepper* time; I'm almost playing lead bass then.

George *The significant thing about your bass playing in the early days was that you played tunes with it.*

Paul Yes, because of writing songs at the same time. First of all my bass playing came from watching bass players – the cabaret guys. After a while I did get into it; I liked the idea of being the backbone of the group. In the very early days I got a friend, Adrian Barber, to build me what we used to call "the coffin", a big cabinet with two 15-inch speakers in it, and black cloth and a big black box; that was the first sound ever really – a great bass sound. It was a quad amp.

Once I got that big bass sound it was terrific because I could actually make a contribution. Later, instead of just playing like the guys in cabaret where they just rooted all the chords, I got interested in this idea of counter melodies in the bass. Having been a guitarist, it was quite easy to switch on to the electric bass; it's just the bottom four notes of the guitar really.

George *And a bass guitar does sustain more than a string bass. You can hear the tunes more; the string bass is just a boomp.*

Paul In fact, if you hear string bass players doing melody, it always gets a bit in the way. They can't do it as easily.

George *What advice would you give to a young bass player?*

Paul The most important single piece of advice is do it a lot, play a lot with people. There's no point in learning all about it and never going anywhere and doing it; that's where the real guts

Paul McCartney and George Harrison rehearsing before an audience in 1964. McCartney is playing a left-handed Hofner bass guitar.

of it starts to come out. I'd suggest they play a lot with a plectrum at first. Anything else is a matter of judgement and personal taste.

George *Have you ever tried fretless bass?*

Paul I've tried. I'm not wild on it, just because I'm so used to fretted basses. It's a bit like the radio mikes on guitars. I feel naked without a lead. Frets, I know where I am. Fretted bass is my instrument, and you've got to be damned good to play a fretless; anybody who's only half good can often go out of tune. If I was going to play fretless I'd actually paint them on in white paint. I don't like to guess it, because you can be just a tiny bit out; the rest of your bass part can be terrific and you've got one stinking thing that's a big sharp. The only advantage of it for me is that you can do nice slides.

George *But you can do that on frets too.*

Paul Yes, not quite so easily.

George *Have you got any bass players that you admire a lot?*

Paul I admire, mainly because it's stuff I can't do, what I call the bumthwacking bass style. The modern style of bumthwacking which you do with your thumb is done really well by Louis Johnson. I really admire him a lot. I also admire George Porter of The Meters, the New Orleans group. They haven't had the hits, but they are a helluva good group, fine musicians, and one of them is Art Neville who's got a great R & B pedigree. George Porter is very fine: I liked him on rock, I liked him in funk and in all the stuff his group normally does – R & B. And, of course, I like Stanley Clarke a lot. ●

Drums

A basic drum kit should consist of a bass drum and a snare drum, at least two tomtoms – you can get away with two – a pair of high-hat cymbals and another two, or ideally three, cymbals: a crash, ride and a crash-ride. While this is the basic kit, a beginner could start with just a snare, bass and high-hats but, obviously, the more you have the more musical options will be open to you.

Drums and drum heads

Of the best and most commonly used drums I prefer Yamaha; my second choice would be Pearl and then American makes such as Ludwig, Ludwig-Gretsch and Slingerland – which are all well made – and Premier, an English company. If you have been playing for a few years but cannot afford a new Yamaha, I recommend finding an old American kit from the late 1950s or early 1960s – particularly a Gretsch – because they are superior to those made today.

For each size of each type of drum there are about 20 to 30 heads available; they come in all weights, thicknesses and finishes, all of which affect the sound of the drum. Although calf heads can still be bought, they are not very practical and since the 1960s plastic heads – some of which feel and sound very much like a calf head – have become the norm.

Cymbals

Rhythms are played on a ride cymbal, also known as a time cymbal, in the same way they are played on a high-hat. A crash cymbal is used for accents and punctuation, and a crash-ride combines the two and is used for rhythm and accent.

Most drum manufacturers also make hardware – bass and high-hat pedals and stands – but do not make cymbals. The three cymbal manufacturers I prefer are Avedis Zildjian, Sabian and Paiste. Avedis come from Turkey but have been based in the United States for some time; Sabian is a Canadian-based off-shoot of Zildjian and Paiste are Swiss. Cymbals are all different and not only in size: 10 Avedis cymbals of roughly equal size will all sound different, even if they weigh the same and are stamped with the same specifications.

It is more difficult to choose cymbals than

drums and I am always looking for a slightly better cymbal. A cymbal is as good as the musician who chooses it and the drummer must know what to listen for, where to hit it, what he is going to use it for and the type of response he is after. The carrying quality is another consideration: whether you want the sound to carry or not, whether you will be playing in a loud band and will have to project to the back of a hall, and whether you will be using microphones or not.

All cymbals have overtones and I try to pick those whose overtones will not clash. Make sure you do not have two crash cymbals whose pitch is too close because it will be difficult to differentiate them; if you already own two or three cymbals and want to get more, take the ones you have with you to the shop so you can be sure they all fit together.

Drumsticks

The traditional method of holding drumsticks was used originally in marching bands and is known as the orthodox grip. At the moment the most common method is known as the matched grip. While in the past jazz drummers used the orthodox grip and rock drummers the matched grip, today it is the other way around. Cozy Powell, Buddy Rich and Steve Gadd all use orthodox; Martin Drew, the jazz drummer uses matched and Phil Seaman used to use matched. I use matched except when playing with jazz friends.

Tuning

An expensive, well-made drum kit will not produce a good sound automatically; it will have to be tuned and over the years tuning has become a fine art. Tuning is complicated because it is dependent upon the location and circumstances the drummer is tuning for; for example, a small room, projection without mikes or a recording studio. If drums are deadened for a small room – as some people believe they must be – they will not project adequately in a large recording studio. In the early 1960s everyone was damping down their drums to get a "studio sound", but nowadays if you tune your drums for a jingle or demo session in a small room that is heavily carpeted and then put them in a large studio, they simply will not carry.

The best approach is to tune to a sound rather than a note, for example I try to have the lowest bass drum sound like a low tomtom and then remove some of the ring. I also tune the snare for

Pang (chinese) cymbal

Crash cymbal

Ride cymbal

Splash

High-hat

Snare

Small tomtoms

Bass drum

YAMAHA

Sticks. 1. Wooden drumsticks. 2. Nylon-tipped sticks. 3. Brushes, usually metal-wired but occasionally nylon. 4. Timpani beaters. *Above left,* matched grip. *Above right,* orthodox or military grip.

1   2   3   4

159

a snare sound rather than a note; although some drummers, such as Bill Bruford, tune to a note and achieve a great snare drum sound, but such people are an exception.

It is extremely important to try and achieve a good melodic interval between the tomtoms so there is a high, a low and something in between. It is also vital that the drummer understands the relationship between the bottom and top heads of the tomtoms and that this will change if different weights are used. Tuning the tomtoms to one note is not a good idea because if they are tuned to an A-chord, for example, and the musicians you are working with decide to play in B-flat, the first time you do a fill it will not sound too good.

Playing

For the right-handed player the subdivisions of the beat are played with the right hand on the high-hat or the ride cymbal while the left hand plays the back-beat, or accent. If the time signature is 4/4, for example, the left hand plays beats two and four, the right foot plays a pattern – perhaps four beats to a bar (each downbeat) or some other fixed pattern – on the bass drum, while the left foot raises and lowers the high-hats as required. Thus while the bass drum plays four beats in a bar, the left hand hits the snare on beats two and four while the right hand plays eight or sixteen beats. If the speed is fast, the drummer may use both hands on the high-hat to fit in the sixteen beats.

Regardless of an ability to play a particular instrument, a musician needs to have an appreciation of musical content; the better a musician understands music as a whole, the better he will play his own instrument. When I play I strive to put the particular musical atmosphere and the material above all else, so that I can play with the greatest possible sympathy for the material in the most musical and complementary way: if it is jazz, I play jazz, and if it is heavy rock, I play heads down and heavy.

Time-keeping – the ability to keep time consistently, evenly and regularly – is more important than technique. While it is also important to have good technique, and the more you have the better, I agree with Bruce Springsteen's drummer Max Weinberg who said that if a drummer has good time he will not necessarily get a job, but if he has bad time, he is less likely to get a job.

Other musicians are usually more concerned that the drummer keep things flowing than with his ability to race around the kit impressing everyone. If a drummer is lucky enough to com-

bine the two – and there are dozens of drummers who have phenomenal technique and time, such as Steve Gadd – that is ideal, but a drummer with good time and average technique is more likely to get work than one with brilliant technique and poor time.

Learning

The range of music from the past 10 or 15 years available on record today is a tremendous learning device; in the early 1960s recordings of so many different styles were not as easy to come by. I started simply by playing with records and listening to many different styles and I recommend that the beginning drummer do the same. If noise is a problem, you can use practice pads, wear headphones and play along to records in your room. This is an especially good way to learn the drums because on most records the time is good and the beginner will learn therefore to control his speeding up and slowing down while understanding what a drummer can do with different styles of music.

Rhythm boxes and clicks

In film music a drummer usually works to a click track, and in contemporary music he often works to a rhythm box. If I am working with a rhythm box, I try to find out if it will be used in the final mix because if the musicians have taped their parts or are overdubbing they tend to drift in and out with the click, and the drummer must know whether he is going to go with the click, with the musicians or stay somewhere in the middle when such drifts occur.

When working with clicks I try not to sound mechanical. Sometimes someone will want a mechanical feel and then I will play semi-stiff, but in general the key to working with clicks and rhythm boxes is to try and sound relaxed and make it swing. A metronome might keep good time, but a drummer needs to make a song feel like it is going somewhere – whether it is a dotted feel, a jazz feel or a regular feel – so that he is not just locking it all in without a sense of occasion or motion.

Electronic drums

At the moment electronic drums are fashionable and, while I think they will be around for a while – Dave Simmons' in particular – I cannot see

Warren Cann, *right,* uses a combination of acoustic and electronic drums for recording. Additional tomtom sounds and special effects are provided by the Simmons kit (right, foreground), the control box of which is in the centre rack behind the player.

Simmons drums: an electronic kit capable of producing a variety of tones through electronic control modules. The drums can be played manually as well as being triggered by a sequencer.

Linn computer: a programmable drum machine, similar to the Roland Drumatix, although it uses microchips of recorded drum sounds. Both pitch and tone can be altered.

them replacing the acoustic drum. The electronic music I have enjoyed listening to most is music where a synthesis exists between the acoustic and electronic. The electronic drum is a threat to the acoustic drummer in some types of music such as jingles and short, concise pop songs where the piece has to be consistent in tempo and have a certain feel. In this case it could be simpler to programme an electronic drum than call in a drummer; however, if this is carried to an extreme, then everyone's music will begin to sound the same and, hopefully, the novelty will wear off.

Performing

I do a fair amount of studio work, so when I perform live I experience greater psychological freedom because, although I know the music has to be right. I also know it is not going down on tape, unless the concert is being recorded.

The band might say you were great and the audience may go wild but, if you know you did not play well, you cannot fool yourself; and, if you make mistakes, you are kidding yourself if you say it does not matter. The great thing is to get in there and forget everything else.●

Playing Drums

I just seemed to lean towards the drums and started playing when I was about three. My uncle was a drummer and showed me how to hold the sticks; I used to bang on everything and he and I would play along with marching records. I started taking lessons when I was about seven, when I also joined a drum corps and played at home as well. My father used to take me to clubs to sit in with various bands, so I was able to practise and play a range of different styles.

Just like when learning a foreign language you must use it because if you don't it never flows and you forget it, so with drumming you must keep playing. I was fortunate therefore in being able to learn, practise and play different styles. I'd come from a drum corps rehearsal where we were using big sticks and go to a club and use small sticks, which was a big change; but after a while I learned not to let it bother me and it became natural, mainly because I didn't have any choice. Once you got up to play you didn't have time to think about whether it was comfortable or not and it was better to think about how much fun you were having. If the sticks were too heavy and I got blisters, I was usually having too much fun with the other guys to stop and think about the discomfort.

Lessons

The teacher I had when I was in music school let us hold the sticks the way that was most comfortable, and that was good. Matched grip became popular because guys could practise snare drumming using the same technique they'd use for xylophone, marimba or timpani. The military, or orthodox, grip is good for technically intricate things and the matched for power and to get to the left cymbal; choice of grip depends on the kind of music you're playing.

The matter of when and whether to have lessons is different for everyone. For some young people – those that are academically inclined – taking lessons from the start can be a good idea; and some people can be inspired technically and mathematically by learning to read music. For another type of person, though, it can be discouraging to become involved in reading and technique and matters that are separate from music itself; once such people get to the point with their music where they can see the purpose of learning then they will benefit from lessons.

I don't feel there's less need for a drummer to have a musical education than any other kind of musician, but it is unnecessary for a beginner to learn the technical side first. Even without lessons a drummer will learn just by wanting to play, and this is the way any musician is inspired to learn, say, how to write music. Lots of famous musicians can't read music, and although they might try to learn when they're older, it's harder; on the other hand if they'd had a musical education they might not have had the same freedom in their writing. People must remember that you don't play with your eyes, you have to be able to hear.

Drums

With my first set of drums I just experimented with different heads – tomtoms with one or two heads and different thicknesses – and eventually I came up with a set that was a good all-round kit to take into a studio; I can tighten them up and they'll speak, or I can loosen them to sound big. I can get pretty much anything I want unless the engineer wants a completely different set, which is to be expected in certain circumstances.

When I started building a set of drums, I bought a whole new set and, while the bass drum felt good, the tomtoms didn't so I took them back

Concert tomtoms

Steve Gadd and Paul McCartney, *left* (Photo: Linda McCartney)

and got another line of drums for the tomtoms. They only had one head so I bought a set of eight chromatic tomtoms on stands, but they weren't made for a bass drum so I had bottom heads put on all of them and hooked them to tomtom mounts that fit on the bass drum. I left them on their floor stands so that they could be used as side gear, then chose the four heads that would give me the most range and hooked them in with the bass drum.

When other people were starting with a 12-inch tomtom I started with a 10-inch, and could get it to sound either high-pitched with a lot of tone or loosen it a bit to sound big. The next one I got was a 12-inch, then a 13-inch which I used to keep up on the bass. I discovered that drums with two heads – small drums which you can loosen – sound a lot bigger, but when you tighten them to get a higher pitch they choke and you don't get any resonance.

The biggest one I was using at the time was a 14-inch which I would change around. Today I'll sometimes use the 10- and 12-inch on top and a 15 and 16 on the bottom; but the basic 10, 12, 13 and 14 – the tomtoms with two heads – have a lot of range on every drum, high or low, and a lot of flexibility. You might not want to use them if you were recording with, say, Led Zeppelin – then you might want to use gigantic drums instead – but these work in a lot of different conditions.

Recording

When I go into a studio and am given a new piece, the road map – the sections of the tune – is the first thing I try to learn: how the artist or producer wants the piece structured (verses and choruses) and in which sections he wants to have a change. I then think about the individual sections and how they might be played. If I have an A-B-a structure, for example, and B is repeated, I try to remember how I played B the first time so it will make sense compositionally. On the other hand, people will sometimes ask me to play it once in one way and then not to repeat it.

The most important thing that the drummer has to do is to keep everything solid, to lay down a groove for the others to play within. There are types of music where the arranger wants the rhythm to breathe with the vocals, or the drummer is just an accompanist, but most commercial work is built on a groove set by the drummer.

Whatever I am playing, I try to begin by giving the minimum amount necessary to make the piece settle down while still contributing something to the music; then if people want more, I can give it. When you start out as simply as possible, you give the thing a chance to settle and you discover where the tune itself wants to be. Music written by really good composers plays itself; it doesn't require a lot of thought.

Keeping everything tight and solid becomes especially important and difficult when a song moves from one section to the next. When you get to the bridge or when the piece moves to another level of intensity there's a natural tendency for the time to speed up if you're not concentrating hard; and at the fade the piece usually starts burning and everyone gets excited so there is even more chance for the tempo to go wrong. Many producers and arrangers use rhythm machines or click tracks along with the drummer; using these can help a drummer discover the natural tendencies in a piece.

Working

Every drummer is unique and every job is a different story. I've gone on jobs where the drums have sounded fine to me but the engineer made me change the bass drum head because to him it sounded like a dampener. Then I'll go to another date without changing the head back and the engineer will say the bass sounds like a cannon. I don't argue because it's important to realize that music is a group effort; it's not just about the individual and everyone has got to be out there working together. I'll even let an engineer put a mike as close to the centre of the snare as he needs to feel comfortable with the sound he's getting, and I'll change my method to accommodate this. For certain types of drumming it would be impossible for him to do this, but if I've just got to play a back beat, and he likes the sound and I like the way he's getting it, then I'm willing to go along.

I don't have any particular sound that I go for, other than what seems best for an individual track. You just have to trust the people you're working with. If they say they want to take the snare down or want to use a bigger one, I understand and that's the way I like it. I'm actually orchestrating my sound to fit the piece. I'll change anything, even the drum set, to go from one tune to the next.

I don't believe in any set approach. I think that you have to find a way that is comfortable and, maybe most importantly when you're doing it for business, the way that's most comfortable for everyone involved. That's what business is: a group of people working towards the same end and when you're working professionally that becomes important. There's no sense in being hard-headed about it: I'm not out to prove anything, I'm just out to play music the best I can.●

Non-Tuned Percussion

The subject of percussion is vast and fascinating; one can write and talk for hours on the instruments, their history and the techniques. However, I have only one chapter in which to try and capture your imagination so I shall select a number of instruments that I feel to be of "popular audible knowledge"; instruments that are comparatively easy to distinguish when they are played in an orchestra, band, or group.

Percussion is the art and skill of striking, and it was an art and a skill at which ancient man was very adept. His very survival depended upon it. He would terrify his enemies, communicate to his friends – by drumming or percussing – his most basic of tools being bare knuckles and a patch of earth on which to beat. It is important to remember that the percussion family, along with the voice, is the most ancient of musical families, and as it has evolved it has been used to set the ambience for all sorts of situations and events – from the religious temple drums to the war drums of the East and West.

Before I begin writing about the instruments and the techniques of performance, I feel it important to say something of my own musical experience and philosophy: the principles which have helped me to structure my performance as both a stage and a recording musician.

Music is the most wonderful form of universal communication; and percussion, as I have already stated, is certainly one of the oldest and most basic tools of that communication. Each man has, in his pumping heart and the graceful flow of the body's movement, an inherent sense of rhythm. Each movement of the body including the use of the voice owes its "form" to the space between action and reaction: to "timing" "Timing" is the common element of the performing arts (theatre, dance, etc). It is "good timing" that determines an electrifying performance. Perhaps the most coveted and respected accolade of praise that it is possible to bestow upon any actor, comedian, dancer, or musician, is that of "great timing".

Percussion playing is audible drama which in performance manifests as visual drama. In the modern symphony orchestra, for instance, players in the percussion section are able to move among their instruments (unlike the main body of the orchestra), thus distracting and then captivating the eye of the audience who watch the timpani and cymbals being beaten and clashed with style and panache.

It is the interpretation and the understanding of the spaces between musical notes that holds the excitement of music for me, and I have always tried to allow my performance to be governed by that tension.

Techniques

There are many books offering advice on technique, and most of them are very useful, but it must not be forgotten that a large part of any player's technique comes from his, or her, own experience – the knowledge assimilated while *playing* the instrument. The physical comforts or discomforts, the effort involved in changing position or posture, all these are personal matters and I shall therefore make brief generalizations with the intention of your using them as a guide rather than a rule.

In spite of there being so many different types of percussion instrument, one basic fact of tech-

Ray Cooper on stage, *below.* Among the percussion instruments are three conga drums, with their distinctive deep, barrel-shaped shells. They can be played with any part of the hand to create different effects.

nique prevails: as a percussion player you will be aware that a large proportion of the instruments are played directly with the hands. The instrument in effect becomes an extension of the body. It is therefore essential for you to learn about, and be aware of, your arms, hands, fingers, and fingertips. Acquiring this knowledge and awareness brings about control and discipline. Only when the correct marriage between player and instrument has been established can practice with techniques really begin to show desirable results.

But moving on to a more specific discussion of the instruments, I must add what I feel to be a very important point: so important that it may appear to be obvious, but as it seems to be the general fortune for the obvious *not* to be stated, and consequently for it to be forgotten, I make no apology for this insertion. Having stressed the necessity for an awareness and control of the arms, hands and fingers, and the duality of instrument and body in the production of sound, I must add that the essence of good music is better attracted to a healthy, disciplined body and a well-kept musical instrument. Both instruments, human and musical, should be well maintained and cared for and should not be abused. The abuse of either instrument will make playing and making music more difficult.

I have become known as a percussionist who specializes in Latin-American percussion. I might argue that point, but it is a good starting place for our discussion. The Latin percussion family includes what are considered to be some of the earliest musical instruments. These are what we know as rattles and shakers.

The maracas are gourds with peas or beans inside. They are held one in each hand and shaken back and forth making the beans strike the inside shell with a sharp precise sound.

The cabaça is a gourd with an outer mesh of beads. The bead mesh is cradled in the palm of one hand while the other turns the instrument to and fro causing the desired sound.

The chocallo is another shaker, this time a metal cylinder containing lead shot or peas. It is usually held in both hands and shaken backwards and forwards, again so that the lead shot or peas strike the inside shell with the desired sound.

The claves are also very ancient instruments made up of two cylindrical pieces of hard wood. They are held, one resting lightly on the finger tips with the palm of the cupped hand acting as a resonator, the other between the thumb and first finger, or first two fingers, of the other hand. One then strikes the "resonator" clave with the other clave to produce a delightfully sharp and clear tone. Practise making the shape of a resonator with your hand; your ear will tell you when the best tone is produced. The famous rumba rhythm (below) is a well known clave part.

The güiro, or scraper, is yet another very old instrument. It is a gourd which has had ridges cut throughout its length, and it is played by running a scraper made of forked cane or bamboo back and forth over the notches of the gourd. The sound produced is very interesting and with experience and experiment can be made to vary enormously.

The tambourine is one of my favourite instruments. This often sadly underrated instrument has brought "life" to many a dull recording track. The back beat or hit on a tambourine is a good example of how player and instrument are united in the creation of sound. For a good back

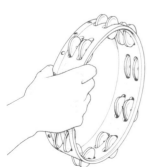

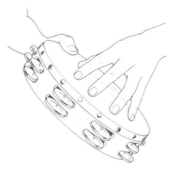

Rhythmic shaking: hold the tambourine firmly in the right hand while moving it to and fro in a parallel motion.

Back beat: the finger pads of the left hand (which should be slightly cupped) strike the tambourine held at an angle.

A sharp tap can be achieved by hitting the fingertips of one hand with the outer edge of the tambourine.

beat, a "headed" tambourine is needed, that is a tambourine with calf or vellum stretched over it. It has been my experience that a plastic head is not able to give as much power to the sound. It is also more difficult to get the important communion of feeling between hand, fingertips and instrument. In my opinion the best sounding general purpose tambourine is a double jingled one of about 10 inches diameter. As I feel there to be an affiliation between weight and good sound, I think that a tambourine should be quite heavy. All my instruments are made of solid components and are heavy in structure. When you hold them, you feel their substance and presence which adds to the important feeling of association between the body of the player and the body of the instrument. For playing a back beat I hold the tambourine in my right hand at an angle. The left hand is held slightly cupped, with the fingers spread. It comes down on to the head of the tambourine, finger pads first.

Rhythmic shaking of the tambourine is executed by holding the instrument almost vertically and moving it to and fro with a parallel motion. By doing this the jingles have a more precise hit than if they are "waggled". An instrument must always be held with assurance and authority; never waggle or hold the tambourine limply; the sound ensuing will also be limp, and lack precision.

The tambourine has become a very important instrument in pop music. The marriage of snare drum and tambourine playing back beats together has inspired many record producers. The instrument can become an extension of the drum hit, its own natural frequency cutting through most other instruments.

I could write much more about the tambourine but I must leave it to you to discover for yourselves its versatility and range through your own extended study of this instrument.

The conga or tumba drum, of the Afro-Cuban family is my other favourite instrument. It is a wooden barrel-shaped shell with a vellum or calf-skin head. It is played with every part of the hand: fingertips and pads, the palm and the whole flat of the hand – each part produces a different effect. As with tambourine-playing, the hand formation and force of impact creates the sound. I play three tumbas, but the technique of producing the differing sounds should be practised on one drum and later adapted to the use of two or three. Like the tambourine, the conga drums fit well into the pop idiom and can become an enhancing extension to the sound of the drum kit.

The bongos comprise a pair of wooden shells

Tabla

Bell tree

Tambourines

Sleigh bells

Chocalho

Güiro and stick

Crotales or finger cymbals

Bongos

Cuica

Mark tree

abaça

Skulls or temple blocks

Modern cabaça

Cow bells

Gogo bells

Triangles

Maracas

Claves

with tightly stretched vellum heads to produce the clear high-pitched notes that are associated with bongo playing. These instruments are small hand drums, held between the knees of the seated player and played with the flat of the fingers, or the fingertips. Pressure from the palm of the hand on the vellum head is used to vary the sounds; the small drum is usually played to the left and the large to the right. The distinctive trill or roll is probably the best known sound to be produced by these two little drums. Many other sounds can be produced by experimenting with the instruments.

The tabla Before I leave the subject of hand drums, I must, with the greatest of reverence, touch upon the art of tabla playing. Nowhere in the world has drumming reached a higher degree of perfection than in India. The drum, in that vast and mystical country, has been and still remains the instrument associated with all the acts of life. The most predominant percussion instruments of Indian classical music are the tabla and the mridangam, although both instruments are also widely used in folk music.

The tabla consists of two drums, the bhaya (lower drum) and the tabla (higher drum). The present day bhaya has a shell of metal. The "head" consists of two skins secured to the shell by a hoop of twisted thongs. A black patch (made from rice, flour, tamarind juice, and sometimes iron filings), approximately three inches in diameter, is fixed to the skin a little off centre, lying – when the hand is in playing position – under the tip of the forefinger. The black patches on both tabla give the drums their unique overtones.

The tabla (small drum) has a wooden body. The "head" is smaller than the bhaya, approximately six inches in diameter, and the black patch is fixed centrally. The heads are fastened to leather hoops and held by leather straps. Wooden dowels are usually placed between the shell and straps putting pressure on the heads. The pitch is raised or lowered by the player making upward or downward strokes of a small hammer on to the wooden dowels. In performance the bhaya is placed to the left and the tabla to the right. The left hand controls the pitch of the bhaya by pressure, adding intricate rhythms with the fingers. The player uses the base of his palm as well as his fingers.

Non-tuned percussion instruments divide into three groups – drums, shakers and rattles, and soft percussion. These instruments can provide a colourful rhythmic addition to many forms of contemporary music.

Timbales, *above,* are slightly larger than the bongos and have metal shells which can also be hit with the playing sticks. The addition of a cowbell creates more rhythmic possibilities.

I would suggest that perhaps the best approach to tabla playing is to watch and listen to the masters. It is still possible to obtain records of the late Chatur Lal, who used to perform with Ravi Shankar (India's master sitar player). Then we must listen and watch the masterly skills of Alla Rakha who performs with Ravi Shankar now. **The timbales** are not my favourite instruments, but I do have a certain soft spot for them even though they can be incredibly loud and cutting. They have a brass shell and look a little like large metal bongos. They are played with sticks – usually thin round untapered rods – and I usually play them in conjunction with a cow bell (experimentation with various rhythms is great fun). However, it is not uncommon to hit the shell of the drum itself which produces a good, clunky, metallic sound.

The triangle I use a triangle quite a lot on pop records. Its versatility never ceases to amaze me. You can cup the triangle in your hand and muffle or open the sound, and employ many other tricks. The triangle leads us on to the softer regions of percussion playing: finger cymbals, crotales, and so on.

Bell trees and mark trees For me, bell and mark trees hold magical qualities. I feel like a delicate water colourist when using these instruments. Suddenly, as a musician, one starts to colour sound, conjuring up sunlight, raindrops, and more. The techniques involved in playing these "bell" instruments are relatively simple; it is the

nuances and subtleties which can be produced that need understanding. The bell tree is a collection of cupped bells of varying sizes and pitch arranged on to a rod, and the percussionist produces sounds by either moving a brass-headed stick up and down the bells, or striking the bells individually (practise to get your desired effect).

Mark trees are like metal wind chimes; various sizes of metal tubes are strung on to a rod and hung vertically. The player moves his hand or a soft stick up and down the hanging tubes. A bell tree tends to be easier to control in terms of sound than the mark tree; after one has set the tubes in motion, hitting each other, one has to wait for the natural decay of sound.

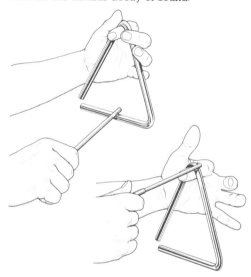

Triangle: the high, penetrating sound can be muffled by cupping with the fingers, *top,* or played "open", *below,* striking the metal beater at the top of the instrument.

Advice for beginners

All I want to do is to impart the magic of these instruments to you, illustrate them, and then ask you the reader to obtain them and experiment with them. There are many, many more instruments which I could write about, but what I hope to have done already in this chapter is to have captured your imagination to the extent that you will want to find out for youself – always the most enlightening and excelling thing to do – more about percussion.

Can I now leave you with this: for those that choose the disciplines of music as their life's work, the way is long and difficult. Such knowledge is not purchased – it must be earned. Thank you, and God bless.●

Tuned Percussion

Tuned percussion has played a major part in the music of non-European cultures for centuries. The South American mixture of native Indian, African and Spanish – hence Moroccan – music, together with the more recent influx of North American jazz and pop, has produced a number of new styles, collectively termed Latin, most of which feature tuned percussion in a big way. In African and Indonesian music tuned percussion creates the pitch element in largely rhythmic music.

Until recently, in European music tuned percussion instruments were used sparingly to create effects, rather than as part of the general sound. Nowadays, however, they are finding a wider and more receptive audience, not just through the work of modern classical composers such as Britten and Stravinsky, but through their increasing use in funk, rock, reggae, Latin-American jazz and indeed in film music.

As well as their individual sounds, which make them effective solo instruments, they make excellent "doubling" instruments: that is to say they can give an edge to, or enhance, the sound of a sustaining instrument such as an organ or flute. A good example of this can be heard on Steely Dan's *Aja*, where the piano and guitar lines are doubled by Victor Feldman's xylophone an octave higher; Feldman's playing gives a sharp edge to the melody and adds brilliance to the overall sound.

The glockenspiel
Sometimes called bells in the United States, the glockenspiel consists of a series of steel or alloy bars arranged in two rows, similar to the keys of

Tristan Fry

a piano but with the "black" notes slightly raised. These rest on felt supports and are held in place by a hole at the top end of each bar. Standard models have a range of two-and-a-half or three octaves.

The sound of the glockenspiel is bright and ringing, and sometimes the notes must be dampened with the fingers after being struck to reduce reverberation. When used in recording sessions, the "white" notes are recorded first and the "black" notes are overdubbed to avoid a "swimmy" sound caused by too much reverb. Some glockenspiels include a damper mechanism, but these are unfortunately rather rare.

The mallets used to play the glockenspiel are of wood, plastic, hard rubber or metal, and each material produces a different tone; hard felt timp sticks are used to produce a sound with little or no attack.

The glockenspiel has featured in many soul recordings, particularly those by Motown, and is usually played two octaves higher than the singer or melody instrument, for example, *Now That We've Found Love* by the O'Jays and *Ain't No Mountain High Enough* sung by Diana Ross in which the bass line is doubled by a glockenspiel.

The xylophone

The xylophone is traditionally made of wood, although some modern instruments are synthetic. It resembles the glockenspiel except that the underside of the bars are recessed to create different pitches, thus eliminating the need for large bars to produce lower notes. Beneath each bar is a tube resonator whose pitch is the same as its bar. Hard beaters produce a bright ring and softer mallets a more mellow tone. A good example of the xylophone in popular music is Tom Jones' *Delilah*.

The marimba

Like the xylophone this is made of wood, or sometimes nowadays from synthetic material. In orchestras and large ensembles the rich sound of the marimba, enhanced by the use of soft mallets, plays the part of a bass xylophone. There is also a bass marimba which is used in street and festival music in Africa and Latin America; it has a deep resonating tone reaching to two octaves below middle C. The xylorimba, as the name suggests, combines the ranges of

Tuned percussion instruments: wooden bars on the xylophone and marimba produce a harder, more mellow sound than the metal bars of the vibraphone. The tubular bells and glockenspiel both produce a ringing tone.

Vibraphone

Xylophone

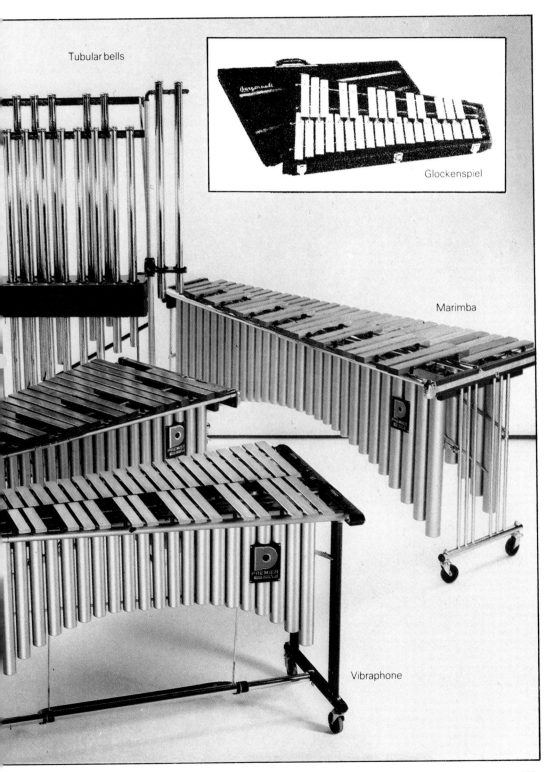

Tubular bells

Glockenspiel

Marimba

Vibraphone

the xylophone and the marimba; this is at least five octaves and some agility is required to get from top to bottom quickly.

The marimba is featured in recordings, almost as often as the glockenspiel. Listen to Lulu's *Morning Dew*, Burt Bacharach's score for the film *Casino Royale* and, more recently, Toto's single *Africa* where it is heard in both solo and supporting roles.

The vibraphone

The vibraphone, or vibes, is approximately the same shape as an orchestral xylophone but the bars, which are flat-mounted, and the resonators are made of metal. Vibrato is produced by revolving discs driven by an electric motor. These are fitted into the upper opening of the tube resonators and turn on a spindle.

While two mallets are used to play the xylophone, marimba and glockenspiel, four mallets are used on vibes, and some players have adopted this method for the former instruments as well. By using a swing technique of holding the beaters between the fingers and widening or contracting the hands, complex, four-note chords can be played. Top vibraphone players such as Gary Burton and Frank Ricotti use a fifth beater to stroke a bar after it has been struck to bend the note and create a bluesy effect. Early Motown records, such as *Baby Love* by The Supremes, often used a vibraphone to double the melody.

The celesta and tubaphone

The celesta sounds like a glockenspiel but, instead of beaters, a keyboard with a modified piano mechanism strikes the bars inside the instrument. The tubaphone is a small glockenspiel-like instrument with metal tubes which are played to produce a bell sound.

Tubular bells

A standard orchestral instrument, tubular bells consist of a set of 18 chromatic metal tubes that are suspended vertically. They produce a "ching" tone. The tubes are struck near the top and a damping mechanism operated by the foot can be used to stop reverberation. They are used to great effect in *I Want Your Love* by Chic.

Timpani

The membraphone family comprises those instruments in which sound is created by the vibration of a stretched membrane or skin. The timpani (timps), or kettle drums, are the most consistently used in classical, jazz and popular music, being capable of low, sustained rumbling as well as loud, dramatic bangs.

There are two types of timps: the traditional, hand-tuned model which has six tension screws for tightening a skin stretched over a copper bowl and held in place by a steel collar; and the more common machine timp for which a single mechanism, such as a master screw, foot pedal or the rotation of the drum bowl, is used to

Steel drums

TUNED PERCUSSION

Hand-tuned and machine timps:
the two types of timpani in
common use are, *left,*, the hand-
tuned timp which uses six
manually operated keys to
produce the desired pitch and,
right, the machine timp, operated
by a foot pedal and incorporating a
tuning gauge.

tighten or loosen the skin head to change the drum's pitch. A tuning gauge on the side of the drum enables the player to know what key he is in without having to stop and tune by ear. The African talking drum, or kalungu, works on the same principle: by rapidly squeezing and relaxing thongs attached to the skin, changes of pitch can be made.

Timp playing sticks are usually made of hickory, but stick heads vary. Large, soft heads are usually made of cork covered in felt; hard felt or wood is used for smaller heads. Rock drummers will occasionally use timp sticks for special effects, such as a swishy cymbal or heavy tomtom sound. Timps are used for effects in rock music; the instrumental section of Earth, Wind and Fire's *Boogie Wonderland* contains a good example.

Steel drums
The unique sound of the steel drums is characteristic of West Indian music. The steel drum sound was originally made on an upturned oil drum with different parts of the drum producing different pitches. On the modern drum the lid is concave and covered with small convex sections which are struck to produce specific notes. After a note is struck an out-of-tune bend may be heard caused by reverberation; tuning the steel drum is an art in itself. The drums come in four sizes; treble, alto, tenor and bass. Striking implements are usually made of metal and, occasionally, have rubber or felt tips. 10 c.c.'s *Dreadlock Holiday* includes an excellent display of steel drumming.

Other instruments
There are many hybrids of standard tuned percussion instruments, such as the vibra-marimba; and several bizarre inventions, which nonetheless have their uses. The waterphone is a strange instrument, which looks like two saucepans held

together with metal strips. It is played with sticks or, more often, a double-bass bow, which is drawn across the strips. The "saucepans" are immersed in water to produce a wobbling sound, as heard in the disturbing soundtrack of the film *Alien*.

Handbells, tuned to a major scale, have been used for 800 years; a modern example is Herbie Flower's *Carillon*. Tuned sleigh bells are struck rather than shaken; and crotales, or antique cymbals, have an enchanting "ching" sound, as heard on John Lennon's *Oh My Love*.

Crotales

Advice for beginners
If you are thinking of taking up percussion, it is a good idea to learn the piano as well, because this will be a great help in understanding the harmonic as well as the rhythmic pattern of music. Use a cushion to practise getting the right kind of stroke with your sticks: if a heavy impression is left in the cushion, you are hitting either too hard or without enough "bounce"; most percussion instruments sound better when struck lightly and briskly so that they can "ring".

Listen to records and try to identify the tuned percussion without looking at the album sleeve. Finally, remember that these instruments do not lend themselves easily to slow, or sustained, music (except, perhaps, for the vibes). It is possible to create an illusion of sustain by rolling with two sticks on one note, but this is only fully effective on the bass marimba. It is best to use this effect to punctuate a rhythm line or to enhance the brightness of the tune in syncopated rhythmic passages.●

Brass

The instruments of the modern brass family have an interesting and curious history stretching back to ancient times. The earliest musical horn, dating from about 4000 BC, was a crude instrument made from a hollowed tree branch. The period between 1400 and 1600 AD saw the birth of the natural trumpet ("natural" because it was restricted to the notes of its harmonics). It was as much as eight feet in length, folding around on itself, with a cup-shaped mouthpiece, flared bell and no side holes or valves. The instrument was capable of only simple overtones, although it could produce a complete scale in the upper partials where the harmonics were closer together; thus early trumpet music was written predominantly in the higher registers. Also during this period, the sackbut – the forerunner of the trombone – appeared with a U-shaped slide making it fully chromatic and therefore the most versatile of the brass instruments of the time.

Horns were often used for hunting, especially in France: hence the French horn. Like the trumpet, the French horn remained non-chromatic until the eighteenth century when it was discovered that the key of the instrument could be altered by inserting different lengths of tubing, or crooks, to change its fundamental note (the lowest tone of its harmonics) and hence the pitch of its harmonics. This cumbersome system was used until the early nineteenth century when the advent of mechanized valves brought about the first family of fully chromatic brass instruments. The tuba also arrived at this time, providing fuller sound at the bottom of the brass section.

Modern brass instruments

Today, brass instruments are sophisticated pieces of machinery and their range is enormous. The family includes: trumpets pitched in B-flat, C, D and E-flat; piccolo trumpets pitched in high F, G, A and B-flat; cornet; flügelhorn; alto, tenor and bass trombones; French horn; Wagner tuba; tenor tuba (euphonium); the E-flat, double B-flat and C tubas; as well as other minor instruments. For modern recording, the B-flat trumpet, trombone (tenor and bass), French horn and tuba are the most widely used.

Trumpet, flügelhorn and piccolo trumpet

The B-flat trumpet, usually found in jazz and popular music ensembles, is a transposing instrument; its music is written a tone higher than concert pitch. Many trumpet players can play consistently in the upper register (and some even higher), but there are many good players who are not capable of this; in recording sessions players are rarely asked to play higher than the normal range.

Most session trumpet players also play the flügelhorn which is, again, pitched in B-flat. It has a wider bore than the trumpet, so to get the best results from its warm mellow sound it is advisable not to write notes higher than G (concert), although higher notes can be played.

The B-flat piccolo trumpet is common in Baroque music, but it has occasionally found its way into popular music; one of the most famous examples is The Beatles' recording of *Penny Lane*. The instrument is pitched an octave above the normal trumpet, and is thus extremely difficult to control; relatively few trumpet players have mastered it.

Trombone

The tenor trombone is written in the bass clef and is a non-transposing instrument. As well as producing notes in its normal range, it is capable of playing seven more tones (usually only used as pedal notes) from low B-flat down to E. However, the first three of these are the most reliable.

The large bore of the bass trombone gives it great depth and power in the lower register. It is

Trumpet mouthpiece: as with all brass instruments, lip pressure on the mouthpiece helps to change the pitch.

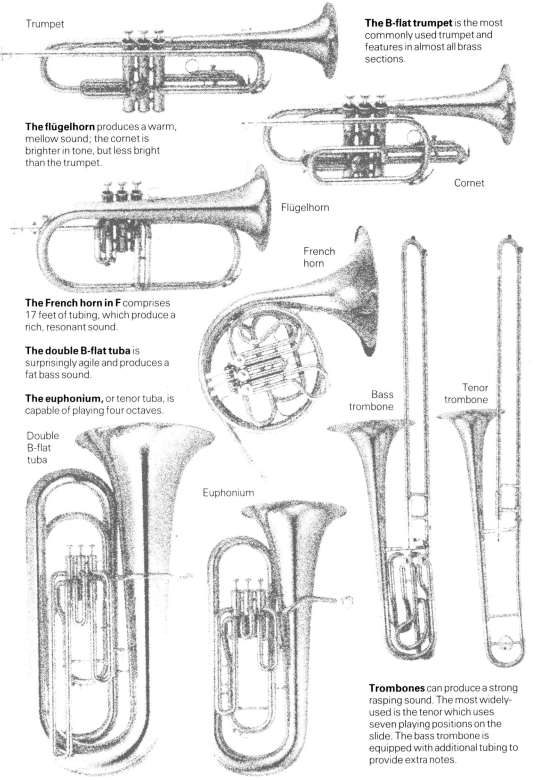

Trumpet

The B-flat trumpet is the most commonly used trumpet and features in almost all brass sections.

The flügelhorn produces a warm, mellow sound; the cornet is brighter in tone, but less bright than the trumpet.

Cornet

Flügelhorn

French horn

The French horn in F comprises 17 feet of tubing, which produce a rich, resonant sound.

The double B-flat tuba is surprisingly agile and produces a fat bass sound.

The euphonium, or tenor tuba, is capable of playing four octaves.

Bass trombone

Tenor trombone

Double B-flat tuba

Euphonium

Trombones can produce a strong rasping sound. The most widely-used is the tenor which uses seven playing positions on the slide. The bass trombone is equipped with additional tubing to provide extra notes.

also equipped with additional, optional, tubing (brought into action by a trigger mechanism), which enables the instrument to play all the notes from the lowest of the tenor trombone's normal range down through all the pedal tones to low E.

French horn and tuba

The French horn is a transposing instrument, pitched in F and written in the treble clef, although the bass clef is used for the lower notes of its normal range. It can also produce pedal tones written below low C, but the practical use of these is generally limited to long sustained notes.

The tuba, on the other hand, is a non-transposing instrument, written in the bass clef. There are many types, of which the most common is the double B-flat. Despite its size, the tuba is more agile than most musicians realize: few composers or arrangers exploit its full potential.

Brass in popular music

The use of brass in popular music has developed from the earlier forms of American jazz – Dixieland through to the Swing Era – and the style of writing for brass has been influenced by composers and arrangers such as Duke Ellington, Ralph Burns, Neil Hefti, Stan Kenton and Gil Evans.

In the 1920s and 1930s the trumpet established

Chicago, *above,* were one of the first rock groups (along with Blood, Sweat and Tears) to use brass instruments as an integral part of their line-up.

Dizzy Gillespie, *below,* with his famous angled trumpet, has developed a distinctive playing (and stage) style. Along with other notable players he has established the trumpet as the principal instrument in jazz.

itself as the principal brass instrument through the playing of Louis Armstrong, and this tradition has been carried through to the present day by players such as Roy Eldridge, Harry James, Dizzy Gillespie, Clifford Brown, Miles Davis, Freddie Hubbard, Cat Anderson and Maynard Ferguson.

In the 1950s, the rock 'n' roll era, brass was heard much less and was confined to small sections playing repeated "riffs". Nevertheless brass playing continued to develop in the distinctive big-band blues style of Lionel Hampton and Count Basie, although instrumental solos were nearly always left to the saxophone, guitar or piano.

The 1960s

The basic style that emerged in the 1950s was exploited and developed by many rock groups, in particular those led by Wilson Pickett and James Brown, which gave birth to the STAX sound. The style was carried through into the 1960s by the brass sections which played with Stevie Wonder, The Supremes and all the artists on the Motown record label.

At the same time, an entirely different type of brass sound was heard in the music created by Herb Alpert, a "pop" version of the Mexican "madriachi" style. The same sound can be heard in other contexts: for example, the trumpet solo in The Carpenters' recording of *Close To You,* and the flügelhorn parts in many of Burt Bacharach's lush orchestrations, such as Dionne Warwick's *Walk On By.*

A further development is to be found in the sophisticated brass writing and recordings of Blood, Sweat and Tears, and Chicago, both of which featured brass sections prominently as an integral part of the band. The Beatles opened another avenue by featuring two members of the brass family hitherto rarely heard in popular music: the French horn in *For No One* and the famous piccolo trumpet solo in *Penny Lane.*

The 1970s and 1980s

Many "funk" bands, such as K.C. and the Sunshine Band, Kool and the Gang, and Tower of Power (which featured one of the most famous brass sections to be heard in popular music since the Memphis Horns) appeared in the 1970s. However, the band which created a new style of brass writing, and had a lasting influence, was Earth Wind and Fire whose recordings sometimes featured as many as five French horns.

Since the mid-1970s brass instruments have been used more extensively and with more and more imagination. The saxophone is still the most common solo wind instrument in pop music, but many more records feature members of the brass family: the trumpet introduction to The Stylistics' *I Can't Give You Anything But My Love,* the trombone solo on Diana Ross' *I'm Coming Out* and the trumpet solo on Herb Alpert's *Rise*

Guy Barker, using an electric "bug" on his trumpet, a device made popular by Randy Brecker. This amplifies the sound of the instrument without the use of a microphone.

are just the tip of the iceberg.

There are now many great brass players involved in popular music in the recording world. Two of the most influential are trumpet players: Randy Brecker, who plays an electric trumpet with the Brecker Brothers; and Jerry Hey who has worked with The Seawind Horns, Michael Jackson, Earth Wind and Fire, Quincy Jones and many others. Both are not only great trumpet players but also innovative composers and arrangers, who have contributed much to the style of brass writing in recent years.

Advice to beginners

When buying an instrument try and obtain professional advice, preferably from someone who knows about the specific instrument you intend to play.

It is very important, when practising, never to overload your schedule: practise for an hour, then rest, then start again. This also relieves the pressure on the lungs.

Whatever the area of music in which you intend to specialize, it is always beneficial to practise classical techniques: studies, tone development, articulation and so on. The majority of jazz musicians have developed their technique through classical study.

Listen all the time to other areas in music and try and keep your mind open to other styles of playing. Finally, do not adopt one attitude for practising and one for performing. Whenever you pick up the instrument, play as though you are giving a live performance.●

Playing Brass

The brass instruments have been around for a long time and have always fulfilled an important musical and social function, be it a brass band in a park, a Munich *Oktoberfest*, or the distinct trumpet playing of a jazz great such as Louis Armstrong. Each of the brass instruments is unique and, when used in combination, they create a bright, engaging sound that justifies their popularity in classical and contemporary music alike.

Qualities of brass instruments

While the tonal colour of the trumpet is brilliant, the dynamics of the instrument enable a player to change from a brilliant *forte* to a subdued and almost pretty *pianissimo*. The orchestral range of the trumpet is from concert E below middle C to high concert C, two ledger lines above the treble staff. Its contemporary range is from low concert E to high concert F, three ledger lines above the treble staff. There are a few players who can play much higher than that: Bud Brisboy, Maynard Ferguson and Derek Watkins can reach concert C, or D above that, with an ease and flexibility which few others have.

The range of the piccolo trumpet is from concert E on the first ledger line of the treble staff to high concert G on the fourth ledger line. The range of the flügelhorn is from low concert E below middle C to approximately concert F, the top of the treble staff. Played much higher it loses its characteristic sound, although some players can make the flügelhorn sound good above concert F. Chuck Mangione, for example, plays in the higher partials of the flügelhorn, an effect he consciously seeks.

The orchestral range of the trombone is from low E, first ledger line below the bass clef staff, to approximately high concert C, sounding C in the middle of the treble staff. In contemporary range there are several players able to play to trumpet range – high concert G on top of the treble staff – and beyond. Bruce Flowers, who has played with Frank Zappa, has unbelievable range, and several other players have a useable range to high concert G.

Trombones and trumpets combined

The use of the trombone and trumpet in combination is as old as the instruments themselves

and creates a full, almost organ-like quality. While trumpets alone have a thinnish sound and trombones alone can be rather heavy, adding a trombone to a trumpet section makes the trumpet sound fuller and creates a spectrum of sound. It is well worth adding a trombone to a small trumpet section; their unison, or octaves, become stronger and the chord notes in the middle register are fuller and respond better on the trombone.

Brass and saxophones combined

Although the saxophone is not considered a member of the brass family, many brass sections include the instrument because it has a bright sound and its middle register quality and reed vibration add a buzz to a brass section. For record dates, the sections I use most frequently comprise: two trumpets, one trombone and two saxophones; or three trumpets, two trombones and one saxophone. Sometimes for a small section I use two trumpets, one trombone and one saxophone.

Trumpet and soprano sax have almost the same range; the combined sound is very brilliant and very bright. The alto saxophone is also bright but, being a little lower, creates a fuller sound when combined with the trumpet. When the middle range of the trumpet and the high range of the tenor saxophone are played in unison, a fairly intense sound is created; trumpet and tenor saxophone are usually played in octaves for greater weight, as heard in the recordings by The Crusaders.

Tenor sax fits in well with trumpet and trombone; it adds the range that is necessary to cover the distance between the two. Alto sax can perform the same role if a higher, brighter sound is required. Two trombones with trumpets and sax add another very distinct colour to the middle of the section.

An interesting and pleasing combination is flügelhorn and alto saxophone, providing the saxophone is not played as intensely as it normally is with a trumpet and the flügelhorn is played very lightly. Flügelhorn and flute together produce a very light sound with a great deal of bounce; a good example of this is Boz Scaggs' *Low Down*.

Baritone saxophone with bass trombone is good for doubling bass parts or adding weight to the bottom of a brass section. The tuba can, of course, be brought into the brass section if a heavy bass sound is required. A good example

Blood, Sweat and Tears, pioneers of brass rock.

of trumpets, trombones and tuba used in combination, and indeed of excellent brass writing, is the Gabrielli Brass as performed by the Chicago Symphony and the Philadelphia Orchestra brass sections, each playing antiphonally.

Contemporary writers and players

There are several good brass and horn writers around nowadays. When I was learning to write for brass, the Brecker Brothers were a major source of inspiration; they created some innovative sounds with just trumpet, alto saxophone and tenor saxophone. I also learned a lot from Tom Washington, whose work can be heard on records by Earth, Wind and Fire, Tom Tom 84, The Jackson Five and many others.

Chicago has had a great influence on brass writing; they use trombone, trumpet and sax,

with trombone generally featured as the main instrument. Some of the writing for the early Blood, Sweat and Tears records is also extremely innovative. The introduction to *In The Stone* on Earth, Wind and Fire's *I Am* album is a good example of my own brass writing.

I tend to overwrite to the ultimate regions of the brass instruments and my music is physically and technically demanding. I therefore hire those musicians who in my view are the best: the trumpet player Chuck Findlay, who also plays a very good trombone and slide trumpet; the trombonists Gary Grant, Lou Mercurian and Charlie Loper; the bass trombonist Bill Riechenbach, who can play all the trombones and slide trumpet. Other excellent brass musicians include the Brecker Brothers – Randy Brecker is a very talented jazz player – John Faddis, Alan Reuben, Tom Malone and Derek Watkins.●

Saxophones

When it first appeared in the 1840s, the invention of the Belgian instrument maker Adolphe Saxe, the saxophone was shunned by most composers, until Prokofiev and Shostakovich began to use it, because its tone was felt to be too brassy and did not blend easily with the other woodwinds. The sax was neither fish nor fowl: although made of brass it was not considered a brass instrument, nor was it a woodwind because its sound was too strident.

Between 1910 and 1930 the sax became a prominent part of the jazz orchestra, rising to the height of its popularity during the swing era in the 1930s and 1940s. From the 1950s onwards popular music consisted basically of rhythm instruments, such as guitars and drums, and it was mainly black R & B groups who continued to use horns and saxophones. King Curtis and Junior Walker exemplify the classic R & B sax, and Curtis, who played solo on Aretha Franklin's hit *Respect*, was the epitome of the "Texas by way of New York" (or, in this case, vice versa) tenor sax sound.

In the late 1960s and early 1970s groups such as Blood, Sweat and Tears arrived with big, fat-sounding horn sections and, after years of being inundated by guitars, drums and amplifiers, musicians were once again excited by alternative tonal colours. Some of the great saxophonists today include Michael Brecker, David Sandborn, Ernie Watts, Peter Cristlieb and Jim Horn, all of whom exemplify the best styles in saxophone playing today.

Types of saxophone

There are a number of different saxophones in common use: the tenor sax is probably the most widely used because of its mid-vocal range and variety of tonal colours. Two exceptional tenor saxophonists are Stan Getz, who has a soft, mellow tone and, at the other extreme, King Curtis with his hard, soulful style. Other sax soloists who have recently gained prominence include Phil Woods, who played on Billy Joel's *Just The Way You Are,* and David Sandborn, who has played with artists such as Carly Simon, James Taylor and Paul Simon.

The soprano sax has the highest range and, having a moodier and more ethereal quality, as heard in *Love Is The Answer* by England Dan

and John Ford Coley, is not generally used in rhythmic music. The baritone sax – a gutsy horn that frequently doubles with the bass and is often found at the bottom of the horn section – was put to terrific use by the group Tower of Power with their technique of switching back and forth between playing high with the horn section and then jumping to a low bass.

Saxophones are made in either the key of E-flat (alto and baritone) or B-flat (bass, tenor and soprano); at one time they were also made in the key of C, but these were felt to lack resonance. They are made in different keys to enable players to use the same fingering on any type. Thus when a player sounds the note G, for example, he uses the same fingering whether he is playing an E-flat or a B-flat saxophone. A G fingered on a tenor sax, however, will sound lower than the same G fingered on an alto sax because the former is a larger instrument.

All modern saxophones are transposing instruments: instruments for which music that is heard as sounding concert pitch is written in a key other than concert pitch. Concert pitch is when a written note is the same as the note heard; in theory, a C-saxophone would play concert C when the player read and fingered the note C. A B-flat sax will sound concert B-flat when the note C is fingered and, similarly, an E-flat sax will produce E-flat when C is fingered. When middle C is played on the B-flat soprano sax, the note produced is B-flat one tone below middle C; and the B-flat tenor sax produces B-flat an octave and a tone lower. Similarly, the E-flat

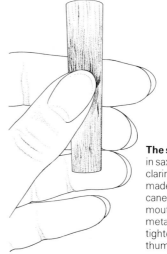

The single reed, used in saxophones and clarinets, is usually made from natural cane. It is fixed to the mouthpiece with a metal band and tightened with small thumb screws.

alto and baritone sax produce E-flat one sixth lower and an octave and one-sixth lower, respectively, when middle C is played. Thus it is the responsibility of the composer or arranger to write the correct notes to obtain the desired concert pitches; if the sound G above middle C is to be produced on an alto sax, for example, it must be written as:

To be able to read or write music the saxophonist should know all of the various transpositions, but unfortunately this is often the last thing he learns. If the saxophone were invented

Saxophones: of the 14 original members of this family these four are the most widely used. The soprano has an ethereal sound while the baritone can add a lot of power to the bass end of a big band or group. The tenor is the most popular because of its mid-vocal range and ability to produce a variety of tonal colours.

Baritone

Soprano

Alto

Tenor

183

today perhaps these complications would be resolved, but tradition has caused them – for better or worse – to become embedded deeply in the framework of music and technique.

Playing

There are a number of ways of playing a saxophone – blowing the cheeks out, hooking the mouthpiece towards the roof of the mouth, or downwards, and all are heard in the different playing styles. One of the most important elements is the use of the diaphragm and this takes a great deal of study and practice; it is control of the diaphragm muscle which enables good sax players to achieve the tone they require, and tone is the essence of the saxophone's appeal. This does not necessarily mean that the saxophonist has to be in top physical condition at all times, but this is definitely an advantage.

The sax sound

Like the human voice, the saxophone has an emotional quality due to the player's mouth being in contact with the instrument. Many of the inflexions and articulations used in speech can be translated into the saxophone's sounds – what I call vocalese – and to translate vocal phrasing the player must listen to these inflexions very carefully. This is similar to the way in which the jazz singer Ella Fitzgerald uses her voice to express an instrumental jazz line, only the saxo-

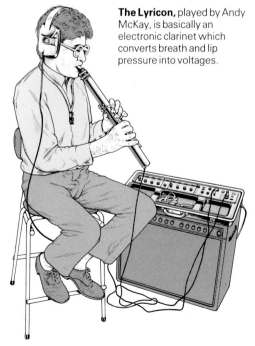

The Lyricon, played by Andy McKay, is basically an electronic clarinet which converts breath and lip pressure into voltages.

phonist must play the way a singer would sing.

There is a language of phrasing common to all instruments and it can be interesting to derive inspiration from another instrument, something I used with the LA Express players. One of our orchestral tricks was to play a melody line using sax and guitar, and the guitarist and I would have to accommodate each others' embellishments. The guitarist might, for example, bend a note – something I would not normally do on a sax – but I would do likewise to keep in unison; the resulting sound was powerful and moving.

The solo sax

Some famous sax solos include Sly Stones' *Dance To The Music,* in which a clarinet lick answers the basic melody line of the chorus, and Phil Woods playing alto sax on Billy Joel's *Just The Way You Are.* The sax is often used to echo a solo voice; it is often used in introductions and/or fades, and there might be a middle solo section as well, as in Gerry Rafferty's *Baker Street.* In such cases the horn section functions both as an accompaniment and as a solo voice. For the record, and because somebody may learn by listening to one or more of them, my own solos include a tenor sax solo on Carole King's *Jazz Man*; soprano sax on Paul McCartney's *Listen To What The Man Said* and tenor on Rod Stewart's *Do You Think I'm Sexy.*

The sax in combination

Saxophones blend naturally with other wind instruments – primarily brass – and can add a great deal of punch to a song. They are often the icing on the cake, because the decision to use a sax is frequently made after a song is already on tape. This makes the saxophonist's job easier because there is then a clearly defined parameter within which to work.

A mixed horn section of saxophones, trumpets and trombones is common in pop music today; James Brown used a hot R & B horn section; Wilson Pickett has been known to use 12 horns in a line; and the famous Sly Stone song *I Wanna Take You Higher* was basically a lick played in harmony by a massive horn section. For Steely Dan's *Aja* album we used a large, mixed horn section of five saxophones, two trombones and a trumpet. Whereas most pop music consists of simple chords of three or four notes, complex jazz chords require many horns and, for this particular recording, the horn section had to match the complexity of Steely Dan's harmonics.

When working with Blondie on *Rapture* I overdubbed four individual horn parts, phrasing each part in the same way to create a quality you

King Curtis

could not achieve with a group because of minute but audible differences in style. When all parts were attacking, releasing and doing vibrato, it had a phenomenal effect.

On Pat Benatar's *Evil Genius* we had a four-man sax section, but worked hard to play as one; this worked and is well worth trying. On a Rickie Lee Jones album David Sandborn played the melody on alto sax, Randy Brecker second harmony on trumpet and I played third harmony on tenor. We then doubled each of our parts: in effect a mixed ensemble, but doubled.

The clarinet

The clarinet was popular in the 1940s in the swing era, but it fell out of favour in the 1950s and 1960s except as a novelty instrument, a good example being The Beatles' *When I'm Sixty-Four* and Paul Horn's solo on Joni Mitchell's *For Free*. The bass clarinet (an octave lower than the standard clarinet) has a distinctive deep, reedy, penetrating sound. Good examples of its use can be found on Herbie Hancock's album *Head-hunters* and Steely Dan's *Babylon Sisters* from the album *Gaucho*. ●

Clarinet

Flute

The flute family and, to some extent, the clarinet family are fairly difficult instruments with which to express individual style, because they require great technical expertise. The achievement of a fine tone can prove a restriction to a player's style, which is perhaps why these instruments have not gained the popularity of the sax in popular music.

Because of its airy, wispy quality the flute is difficult to use with electric music and, while I have played the instrument a great deal, it has been used mainly for sweetening rather than as a dominant solo. I remember being fascinated with Jethro Tull because the flute, being largely confined to jazz, had not figured so prominently in popular music for some time. Roland Kirk popularized the "grunt" flute, as Quincy Jones named it, which is basically singing into a flute as you are playing. Herbie Mann did a country and reggae album with the flute as a secondary instrument but, while he did very well by it, the flute did not break any new ground.

The piccolo – the highest instrument of the orchestra – can add a sharp edge to the sound of a large horn section with its brilliant and penetrating quality. The alto flute (in G) produces a warm, mellow tone and is much used in jazz and film music for its atmospheric qualities. The bass flute (an octave lower than the standard flute) is rarely used, but it has a haunting, ethereal sound, quite different from that made by any other instrument.●

Jethro Tull

The flute, *top,* **and piccolo,** *above,* use similar fingerings, but the piccolo's range extends one whole octave above that of the flute. The instruments have no reed, simply a blowhole, *left,* which contributes to their characteristic breathy sound.

Double-reeds

The instruments which are classified in the double-reed group are the oboe, cor anglais, bassoon and contra-bassoon (bass bassoon). All four have very long histories; the oboe has Eastern origins and the bassoon can be traced back to medieval times.

The bassoon is associated with two popular characters or moods. First, the clown: the instrument is used many times in classical music to portray clowns or a clown-like jollity; *The Sorcerer's Apprentice* by Dukas is a well-known example. The bassoon also takes on this role in popular music; its prominent part in *Tears Of A Clown* by Smokey Robinson is a memorable example. The bassoon's other mood is delicate as in *Northern Lights* by Renaissance.

However, except for a few instances, the double reeds have always been regarded as orchestral instruments. Most popular composers and musicians have ignored them: they are rarely included in contemporary popular music, nor have those techniques been developed which, despite being avant-garde, are now commonplace with many other instruments. An isolated exception is Berio's *Sequenza* for oboe.

As a bassoonist I find this very disappointing. I have experimented with electric as well as technical effects and have found the results at least satisfying and at most incredible. The first technique I mastered was microtone trills. These can be done in two ways: by fingering changes on the same note, which alters the pitch less than a semi-tone (this can be done to produce an actual, as well as a microtone, trill); and "lipping" the note up and down with alternating lip pressure on the reed. I found that, done slowly, this produces a very sexy effect.

Electronic effects add a major new dimension to the bassoon. The wah-wah can be applied with the help of a good contact mike (I use a Barcus Beri or a Frap) and makes a significant difference to what is normally a full-bodied sound, by making it more "nasal".

I found phaser effective, depending on the acoustics of the room. Tape delay has proved very successful, although much mental prepara-tion is needed before committing oneself to tape to ensure decent harmonic relations, and of course because any mistake made is repeated over and over again while the sound fades.

Synthesizer seems to have unlimited potential for the bassoon. I tried it through a ring-modulator, and even more effective, the technician dropped a low note two octaves, and raised a high note two and then three octaves. The sounds obtained in this way are totally unlike any other musical instrument. By super-imposing one bassoon track on another or on more than one, it is possible to build huge shifting chords which can create an uncanny, perhaps unearthly effect. In a piece by Gordon Jones, this was combined with gamelan gonglike instruments from south-east Asia, which together produced just such an effect.

So, although double reeds are used much in classical music and occasionally in rock music – examples are the cor-anglais solo in the second movement of Dvorák's *New World Symphony* and the oboe in *Sometimes Late At Night* by Carol Bayer Sagar – the potential for these instruments is enormous and ripe for development.●

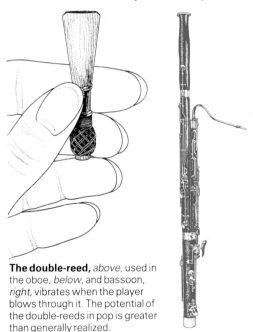

The double-reed, *above,* used in the oboe, *below,* and bassoon, *right,* vibrates when the player blows through it. The potential of the double-reeds in pop is greater than generally realized.

Harmonica

The harmonica is probably one of the most widely-bought instruments in the world, largely because of its size and cost. It first appeared as the non-chromatic mouth-organ in about 1830, with the chromatic version becoming popular in the late 1920s. While the harmonica is often relegated to the status of a child's toy, in the right hands it is capable of a virtuosity equal to that expected from the violin, cello, flute, or any other "serious" instrument.

Construction

The harmonica is made of a number of fine reeds that move back and forth. These are fixed in slots to a metal plate attached to a hollow box. Each reed has its own resonating chamber, and blowing or sucking through the top of the base causes the reeds to vibrate. A chromatic harmonica has two sets of reeds that are tuned to a diatonic scale of C major and C sharp major, respectively. When one scale is in use, a spring device activated by a button blocks off the other scale, similar to the pedal action of a harp.

The range of a chromatic harmonica is from middle C to three octaves above, but some larger instruments cover four octaves. Harmonicas are available in different sizes for use by marine bands or harmonica groups requiring bass or tenor instruments. They can also be bought in different keys for, say, a blues player who might not wish to use a chromatic instrument, or for players who find extreme keys difficult to manoeuvre.

Advice for beginners

To learn to play most instruments the student can usually find a teacher, but there are no harmonica teachers as such – just a few excellent musicians who have learned to play as well as they do through experimentation and hard work.

The most important thing to bear in mind is that it is the music itself that counts, rather than just the technique. Many players believe, for example, that the "cowboy" vibrato achieved by flapping the hands over the harmonica improves the sound. This is not so: creating a good, solid tone is what the player should aim for. When I use a throat vibrato, it is only after the note has the solidity of one produced by an excellent string musician. Vibrato is an embellishment, not a substitute for technique, which is why people like Stevie Wonder and Toots Thielman are considered exemplary players.

As a disciple of Heifetz, I have attempted to emulate his musicality on the harmonica. I began as a violinist and so I always try to play the harmonica with a feeling appropriate to the music, be it Bach, Handel or Stanley Myers. With a developed ear and a feeling for the instrument, it is possible to hear the difference between someone who simply *plays* the harmonica and someone who plays *music,* using the harmonica as a means of expression. The latter is the true musician.●

Vibrato, *below:* a simple vibrato is obtained by flapping the right hand behind the instrument. A throat vibrato is harder to achieve but gives a better tone and a greater control of dynamics.

Chromatic harmonica: when the button is pushed in, the holes for C major are closed off while those for C sharp major are opened. Hence all semitones are possible.

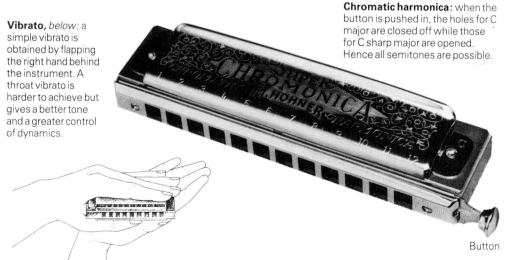

Button

Accordion

In 1822 in Berlin, Friedrich Buschmann developed a portable bellows organ, named the handäoline. In 1829 Cyril Damian of Vienna improved upon this and called his instrument the akkordion. Both these instruments were developments of the mouth organ: Damian's produced different notes according to whether air was blown in, or sucked out, through the reeds by the bellows. Also in 1829 Sir Charles Wheatstone constructed a hexagonal concertina which, although it could produce only one note from each press and draw action of its bellows, was considered an improvement in terms of tone and clarity and is still favoured by folk musicians the world over.

Notes were obtained on all these instruments by pressing buttons. The great innovation in accordion design occurred in 1852 when a Frenchman substituted a keyboard for the buttons on the right-hand side of the instrument – hence the name piano accordion. Since then keyboard players have been able to play the instrument with comparative ease.

Cajun music

Like the pedal steel guitar and the dobro, the accordion came to be used in popular music through the merging of cultures. When the French settlers in Nova Scotia, who were known as Acadians, were deported to Louisiana at the turn of the century, they took their folk music – which was similar to Irish jigs and other European folk dance styles – with them. The word "cajun" is a southern corruption of Acadian. The merging of the blues sound, prevalent in the south at that time, with Cajun music produced an R & B style of playing (with flattened thirds and sevenths) known as zydeco. The master Cajun player is Clifton Chenier, a piano accordion player, who performs with Rockin' Dopsie (a zydeco specialist) and Queen Ida, both of whom play button accordions. Together they present the most exciting aspect of Cajun music.

The accordion in popular music

There are a number of great accordion players in Mexico. On the Mexico-Texas border they even hold all-night competitions, where the bands attempt to upstage each other with ever more impressive shows of brilliance. A notable Mexican accordion player is Flaco Jimenez, who has worked a great deal with Ry Cooder.

The accordion appears on many well-known popular recordings: The Band's *Rocking Chair,* Shakin' Stevens' *Julie* and two versions of *How Can I Be Sure?,* by Dusty Springfield and The Young Rascals, are prime examples.

Advice for beginners

Some kind of formal training is likely to help many would-be accordion players; but finding out how it works, practising, experimenting and listening to the music of good players is the real way forward. Be sure to listen to Chenier and Jimenez; and remember that Charlie Parker was a self-taught sax player who took the art further than anyone previously and perhaps since – simply by practising.●

Geraint Watkins performing on piano accordion.

The piano accordion, *right,* is controlled by: a keyboard, 1; treble registers, 2, and bass registers, 3, which change the tonal quality; bellows, 4; and bass buttons, 5, which produce either bass notes or chords.

Strings

Strings have always been used in "popular" music. In fact the earliest cello, made in the mid-seventeenth century, had a peg inserted in the back of the instrument with a string attached so that it could be hung around the player's neck as he marched in the local band.

The modern use of strings in popular music derives from the lush Hollywood string sounds used on certain early Frank Sinatra records. These were carried through by pop artists of the 1950s like Pat Boone and Buddy Holly. On Holly's *Raining in My Heart,* for example, there is an imaginative use of *pizzicato* (plucked strings) to imitate falling raindrops. This effect was developed on the Holly-influenced Adam Faith records scored by John Barry, for example *What Do You Want?* and *Someone Else's Baby,* which combine punchy *pizzicatos* with *tremolo* bowing (very fast, short bows on the same note).

Several Beatles records feature strings: *Eleanor Rigby* and *Yesterday* are especially

good examples. On early rock 'n' roll records (Gene Vincent, The Crickets) a string bass was used to pluck the bass line, but this gradually gave way to bass guitar.

Solo strings have often been used in pop music, usually to introduce a touch of romance to hard hitting drums and guitars, and sometimes to provide an alternative to guitar solos: listen to Gerry Goodman's playing, initially with The Flock and later with The Mahavishnu Orchestra. Folk and folk/rock bands, like Fairport Convention, used both acoustic and electric violin in their stage act; and the violinist Jean-Luc Ponty is in the forefront of the electric jazz movement, using a mixture of a classical and a *glissando*-style (sliding) blues technique.

Almost without exception (a notable one being Stephane Grappelli) string players have had a classical training, and it can be difficult for players brought up on a strict diet of classics to suddenly acquire the freedom needed to play jazz or rock music. This is mainly because a classical player is taught to interpret note values exactly and precisely as printed on the page, whereas rock, and particularly jazz, music require a great sense of freedom and "across the barline" phrasing. In general a lot of *portamento* (sliding from one note to another) is frowned upon in present-day classical music, but this is an important feature of jazz and other modern string-playing.

String sounds

The string family consists basically of four instruments: violin, viola, cello and double bass. All of these have been used extensively in popular music. The range of sound and tone colour they offer is immense and many different techniques can be employed in writing for them. Strings are usually played *arco,* meaning "with the bow". When the strings are plucked as on a guitar, this is called *pizzicato.* Double-stopping is when two or more notes are played at once, and *sul ponticello* is when the player bows right on the bridge of the instrument, producing a grating sound. *Col legno* means playing with the wood of the bow and is often used as a rhythmic effect.

There are a number of ways of playing *arco.* The bow can be bounced on the string for a springy, light effect known as *sautillé* or *saltando* (jumping). A similar technique, *spiccato,* involves dropping the bow on the string and lifting it again before the next note, usually at speed. *Jeté* is a term used to denote the thrown bow,

Tuning: the double bass is the only string instrument tuned in fourths; the violin, viola and cello are all tuned in fifths. Open cello strings sound an octave below those of the viola.

Double Bass

E · A · D · G

Cello

C · G · D · A

Viola

Violin

G · D · A · E

Jean Luc Ponty, *above,* the virtuoso jazz/rock player who uses an electric violin. The violin, *below,* incorporates both soft and hard woods in its body, while the fingerboard is usually made of ebony or vulcanite.

a fast skimming movement for fast detached passages using the upper third of the bow. Add to these *staccato* (short, sharp) and *legato* (joined, smooth) and a host of variations in between, and the enormous variety of possible sounds begins to be apparent.

Harmonics can produce an ethereal, other-worldly quality. A simple example of this is achieved by stopping a note halfway along a string at the point of the octave above the open string. If the string is pressed down on to the finger-board, the note will sound in tone in the normal way. If, however, the string is touched lightly without being stopped on the finger-board, a flute-like note, less strident and more ghostly, is produced.

String combinations

The classical string quartet, a combination which is also frequently used in popular music, comprises two violins, viola and cello. A chamber orchestra may consist of four first violins, three second violins, two violas, two cellos and a double bass, or something close to this structure. This is the approximate size of a section used in recording many forms of pop music from Frank Sinatra to Procol Harum. Sometimes an arranger or producer will reduce this to a smaller section of seven or eight players, dispensing with the double bass altogether and using just one cello, one viola and fewer violins. A full symphony orchestra may use a complement of 50 strings, but this is rare in popular music.

Some popular groups use unorthodox combinations. The Electric Light Orchestra uses one violin with two cellos, creating a highly distinctive string sound with more weight at the lower end of the scale. For most forms of popular music, however, the conventional balance, which is broadly based on volume (the volume of one cello is equivalent to that of two violins), offers greatest scope to the arranger.

Bowing: 1. Normal hand position for all string instruments. 2. Alternative double bass hand position.

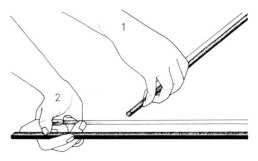

The gittarone, or acoustic bass guitar, *left,* is used mainly to provide the bass line in folk guitar ensembles. Its tuning is similar to that of the double bass, but its volume is not as loud.

Charlie Mingus, *right,* one of the great jazz bassists.

Advice to beginners

I would advise anyone who wants to play a stringed instrument to begin at the earliest possible age. I first played a cello at five, even though I didn't take it seriously until I was thirteen or fourteen – and by seriously I mean three to six hours practice a day. But I am always grateful that I played so young, because by starting young your fingers take on the required shape! On the cello, and even more on the double bass, you need a large stretch to reach some notes cleanly, and a well-developed left hand with a big stretch will always be an asset, giving the player a greater choice of fingerings. However, adult beginners should not despair. As long as they are prepared to put in regular practice, they can learn and get enormous enjoyment from playing alone and with others.

In the initial stages I would advise getting as fine a teacher as possible, because a good basic technique is absolutely essential for string playing. It also can't be overemphasized that only the most dedicated will make it professionally in what is a highly competitive field. Playing a stringed instrument is not something to be half-hearted about – you can't expect to leave it for seven days, pick it up again and then play just as well as you did the week before – regular practice is an essential part of good string playing. It is hard at first, because of the lack of frets or keys, to play well in tune, but perseverance – and that means practice – will be rewarded ●

Electric Light Orchestra

Harp

The harp is an ancient musical instrument: remains have been found in Egyptian tombs and it is documented in records dating from biblical times. It was widely used in the British Isles, especially in Ireland, in the Middle Ages; and sixteenth-century Italian composers adapted the Irish harp for use in their orchestrated operas.

The double-action harp

The modern orchestral harp – known as the double-action harp – was first introduced at the beginning of the nineteenth century. The best examples are made in Germany, Italy and the United States, and even the least expensive can cost the equivalent of an expensive car.

The double-action harp has a range of six and one-half octaves, from C-flat to four octaves above G-flat. It is tuned to a diatonic C-flat major scale, and there are therefore seven notes in a scale. It is thus non-chromatic in the sense that it cannot play all twelve semitones consecutively as a piano can. To provide semitonal action there are seven pedals for each set of notes which enable the player to raise a note by a tone or semitone, hence the name "double-action".

Technique

The pedals of the double-action harp are used to create chords when playing *glissando*, probably the most widely-known harp technique. On one occasion when I arrived at a recording session, the producer said he wanted us all to listen to a particular song. At the beginning of the song was a simple harp *glissando*. This was all the producer wanted, but he was unable to describe the effect in words. This incident illustrates a common problem for the harp player. Composers often write music for the harp that reveals their lack of familiarity with the instrument. Similarly, arrangers often have an idea of what they want but are unable to put this into words or music. The producer often just wants a simple, self-contained sound or effect – one or two *glissandi* – they do not want a concerto.

Advice to beginners

In some ways the harp is more difficult to learn than other instruments because it can take a long time to develop a reasonable technique. Unlike

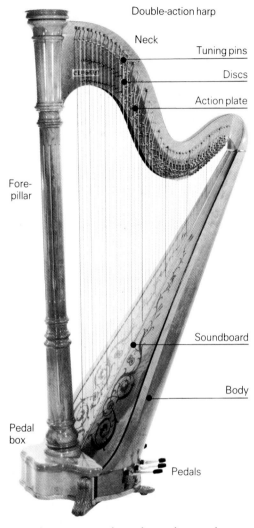

Double-action harp
Neck
Tuning pins
Discs
Action plate
Fore-pillar
Soundboard
Body
Pedal box
Pedals

some instruments, where the student can learn a few chords and then accompany him- or herself while singing, the harp requires time and committment. I recommend all aspiring harpists to learn chord symbols because most pop musicians work with these.

It is often twice as hard for the harpist to break into professional playing as it is for other musicians. On your first engagement, be co-operative. Learn to play with headphones, experiment with jazz and pop phrasing, and try to get the feel of the piece you are playing, even if it is not something you would normally choose to play. Lastly, always remember that you are only as good as your previous performance.●

Banjo

The banjo is believed to have originated in northwest Africa and was probably brought to the United States on slave ships in the eighteenth and nineteenth centuries. The roots of American jazz began in the deep South with a mixture of hymns and work songs, and the banjo was a predominant instrument. In the late nineteenth and early twentieth centuries it was used by minstrel bands, and was later adopted by traditional jazz bands as an alternative to the guitar. Today, the banjo is most widely used and identified with country and western, bluegrass and country rock music.

Construction and uses

The banjo is a plucked instrument consisting of a fret board attached to a metal hoop over which parchment is stretched. The body of the banjo acts as a resonating chamber to create the characteristic bright, snappy, non-sustained sound associated with the instrument. Its dry tone, limited chord variety and penetrating tone make it especially well-suited to rhythm work in unamplified bands.

A banjo can have from four to nine strings, the most popular types today being the five-string and the tenor banjo, which has four strings. The five-string has four of its strings tuned to C, G, B and D, from the bottom upwards, plus a high string tuned to G which is positioned next to the lowest. This is shorter than the others and is often used as a drone string, but is sometimes fretted as well. Like the violin and mandolin, the tenor banjo is tuned in fifths.

The five-string banjo is the most widely used in big-name country rock and country and western bands, but many Dixieland and Irish folk bands prefer the four-string tenor banjo.

Technique

Although some banjo players use a pick, and, on gut-string banjos, others play solely with the fingers, the predominant method of playing used in country music today is a style evolved by Earl Scruggs which involves the use of a thumb pick and two, or sometimes even three, finger picks. Scruggs is also the inventor of special tuning pegs, incorporating mechanical cams or gears that enable the player to raise or lower the pitch of a string while playing.

The banjo is frequently used for film and television music – usually for chase sequences or fast-moving action, because it has a sound that lends itself to light, quickly-paced themes.

However, from time to time I am asked to play something very different from the usual type of assignment: for example I was once asked to play a reggae session for The Pioneers. I thought the idea of using a banjo with reggae very odd, but it worked well and the producer obviously knew what he wanted. On the other hand, people sometimes write music for banjo that is totally unsuitable because they do not understand the technique involved. They might not realize, for example, that the player must move his fingers continuously in a distinct pattern to create the characteristic happy sound.

Advice for beginners

There are few banjo teachers, and probably the best way to learn is, like most players, through simple experimentation. Start by learning one style, such as Scruggs' or Don Reon's, and listen to as many of the banjo "greats" as possible.●

The Gibson RB250, *left,* is a five-string banjo with traditional violin-shaped pegheads. The fifth string incorporates a geared peg (for accurate re-tuning during performance) an invention of **Earl Scruggs,** *right,* a pioneer of country banjo playing.

Mandolin

The mandolin is the youngest member of the lute family and, while it has never obtained the prestige of the major instruments, a few famous composers have considered it worthy of special attention. In the 1940s in the United States Bill Monroe introduced the mandolin to pop music, by cross-breeding it with old-time dance and country songs, and it has remained a popular instrument ever since.

Construction and technique

The mandolin has eight steel strings tuned in four pairs to the notes G, D, A and E. Because of the tuning – open fifths – a different set of chords is available than on the guitar. Although I play both mandolin and guitar, I find the mandolin especially good for creating the open-tuned progressions which Joni Mitchell and a few others perform so well.

The mandolin is best known for the *tremelando* effect, which was developed in southern Italy as part of the "serenade" style of playing. The effect is achieved by moving a pick rapidly back and forth on the strings and must be performed at the right speed with the right number of subdivisions of beats to achieve a true mandolin sound. The technique is difficult to master, because the frets are very small.

Because of its brilliant sound, the mandolin is as well-suited to rock as to bluegrass or country music, and I find that I play differently depending on the type of music. Bluegrass, for example, does not require *tremelando*, but fast picking like a banjo.

Advice to beginners

The mandolin is a useful adjunct to a guitarist's or violinist's repertoire because it is a specialist instrument rather than a main rhythm section instrument. Because it is such a percussive instrument, the mandolin player must have a good sense of rhythm and a proficient *tremelo* technique. Learn to read music, but also learn to listen. When you are listening to a song, try to imagine what you would play if asked to add a mandolin part.●

Julian Littman, *right,* performing on a custom-made, solid electric mandolin.

The mandolin: four sets of double strings produce a bright, penetrating sound, suitable for rock, bluegrass or country music.

Instruments in Combination

Rhythm, melody and harmony are the basic elements which make up Western music, and this inevitably leads to the combining of instruments. The combinations which are widely recognized as successful have been discovered through trial and error, sheer necessity, or sometimes by someone making a fortunate mistake. Before the days of the microphone and the amplifier, when all music was played acoustically, instruments were developed to explore the high, low and middle pitch ranges of a particular instrumental timbre. Hence families of instruments evolved with uniformly complementary sounds. The obvious example is the string section of an orchestra where violin, viola, cello and bass fill the high, upper middle, lower middle and low ranges respectively. In the woodwind section the flute, oboe, clarinet and bassoon cover similar ranges. That the instruments within each family can overlap each other's ranges to a certain extent (for example, sometimes the cello plays higher than the viola) only serves to heighten their congruity. A string quartet with a bassoon substituting for the cello produces a slightly strange if not totally incongruous effect. Likewise a flute substituted for a trumpet in a brass quintet might sound equally out of place. The problems of achieving balance in terms of tone, volume and range is faced by all composers and indeed by many musicians.

There are many fine instrumental pop groups producing non-vocal music, but most popular music is an accompaniment to singing, although sometimes the voice itself is used like an instrument. The majority of those who write or arrange popular music started as soloists experimenting with an instrument and a song or melody.

Solo performers

There are many solo performers who can capture a mood or recount an experience with the aid of only a guitar or piano: Bob Dylan, Joni Mitchell, Donovan, Joan Baez and Randy Newman all began in this way.

Great technical expertise on an instrument is not of paramount importance for putting a song across effectively. In fact it is often the simple accompaniment that has the most telling effect. For example, Dylan's *Blowing In The Wind* and Joan Baez's *Plaisir D'Amour* are most effective

with simple accompaniments: elaborate arrangements of such songs detract from the realism of the lyrics.

Guitar and piano are well suited for solo accompaniment because they are capable of providing both harmony by the use of chords, and rhythm by percussive playing. The results can be sustained and languid or bright and choppy, and the notes of chords are easily arpeggiated, made to flow quickly one into another. The accordion and concertina, which are widely used in European folk music, can also provide harmony but they have fewer percussive qualities and the range of available sounds is smaller.

One-man bands

A guitar or piano soloist can only expand the range of sounds at his disposal with instruments that do not require the use of his hands. In his pre-electric days Bob Dylan often performed on guitar and harmonica simultaneously. The harmonica is perfectly suited to acoustic music and blends well with almost any combination. It has sustaining properties which contrast with the strumming guitar or chunky piano sound. Also, by "over-blowing" or "over-sucking" a good player can flatten or "bend" the notes on the harmonica producing the blues-style effect

Randy Newman, who began as a solo performer

Jesse "Lone Cat" Fuller, *left,* could play five instruments simultaneously, including an upright string bass of his own invention which he played with the big toe of his right foot. One of his most famous songs, *San Francisco Bay Blues,* has been recorded by Bob Dylan, *above,* who used the combination of guitar and harmonica extensively in his own songs.

beloved by country and rock musicians alike.

One-man bandsmen add percussion to the guitar and harmonica combination with a bass drum and/or cymbal. The bass drum is strapped to the player's back and played with a spring-loaded foot-pedal connected to the drum stick with a wire; one cymbal is attached to the side of the player's body, the other to his elbow and the pair are brought together by flapping the arm. Don Partridge used this sort of set-up for his hit single *Rosie* in the early 1970s.

One of the greatest one-man bands ever was Jesse 'Lone Cat' Fuller who was born in 1896 in Atlanta, Georgia and was still working in the 1960s. He played 12-string electric guitar, harmonica and kazoo, these last two fitting into a metal frame which he wore around his neck. With his left foot, he played hi-hat cymbals, while with the big toe of his right foot he played a bass instrument of his own invention, which he called the "Fotdella". This consisted of an upright string bass with six piano strings struck by hammers, which were activated by six pedals which Jesse played with his toe. He could thus provide himself with a simple bass accompaniment. His famous song *San Francisco Bay Blues* has been recorded by a number of other people including Bob Dylan, but Jesse Fuller's version has the sound of a three-piece band albeit produced by one man.

Small ensembles

Although a one-man bandsman can play up to four instruments at the same time, obviously a small group of players has considerably more scope. Which instruments are used by small groups depends largely on the type of music being played. There are certain line-ups which are considered standard for each field. Folk groups use mainly acoustic instruments, although in folk/rock and non-traditional country music electric guitars, bass and drums often form the basis of the sound. However, violin, banjo, string bass, flutes and recorders are usually preferred to synthesizers and organs, although violins and banjos are sometimes electronically amplified by folk bands such as Steeleye Span and the Hank Wangford Band. While in some folk bands, such as the jug bands of the skiffle era, a tuba may well replace the string bass, this would not be considered suitable in a rock band. Similarly, although guitar is used extensively in jazz, it does not appear to be as indispensable in this field as the piano which seems omnipresent in all but the most avant-garde jazz. However, popular music is a living, growing, ever-changing field. It is not based on a set of rigid formats and many types of music borrow from each other in the course of experimentation. Let us look first at the smallest ensemble, the duo.

Dire Straits, *above* and Kiss

Line-ups for rock

The first successful rock 'n' roll sound, produced by Bill Haley and the Comets around 1955, was a mixture of black blues and white country music. Electric guitars, drums, piano and acoustic "stand-up" bass formed the basis of the sound and saxophones were sometimes added. Bands like Buddy Holly and the Crickets and singers like Eddie Cochran and Ritchie Valens used the same type of rhythm section. The rockabilly bands of today are making a conscious attempt to revitalize this sound and are once again using acoustic bass. However, electric bass is more versatile and easier to transport; and all-electric bands had in the main superseded the electro/acoustic ones by about 1966.

The two guitars, bass and drums combination initially gained popularity with instrumental groups like The Shadows and The Ventures, although the piano remained popular with rock 'n' roll bands and continues to be so. Cliff Richard used The Shadows as a backing group and The Beatles and The Rolling Stones followed this

format, adding vocals to the four-piece line-up. The combination has now been popular for almost twenty years. Dire Straits, The Pretenders and Kiss carry on the tradition as do many New Wave and Heavy Metal bands, such as Girls School, Rainbow and Motorhead.

In the mid-sixties, however, many groups appeared which used an electric organ instead of a rhythm guitar. The organ can produce a greater variety of sound than the rhythm guitar, and it quickly became commonplace with soul groups, keen to obtain some semblance of the string and horn lines featured at that time on Tamla Motown and Atlantic soul records.

The first hit record from a four-piece band using organ was *Green Onions*, released in 1962 by Booker T. and the MGs. The band was the instrumental backing or "house" band of the Stax Record label and had featured on all the early Otis Redding and Carla Thomas records. In England the sound was taken up by mod bands, such as The Small Faces, Manfred Mann and The Animals, whose hit version of the traditional *House of the Rising Sun* firmly established the organ in British popular music.

West Coast rock

This term, and also acid rock, was used to describe the music of the American west coast groups of the mid-1960s, such as Jefferson Airplane and Grateful Dead. The sound is very electric: often weird, sometimes ethereal, occasionally violent. Groups would use three or even four guitars plus a mixture of acoustic (bongos, recorders) and keyboard instruments. The first worldwide hit to feature the sound of a synthesizer was The Beach Boys' *Good Vibrations*. A precursor of the early, string synthesizer was the mellotron, used by British Bands, such as King Crimson and The Moody Blues. Acid rock is now almost defunct, but it points the way to many contemporary sounds.

Modern rock

Modern rock combinations really began in the late 1960s. The development of pedals to produce all sorts of effects, initially from guitars and keyboards, expanded the small group's range enormously. Early gimmicks such as the fuzzbox, which is used on The Rolling Stones' *Satisfaction* and the wah-wah pedal, used to great effect by Jimi Hendrix and The Cream, forced the electronic hardware industry to examine musicians' needs and even to begin to dictate to musicians what they needed to be up-to-date and progressive. Modern rock has numerous styles, including heavy-metal, jazz-rock, rockabilly, punk and new wave, but all share an enthusiasm for sound effects, both in the studio and on-stage. Simple line-ups like that of The Who (guitar, bass, drums and vocal) are still popular, while many new wave groups consist of guitar, bass, drums, and keyboards. However, the organ has usually been replaced by a synthesizer, and it is normal to expect the keyboard player to play piano and synthesizer simultaneously. This provides great scope for interesting sounds, and many bands employ two keyboard players sharing a variety of synthesizers.

Additions to the small ensemble

The small ensemble (usually three to five players) is particularly well suited to touring and making a living from personal appearances. Larger groups find this harder to do, and not just because the public cannot be expected to pay more for a few additional instruments. For, unlike classical music or big-band jazz, the sounds of the instruments used in popular music are not as important as the "message" or "flavour" in the music: a band that has rhythm (drums and bass), melody (singer or lead instrument) and harmony (bass and supporting instruments) is all set to go and make music: additional instruments are a luxury, albeit often an effective one. The flavour of the music often colours the way the instruments are played rather than determining which instruments should be used. Reggae bands use quite standard rhythm sections: they line up with drums, guitar, bass and keyboards (with optional sax, trumpet or percussion) and play in a totally different style from, say, Status Quo or Steely Dan who often use the very same instruments.

However, there are preferences for certain additions to the four- or five-piece band which

reflect the musical genres of the late 1960s and early 1970s. Bands like Chicago and Blood, Sweat and Tears added a brass section, consisting of saxophone, trumpet and trombone, to the rhythm section: Santana, on the other hand, used four percussionists and made Latin-rock the precursor of Latin funk and jazz-funk. Tower of Power, a five-piece horn section, consisting of two saxes, two trumpets and a trombone added a fatter, bigger and tighter sound to soul music. Brass arrangements had been part and parcel of the American soul scene since the emergence of the Stax and Atlantic labels at the end of the 1950s, but these were more often heard on record than live. Most record companies found it more economical to send their artists out on the road with an organ substituting for the horn players. From the late 1960s on, however, soul bands included horn players and a rhythm section and frequently numbered about nine people. The Rolling Stones borrowed Jim Price (trumpet) and Bobby Keys (sax) from Leon Russell's Mad Dogs and Englishmen to take a horn section on the road as part of a rock 'n' roll band in 1970. They thus came full circle back to the line-up used by the combos of the 1950s, but, of course, the sound was totally different largely because of electrification.

Large groups and orchestras

Until fairly recently, although string sections were heard on records, they were rarely taken on the road because of the problems of providing them with microphones, the additional space required on stage and the extra expense. To get a good rich string sound the minimum requirement is three first violins, three second violins, two violas, one or two 'cellos and (optional) double-bass. Groups would therefore usually

Santana

replace a string section used in the studio with an organ or synthesizer when performing live.

However, the excellent New York band, Chic, manage to recreate their recorded sound when playing live. They have three violins and a viola, four, sometimes five, brass instruments, a five-piece rhythm section and three backing vocalists in addition to their principal performers, who comprise guitar, bass, drums and two "frontline" girl vocalists. By writing their arrangements for their "chamber" ensemble and recording them with little overdubbing on tape, they can carry their sound with them on stage. By using contact mikes on the strings the problems of feedback are eliminated and the sound can be expanded using electronic devices such as "chorus" effects.

The ultimate ensemble, and one that can only be afforded by the most successful acts, such as Barry Manilow and Diana Ross, is the thirty-, or more, piece orchestra and mini-choir. Earth, Wind and Fire and Barry White take very different bands on the road. The former uses a large brass complement (up to 15 players), a small string complement, backing vocalists and a complete rhythm section which includes three percussionists. Barry White's orchestra, known as The Love Unlimited Orchestra, uses more than twenty string players, three French horns, saxophones, flutes, a three-girl singing group, and a large rhythm section with two or three guitars and three keyboards. At first sight it appears that these two orchestras are very similar, but in fact the Barry White sound is more lush: strings and French horns used in combination provide a Mantovani-style back-wash against which the singer grunts his message of love. Earth, Wind and Fire feature punchy, elaborate rasping saxophone licks and staccato trumpet tattoos. Hence their sound uses more brass and percussion to kick the music along.

The spectrum of possibilities available with a band of this size is an arranger's dream; and because of the size of the forces being used a concert-master or conductor is usually employed to keep the musicians playing tightly together. He works in conjunction with the drummer and the star, cueing the various sections. If there is a choir, a separate choirmaster may also be used. This may seem superfluous, since the drummer will be controlling the tempo. However, on a large stage some members of the band may be fifty feet from the drums, possibly with a restricted view of the front of the stage. The concert-master guarantees that everyone plays together.

A large orchestra will still combine instruments according to sections. String lines will rarely be the same as those for brass, and each will usually be treated as a separate entity supporting the whole. However, arrangers and writers have always striven for original twists that will delight the musicians and the audience. Certain special combinations have been used on records which have become milestones in pop history.

Special combinations

Without doubt The Beatles had an enormous influence both on lyric and songwriting and on the use of instruments. It is almost impossible to pick on any Beatle track after the release of the Album *Rubber Soul* in 1965 without discovering some new sound. A major example is the most famous of McCartney's ballads, *Yesterday*, which featured a string quartet playing, on Paul McCartney's insistence, without the finger-wobbling technique known as vibrato. Strings had been used on pop records for 50 years, but only as additional icing to the parts played by rhythm sections. Here they supported a solo voice and an acoustic guitar and constituted in fact the basis of the backing track.

From *Rubber Soul* came the strange Lennon

anecdote *Norwegian Wood*, on which George Harrison played sitar. This apparent flirtation with Indian music spread to The Rolling Stones who used it on *Paint It Black*, and to Stevie Winwood's Traffic with *Paper Sun*. The sitar is a haunting, echoing instrument capable of great emotional expression in the hands of a master. Sadly, most rock musicians had not the time or inclination to work at it for long and Harrison's *Within You Without You* is a brilliant blend of Indian and western styles, but unique in this respect in rock music. Those musicians who liked the sound, but not the practice, quickly found a substitute in a special kind of guitar. The sitar owes much of its echoey sound to sympathetic strings, usually 12 of them, which are not plucked but literally ring "in sympathy" with the notes being played on the main strings. Sympathetic strings were added to an electric guitar and suddenly the sitar sound could be captured by a guitarist. The sound was never totally convincing because the elaborate Indian string-pulling techniques could not be employed on the more tightly-strung guitar. However, the best example of this instrument on record is Steely Dan's first single *Do It Again*. Other Indian instruments used in pop are the tabla (hand drums) and the dilruba (a small instrument, similar in construction to the sitar, but played with a bow) which was used together with 'cellos on *Within You Without You*.

The Rolling Stones, following hard on the heels of The Beatles, also utilized new combinations of sound. *You Can't Always Get What You Want* from the album *Let It Bleed* had the London Bach choir joining forces with The Stones plus Al Kooper playing organ and French horn. This last instrument was played on the overture of The Who's *Tommy* by John Entwistle, the group's bassist; but the most famous French horn solo in pop came on a Beatle tune from *Revolver, For No-one*.

A number of unusual combinations of instruments have been used by experimental, but successful, bands, and some of the most interesting combinations have been used by bands who have sought to mix styles of music from very different cultures in order to create their own special sound.

In the early 1970s the American saxophone player Paul Winter led a group of musicians known as The Winter Consort, playing music from a wide variety of cultures and spanning half a millennium. Fifteenth-century Italian frottolas were played alongside third-stream jazz (similar in style to the Modern Jazz Quartet), folk rock and pure avant-garde music. They would play new arrangements of Bach as happily as the bossa-novas of Carlos Antonio Jobim. The line-up consisted of Paul Winter on alto sax and a variety of players who doubled on acoustic and occasionally electric instruments, including oboe, cor anglais, flute, Spanish guitar, lute, cello, bass (acoustic and electric) and drums. It was altogether a rich and varied sound with often virtuoso playing.

Another, more recent, example is the English band Monsoon. Their line-up comprises Steve Coe on piano, Martin Smith on guitars, Jhalib on percussion and tabla, Davi Mankoo on sitar and vocalist Sheila Chandra. They consciously mix Indian musical ideas, a Western beat (usually provided on a snare-drum) and a mixture of electric and traditional acoustic sounds provided by the sitar and tabla. The music has some of the hypnotic quality of the synthesizer bands, but with the rhythmic variety of Asian drumming and the atmospheric rhythmic drone of the sitar's chikkari strings. Their first hit *Ever So Lonely* has a haunting, Eastern quality in the modal scale used, but the song is nevertheless pop music for Western ears. The Winter Consort, Monsoon and some other equally inventive bands prove that good music can be presented in a variety of interesting ways.

One of the most striking of the recently developed gadgets is the voice-box, where the sound of the guitar is sent to a small electronic box attached to a tube, one end of which the player keeps in his mouth; he moves his mouth so that the guitar sound is given speech-like articulation, coming through the tube to be picked up by a microphone. The effect is brilliantly displayed in Steely Dan's *Haitian Divorce*.

Solo violin was the main attraction of CBS's group The Flock during the late 1960s. Gerry Goodman, an expert in electric jazz violin, subsequently left the band to team up with guitarist John McLaughlin, keyboard-player Jan Hammer, bassist Rick Laird and drummer Billy Cobham. This quintet, The Mahavishnu Orchestra, put the idea of jazz-rock fusion firmly on the map.

Electropop

Many of the most inventive ideas of recent years have been added, not by conventional instruments, but by synthesizers and at the mixing board. Bands like Pink Floyd and Genesis depend on extremely skilful sound engineers for the success of their stage shows. Synthesizers can be programmed to play a recurrent sequence of notes at the touch of a button, leaving the player free to play on another keyboard.

With echo, delay lines, phrasing and vocoders (see: synthesizers), as well as a host of effects pedals, bands can get a range of timbres and blends hitherto unknown in music.

Because synthesizers can produce such a variety of sounds which cannot be obtained with other instruments, a number of bands use a completely electronic line-up comprising Simmons drums, synthesizers and effects devices. Groups such as Kraftwerk, Yellow Magic Orchestra, Depeche Mode, Orchestral Manoeuvres in the Dark and the duo Soft Cell may add brass or strings on record, but they frequently play live with just electronic equipment.

The synthesizer cannot of course replace acoustic instruments. For example, however good the quasi-string sound which can be obtained from a top quality synthesizer (and with subtle mixing on tape some people cannot tell the difference), the synthesizer cannot reproduce the extremely varied articulation of human string players or their irregular vibrato. A major ingredient of the sound made by a string section results from the differences in the players' vibrato, the tonal variations of the different instruments and the sound of horsehair and resin meeting strings. No synthesizer can produce that constant variation. So, if you want the sound of real strings, you have to use them; the same applies with brass and acoustic instruments.

The use of sequencers and arpeggiators enables musicians with no great technical ability to create fast and hypnotic bass lines which are very much a part of the futurist and new romantic pop styles. Rock music has always leaned more towards melody and rhythm than towards atonality and the marriage of the new sounds with the old harmonic and structural techniques is frequently effective. Human League's rock song *Don't You Want Me Baby* was recorded using a Roland MC8 micro-composer. This is a device which drives synthesizers with an electronic pulse, so that several different sounds laid down on tape can be recorded in synchronized rhythm and without wrong notes. Human League also used the MC8 to drive a Linn drum machine in synchronization with the tracks laid down by the synthesizers.

Some musicians find the use of electronic machines distasteful because they deprive music of the human element. Some electronic music certainly lacks emotion, but a singer can add this element to an otherwise rigid track simply with his voice, for example Phil Oakey's vocal on Human League's *Don't You Want Me*.

Synthesized sounds can take on the roles of more traditional instruments in popular music, but they cannot replace the sounds made by those instruments. A low sustained organ-like sound can convey the mood of a low string section, but it will not display the sound or the agility of the latter. This is not to say that it is wrong to use such an effect. *Maid Of Orleans* by Orchestral Manoeuvres in the Dark was a good pop record, but the quasi-string sounds were never intended to be mistaken for the real thing. They merely created an effect which was in keeping with the mood of the song.

The merits of electro-technical pop lie in its ability to create hypnotic and tonally extra-normal sounds which can add to the enjoyment of the music. The dangers are that it is very easy to produce unpleasant sounds or worse still boring ones.

Advice to beginners

Experiment with even the most seemingly insignificant effects. A twanging Jew's harp or a milk bottle struck with a screwdriver may make all the difference to what you are trying to create. And if you think that last idea is crazy, Bob Marley used it on his recording of *Jamming.*●

Forming a Group

"So you wanna be a Rock 'n' Roll star/then listen now to what I say./Just get an electric guitar,/and take some time and learn how to play." These lyrics are from a hit single by the Byrds and reflect an attitude towards popular music which accounts, at least in part, for its enormous mass appeal: the pop musician can play what ever he or she likes, at whatever standard he or she can achieve and make of the music anything from a hobby to a professional career. This sounds terrific in theory, but as with all theories there are some negatives to consider.

The lives of most professional musicians are, to say the least, irregular. This year's shining star can easily become ancient history next year – or next month. If you are talented or lucky enough to achieve a modicum of success, you will have to work twice as hard to maintain that success as you did to achieve it. This can mean gruelling tours, weeks or months away from home seeing little of the exotic places you might visit, because all there is time for is sound checks and the inevitable airport lounges.

You might, of course, never make it to stardom, which is not necessarily a tragedy. Many professionals, particularly session musicians, are happy to work on a fee-per-gig or per-recording basis, free from contractual obligations and therefore able to pick and choose their work and run their own lives. This, however, can only be achieved by the more successful musicians. For those less in demand, the work is not so highly paid and consequently they do not have the freedom to refuse work that they do not particularly enjoy.

Every musician's dream is to express his or her own style, but because of the competition and the lightning changes in fashion this is not always possible. Many musicians, however, discover that they can derive a great deal of satisfaction from playing with other people, even if this does not involve playing their own music. Many professionals are free-lancers who, after years of experience, go to gigs and play with musicians they have never met before by using simple chord charts or playing by ear. Musicians often prefer this type of work because they are paid to do a job they enjoy and avoid time-consuming rehearsals. To do this successfully,

however, your standard of musicianship must be high and, as in all competitive areas, if you can't deliver the goods, word soon gets around.

Starting out
Bands usually begin when a few friends decide to get together, and the first thing they do is figure out which part of the band is missing. If no one knows of anyone to fill the remaining place or places, one solution is to read the ads in the music papers to see if there is anyone available who might fit your needs; or you can always advertise yourselves.

Equipment
When buying equipment, try to get the best you can afford, but there is no need to take out a massive loan for, say, a Prophet V or Jupiter 8. It can be hard enough finding any extra cash in addition to your living expenses when as yet you have no income from your music. There is nothing wrong with buying secondhand equipment: many excellent pieces are sold, not because there is anything wrong with them, but because musicians are constantly upgrading their gear. Charlie Parker started on a really old alto sax that was almost held together with rubber bands.

Rehearsals
There are no rules on how to run a rehearsal. After 15 years of playing with bands from three to 50 pieces, I can only suggest what might work in certain situations. One thing is certain: the larger the band, the more difficult it will be to control what is happening. For this reason, professionals prefer to use either written music or simple chord charts that give the harmonic and rhythmic framework of a piece. With small groups it is often easiest to rehearse with one member telling the others the chords and structure of the piece, bit by bit. By using a chord chart as well, the entire song can be played through from beginning to end with comparative ease.

Noise is an important factor to consider. Acoustic band rehearsals are no problem for obvious reasons. Should neighbours complain about the noise of an electric band you can rent a garage, talk to the local minister about using the church hall, or use a room in the local school. Use your imagination and you should find somewhere suitable.

Whatever your band consists of, and wherever you play, do it quietly; you are not yet in

Madison Square Garden and you should be rehearsing for yourselves. Ears tire quickly when buffeted with volume, especially in a confined space; concentration goes, tempers fray and timing is impaired. This is not to say that you should not have a good blow now and again, especially at the start of a rehearsal. Music is exciting and intoxicating and you will probably arrive at a gig or rehearsal with a great deal of adrenalin so it is good to let off some steam. When you get down to serious work, however, you will find that you have more staying power if you rehearse at a reasonable volume.

Vocal rehearsals should take place separately from main band rehearsals, because it is often difficult and irritating to stop a band going full tilt to correct a bit of phrasing or harmony. If once or twice a week you get together around a piano or with a guitar and practise the vocals, at the next full rehearsal your band will sound tighter because everyone will know what they are supposed to be doing.

Decision-making

There are two basic approaches to decision-making within the band; the democratic and the autocratic. If you are hired to join a band that already has professional status, you will probably just have to do what you are told because the major decisions will either have been resolved or will be made by the lead singer or

Rehearsals: as well as holding full rehearsals regularly, it is a good idea to arrange separate vocal rehearsals. With well prepared and tight vocals, rehearsals with the full band will run more smoothly.

bandleader. This is acceptable to people who have no need for authority and who are happy to comply with others' wishes in return for a good income and freedom from the problems of running a group.

In a newly formed band, however, there may well be two or three strong personalities contributing to the band's musical policies. Inevitably there will be differences which might involve small matters but which nonetheless contribute to the shaping of the band's image. I suspect that the bands that have lasted the longest were formed on this basis. The Who, The Rolling Stones, even The Beatles probably made their basic decisions by discussion and, very likely, argument between at least two opinionated members.

Such band members often stamp their personalities on their own material and give the entire group a recognizable sound. The backing on a Barry Manilow recording can vary so enormously that, if Manilow's voice were removed, the remaining sound would not give a clue as to who the artist was. Remove the vocals from a Who, Stones or Santana track, however, and enough of the individuality of the players' styles remains for you to easily recognize the band. Discussions between band members then, though they take time, will establish the direction of the band more constructively than will simply going along with what the strongest member dictates.

Matters unrelated to musical direction can also cause problems: for example the purchase of a PA system. If your band uses vocals, you will obviously need a PA, which you might have to rent and pay for out of gig money. You may all agree to use half of this money to pay for the PA, but say the drummer needs new sticks and the lead guitarist needs strings and *they* do not sing, so why should they contribute to the PA? A fair argument, and a typical one. One solution might be to own the PA collectively. However, then there is a problem if someone leaves the band and demands the return of their contribution.

You can begin to see the problems that can arise, and it is important therefore to discuss every member's views early in the formation of the band, particularly those involving money. Decide upon the rules by which you all agree to be bound, and then you will be free to concentrate on your music. Grievances should be aired – it is much more constructive to discuss, or even argue, a point and reach an agreement than to have a lot of grumbling that will adversely affect your playing. If you all truly want to be successful, you will have to learn to overlook the small change spent on items like a new fanbelt for the van. By sticking together, your band might also last 15 years.

Developing style
As in all of the arts, there is no such thing in music as true originality. All musicians are continuously assimilating influences and using them, consciously or unconsciously, to shape their own music. Every member of every band has strong feelings about certain types of music, and all have favourite artists who influence their style. If you can accept the fact that you will never be totally unique, you can set about developing a style by experimenting with other people's songs and doing impersonations of artists you like, all of which will slowly reveal the direction in which your band is moving.

Do not be afraid of working with teachers or people outside of the band who can only add to your growth and self-awareness. If you are an instrumentalist, consider taking lessons from a professional. If you are a vocalist, a few months with a singing teacher who is classically trained but sympathetic to popular styles can often work wonders. Not all singing teachers wish to turn you into a Caruso or Sutherland, and there are many useful things that any singer can learn about breathing and voice production. A local choir can also be an enjoyable way of supplementing your lessons and can help you to learn to read music and sing in harmony. Do not be too proud to sing in a choir – many great soul singers, such as Otis Redding and Aretha Franklin, gained their groundwork there.

The whole being more than the sum of its parts, much of your band's style will emerge from the way each member plays and from their individual influences and aspirations. Often a band's sound is memorable because of the merging of its members' particular styles. So be aware of each others' ideas and try to incorporate them into your music's basic structure.

Becoming semi-professional
When your band can produce an hour of good, solid sound – either your own or a mixture of your own and well-known material – you will want someone to hear you. Before running to the telephone to contact the big agencies or to place ads in the music papers, get some local reaction. There may be bodies such as sports or social clubs that give an occasional dance, bars or restaurants that would welcome some music. Ask if they would be interested in booking you for an evening. At this point, you cannot afford to be greedy and name an exorbitant fee. Play for free if necessary; you need the experience and they are doing you a bigger favour than you are doing them. The first paid gig I did was for such a dance for which five of us received a paltry fee that went towards gas for a borrowed van. If you are lucky, there will be plenty of opportunity to name your price later on.

On your first gig you are unlikely to bring the house down, because what *you* think sounds great may not appeal to everyone. Watch audience reaction and learn to take criticism. You will be trying to improve your music for the rest of your life, so why not start now.

Finding an agent
Once you have ironed out the problems that will inevitably arise from your first few gigs and feel you have reached a satisfactory level of performance, it is time to call a few agents. You need an agent because they are the people who have contacts with the places where you will want to be heard. It is myth that every agent only wants to take advantage of you; many are straightforward, reliable people who have the band's best interests at heart. As in every business, however, there are "sharks" about and you will probably

be bitten but will learn from the experience. Treat your booking agent like any other agent, say a travel agent: someone who provides a service between supplier and consumer for which he or she receives a portion of the profit. Whatever you do or do not do, make sure you get legal advice before signing anything.

Managers
If you are looking for a manager, or someone offers to manage you, first make certain that they can offer you the services you require and do not sign with anyone until you have seen the results of their work. In my view, you do not need to even consider a full-time manager until you are at the stage of recording masters or have a large enough following to warrant seeing record companies. A manager can be extremely useful, taking care of business hassles so that you can concentrate on your music. However he or she may well ask as much as 30 per cent of your total earnings from gigs, recordings and publishing. If you are going to pay someone a third of your earnings, you should be certain of getting results. Always have a legal adviser on hand to keep a check on the business and financial side.

Stage set-up
At the highest professional levels stage sets are designed primarily on aesthetic criteria because most of the technical difficulties have been resolved; for example the use of a high-quality monitoring system will eliminate the problem of sound balancing. For the majority of bands, who do not have the funds for such luxuries, there are two basic facts to consider. First, as many small bands know, stages can be inadequate or even non-existent and you will simply have to set up as best you can while ensuring a reasonable balance and spread of sound. Secondly, you must be able to hear yourselves.

The drummer and bass player work together to lay down the beat, and because the subdivision of the beat occurs most frequently on the hi-hat, or sock, cymbals the ideal place for the bass player is on the hi-hat side of the drummer. This is not a hard and fast rule, but if the rhythm unit is kept physically together, it will help to keep the sound tight.

For melody instruments, consider as an example a five-piece band consisting of keyboards, guitar, singer, or some additional instrument, and the bass and drums. It makes sense to have the two treble instruments on opposite sides of the stage to create a natural stereo sound, and to avoid the two becoming cluttered by emerging from the same side of the stage. The bass and drums should be positioned in the middle, and the guitar and keyboard amps should be angled in slightly so that there is a balanced sound which the whole band can hear. The singer or wind instrument will go through the PA, which will usually come from both sides of the stage. In some venues where there is no proper stage, or a very small one, the PA may be set up so that the audience can hear the vocals but there are no speakers near the band. In this case a vocal monitor on the stage will help to keep your singing in tune and to give you an idea of the general blend of sound.

There are many ways in which a band can set up and the suggestions above are only guidelines towards achieving good sound. A high-quality stereo PA system will obviously enhance the vocals and acoustic instruments. Once you have good equipment and an adequate PA, you may be tempted to turn fully professional.

Image
A band's image supports its style of music. Exceptions to this abound, but if you go to see a country and western group, for example, there will probably be a lot of boots and Stetsons around, while soul and disco acts will display their fair share of flashy suits, glittering dresses and complicated dance steps.

The public expects to be entertained in a fashion appropriate to the style of music they are listening to. They also expect the artists to wear clothes that reflect their own involvement with the music. A heavy metal band would look incongruous dressed in gold lamé suits, and it is doubtful that someone like Smokey Robinson could carry off the leather armband, steel knuckle-duster image of Ian Gillan.

On the other hand, there is no formula for dress or image. Being yourselves may suffice, but to attract attention it may be necessary to overdo it a bit, remembering that your audience will expect you to keep your image consistent. It does not matter today whether Pete Townshend wears a boiler suit or a smart Italian three-piece, but in the early days of the group the mod image was important for audience identification with The Who generation. Contrasts can also work: remember that, in spite of the Stones' studied scruffiness, Bill Wyman has always looked impeccable, and still does.

You will receive more attention from prospective agents and clients if you have a definite stage presence. It is not important that your image be stunning, but it should be recognizable both in sound and vision so that you become identifiable. Then you are on your way.●

CHEAP BUT GOOD ADVICE
FOR PLAYING MUSIC IN A GROUP

1) PLAY ONLY WHAT YOU HEAR.

2) IF YOU DON'T HEAR ANYTHING, DON'T PLAY ANYTHING.

3) DON'T LET YOUR FINGERS AND LIMBS JUST WANDER - PLACE THEM INTENTIONALLY.

4) DON'T IMPROVISE ON ENDLESSLY - PLAY SOMETHING WITH INTENTION, DEVELOP IT OR NOT, BUT THEN END OFF TAKE A BREAK.

5) LEAVE SPACE - CREATE SPACE - INTENTIONALLY CREATE PLACES WHERE YOU DON'T PLAY.

6) MAKE YOUR SOUND BLEND. LISTEN TO YOUR SOUND AND ADJUST IT TO THE REST OF THE BAND AND THE ROOM.

7) IF YOU PLAY MORE THAN ONE INSTRUMENT AT A TIME - LIKE A DRUM KIT OR MULTIPLE KEYBOARDS - MAKE SURE THEY ARE BALANCED WITH ONE ANOTHER.

8) DON'T MAKE ANY OF YOUR MUSIC MECHANICALLY OR JUST THROUGH PATTERNS OF HABIT. CREATE EACH SOUND, PHRASE, AND PIECE WITH CHOICE - DELIBERATELY.

9) GUIDE YOUR CHOICE OF WHAT TO PLAY BY WHAT YOU LIKE - NOT BY WHAT SOMEONE ELSE WILL THINK.

10) USE CONTRAST AND BALANCE THE ELEMENTS:

> HIGH - LOW
> FAST - SLOW
> LOUD - SOFT
> TENSE - RELAXED
> DENSE - SPARSE

11) PLAY TO MAKE THE OTHER MUSICIANS SOUND GOOD. PLAY THINGS THAT WILL MAKE THE OVERALL MUSIC SOUND GOOD.

12) PLAY WITH A RELAXED BODY. ALWAYS RELEASE WHATEVER TENSION YOU CREATE.

13) CREATE SPACE - BEGIN, DEVELOP AND END PHRASES WITH INTENTION.

14) NEVER BEAT OR POUND YOUR INSTRUMENT - PLAY IT EASILY AND GRACEFULLY.

15) CREATE SPACE - THEN PLACE SOMETHING IN IT.

16) USE MIMICRY SPARSELY - MOSTLY CREATE PHRASES THAT CONTRAST WITH AND DEVELOP THE PHRASES OF THE OTHER PLAYERS.

Staging Concerts

"Ladies and gentlemen, will you please welcome – The Rolling Stones!" Backstage – Roy Lamb, stage manager: "Stand by all stations, go house curtains, go balloons." Fifteen thousand balloons float heavenward and Balloon Crew 1's work is over. The Auditorium – Patrick Woodroffe, lighting designer: "Stand by stage lights, bump to cue 1. Stand by spotlights 1, 4, 6 and 8. Colour to 4 to pick up lead singer moving downstage. Go 1." Jagger moves stage right. B. J. Schiller, sound: "Vocal monitor position 2. Local monitors no feedback." Stage manager 1: "Stand by scrim reveal. Go!" The singer rides a cherry picker 30 feet over the heads of the audience. Backstage – the Ambience Crew have put the final touches to the backstage decor, truck drivers relax before tonight's haul. The Box Office – Bill Graham, tour promoter is settling up with the hall manager: takings, production costs, local crew, transport, hotels, entertainment – each item is checked against a budget.

Fifteen years ago, when they played Shea Stadium, The Beatles' equipment arrived in a pick up truck; today The Rolling Stones use a convoy of 32 trucks and a staff of 150. Shows have grown up and an industry has evolved along with them. Not every act could or would want to tour on this scale, but with more than 50,000 acts competing for the audiences and stages of the world, shows are big business.

To the average fan, a concert is a few hours of entertainment provided by their favourite artist. The audience is unaware of the months of work and planning that have gone into those few hours, nor the number of people who are responsible for making or breaking a show.

The promoter

A successful group plans its activities up to a year ahead, the time being divided into recording, promotion, touring and short breaks for recuperating. To the promoter, a gambling man, every group wants to play larger audiences, earn larger grosses and be more successful. The promoter is responsible for filling the halls: "bums on seats" is his game and, if a hall is too small, he has underestimated the group's potential; if it is too large and there are too many empty seats, it is demoralizing and unprofitable.

Lighting design is one of the most important considerations when staging a concert, especially with large rock groups like The Rolling Stones. Patrick Woodroffe's cue sheet, *right*, for their 1982 U.K. tour, details each number in running order enabling him to direct his technicians accurately.

Show ROLLING STONES
Designer P/W.
Date 8/82.

Control	Colour	Lamp Type	Focus or Function	Watts
			Page No. ⑥ of	
			MISS YOU	
(SAX LINE) —			STRAIGHT IN — ADD AFTER 4 BARS.	
WATCH ACCENTS —			▶ VOX	
			▶ SAX SOLO. → BREAK DOWN → BUILD UP W/ SAX SOLO + GUIT LINES.	
	▶		VERSE → ▶ GUIT/SAX → LONG VAMP (VOX/GUIT/SAX.)	
			FADE OUT.	
			HONKY TONK WOMEN	
			KEITH INTRO	

211

A promoter knows that a group's manager will want his band to give concerts whenever an album is released. A touring itinerary must be planned so that four or five shows can be played each week, with travelling time allowed for. The promoter will block-book halls even before booking the acts and will then juggle his clients to fit his bookings. The promoters compete to offer acts the best deals and venues, although in the case of a show such as Bill Graham's outdoor "Day on the Green in San Francisco", the tides reverse as groups clamour to play such a well presented and organized event.

Stage production

As the touring date approaches, ideas for the stage show are discussed, with inspiration likely to come from several directions: an album cover, another show, or the manager producing an idea that fits with his promotion of the group. A designer who specializes in scenery and lighting liaises with the group's production manager and a concept slowly emerges. It is the designer's job to realize the idea for final presentation, costing and approval; usually he produces a scale model, an artist's impression or a drawing. Designing for a touring rock stage is as much a feat of engineering as a creative process, be-

Touring itinerary: each day of a group's concert tour is itemized on an itinerary sheet which lists dates and places of concerts and the days travelling in between. *Left*, the itinerary sheet for Earth Wind and Fire's 1982 European tour.

Stage design has to take into consideration technical, engineering and lighting problems. Artwork, like that used for 10CC, *below left*, and scale models, of the type produced for Ozzy Osbourne, *above*, are submitted for approval before a finished blueprint, such as the one used for a Rod Stewart tour, *below*, is drawn up giving full stage and rigging details.

cause each piece must be able to withstand the rigours of being put up and taken down every day; a show that looks impressive at rehearsals must still look good six months later.

Eric Barrett is credited with having first used coloured lights – for Jimi Hendrix and The Beatles – but it was the flamboyant Californian Chip Monck who conceived the first rock show spectacle as we know it today. Monck didn't do things by halves; the story goes that his budget for The Rolling Stones' world tour was spent well before the entourage left rehearsals in Hawaii.

The 1970s was an age of mechanical shows: Electric Light Orchestra toured with a space ship that supported the lighting of the show; David Bowie floated over the audience in a mechanical hand; Alice Cooper magically stepped out of a movie screen (a trick invented by Walt Disney using a screen made of stretched elastic); Donny Osmond flew out over the audience (and nearly got stuck swinging over the 20,000 fans below); and Keith Emerson played a grand piano rotating through 360 degrees. All of this required planning, designing and engineering, and rock shows borrowed heavily from the mechanical expertise of theatre and film until by the 1980s rock stage production became a business in its own right.

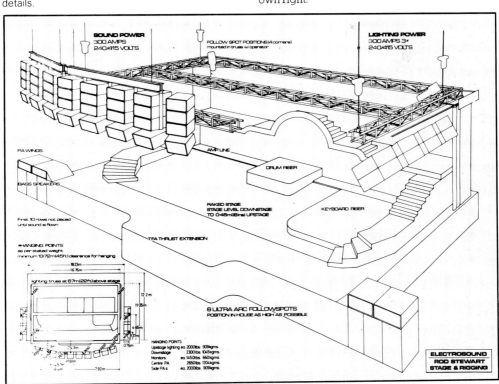

The tour manager

Once the production of a show has been planned, two key personnel – the tour manager and the production manager – are hired.

The tour manager is responsible for the logistics of getting the entourage from one place to the next, and will work with a travel agent who specializes in the music industry. In the United States nearly all travelling is done in buses that are fitted with various degrees of luxury. All have sleeping bunks – an overnight run can be as far as 500 miles with a show at both ends – and cooking facilities, shower, video and hi-fi are all standard and necessary equipment because this will be home for up to ten people for three months.

Some groups charter aeroplanes, such as the Starship range, which are equipped for a group's needs; in Europe flying is generally the rule, whereas in Japan the bullet trains are more convenient. Needless to say, checking in and out of airports can be strenuous if done every day, especially for the tour manager. The tour manager will also book hotels, and the larger shows will have a tour accountant to look after their finances.

And so the show goes on the road. Each hall will have what is known as a technical rider which specifies all of the group's requirements from the amount of equipment to be hung from the roof, to the food and drink needed in the band's dressing rooms.

The production manager

The production manager is in charge of the technical crew who move independently of the band because they must arrive at a gig early on the morning of the show. In the planning stages, the production manager will contract services such as lighting, sound, trucking, rigging, bussing, and catering. There is stiff competition between companies providing these services and decisions are made on the quality of the equipment, management and crews, as well as the prices bid.

When all of the major decisions have been made, a final production meeting is held prior to rehearsals and it is here that, for the first time, all key personnel meet. The tour manager presides; it is an important time because the technical success of a tour is dependent upon the crew working together efficiently and happily.

Rehearsals

Rehearsals may be held in an unused theatre or film studio; Rod Stewart once rehearsed a European tour in an RAF aircraft hangar, much to

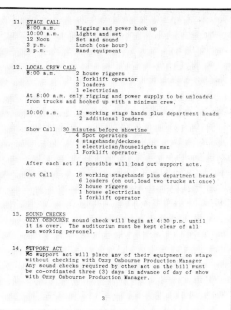

```
11.  STAGE CALL
     8:00 a.m.        Rigging and power hook up
     10:00 a.m.       Lights and set
     12 Noon          Set and sound
     2 p.m.           Lunch (one hour)
     3 p.m.           Band equipment


12.  LOCAL CREW CALL
     8:00 a.m.        2 house riggers
                      1 forklift operator
                      2 loaders
                      1 electrician
     At 8:00 a.m. only rigging and power supply to be unloaded
     from trucks and booked up with a minimum crew.

     10:00 a.m.       12 working stage hands plus department heads
                      2 additional loaders

     Show Call   30 minutes before showtime
                      4 Spot operators
                      4 stagehands/deckmen
                      1 electrician/houselights man
                      1 Forklift operator

     After each act if possible will load out support acts.

     Out Call         16 working stagehands plus department heads
                      6 loaders (on out, load two trucks at once)
                      2 house riggers
                      1 house electrician
                      1 forklift operator

13.  SOUND CHECKS
     OZZY OSBOURNE sound check will begin at 4:30 p.m. until
     it is over.  The auditorium must be kept clear of all
     non working personel.

14.  SUPPORT ACT
     No support act will place any of their equipment on stage
     without checking with Ozzy Osbourne Production Manager
     Any sound checks required by other act on the bill must
     be co-ordinated three (3) days in advance of day of show
     with Ozzy Osbourne Production Manager.

                              3
```

Setting up a concert: everything, from unloading trucks, *top*, to rigging up sound systems, *right*, is listed on a detailed schedule or "rider", *above*.

214

the pleasure of the inhabitants. Two days are normally set aside for technical rehearsals, although two weeks were allowed for Pink Floyd's "The Wall" show. Rehearsals are the culmination of many weeks' work, and preparation is essential because once the show is on the road it is difficult to make changes. New equipment can be extremely expensive to ship and so spare parts – from strings and speakers to light bulbs and tiny electronic circuits – are essential. Despite checking and rechecking, as in Murphy's Law, anything that can go wrong will; and as far as rock 'n' roll touring goes, Murphy was an optimist.

With all of the equipment finally set up, the group arrives for the first day's rehearsal. By now the group should be together musically; these rehearsals are used mainly to integrate the group's performance with technicalities such as stage positions, and to give the sound and lighting crews an opportunity to test their plans in practice.

Setting up

Early in the morning on the day of the show, riggers will be in the ceiling of the hall hanging cables from which to suspend sound and lighting equipment. The rigger's job developed in the early 1970s when rock shows moved out of theatres, with their sophisticated technical facilities, into halls and sports arenas which had not been built to house a stage and the technical equipment most shows require. The riggers borrowed heavily from techniques used for shows such as *Holiday on Ice* and *Disney on Parade*, adding their own innovations and setting high standards of technique and safety.

While the riggers are at work, local crews will have been split into teams to work in various departments: truck unloading, lighting, sound and stage set up. Lighting will usually first be assembled on the ground in preparation for lifting by electric chain hoists. The tour electrician will tap into the mains of the building, since most shows require enough electricity to run a small town. For one show in South America the promoter of the group Queen arranged for part of the town in which they were playing to be blacked out for the duration of the concert to provide enough electricity for the 500 lights used in the show. To date, Van Halen holds the record, having carried more than 1,000 lights on tour, some million watts of electricity. Rock 'n' roll has always had a tendency towards the excessive and, of course, quality and quantity do not always go hand in hand.

The acoustics of every venue, unlike those of

recording studios, are different, and even with the best equipment in the world the sound mixer's task of using the acoustics to their fullest potential is crucial. Speakers must be angled to give even coverage to every seat and the engineer can then compensate for peaks and nulls in the frequency response of the room by using a graphic equalizer. Short of covering the walls and ceiling with deadening material, which has been done on occasion, the mixer has to cope with the natural echo of the room.

A musician obviously never sees or hears his own show and can only hear himself through his own speakers, and so monitors are of paramount importance. The performers rely upon the monitor mixer who is the most important person with regard to the performer's on-stage confidence.

The eleventh hour

By late afternoon everything should be up and working: sound equipment in position, lights focused and the stage made ready for a sound check which usually takes an hour or so to allow monitor levels to be adjusted and the sound engineer to set up his mixer. For the performers, this is a pre-show rehearsal and, if everything has gone smoothly, there may only be minor repairs or spare parts to be replaced. By six o'clock the technicians and crew can take a break until showtime.

During the few hours preceding the performance the house crew make final adjustments: barriers are placed in front of the stage, seats that have been removed for set-up are replaced, the security staff are briefed, spotlight and houselight operators meet the lighting designer, and stage hands are given the cues needed during the show.

Once the doors are opened, the show is rolling. The stage manager will organize the support acts until the final call to the band's dressing room. The houselights will then go down, and the show is on.

The moment the group leaves the stage after their final encore, the team that has been at work since 8 a.m. takes down all the equipment that has been up and working for only a few hours. Three hours later, the doors are closed on the last truck, and it is on to the next show. ●

On stage: surrounded by a battery of lights and supported by a massive sound system, Queen give one of their unique concerts: the end result of hours of preparation by crews of lighting technicians, electricians, sound engineers and numerous others.

Performing Live

In Ultravox we get our greatest thrills from live performance, above all because it's immediate. Working in a studio is fascinating, but it's lengthy, and the best moments come rather unpredictably – when someone just happens to hit peak performance. On stage, you can deliberately work towards achieving that buzz. And you get feedback from the audience, although you don't always. We can belt it out for 45 minutes and know we've got the audience right with us, but there's another 30 minutes to go and then you have to really work at it to hold them through to the end.

Some nights it works, and some it doesn't. When we feel it hasn't worked, we come off stage feeling absolutely miserable; but often what we think has been a rotten show turns out to be one of our best. This shows what a barrier there is between us and the audience; although the space between us on stage and the front row of the audience is only about six feet, it is, in effect, an invisible wall. The people sitting out there get a completely different feeling about the concert to the one we get on stage.

Projecting an image

Ultravox is a band with a certain sense of style, not only musically, but in other ways. We try to project this style into everything we do, but it comes across best in concert. We like to have really close control over every aspect of our live performances, including every detail of the set, the clothes, the equipment, even the posters.

We put an enormous amount of groundwork into our stage performances. Being in control of what happens means thinking of everything and then supervising all the work yourself. We present complete shows, not simply a series of isolated numbers.

It all comes down to being extremely image-conscious. Live performance means a great deal more than just standing on stage, especially today when the opportunities for projecting oneself are so varied. Taking advantage of these opportunities means thinking about, and working at, every little detail.

Set design

You could say that the process of live performance starts right back at the songwriting stage,

because when we compose, we introduce visual themes into our songs – mainly romantic imagery. We think up songs almost as a series of images, rather like a film – frame by frame – and these transform well into visual ideas for stage sets.

The nature of our music means that we spend much of the time sitting at keyboards, rather than cavorting about the stage. In order to make up for the low level of physical action, we have to make as much as we can of the sets. They have to be pleasing visually, and adaptable in terms of lighting. We use professional builders to put them together – on our last tour we used the people who built the wall for Pink Floyd. The basic design comes from us; this year we used a 40-foot structure at the back of the stage. Everything was painted grey, right down to the keyboards and the carpet: the effect was very theatrical – more like a 1920s theatre than a 1980s rock show.

We do a vast number of rough sketches, and we frequently involve an architect to make sure the sets are structurally sound. We often consult the designer of the album sleeve because many of our tours are linked to a particular album, and we like to see the set as an extension of the sleeve.

Lighting

The lighting is extremely important, and always very expensive. In order to get it the way we like it, we arrange a whole week of stage rehearsals, going through each number over and over. We regard the lighting control man as a performer in his own right. He has his own set pieces, just as we do, and he has to project the same type of atmosphere with the lights as we do with the music. He can't flash around lots of bright lights when we're playing something moody or sad. Getting the lighting right is extremely time-consuming, but it is worthwhile because the result is always something unique – tailor-made for the music.

Live sound

Obviously, you have to modify the sound produced in the studio in order to make it suitable for live performance. When recording, we use

Ultravox – *from left:* Billy Currie, Midge Ure, Warren Cann and Chris Cross – waiting the cue to go on stage, the culmination of months of thought, planning and rehearsal.

overdubs and multitrack in the usual way, but when we perform there are only the four of us; we refuse to use backing tapes. Many bands who use electronics do this, because its simpler to have your sequences on tape. We prefer a more natural approach, and this means being selective, picking out the main themes of our numbers, and not attempting to reproduce studio sounds on stage. It's impossible, in any case, to do this perfectly. In my view it doesn't matter if a sequencer isn't there, or isn't as loud as it should be, or isn't playing as tightly in time as it does on the record. What people want from a concert is reasonable sound – basically the same as the album without being identical – and strong visual excitement. If the performance is good enough in its own right, the audience is going to be too excited to notice the difference.

Expense
In order to justify the cost of the sets, the lighting and the time spent rehearsing, we often have to do two performances a night. It wouldn't do to just raise the price of the tickets; the fans pay enough as it is.

Our basic equipment fills several articulated trucks. There's a limit to where we can take it because of the shipping costs. Obviously it is worthwhile shipping everything you have got to the United States, but when it comes to performing in Australia and Japan, we have to devise less ambitious sets. However, they still have to be strong visually, and they therefore present a different set of problems.

Audience characteristics
Audiences in different countries, and even in different cities, respond differently. Within England, Manchester, for example, tends to produce a reserved audience, while Liverpool and Glasgow generally give us a warm reception. The Germans haven't seen anything quite like us before; we get strange reactions there – they don't really know how to take us. They know Kraftwerk who are similar to us, of course, but Kraftwerk don't tour a great deal and their image is very robot-like, whereas despite our electronics we are basically a rock 'n' roll band.

We have always got very warm responses from American audiences in small clubs. When we go there in future we will be taking the show we really want to give them and playing the major concert halls.

Television and video
We don't enjoy television performances simply because we can't control the production. There

Ultravox on stage in front of the set designed for their 1982-83 world tour. The band and the designer of the sleeve for their album *Quartet*, Peter Saville, worked together to create a set which would reflect the sleeve design.

is something horribly stale about appearing on British pop programmes. The format is always roughly the same; the producer says what the camera angles are to be; it is always rushed, and we can't choose how we look.

German television is worse; you get a director who wants you to go on stage with giant bananas

hanging down all around you. To avoid this sort of problem we make "promo" films – small four minute movies. A lot of people use video cameras; we use 16 mm film and edit on to video tape. This is more expensive and it takes longer, but the final result is vastly superior. Unlike video, you can't see what you're doing as you do it, so you have to take a lot of trouble when you're constructing the sets.

Some of the films have actually won awards, and we suspect that many people, who were not particularly interested in us previously, turned on to our music after seeing the films.

Advice for beginners

Bands starting out on live performance should be aware that audiences may take time to get used to them – especially if their music or image is something new and unusual. They must not take an unresponsive audience too much to heart, and remember that it is extremely difficult from the stage to get an accurate idea of how you are coming over.

Nowadays, for better or worse, image – as well as sound – is important. You must perform – not just play your instrument – and be positive about everything you do on stage.●

Making Promotional Videos

The promotional video has become an essential part of the music industry. My own career has been greatly enhanced by the recent video boom, and my work is much more challenging and enjoyable as a result.

The strength of any video "promo" lies in the complementary quality of three basic elements: the words and music of the song, the "live" performance, and the distinctive imagery of the artist. Together these offer unlimited opportunities for visual interpretation that can help establish the personality of a performer in a colourful and individual way. At the same time, the artist escapes the restrictions of the touring circuit and the recording and television studios.

Live television performances can be disappointing because of their format and the limited rehearsal time for camera run-throughs. Video, by contrast, offers complete control and makes for more exciting television. When people watch music shows on television the music inevitably takes second place to the image because a television set produces such a compressed mono sound. Video can successfully overcome this discrepancy. In every other aspect of promotion a performer is judged by musical content alone, but with video the music serves the picture. It becomes the soundtrack to a "mini-epic".

When I began making videos privately in 1979, I soon realized the possibilities were endless and that one could produce visual ideas otherwise impossible for an audience to see. I had been influenced by the diversity, humour and glamour of The Beatles' *Magical Mystery Tour*, their films with Dick Lester, *Help* and *A Hard Day's Night*, and The Monkees' weekly television show which included three minute sketches of their songs. Add *West Side Story* and the talents of Fred Astaire, Gene Kelly and Bob Fosse, and I had a pretty rich mix of influences to draw upon for inspiration. It was an entirely new challenge: "A Three-Minute Hollywood".

Making a video can be a hard, time-consuming operation, the organization of which many performers find too demanding. Consequently, many small independent video production companies now exist to serve artists, package performers and handle everything from thinking up a story line onwards. Personally, I prefer as much artistic control as possible and use the video companies only for technical services.

Constructing the story

First comes the story. About a month before a single is released I make sketches and rough notes for a script. However bizarre, disjointed or abstract the lyrical content of the song, I always try to include a small dramatic story with a beginning, middle and end, the simpler the better. A story-board is made with small cartoons illustrating the proposed action. This is very detailed work, dissecting the lyric of the song word for word, phrase for phrase, breaking it down into individual scenes. It is here that the most creativity is needed. Laziness makes for a much harder (and more expensive) time later.

Working with a director

It is then time to approach the director, whom you must trust as you would a record producer. Many groups undervalue a director's role by thinking that all they need do for a music video is to present their usual live stage show to a camera. A good director, like a record producer, takes a detached but constructive attitude, and concentrates on drawing the best performance from you. Having directed myself in the video of *Friend or Foe*, I now truly appreciate the amount of responsibility, vision and patience needed to direct successfully. I have

Right, Adam Ant on set for *Goody Two Shoes.*

Adam Ant's original sketch for *Friend or Foe.*

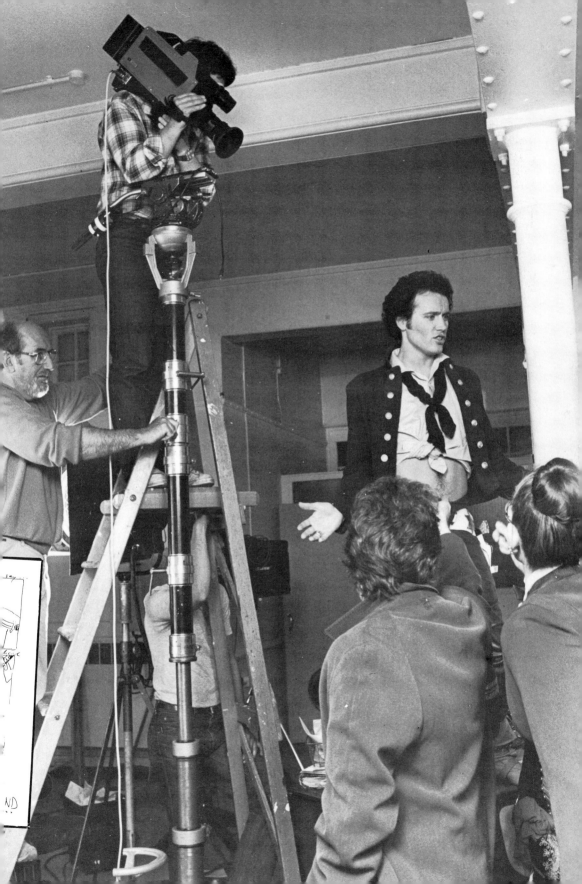

been fortunate to work with Mike Mansfield who immerses himself in each stage of the video from storyboard to completion. Over the two years we've worked together a trust has developed which allows me to concentrate entirely upon my performance during filming. His ability, quite apart from his enormous experience, lies in the careful way he understands my ideas, orchestrates them and puts them on the screen. Long discussions take place during which ideas are added or thrown out. The director then has to co-ordinate all of the artist's ideas into a practical and economically feasible structure. The script is cast, budgets allocated and location sets constructed.

Shooting the video

Without a doubt, making videos is the most exhausting part of my working schedule. Usually a three day shoot will start at 6.30 in the morning and continue late into the evening. In *Stand and Deliver*, *Prince Charming*, *Antrap* and *Goody Two Shoes* I pushed myself out of the role of singer into that of lead actor. The group became characters in the film instead of being locked behind their instruments. Sometimes we used established stars like Diana Dors, Lulu, Graham Stark or the James Bond girl, Caroline Munro, to adorn the story with cameo appearances. All of this, I hope, makes the audience wonder if they are watching a group trying to sell them a seven-inch piece of black plastic or a lavish, three-minute epic commercial. What is important is to grab their attention, make them watch, remember it, want to see it again, and perhaps buy the record. People now expect to "see" records as much as listen to them.

I have jumped out of trees, crashed through windows, swung on chandeliers and dived over tables to keep an audience watching. I've found myself singing in an English wood in mid-winter when a burst of hailstones brought an abrupt end to the chorus, and on the battlements of a castle rescuing Lulu, my lady in distress. (At the start of *Antrap* I was so frozen in my suit of armour that I had great difficulty moving my lips. I felt like a ready-frozen sardine.)

Video's versatility and mobility allow you to get through an enormous amount of work in a very short time. Stunts or choreography can be judged immediately after the take on playback, allowing improvements to be made on the spot, unlike with film where you have to wait until the next day to see the rushes. If there is a drawback it's that the technology threatens to take over as it can in record production. There are so many video tricks and techniques to make a slack or uninspired performance look special. In the end, however, these exhaust themselves and you're back with the human element. I rely heavily on physical work, dance, and other human skills when I make videos, and use the available technology to serve them – working with the technology, not falling prey to it.

The economics of video

My videos cost between £10,000 and £40,000. These apparently enormous sums pay off in many ways. With inflation and recession, touring has become very expensive and an artist may only be able to visit each territory once a year at most. A video makes worldwide simultaneous release of a single possible because the overseas audience is immediately up to date and in tune with the artist's latest development, and the colour, imagery and style of the performer remains familiar until the next live appearance in that territory. During *The Prince Charming Revue* in 1981 I incorporated 20 minutes of video film into the intermission. The audience reaction was tremendous and as attentive as in any cinema. Many clubs and discotheques now present videos as part of the evening's entertainment. In short, video provides an historic and visual biography of the artist, showing developments, mistakes and triumphs alike.

Video discs

Which brings us to the video disc. Video discs are virtually indestructible and unscratchable, and excellent quality video film can be accompanied by stereo sound. I feel that the possibilities are enormous, especially for the "concept" album. Had the video disc been available when The Who released *Tommy*, or Pink Floyd *The Wall*, we probably would have had a simultaneous release of album record, cassette, video disc and video cassette, instead of having to wait years for both to materialize into feature length films.

Once the teething troubles are overcome and a competitive price is reached, I'm sure the public will be swift to adopt the video disc. With the amount of research being done on video single and LP discs, it may not be long before they become a household feature, and remarks like, "Have you seen and heard so-and-so's new single?" become commonplace.

I don't believe that video will replace its counterparts, records and live shows; this has never been my intention. I do believe, however, that it will take its place beside the record rack and auditorium to become another form of popular entertainment in its own right.●

Recording Music

*". . . it's best to lead with your instincts
and support them with your craft."*
QUINCY JONES

Sound Reproduction

Recording music involves three ingredients: musical instruments or voices to create sound waves in the air; one or more microphones to transform these sound waves into an electric current; and a machine that can record or "freeze" the musical signals for replay.

How sound is produced

To understand how the process described above actually happens, let us follow the recording and playback process of an acoustic guitar with a single microphone. When the player plucks or strums the strings, they vibrate and in so doing compress and release layers of air particles around them. This back-and-forth motion radiating outwards through the air is often compared to the effect of a stone dropped in the middle of a still pond. However, sound waves spread in three dimensions in the air to create a continually expanding sphere. Succeeding waves will follow the initial wave for as long as the guitar string continues to vibrate.

Sound into energy

Sound waves travel through the air at a speed of approximately 760 miles per hour, or 1,115 feet per second, reaching the microphone, and the ears of the player, in a fraction of a second. The minute up-and-down changes in air pressure set the light-weight diaphragm of the microphone vibrating. This is part of an electrical generator system capable of producing an equivalent alternating electric current, similar to the mechanism that converts the vibrations of the player's eardrums into signals reaching the brain.

Once the signal is in the form of an electric current, it can be boosted by an amplifier and impressed on to a recording medium. In disc recording the alternating current is transformed back into vibrations, which a cutting stylus then inscribes as an undulating pattern, or waveform, imitating the original sound wave. In analogue tape recording, the pattern of the continuously reversing polarity of the magnetic particles in the tape's coating records the sequence of sound waves.

To play back a recording, the disc or tape must be set in motion at the original speed and

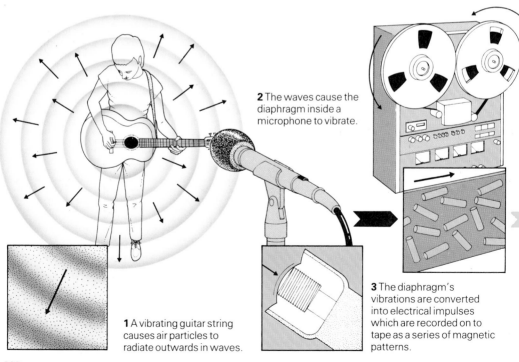

2 The waves cause the diaphragm inside a microphone to vibrate.

1 A vibrating guitar string causes air particles to radiate outwards in waves.

3 The diaphragm's vibrations are converted into electrical impulses which are recorded on to tape as a series of magnetic patterns.

create vibrations in a cone or diaphragm. These vibrations once again send sound waves through the air, and thus we hear sounds resembling the original guitar.

The sounds of music

How closely a reproduced sound resembles the original will depend on the accuracy, or fidelity, with which the recording and playback chains manipulate the musical signals. Our guitar player changes two main sound characteristics as he plays. First, he selects notes of different pitch on the musical scale, which is the same as producing changes in the rate, or frequency, of the vibrations. High-pitched notes correspond to higher frequencies, which the guitarist selects by plucking the lighter, more tightly stretched strings and shortening their effective lengths by pressing on the frets. The note "A" on the treble clef, for example, corresponds to a frequency of 440 vibrations, or cycles, per second (cps), and is written as 440 Hertz (Hz). Going up or down an octave means multiplying or dividing the frequency by two, which gives us the frequencies for all the "A" notes on a piano. Although this range encompasses nearly all of the notes on a piano, a recording that incorporates only a 4,000Hz bandwidth would not necessarily sound life-like.

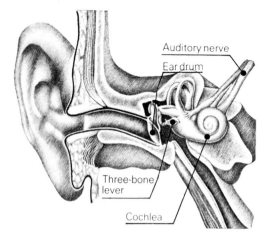

The human ear is like a highly sophisticated microphone. The ear drum vibrates when stimulated by sound waves; the stimulus is transferred via three tiny bones to the cochlea where it is converted to electrical impulses which travel to the brain via the auditory nerve.

scanned by a device capable of converting the recorded waveform back into an equivalent alternating current. This can again be amplified as necessary and fed to a loudspeaker or headphones whose job it is to convert the current and

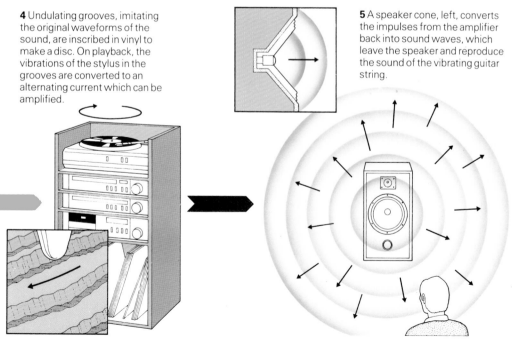

4 Undulating grooves, imitating the original waveforms of the sound, are inscribed in vinyl to make a disc. On playback, the vibrations of the stylus in the grooves are converted to an alternating current which can be amplified.

5 A speaker cone, left, converts the impulses from the amplifier back into sound waves, which leave the speaker and reproduce the sound of the vibrating guitar string.

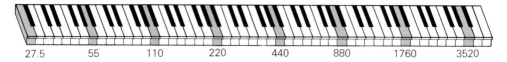

27.5   55   110   220   440   880   1760   3520

All musical instruments generate complex sound waves containing overtones, called harmonics, which are exact multiples of the fundamental note frequency extending to the limits of

Overtones: when a note is played, certain harmonics of that note, known as overtones, are sounded as well. Overtones are always in ratio to the fundamental in terms of frequency. The octave (1st harmonic) is exactly double; the 5th (2nd harmonic) is in ratio, 2:3.

Fundamental

1st harmonic

2nd harmonic

Frequencies of the A notes on a piano measured in Hertz (vibrations per second), *above*. The higher the frequency of vibration, the higher the note; doubling the frequency produces a note an octave higher.

human hearing – 20,000Hz – and beyond. Different instruments produce harmonics in different numbers and different relative strengths, giving them their special tonal quality, or timbre. This enables us to tell the difference between, for example, a guitar, a trumpet and a clarinet, even when the same note is played on all three. Stringed instruments are usually rich in harmonics, some flute notes are almost purely fundamental, and the clarinet emphasizes the odd-numbered harmonics – thirds, fifths, etc.

Designers of electronic organs and synthesizers try to imitate the timbre of various instruments by adding suitable harmonics, but they are only partly successful. One reason why synthesized timbres do not adequately recreate true instrumental tone is due to the initial attack, or transient, which characterizes each instrument and must be included in any synthesized or recorded sound if the instrument is to be reproduced realistically.

The other main sound characteristic which our guitarist varies as he plays is, of course, volume. This is determined by how strongly he sets the strings vibrating and, therefore, the extent, or amplitude, of the resulting air-particle vibrations. As the sound waves spread out from the source, the total energy is spread over a greater

wave-front area, and so the energy per square metre, or intensity, becomes progressively weaker. The human ear can respond to an enormously wide range of sound intensities.

This range is conveniently divided into a scale of 12 steps, called Bels. Each Bel is divided into decibels (dB) so that 10dB equals one Bel; there are 120dB between the faintest sound we can hear and the loudest we can tolerate.

Of course this full 120dB dynamic range is not used in music. Even a symphony orchestra extends to only about 75dB, and an amplified rock band to about 80dB. A professional analogue tape recorder can cope with 70dB, but records usually have to be restricted, or compressed, to about 55-60dB, and AM radio has a dynamic range of only about 30dB, so limiters or compressors are needed.

Acoustics

The room or hall in which music is being played or reproduced through loudspeakers has a considerable effect on the quality of the sound. This is because we hear, not only sounds that travel directly from the source to our ears, but also the countless sound waves that bounce back and forth between the walls, floor and ceiling. These reverberations prolong the sounds and can also change their character: if, for example, the walls are covered with soft, absorbent material that damps out high frequencies, low frequencies will predominate.

Reverberation time is defined as the time it takes for sounds to disappear through 60dB, or to one-millionth of their original intensity. A good concert hall will have a reverberation time of about 1.8-2.4 seconds, at all frequencies, depending upon its size. If a close microphone technique is used to record in such a hall, the recording will sound less reverberant because the direct sound has been favoured rather than the ambient, or reverberant, waves. Pop recording studios are designed to have a short reverberation time of 0.4 seconds or less to improve the attack and separation between the microphones used on different instruments.●

Home Recording

Forty years ago, an American guitarist searching for a new sound, discovered the techniques of multitrack. He was the prototype of the home recording musician.

In the early 1940s Les Paul first had the idea of recording one guitar part over another. At that time he experimented in mono, playing along with one tape while recording on to another. These were the first attempts at overdubbing.

Seven years later he achieved recognition with the release of *Lover*, and by 1954 had built a prototype eight-track recorder.

The recording industry was slow catching up. First two-track, then three, and it grew to four by the mid-1960s, culminating in The Beatles *Sergeant Pepper* album being recorded on two four-track recorders linked together. The number of tracks grew rapidly, and today studios employ twenty four tracks or more. Digital recording takes us into the 1980s. As someone said recently, "if you think digital's just around the corner, then you're already one step behind".

Basic home studio set-up:
quality demos can be produced with a combined mixer and four-track recorder linked to a domestic stereo system, microphone and headphones. Synthesizer, rhythm machine and guitar are commonly used.

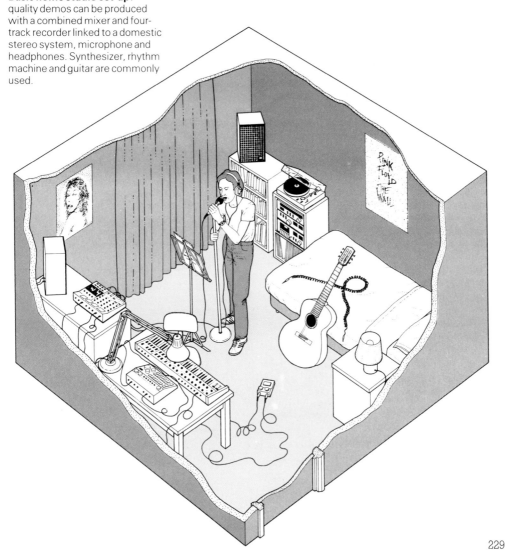

Multitrack for every musician

Musical ideas and compositions are influenced by what we hear. Because what we hear is made with multitrack, it was obvious that musicians would demand these facilities to record, and create music for themselves. As it turned out, when the hyped-up quadrophonic market collapsed in the 1970s, redundant recorders were modified for multitrack. Les Paul's way of making music became affordable for every musician.

There has been tremendous progress in the last few years, and now we see the latest generation of combined mixer recorders making the basic tools of multitrack easier to use and easier to own.

A musician, band or songwriter can make excellent, professional-sounding demo tapes at home. One harmony vocal line in a chorus can lift a song's presentation above the ordinary, and with low cost ancillary equipment it can be turned into a fine, impressive demo recording. People in the music industry rarely have the time to conceptualize an entire arrangment from listening to a piano and voice demo tape, and a musician should try to give them as full an understanding of the final product as possible by putting his ideas on to tape. While a rhythm box does not replace drums any more than a cheap synthesizer replaces strings, people listening to the demo will know what is intended, which is half the battle.

And it's possible to achieve even more. Flying Lizard's hit *Money* was recorded in a living room on a four-track reel-to-reel recorder; Bruce Springsteen's album *Nebraska* was made on a four-track at home and many other musicians from Mike Oldfield to Paul McCartney have studios in their own homes.

Home recording is now within easy reach of every musician. Personal multitrack is as important to the thinking musician today as manuscript paper was in the past. If Bach were alive now, he would probably be using home recording equipment for creation as much as for demonstration.

Multitrack is not just a way of making records. Alone you can sound like a complete orchestra, adding parts and arrangements to a basic idea. And as you work with it, you discover new ways to help you make better music.

The musician can pay close attention to individual parts because not everything has to be recorded perfectly the first time around. Recording instruments and voices at different times means that the problem of separation is almost entirely eliminated.

The musician always has a second chance with multitrack. If mistakes are made on one track, they can be corrected without having to re-record everything, and you can take as long as you like to perfect the vocals or harmonies.

The final mix can be achieved without having to play the music live over and over again. It is a fact that a performer's first take is usually his best, although the overall mix may not sound perfect while recording. If the tracks are laid down the first time around, the performer can then concentrate on the mixdown, making as many practice runs as necessary to achieve the desired mix. Effects such as flanging and echo can be added, and tones and dynamics adjusted after recording has taken place.

As with all modern recording equipment, multitrack recording becomes a creative tool in the hands of a musician. You can record the essence of a musical idea – perhaps just a voice and guitar – play it back, and then build with rhythm, keyboards and ancillary equipment to realize the sound desired.

Overdubbing and sel-sync

The process of recording a series of instruments or voices separately one over the other is called overdubbing. In order to overdub accurately,

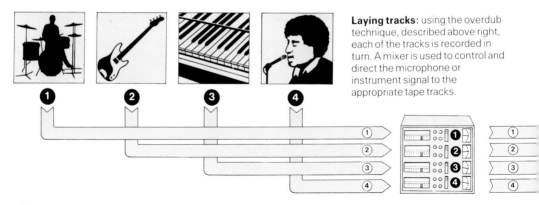

Laying tracks: using the overdub technique, described above right, each of the tracks is recorded in turn. A mixer is used to control and direct the microphone or instrument signal to the appropriate tape tracks.

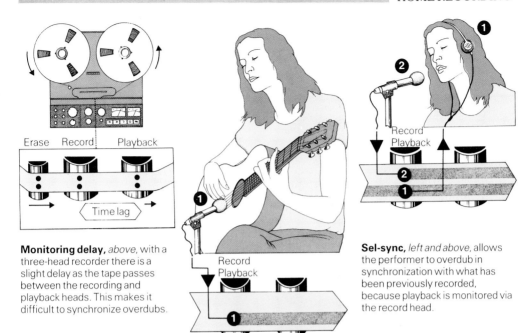

Erase   Record   Playback

Time lag

Monitoring delay, *above*, with a three-head recorder there is a slight delay as the tape passes between the recording and playback heads. This makes it difficult to synchronize overdubs.

Record
Playback

Record
Playback

Sel-sync, *left and above*, allows the performer to overdub in synchronization with what has been previously recorded, because playback is monitored via the record head.

the musician must keep in time with whatever was previously recorded on the tape. The most important feature of the multitrack recorder enabling the musician to do this is selective synchronization, or sel-sync.

Standard three-head recorders allow monitoring (hearing what is already recorded) only through the playback head; because this head is separated from the recording head, the sound being monitored from one track is delayed relative to what is being recorded on to another; the delay is enough to spoil any dubbed recording. The solution is to provide a means of monitoring from the record head. In the multichannel recorder, electronic circuitry and switching allow the record head to function in both the record and playback modes simultaneously. Every multitrack machine has sel-sync.

Tracks and formats

The major difference between expensive and lower-cost machines is the width of tape used for different track configurations. In general the wider the tape, the better the quality and the greater the expense. However, for demo recordings the results achieved by even the narrowest of tapes are more than adequate.

A few years ago eight tracks per inch was the most popular format; this was expensive and required complex tape transport systems with large motors. Advances in tape formulation, head design, noise reduction and electronics have made it possible to achieve similar results with half and one-quarter inch tape. This makes two or four times the number of tracks available to the musician for a similar cash outlay, and also cuts his running costs.

Recording overdubs: using the sel-sync function the musician hears exactly what was recorded earlier. At any time, any track can be recorded again and corrected. With multitrack you only have to get it right once.

Mixing down: when the basic tracks are complete, the playback signals from the recorder are fed through the mixer and combined. Subtle balance, tone control, echo and other effects are all achieved at this time.

Stereo mastering: the final mix is now recorded. Although the word "master" seems to imply the need for an expensive stereo machine, the final stereo master can often be made on a good quality cassette recorder.

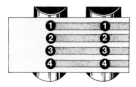

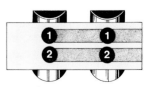

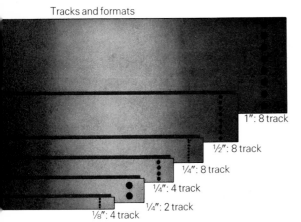

Tracks and formats

1": 8 track
½": 8 track
¼": 8 track
¼": 4 track
¼": 2 track
⅛": 4 track

Most people begin to record using four tracks, which is adequate for most demo tapes. With planned use, up to ten individual tracks can be recorded without ever going beyond second generation – when, for example, three tracks have been recorded and are moved onto the fourth track, the first three tracks can then be used again, making them second generation. Thus there are many possibilities before the number of tracks becomes a creative limitation. Of course, eight and 16 track recorders are more capable luxuries, and, for certain types of electronic music, a necessity.

Multitrack tape recorders
The multitrack recorder is similar to a standard stereo tape deck, with the difference that tracks may be recorded individually or in any combination while any tracks already recorded are monitored via the sel-sync function. In general, most multichannel recorders accept NAB metal reels, although with quarter-inch machines there is a trend to revert to seven-inch spools. Not only is the deck cheaper to make but the tape costs less pro rata on smaller spools.

The electronics of a multichannel recorder are usually modular, allowing quick access for service and regular alignment. Microphone inputs are omitted from many machines because the tape recorder is usually used with a mixer that provides a high level signal. In addition to input and output level controls, switches are provided to allow individual tracks to be put into record or playback and a monitoring system allows the musician to hear either what he's playing or what has been played before. In many cases this switching is automatic: that is, in the playback mode all the outputs come from the tape, and in the record mode the channels being recorded are heard from the record head via sel-sync. Most recorders feature some form of remote control containing tape motion controls and perhaps a record/play function selector.

The mixing console
The mixer is the control centre for multitrack. It always provides these basic facilities:
1. Mixing live signals and feeding these to the tracks on the recorder; and mixing the playbacks for the final mix.
2. Metering and monitoring to listen selectively to what is going on to tape.
3. Send and return facilities to add echo and effects to enhance the signals.
4. Cue or foldback signal for the musicians, so that they can listen to the live signal or the sel-sync playback when overdubbing.
5. Bigger consoles have extra facilities for talkback, signal checks, recorder remotes etc.

On the surface, mixers appear as a series of channel strips. Inputs include a signal selector, tone control, echo send and a slide fader. Then there is pan control (to position the signal between left and right) and switching to direct the signal to the appropriate output strip: fader, amplifier, and finally to the recorder.

Monitoring is a vital aspect of recording, performed by an internal "monitor mixer", which combines the various signals for checking on headphones or speakers.

All mixers essentially work this way, the dif-

Bouncing: instruments A, B and C on tracks 1, 2 and 3 can be "bounced", sent to the spare track 4, collectively while instrument D is being recorded on to the same track as a live overdub. Instruments E and F can then be recorded on the freed tracks 1 and 2 and bounced together with another live overdub, G, on to track 3. In this way it is possible to record up to 10 tracks on 4-track tape without ever going beyond "second generation" (bouncing a track on to another more than once).

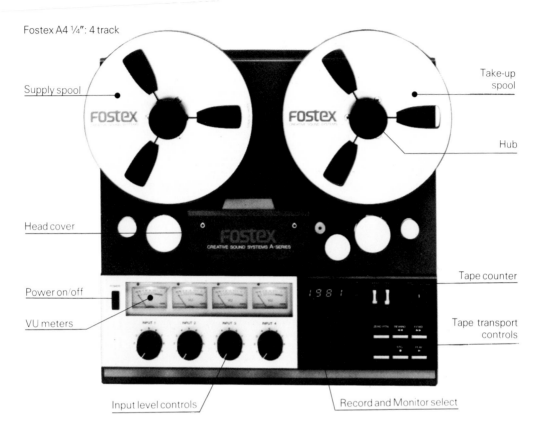

Fostex A4 ¼": 4 track

Supply spool

Take-up spool

Hub

Head cover

Power on/off

VU meters

Tape counter

Tape transport controls

Input level controls

Record and Monitor select

Teac 32-2B ¼": 2 track

Fostex A8 ¼": 8 track

Tascam 38 ½": 8 track

Open reel recorders give better quality, but are more expensive, than cassette recorders. The Fostex A4, *top*, has full overdub facilities and automatic sel-sync switching; maximum spool size is 7". The Teac 32-2B, *above left*, is a stereo mastering machine with outstanding running stability. It includes switchable NAB and IEC equalization. Apart from automatic sel-sync and individual track monitoring the Fostex A8, *above*

centre, features remote punch-in for the solo worker, and the Dolby 'C' noise reduction system is a built-in feature. The Tascam 38, *above right*, is a machine with an optional dbx noise reduction facility. The Soundcraft SCM 381-8, *right*, is capable of master quality recordings making noise reduction systems dispensable. It can be used in professional studios and is completely portable.

Soundcraft SCM 380 1": 8 track

ferences being in size, layout and degrees of sophistication.

When choosing a mixer it is useful to remember that too many inputs are not necessary. After all, each channel is available at every overdub, so in effect you multiply the number of inputs by the number of tracks. Your minimum number of inputs will be determined by the number of tracks for mixdown. Similarly, since with most multitrack work you are only recording a few tracks at a time, you don't need as many mixer outputs as tape tracks, though full monitoring is essential. One final point to remember is that it's better to buy external signal processing – such as equalizers and compressors – rather than over-invest in an effect loaded console.

Cue systems
From headphones or from a loudspeaker, performers need to hear their own or other musicians' music when recording, and a sel-sync signal when overdubbing. What they hear is called the cue, or foldback signal; it is obtained from a separate submix in the mixing console which combines the outputs of the cue send controls in the individual input channels and the tape cue controls connected to the playback of the multichannel recorder.

Echo systems
Reverberation is part of everything we hear in everyday life. Its absence is unnatural. Having avoided reflections and encouraged separation in the studio, at mixdown the reverb effect is carefully added to give body and warmth to the mix. It is essential to have a quality reverb device as part of the basic studio equipment. An echo plate is the classic choice for big studios, but its cost and size are prohibitive for small set-ups. Spring units are an acceptable alternative, and high quality mono and stereo versions are available. Cheap, all electronic units tend to emit alpine echoes, and a fuller, concert hall effect is still expensive to produce this way. The reverb unit connects to the echo or auxiliary send and return jacks on the mixer.

Speakers and amplifiers
By definition, monitoring is simply listening to sound. There is no such thing as a perfect monitoring system; it is a matter of preference and application. Standard reference monitors are highly accurate speaker systems, but even these may give deceptive results if studio acoustics are incorrect.

Positioning of the loudspeakers is critical. The tweeters, for example, should always aim towards the ears because off-axis monitoring can give a false impression of balance and stereo spread.

The size of power amplifier necessary will vary with the material to be recorded, the room

Home mixers: a simple home mixer, such as the Seck 62, *below,* is suitable for basic home recording. It has six inputs, two outputs and two auxiliary sends which can be used for effects, foldback or overdubbing. Extra monitoring facilities are required for 4 or 8 track use. More sophisticated home mixers include four outputs, and full monitoring, which make multitrack recording more straightforward. The Fostex 350, *right,* is compatible with the Fostex A8 recorder (see p. 233) and can accommodate eight tracks.

The **SM58,** is a good all-purpose mike with a wide response and low/high impedence.

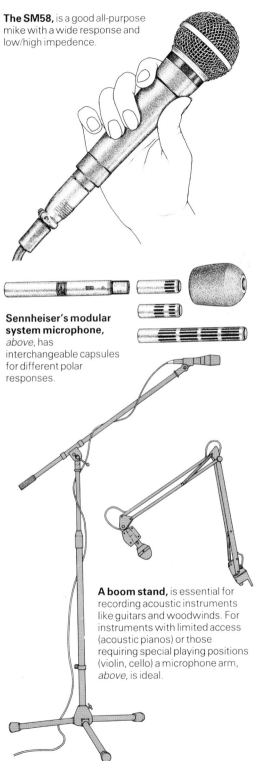

Sennheiser's modular system microphone, *above,* has interchangeable capsules for different polar responses.

A boom stand, is essential for recording acoustic instruments like guitars and woodwinds. For instruments with limited access (acoustic pianos) or those requiring special playing positions (violin, cello) a microphone arm, *above,* is ideal.

size and the efficiency of the loudspeakers. Generally speaking, 40-watts per channel is adequate for most monitoring; remember that a 100-watt amplifier only sounds twice as loud as one delivering 10 watts.

Microphones
It is normal to have a selection of microphones for recording, because different types are preferred for different instruments. The only way to choose is by hearing them and gaining from others' experience, but there should be at least one top-quality microphone for vocals. Low impedance, balanced microphones prevent signal loss and hum pick-up on long runs. Stands and booms are not worth skimping on; there is nothing worse than having a valuable mike come crashing to the floor.

Signal processors
Control beyond mixer facilities helps to achieve more "polished" results.

Graphics or sweep equalizers allow boost or cut of specific frequencies to lift or lose some-

Signal processors, *right,* can enhance sounds and reduce problems of level fluctuation or overload.

thing in a mix. Level control with compressors, expanders and limiters can "tighten" sounds, a third hand that maintains levels of instruments or voices automatically. And delay provides time shift effects. Short delays create phasing and flanging, longer ones doubling and chorus, and half a second or more results in distinct repeats.

These effects can be used alone or in combination, and what can be achieved is only limited by imagination.

The patchbay
Interconnecting this array of electronics can prove to be a rats nest, but a patchbay solves all that. Equipment inputs and outputs are all brought to one array of sockets. It works like a telephone switchboard, permitting any signal path or combination of effects. Switched, plug in types are quick to install and easy to use.

Recording solo: it is advisable to follow a routine. Begin by putting down some kind of rhythm that you can work with. Bass, harmony and melody instruments should follow (guitars, keyboards etc); and then the voices. Put harmony vocals down first (because you will probably need to bounce down), leaving the lead vocal until last. When all you need is on tape, mix down on to a stereo machine.

1 Putting down the drum track, *left*: a tight rhythm is an essential foundation for a good demo recording. It can be laid down with a drum kit or a rhythm box.

2 Adding the bass, *below*, you will need to play along with the drum track, which can be heard through the headphones via the monmix (monitor mix) control. Tracks 3 and 4 are not in use yet, so those faders should be kept down to avoid accidental spillage or noise.

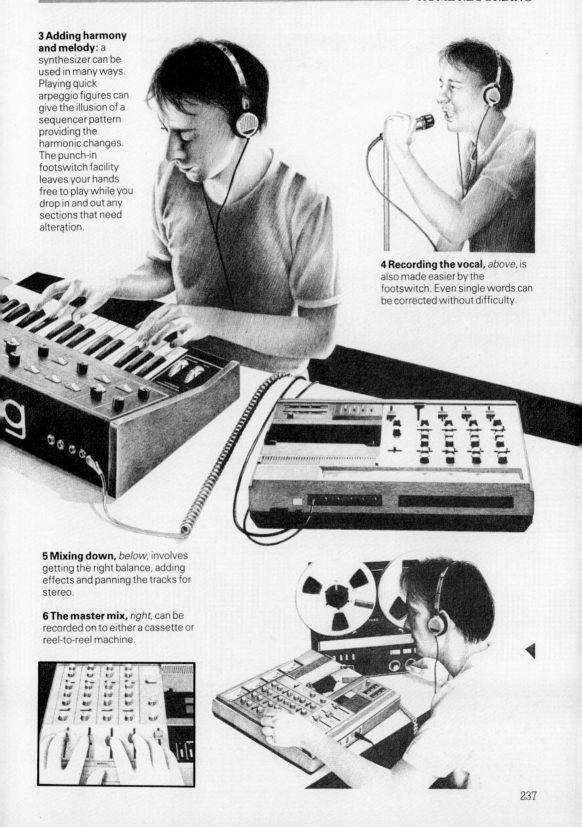

3 Adding harmony and melody: a synthesizer can be used in many ways. Playing quick arpeggio figures can give the illusion of a sequencer pattern providing the harmonic changes. The punch-in footswitch facility leaves your hands free to play while you drop in and out any sections that need alteration.

4 Recording the vocal, *above*, is also made easier by the footswitch. Even single words can be corrected without difficulty.

5 Mixing down, *below*, involves getting the right balance, adding effects and panning the tracks for stereo.

6 The master mix, *right*, can be recorded on to either a cassette or reel-to-reel machine.

Fostex Multitracker 250, *left:* a combined four-track cassette recorder and mixer, a home studio in one compact unit. The cassette section is special format: four tracks move in one direction at double the normal cassette speed.

Fostex 150, *below:* an almost pocket-sized portable studio, with all the essential features of the bigger models.

Tascam 244 Portastudio, *below left:* a complete portable recording system with four-channel mixer and built-in four-track sel-sync cassette recorder with dbx noise reduction.

Tascam 244

Fostex 150

Connecting up a home system

Most home recording equipment interconnects with ready-made, and readily available, phone, pin jack cables. Only microphones have "phone" jack plugs. The central mixer accepts signals from microphones or instruments directly, 1, and feeds them to the multitrack recorder, 2. It also accepts the multitrack playback for mixdown, 3. In the new generation of "suitcase" studios, recorder and mixer are one, and all these connections are internal. The mixer feeds the stereo mixdown recorder, 4, and accepts its playback, 5, to switch to the monitor amplifier or headphones for listening, 6. The monitor amplifier and speakers may be specifically bought or a quality domestic stereo system will suffice at first. Echo and other effects are connected as required, 7, and the cue amplifier, 8, is often integral to the mixer. Connecting up is no more difficult than wiring a hifi system.

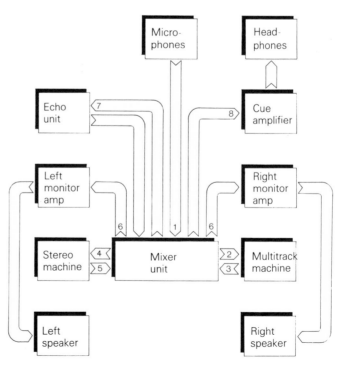

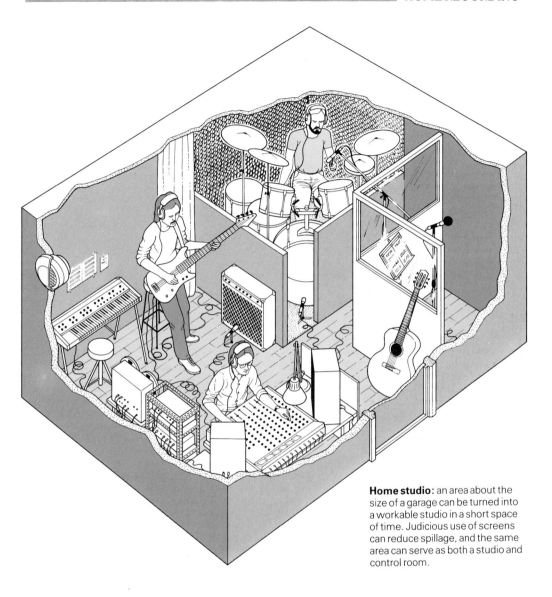

Home studio: an area about the size of a garage can be turned into a workable studio in a short space of time. Judicious use of screens can reduce spillage, and the same area can serve as both a studio and control room.

Studio layout

While large installations can take weeks of wiring, a basic four- or eight-track system can be put together in an afternoon. A musician working primarily alone, will need all the equipment grouped together and close at hand. Studio and control room are one and the same.

There is a popular idea that the room should be "dead", eggboxes or absorbers on the walls. This is not strictly true. Certainly dead areas are useful to prevent spillage, but a certain amount of reflection is necessary to give a natural sound. Acoustic problems tend to appear mainly at low frequencies, so a screen or "gobo" can prove useful. Avoid parallel walls in the room as these can cause standing waves, peaks in the bass response. Taking into consideration the use of close miking techniques, and the direct connection of instruments, soundproofing in its popular sense is not a major worry.

Recording equipment is now within the reach of every musician wanting to develop his or her music. The basics of multitrack recording are no more complex than a music centre and there are no limitations as to what can be achieved; remember what George Martin achieved with The Beatles on their early four-track recordings in the mid 1960s.●

239

Recording Equipment

It is impossible to talk about recording equipment today without also talking about advanced technology. While the music industry is responsible for many new technical advances, it has also borrowed from the world of technology as a whole. Telecommunications, for example, are on the brink of a revolution and recording studios are already feeling the impact of the latest developments in digital electronics.

While it is not necessary for the musician to understand all the intricate inner workings of recording equipment in detail, it is definitely to his advantage to know of what the equipment is capable, how it can help him to produce better music and what will be available in the near future.

Microphones

A microphone is used to convert acoustic energy produced by a musician into electrical energy that can be used by the engineer in the control room. Inside every microphone is a diaphragm. Sound waves produced by a musician's instrument or voice cause the diaphragm to vibrate which in turn produces a variable voltage. The area of sensitivity, or pick-up, around a microphone is known as polar response.

There are four main types of microphone, all of which can be used in the recording studio.

Dynamic or moving coil The diaphragm is connected to a coil set in a magnetic cap which produces a voltage as it is moved. This type of microphone does not have an amplifier built in,

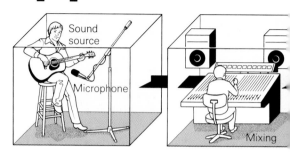

Studio recording process, *above:* the sound is fed via a microphone to the mixing desk where it is equalized; at the same time it is recorded on to a 24-track machine. When all the required tracks have been laid down and overdubbed, the final mix is recorded onto a 2-track master machine in stereo. Using this tape, the master disc is cut from which records are pressed.

The Neumann U87 *left,* a type of microphone highly recommended for studio work.

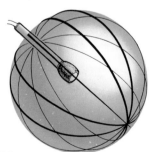

All-round response: sound waves are picked up from all directions in a positive field.

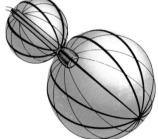

Figure-of-eight response: sound waves are picked up from the front and back in opposite phases (positive and negative).

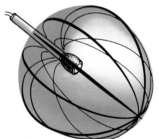

Cardioid pattern is a combination of all-round and figure-of-eight responses. The front pick-up area is strengthened by adding the positive to the negative field.

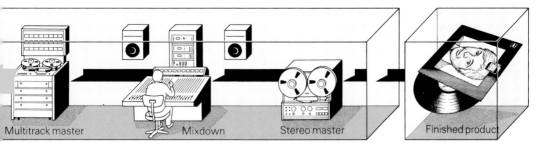

Multitrack master   Mixdown   Stereo master   Finished product

but can have a transformer to increase the output voltage.

Ribbon This uses a large magnet with a ribbon of metal set into it which acts as both a diaphragm and a coil. As it moves, a low voltage is obtained across the ribbon. This type also needs a transformer to increase the output voltage.

Condenser and electret The diaphragm is made of a thin plastic material coated with a microscopic layer of metal with a backing plate. Between the two exists a high voltage known as the polarizing voltage. As the capacity varies with diaphragm movement, a variable voltage is produced which must be amplified within the microphone.

This is the most widely used microphone in professional recording studios. Because the diaphragm can be constructed to have a very low mass, its frequency response and distortion performance can be excellent. Its polar response is generally all-round because the diaphragm is collecting sound at one point only.

If an extra diaphragm is added to the reverse side of the backing plate within a microphone and faces in the opposite direction, the polar response can be varied from a figure-of-eight to an all-round pattern by varying the amount of polarizing voltage applied to the second diaphragm. In this way another popular polar pattern, the heart-shaped cardioid, can be introduced by combining the all-round pattern with the figure-of-eight pattern.

PZM A new and interesting development, the pressure zone microphone, uses a small diaphragm connected to a special electret capsule to produce the output voltage; the sound waves are picked up through a small slit adjacent to a plate. The pick-up pattern is hemispherical and is maintained down to a frequency determined by the size of the plate.

The mixing console

The mixing console exists to help engineers and producers create the sounds and musical balance they require. It is therefore not surprising that it is considered to be the heart of the

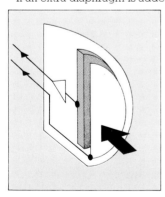

A condenser microphone has an electrically polarized diaphragm which moves in relation to its backing plate.

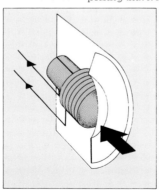

A dynamic microphone uses a coil which moves in a magnetic field.

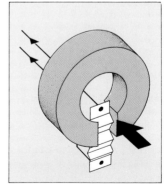

A ribbon microphone uses a metal ribbon, acting as both diaphragm and coil, moving in a magnetic field.

recording process.

During recording, every recorded sound passes through the mixing console at least once, and sometimes twice or even three times. For this reason the console's circuitry must be of a very high standard contributing as little deterioration as possible to the signals passing through. It must also ensure that little noise and distortion is produced and that adequate volume, or gain, is available to allow for occasional peaks of signal without clipping.

The input circuits A signal generated by a microphone passes through an output transformer into a balanced line – a screened wire containing two conductors – to the mixing console. By placing a centre-tapped transformer, or special electronic circuit, at each end of the line, unwanted signals or hum picked up along its length will be eliminated, because the unwanted current will flow in the same direction in both wires.

Because most circuitry in electronic equipment is unbalanced – that is, one side is live and the other earthed – a transformer is needed to convert the balanced input signal into an unbalanced signal within the console. The unbalanced signal is then passed to the microphone amplifier which has a stepped volume control known as the course attenuator. The attenuator can be used to adjust the microphone output voltage to the correct working range of the desk electronics so that acoustic instruments – which usually have low volume – can be boosted, or a loud electric guitar can be recorded at a lower volume without losing the sound quality or overloading the circuits.

Following amplification the signals are passed through low- and high-pass filters which, as the name implies, are used to remove unwanted high and low frequencies and the rumble and hiss from incoming signals. Because their cut-off points are designed to be very sharp, their effect on the sounds which are wanted can be kept to a minimum.

The equalizer Most consoles have several controls that are associated with different areas of the frequency spectrum and it is common practice to split these frequencies into four: bass, mid-low, mid-high and high. The equalizer is

Control room No. 2, *right,* at AIR Studios, London, showing a Neve Electronics 52-input console, JBL speakers, signal processing equipment (at left) and a Bösendorfer grand piano in the studio. The assistant engineer (left), engineer (centre) and producer (right) work as a team.

used to achieve the desired balance between these four frequencies.

Associated with these controls, which are usually switched to select the required frequency, are the cut and boost controls, used to determine the amount of "presence" or "absence" for each frequency band. Usually the equalizer circuits provide an increase or decrease of output (gain) at the selected frequency only, with varying amounts of output on either side of the selected frequency. If the control setting produces a very sharp peak, then the circuit is said to have a high "Q" factor, and will probably have little musical value because it affects only a narrow portion of the sound. If, however, the curve of the frequency band is broadened, then it has a lower "Q" factor and, because a larger range of frequencies is boosted, the equalizer will have a greater musical effect.

There are many and various types of equalizer; for example, if the frequency and "Q" can be continuously altered by rotary controls, the equalizer is parametric. If the level control is replaced by a fader with centre "off" facility, one for each frequency required, then this is known as a graphic equalizer. Instead of peaking at the desired frequency, the circuit can be made to operate at all frequencies above or below the stated centre; this is called shelving.

Foldback On its way from the equalizer to the fader, the signal may be sent to a smaller mixer which sends it to the foldback and echo-send circuits.

Foldback, or cueing, is the process of returning a signal to a performer during a live performance, recording, or when overdubbing, to allow the performer to hear himself or his fellow performers more accurately.

Through the mixing console the engineer selects a small amount of the signal on each channel and, by using the foldback or cue-send control, returns it to the headphone circuits in the studio via a power amplifier. The musician can thus be fed a separate mix of material, independent of the mixing desk faders, and thereby receive a clear representation of his own performance.

In sophisticated systems, the foldback circuits can have up to eight separate outputs: the musician can have his own small mixing console with eight faders, containing a headphone amplifier allowing him to mix his own foldback signal.

Faders An engineer uses a console fader to control the level of the signal in each channel. The scale on the fader is marked in decibels from +10 amplification through 0 to infinite attenuation. A long scale on the fader provides the engineer with fine control and allows him to achieve an accurate and subtle mix of the musical material received through the different channels. Faders are also often used in the monitor section of the desk for balancing outgoing (i.e. to the monitor loudspeakers) and returning signals, independent of the level recorded on to tape.

A desk fader may not always carry the audio signal; sometimes it is used to vary a control voltage, altering the gain of a voltage-controlled amplifier, or VCA. The VCA gain can be changed by varying the voltage at its control input, and therefore the fader can be remote from its VCA.

In certain instances one fader can be used to alter the gain of several voltage-controlled amplifiers (VCAs) at once by combining their control inputs. This is known as grouping and is used to vary the level of an entire section of the mix simultaneously, thereby simplifying the overall process. In some consoles it is possible to use the above method to interchange the function of the monitor and channel faders when these are present in the same channel strip. Such mixing consoles are known as in-line consoles; the equalizer circuit may also be switched from the channel to the monitor.

Once the signal has passed through the fader, it can be directed by a series of push-buttons to the appropriate output of the mixing console, via the mixing "busses".

Most mixing consoles designed for multitrack use have up to 24 outputs, sometimes called groups, that are suitable for connection to a 24-track tape recorder. For example, if the engineer requires channel 7 of the console to be connected to channel 12 of the tape machine, he will select button 12 of the group select unit of channel 7. This output signal will be displayed on the desk meter associated with track 12, and on the monitor with channel 12. Some of the output groups may contain a fader in their circuits, particularly those used for stereo or 4-track work, and group faders may be used to subgroup instruments if the desk is not equipped with individual VCA faders.

Monitors To enable the engineer to hear and measure the output and return signals of the mixing console, a special monitoring section is provided to feed the control room loudspeakers and metering systems (see below). The circuit is usually in the form of a 24-channel mixer, feeding two or four separate outputs, and each channel is equipped with its own fader, foldback-send cir-

Input section and switching attenuator

Filters

Built-in limiter and compressor

Direct output

Aux sends for echo and fold back

EQ section

Computer control panel on the Solid State mixing console. The computer memorizes the mix and controls the tape machines.

Pan pot listening facility

A Channel strip, *left,* from a Neve Electronics mixing console.

cuit and "echo on monitor" level control.

Sometimes it is necessary to produce, say, an echo effect on an instrument or voice without this being recorded onto the multitrack machine. To provide this facility, the echo can be sent and returned solely within the monitor circuit, leaving the recording dry until the echo is added during the final mix. The monitor can be switched to either the 24 mixer outputs or the 24-track recorder outputs. To check that the tape machine is functioning correctly, the 24 meters are switched separately between these same two signals.

Meters There are several types of meter in use and the two most common have different functions. For normal recording, the volume unit (VU) meter is the most common. Because it is simply an AC voltage meter indicating the average level of volume, the VU meter is incapable of reading true peak level. If the signal is fairly constant (bass guitar or similar) the reading will be a fair representation of the level being recorded on to tape, but if the signal is percussive or transient (snare drum) the meter tends to give an indication far lower than the true level. This means that short duration peaks will go unnoticed on to the tape machine, possibly giving rise to distortion.

While some short peaks can be tolerated in the recording process, they create serious problems for the broadcasting industry because transmitter overload is not permitted. The standard device for most broadcasting organizations is the peak reading meter (PPM), which is a true peak reading device: the needle rises very quickly and there is a delay on the return, allowing the operator time to read the level and thus keep the sound below the overload margins.

There are several other types of level indicators used in modern recording consoles. The simplest is a line of light-emitting diodes (LEDs) arranged so that each lights progressively as the level is increased. This system has the advantage of being cheap and occupying little space and, in addition, can be switched to give either a VU or PPM reading.

More sophisticated than this are the bar-graph and plasma-displays, into which can be added facilities to provide visual indications of frequency response and of VCA fader positions, both of which can assist in mixing.

Overdubbing As well as being an aid to recording, the mixing console must provide overdub facilities. After the basic tracks have been laid down, the signals from these can be injected into the monitor section and passed via headphones to the performers, who can then overdub additional material on to clear tracks. In this way even a full orchestra can be recorded section by section until every piece of the musical jigsaw is complete.

Remixing After all of the material has been recorded on to the multitrack recorder, the console is used to reduce the signal to a stereo format suitable for domestic use. To do this, the signal comes from the multitrack recorder to the line input. The recording chain described above is now re-used, except that the foldback sends can be used for echo and ancillary effects to augment the performance. The 24 channels are reduced to two group outputs that often have

their own metering and monitoring circuits separate from the multitrack circuits.

In order to help the engineers create the ultimate mix of all the tracks and facilities at their disposal, various types of fader memories have been devised to remove some of the more repetitive actions required during the remix or reduction process. The various control voltages of VCA faders are constantly memorized by a computer and related to a time code from the multitrack tape machine. As the faders are moved by the engineer, the control voltages are monitored digitally by the computer, and the information is stored.

Simpler systems record this information on a spare track of the tape machine. When the tape is spooled back and replayed the information is reprocessed and the same control voltages are applied to the VCAs, thus recreating the original mix. Usually a button on each fader will allow the engineer to update its position in order to correct small portions of the mix; the updated information is mixed with the original and transferred from one spare track on the tape machine to another. The correct position of the fader for its update is indicated by meters on the mixing console, or by a small meter on the fader itself.

Instead of using tape machine tracks for data storage, more sophisticated systems use a separate storage medium – a floppy disc or something similar – and a time code is recorded on to the tape machine for position reference. When VCA faders are not in use on the mixing console, motorized audio faders are fitted. The fader knobs are touch-sensitive, and an instant update is attainable, without the need to zero the fader or select the appropriate button. Information regarding the mix in progress is displayed on a video screen situated in the mixing console and data storage is on floppy discs related to the time code recorded on the multitrack machine.

Tape machines

Recent tape machine developments have contributed greatly to the versatility of the modern recording studio and its associated equipment. Most records are made using two types of tape recorder: the stereo machine with two inputs and outputs, and the multitrack machine which may have up to 24 channels.

Since the introduction of the tape recorder in the 1940s, its development and uses have spread far and wide in the world of audio. The first magnetic tape recorders were developed in Germany during the last war and were single channel machines using one quarter-inch tape. Other manufacturers were quick to realize the

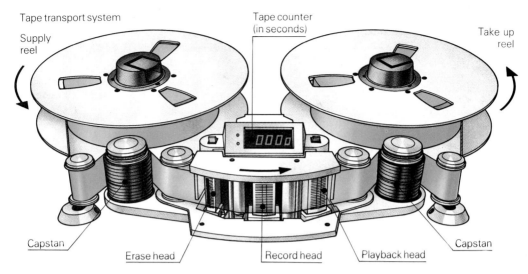

Tape transport system

Supply reel

Tape counter (in seconds)

Take up reel

Capstan

Erase head

Record head

Playback head

Capstan

potential of these devices, and the tape recorder was introduced into studios to replace disc cutting machines. The great advantage of tape was that the programme could be replayed instantly without damaging the master, and could also be cut and edited easily.

With the introduction of the two-track tape recorder in the 1950s, stereo and twin-track recording was made possible and, with the new vinyl disc, the LP was launched. Multitrack techniques arrived in the early 1960s with the introduction of three- and four-track machines which were capable of "sync" recording. Using the record head for replaying previously recorded material, such a machine could record new material at the same time on a spare track. Eight,

16 and 24 track recorders followed.

Basically, a tape recorder consists of a tape transport system designed to move tape from one reel to another while passing over the recording heads at a constant, selectable speed.

The tape is driven by an electronically controlled capstan motor; it passes between the capstan spindle and a rubber idler roller and is pulled across the heads, usually from left to right. Three heads are used on professional tape recorders: one to erase, one to record and one to play back. Recording tape is basically a thin, flexible plastic film, coated on one side with magnetic material which usually contains iron oxide. This is designed to be easily magnetized and to retain the magnetism with little or no

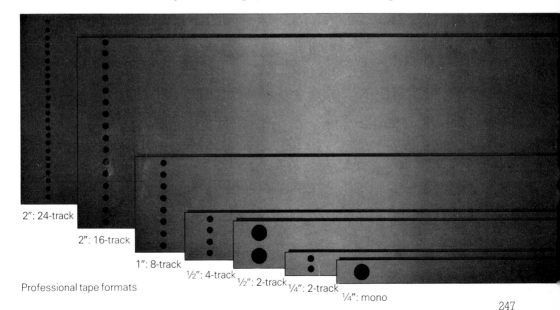

2": 24-track

2": 16-track

1": 8-track

½": 4-track

½": 2-track

¼": 2-track

¼": mono

Professional tape formats

Ampex ATR 102 stereo master recorder, *above*. The tape transport system does not require an idler and is electronically controlled.

Studer A800 24-track audio tape recorder, *below*. This machine uses the very latest technology for high quality studio recordings.

degradation over long periods of time. Tape manufacturers have to ensure an accurate consistency of magnetic properties from one end of the reel to the other, and from reel to reel. Constant sensitivity must be maintained to ensure little variation in replay output and to minimize faults in the coating that cause "dropouts" and magnetic "plops".

The electrical properties of the recording process mean that distortion is produced in the signal on the tape unless a high frequency bias signal is introduced into the recording head, along with the recorded signal. This ensures that the output signal closely resembles that of the input. The bias waveform must be pure and equal on each side of the cycle to avoid creating unwanted magnetism on the tape. Because different tapes have different characteristics, each one needs its own bias setting to achieve optimum performance from the recorder.

Synchronization to provide 46 tracks The newest recording machines are designed for 24-track operation. However, nowadays, for complex recordings, 24 tracks are often felt to be inadequate. An accurate 46-track recording system can be devised by using two tape machines and a reference time code – usually the Society of Motion Picture and Television Engineers (SMPTE) code recorded on to a spare track of each machine. The codes are synchronized by a device known as a Q-lock synchronizer. One machine becomes the master and controls the speed of the other, known as the slave, keeping the two in step. This method is invaluable for recording live concerts; the greater number of tracks gives the engineer a greater chance of achieving a good recording.

Synchronization with a time code is also a great aid when multitrack machines are used in conjunction with video recorders. If necessary, the audio recorder can be operated at a distance from the video recorder, and the two married at a later dubbing session.

Q-lock synchronizer

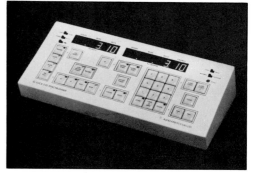

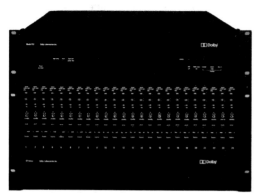

Dolby noise reduction unit

Noise reduction Even the best tape machines contribute a certain amount of noise to every recording. This can be reduced by either increasing the volume of recording on the tape, or running it at a higher speed. There are also noise reduction systems available that can be used in conjunction with the tape recorder; the best known of these is the Dolby system, which is now available for studio, home and film recording. When used for recording, the system splits the signal into four audio frequency bands and raises the volume of the quieter passages to ensure that the low level signals are recorded at a much higher level than usual. In the playback mode the quieter signals are lowered to their

original levels, and noise and hiss are greatly reduced.

In storage, tape can suffer from a phenomenon known as print-through. This is due to the layers of tape being in contact with each other on the reel, causing certain magnetic fields to overlap, transferring information from one layer to the next: this will be heard as pre- and post-echo when the tape is replayed. Noise reduction systems render this effect negligible, as does storing the tape end-out, that is, with the end of the tape – not the beginning – on the outside of the reel.

Speakers

In many ways the studio monitoring loudspeaker system is the most important link in the recording chain. It provides the yardstick which the sound balance engineer uses to evaluate the sounds he is putting on to the tape, as well as to compare the balance of one instrument with another. Therefore, a monitor system must be capable of reproducing all frequencies at similar output levels without any large troughs or humps in the response curve.

With modern studio equipment, noise reduction and digital recording systems, a very low system noise level is attainable. Since most modern bands are able to produce high levels of sound in the studio, the control room monitor system must be capable of reproducing similar

Studio monitor loudspeakers:
right, JBL 4355; *above,* Urei 813.

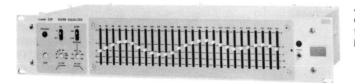

A Urei 539 graphic room equalizer, *left,* can adjust the frequency response of a loudspeaker system.

Eventide H949 harmonizer, *right,* a machine capable of altering the pitch of a piece of music without changing the speed. It is especially useful during mixing.

The RMX 16 digital reverb system, *left,* synthesizes reverberation by using a microprocessor, enhancing the sound of music or simulating the natural ambience of an auditorium.

The DMX 15-80S digital delay line, *right,* repeats a signal without any audible degradation, thereby "thickening" the sound.

Kepex II noise gate, *left,* cuts off any unwanted noise below a preset level.

be changed, again relative to the speed.

A digital harmonizer can alter the pitch of a signal without affecting the tempo and can therefore produce a multitude of effects during the mixing process. The harmonizer uses a constant sampling frequency to determine the number of times that a signal is turned into digital pulses in each second. The harmonizer can then reprocess the signal using more, or fewer, pulses per second. This can be used to produce a change of pitch or even to retune an entire track.

Acoustics

When a studio and control room are designed, certain parameters are applied both to the structure and the internal fittings in order to optimize acoustic performance. Of primary importance is the ambient noise level. A relatively high background noise level can be permitted for a studio and control room used only for recording loud groups, but would be unacceptable for a studio designed for, say, drama or solo piano. An acoustic engineer can specify to an architect the background noise level he requires. This is expressed in International Noise Rating (NR) curves and will determine the maximum permitted noise level in the studio area. In general, the lower the noise required, the greater the cost of construction to achieve it.

Isolation from external noise is essential, heavy walls and roofs provide this, concrete being a popular medium. Floors, walls and ceilings can be isolated from the outside world with acoustic mountings, made of either rubber or metal springs. Air conditioning must be separated off and fitted with silencers, and grills must be of sufficient size to ensure low air velocity. Windows should be double-glazed and all doors fitted with a good sealing system. The control room and studio must be isolated from each other; the window between them should be double-glazed and two separate doors incorporated to provide a sound lock.

Several factors influence the performance of loudspeakers, and good acoustic design pays. Most monitors, for example, benefit from being flush-mounted into the wall of the control room to ensure that the lower frequencies generated will be radiated within 180 degrees, avoiding unwanted reflections from the walls. If the speakers are mounted near the ceiling, then low frequencies will radiate into 90 degrees, helping the bass still further. It is best to design the room around the position of the loudspeakers so as to achieve symmetry.

Unwanted sounds and resonances must be absorbed. It is a good idea to avoid parallel surfaces; curved or sloping walls and ceilings and a variety of acoustic treatments can be used to obtain a reverberation time which exhibits a smooth response. Reverberation can be altered by attaching absorbent materials and panels to the walls and ceilings; the more treatment applied, the greater the absorption and the shorter the reverberation time. This is why rooms with few or no absorbent surfaces, such as bathrooms, tend to echo more than rooms with soft furnishings. Different finishes have different qualities of absorption; for example, soft surfaces tend to absorb more sound than hard surfaces, especially at higher frequencies. The thickness of the material used will determine the lowest frequency absorbed. Absorbing bass frequencies usually involves constructing tuned, hardboard-faced boxes or untuned labyrinths, known as bass traps.

It is wise to keep the absorption characteristics in the monitor area of the control room symmetrical to preserve a good central image for stereo. Different areas of the studio can be treated randomly to obtain a range of acoustic environments for the musical instruments.

The digital age

In the latest digital recording equipment the conventional audio signal, which in its present analogue form has been in use for many years, is converted into a code of pulses similar to Morse Code. With this process, the signal can be treated in a number of ways by using modern circuitry. The digital recording engineer has an entirely new technology at his fingertips.

Digital processing A digital processor converts audio, or analogue signals, into a series of pulses that correspond to the voltage level. The number of times per second that the processor changes the analogue signal into a pulse is determined by the highest frequency needed. Because the limit of most audio equipment is around 20Khz or 20,000 cycles per second, the audio signal must be sampled at least twice this rate, or frequency, which is usually around 40-50Khz. This is known as the sampling frequency.

Because digital language is represented by either "on" or "off" (1 or 0), each pulse is divided into a series of vertical steps in order to tell the memory system of the machine the height of each pulse. The more steps, the greater the accuracy of the system in recreating a pulse of the correct height. A professional digital system will usually use a minimum of 16,000 to 65,000 steps, depending upon the number of bits (*binary digits*) that the processor is capable of handling. Thus, 16,000 steps will require 14 bits

Neve Electronics computer-controlled recording console, *right*. Digital technology has given the recording engineer more versatility than ever before. A colour video screen displays much of the essential information while the manual controls are kept to a minimum on the desk.

Sony PCM 3324 24-track digital tape machine, *below*, Digital recorders have excellent sound quality, wide dynamic range and virtually no distortion.

The Sony compact disc player, *above*, represents the very latest in audio hardware. An optical laser reads metallic pits on the disc (which is about 4½ inches in diameter) and converts them into sound.

and will produce a signal corresponding to a noise ratio of 84 decibels; 65,000 steps will require 16 bits and will correspond to a theoretical noise ratio of 96 dBs.

The digital "words" that make up the ons and offs can be stored on tape or any other memory system. Tape is useful because it can store a large amount of information. Access is slow compared with magnetic discs, but this is relatively unimportant when recording music.

An average magnetic tape machine is capable of satisfactorily recording only up to around 20Khz and, because digital information requires a band width one hundred times this, a special machine is needed. Video tape recorders can be used, but their capacity is inadequate for multitrack and so new machines have been developed. Sony and JVC have developed processors for use in conjunction with their three-quarter inch professional video recorders.

There are also several multitrack digital recorders available, including the American 3M machine which uses one-inch wide digital tape running at 45 ips and is capable of recording up to 32 tracks; and the Japanese Sony model which uses half-inch tape running at 30 ips which can record up to 24 tracks of digital information, two analogue audio tracks and a code track.

The main problem with digital recording is a momentary loss of signal (drop-out) encountered when tape is passing across the tape heads, caused either by dirt or a faulty tape. To minimize this effect, error correction systems have been developed which fill in the "holes" in the digital system to the extent that drop-outs are no longer noticed. It is also possible to splice two pieces of digital tape together to create a musical edit, and the error correction system is now such that the join will not be heard.

Recording companies and studios will gain a great deal by using digital recording because the signal is stored in pulse form and can be reshaped and corrected when necessary. It is thus possible to copy information digitally many times to send to outlets all over the world, while still maintaining a high level of quality.

The digital audio disc Philips and Sony have devised a replacement for the common vinyl record known as the digital audio disc. This compact disc is four and a half inches in diameter and can be played on a turntable revolving at about 250 rpm. The digital signal is recorded on to the disc as a series of metallic pits enclosed in PVC that are read by an optical laser system of great accuracy. The resultant pulses are then converted into analogue signals, or sound. Up to one hour of stereo sound is available on each

The digital
audio disc

side of the disc, and the quality is equal to that of a studio master recording.

Digital mixing Soon the all-digital studio will be a reality. Neve Electronics of Cambridge in England have already developed the first commercially available digital mixing desks.

The main advantage of the digital system is that, because analogue-to-digital conversion occurs early in the recording chain, the signal remains in digital form until it reaches the consumer – apart from reconversion to analogue for monitor and ancillary purposes. Thus the digital signal is sent directly to and from the tape machine without reconversion. A further advantage is that the mixing desk is more versatile than the standard type, and greatly simplified. All of the controls, for example, are assignable to each track, including the faders if necessary, and information is displayed on a colour video screen in front of the engineer. This means that only a few equalizers and switches are needed to control the entire desk, and the bulk of the electronics can be controlled remotely from the console via a single fibre optic cable. Data storage is on a standard floppy disc which is also used to automate any function during replay.

An interesting practical development is the availability of a delay line in every channel allowing all studio microphone outputs to be brought to a single phase point to give greater reality to the recording. Built-in desk limiters can be programmed externally to act and sound like any limiters on the market by feeding the characteristics into the control system. Eventually, all data and music storage will be part of the recording console, using a disc recording medium for quick access.●

Recording Techniques

The sounds produced in the studio must be captured and faithfully reproduced, and this is where the recording engineer comes in. To make sure that the sounds are being recorded at the correct levels and that things are in phase with each other, he will be constantly alert to any distortion and break-up in the incoming audio signals, and must be able to quickly diagnose any faults that may be occurring. The two most important things any good recording engineer must bear in mind are: first, not to create a panic which might unnerve the artist and/or producer; and, secondly, to use his discretion if he does discover a fault. He may even have to take preventive measures during the recording session itself.

Painting with sound

Probably the easiest way to understand the recording process from the engineer's point of view is to think of it in terms of photography, the difference being that a photographer captures light and an engineer captures sound. Just as a photographer must set the film speed on his camera before exposing his film to light, so the recording engineer must set up his tape machine correctly before exposing his tape to sound.

In the same way, microphones can be thought of as camera lenses. They can be bright or dull, and can have a wide sensitive pick-up area like a wide-angle lens, or a narrow sensitive area like a telephoto lens. Like the photographer, the recording engineer will use whichever is most appropriate for the job in hand.

Tone, or equalization, is added to the mikes to enhance the sound, and I often think of this in terms of colour: treble brings out the greens, high treble brings out the blues and silvers, and the bass can be described in shades of browns and golds. As a recording engineer, therefore, you are painting a picture with sound.

Personally, when recording multitrack I prefer not to do the finished equalization at the outset, but take it about half-way – rather like making a very good sketch with only some of the colour added. The reason for this is that in the early stages of multitrack recording we don't yet know what overdubs are still to come, and if I were to add a lot of equalization at the beginning,

The control room at AIR Studios: *from left,*
producer George Martin, engineer Geoff Emerick and
tape operator Jon Jacobs.

I might find it difficult to remove later on (this is known as over-exposure).

In the studio

The type of studio used will largely depend on the requirements of the particular recording session. Small studios tend to be used mainly for group work; larger ones if, say, an entire orchestra has to be accommodated. Both types usually contain booths, which are always used to record individual instruments since they ensure total separation of one instrument from another.

Separation, as we call it, is a source of constant concern for engineers, because if echo is added to, for example, a guitar, and there is a great deal of vocal pick-up onto the guitar mike, the vocal begins to sound swimmy and will lack presence when the vocal mike and echo are mixed with the guitar mike. To avoid this problem, acoustic screens are often used to absorb the sounds of other instruments. These are normally heavy and can come in various shapes and sizes, some with windows and some without. Screens with windows will allow the musicians, and especially the conductor/arranger, to have visual contact with each other, which will be useful for sending or receiving any necessary musical cues.

Small studios are normally deadened with special acoustic treatment; larger studios have a dead area, normally used for the rhythm section, and a live area, which I would normally use for an orchestra, since it will add a sense of space to the type of sound they produce. The control room is linked to the studio by a large window, which enables you to keep a continuous check on what is happening in the studio.

You can't just stay in the control room, however. You must be fully aware of what is happening in the studio, listen to the tonal colours being created, and use the studio acoustics to their best possible advantage to capture, and even enhance, the sounds being produced. Engineers are always listening for sounds that they particularly like, and will often use a different recording technique from the usual one to bring out a sound that they find particularly interesting.

Simple recording

Voice and guitar An example of a simple recording might be a solo voice and acoustic guitar. The first problem to overcome here is the pick-up from the vocalist on to the guitar mike, for which I might use an AK5451 with a narrow pick-up area angled down towards the guitar and away from the vocalist. Conversely, angling a U670 mike away from the guitar and towards the vocalist will minimize pick-up from the guitar on

Recording session: the control room is acoustically isolated from the studio. Contact between them is maintained visually, and verbally via the musicians' headphones. Soundproofing screens have clear panels, because it is important for the musicians to maintain eye contact with each other.

The vocal area is screened off to prevent "spillage", sound from other instruments being recorded on the vocal track. Here, guitar and bass are recorded through microphones, while the synthesizers are "direct injected" into the mixing desk.

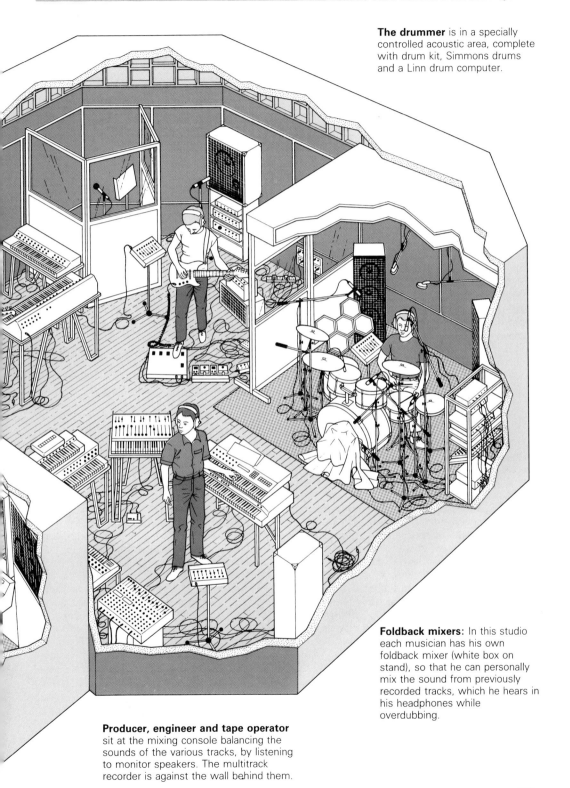

The drummer is in a specially controlled acoustic area, complete with drum kit, Simmons drums and a Linn drum computer.

Foldback mixers: In this studio each musician has his own foldback mixer (white box on stand), so that he can personally mix the sound from previously recorded tracks, which he hears in his headphones while overdubbing.

Producer, engineer and tape operator sit at the mixing console balancing the sounds of the various tracks, by listening to monitor speakers. The multitrack recorder is against the wall behind them.

259

to the vocal mike (though this would be unlikely, as the vocal would normally be louder than the guitar).

Jazz trio A slightly more complex recording might involve a jazz trio consisting of, say, lead piano, drums and acoustic bass. Here it is especially important that the musicians have visual contact with each other, and that the acoustic screens be carefully manipulated in such a way that the musicians can hear each other easily and therefore get a feel for the music. It is common practice nowadays to give each musician headphones to help him hear what the other musicians are playing. As far as I'm concerned, however, it is what is being created in the studio that is of primary importance: the natural dynamics must come through at all costs, and the wearing of headphones for this type of recording must take second place.

The piano lid will prove useful in setting up the group of jazz musicians, since it will act as a screen, shielding the piano mikes from the drums. The bass should be covered by a small screen hinged in the middle and the drums should have two similar screens joined together around the front. All this, together with skilful use of the studio acoustics and the microphone technique described earlier, should be adequate. The actual choice of microphone will be purely subjective: no two engineers will record sound in exactly the same way, just as no two people will photograph or paint a subject in exactly the same way.

Having obtained the correct tonal qualities of the instruments, you can now begin to combine to create a two-track stereo picture. The acoustic bass should be positioned in the centre, and the drum kit spread symmetrically on either side of the bass, but not to the extreme left or right. (The drum kit should be treated as one instrument; too much stereo spread will make the drums sound disjointed.) Finally, you can blend in the piano, which is spread across the entire stereo picture. Once you have listened to the three instruments mixed together, you can then make your final alterations to the equalization, and any other technical adjustments which may be required.

Multitrack recording

A multitrack machine will normally accommodate 24 separate tracks of information on a two-inch tape, which is rather like having 12 ordinary stereo tape machines stacked on top of one another.

Over the years, tape machines have gone through several stages: from four to eight tracks on one-inch tape, then to 16 tracks on two-inch tape, and, finally, to 24 tracks on two-inch tape. Nowadays, by recording a code known as SMPTE onto the twenty-fourth track of two or three multitrack machines, you can run them side by side in lock and, providing you have enough tape machines and a large enough mixing console, you can have as many tracks as you want.

Using the 24-track system

This recording technique gives engineers great flexibility. For one thing, there is room for afterthought because final decisions can be made at the mixing stage rather than at the actual time of recording as is the case with two-track stereo recordings. The multitrack recording system allows each instrument to be recorded on to its own track, enabling you to alter the tone, add effects and adjust the level in the final mixdown. You can also overdub other sections of the instrumental make-up at your leisure, and, when recording vocals, you can pick the best of a number of takes, or build up a vocal track from the most successful parts of several takes.

Laying down the rhythm tracks Of course, some decisions will still have to be made at the time of recording. If, for example, you were recording eight tomtoms, you might easily run out of tracks if you used one track for each of them. I would mix the eight tomtom mikes down to a stereo picture on two tracks of the multitrack, split the rest of the drum kit into two tracks so that the left and right overhead mikes can pick up the cymbals and ambient tones of the entire kit, use a further track for the snare drum and another for the bass drum. I don't normally mike the hi-hat because it is really only there to keep time, and in any case there will be enough hi-hat pick-up from the overhead and snare microphones; the only exception to this would be if the hi-hat were a special feature in the music.

Assuming that you are now recording a basic rhythm track (drums, bass, piano, rhythm guitar), you have so far used six tracks for the drums. I would use another track for the bass guitar. I don't like taking a direct feed from the bass guitar pick-up, much preferring to hear the combined tone of the guitar and bass cabinet because it has its own tonal character. These days, many musicians prefer to take a direct feed, which in my opinion, is lazy: people can become too accustomed to relying on the control room and not on what happens in the studio, which is where it all starts.

I would record the rhythm piano on two tracks as stereo, with the lead parts done at a later stage

as an overdub. Finally, I would use a tenth track for the electric rhythm guitar to make a nice tight rhythm recording.

If you want to preserve the basic feel of the rhythm section, it isn't a good idea to keep on recording it over and over again. Musicians will sometimes keep going back and re-recording because of, say, a slight error in the drums, which is a shame because it might have been a good overall performance. Personally, I would rather go for performance than perfection: the odd error is human, and I like to hear it. In the case of a bad error, however, it is no problem with multitrack to re-record the section in question by overdubbing, keeping the other instruments in their original form.

Guide vocal and instrumental overdubs Having recorded the master rhythm track, I would next record a guide vocal to help connect the various parts of the song for the other musicians who have yet to do their overdubs. These might consist of strengthening the rhythm track by double-tracking the electric guitar to add fullness, and solo work for the instrumental section, such as lead guitar, keyboards or saxophone.

Lead and harmony vocals When all of the overdubs are finished, I would go for the lead vocal. Here the producer will be critical of pitch and the general interpretation of the song. Next come the harmony vocals, each part again being double-tracked to create a fuller sound. As the double-tracking technique uses up a great deal of tracks, once the harmony sections were finished I would then mix them down to two available tracks, and wipe the original tracks in order to accommodate any orchestral overdubs that might be necessary.

Recording studio during an orchestral overdub session. The piano is closely miked and the guitars well screened from the string section. The conductor is positioned so that he can be seen from both sides of the screen.

Headphones These become a necessity in multitrack work because of the number of overdubs involved. When overdubbing a large string section on to a recording similar to our hypothetical one, the volume of the headphones will be an important consideration. Each musician will have a pair of headphones, and, because the string mikes will be some distance from the instruments and the gain fairly high, it could be distracting to hear the cue mix picked up from headphones playing at too high a volume. Ideally, each musician should have his own small mixer whereby he can hear his own mix. In the past, due to the fact that everyone hears things differently, a good deal of time has been wasted in the studio, trying to reach a happy medium with just one overdub or cue mix from the engineer.

Mixdown to two-track When the orchestral overdubs are completed, the next stage is to begin the mixdown to two-track stereo, which will be the master tape from which the final record will be cut. It is at this stage that the "painting" of the "picture" begins, with the addition of echoes and other effects, stereo positioning and equalization. This is a highly personal process and is impossible to put into words: the possibilities are virtually endless.

Editing This is a natural part of the recording process, and there should be nothing intimidating about it. You might, for example, want to edit

Continued on page 264

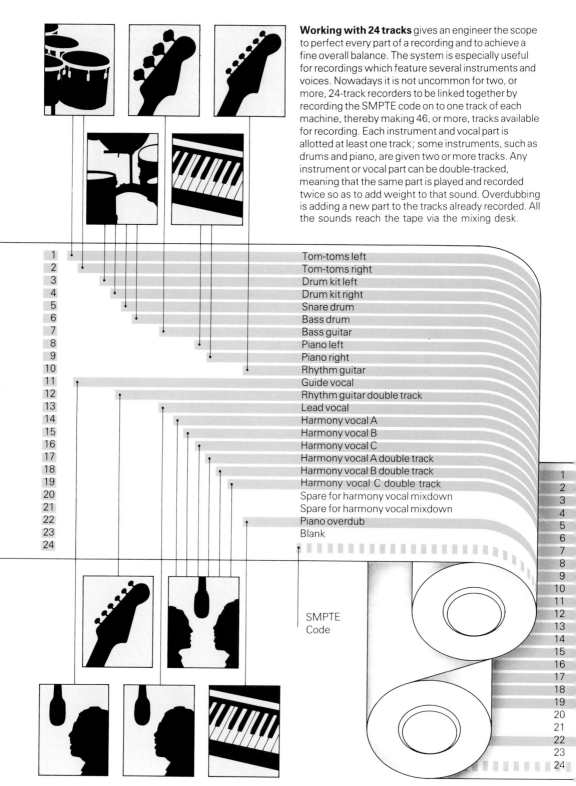

Working with 24 tracks gives an engineer the scope to perfect every part of a recording and to achieve a fine overall balance. The system is especially useful for recordings which feature several instruments and voices. Nowadays it is not uncommon for two, or more, 24-track recorders to be linked together by recording the SMPTE code on to one track of each machine, thereby making 46, or more, tracks available for recording. Each instrument and vocal part is allotted at least one track; some instruments, such as drums and piano, are given two or more tracks. Any instrument or vocal part can be double-tracked, meaning that the same part is played and recorded twice so as to add weight to that sound. Overdubbing is adding a new part to the tracks already recorded. All the sounds reach the tape via the mixing desk.

1	Tom-toms left
2	Tom-toms right
3	Drum kit left
4	Drum kit right
5	Snare drum
6	Bass drum
7	Bass guitar
8	Piano left
9	Piano right
10	Rhythm guitar
11	Guide vocal
12	Rhythm guitar double track
13	Lead vocal
14	Harmony vocal A
15	Harmony vocal B
16	Harmony vocal C
17	Harmony vocal A double track
18	Harmony vocal B double track
19	Harmony vocal C double track
20	Spare for harmony vocal mixdown
21	Spare for harmony vocal mixdown
22	Piano overdub
23	Blank
24	

SMPTE
Code

1
2
3
4
5
6
7
8
9
10
11
12
13
14
15
16
17
18
19
20
21
22
23
24

Which sound goes on which track is obviously crucial. Normally the rhythm section will be recorded first, spread across several tracks. The drums alone might be given six tracks: tomtoms on tracks 1 and 2, the sound from overhead mikes to left and right of the kit on tracks 3 and 4, snare drum on track 5 and bass drum on track 6. Bass guitar can be recorded on track 7, piano on tracks 8 and 9 as stereo, and rhythm guitar on track 10. A guide vocal, which will be left out at final mixdown, might be recorded next on track 11. This would be followed by instrumental solos, if required, and, as in the case illustrated here, double tracking the rhythm guitar on track 12 to beef up its sound. Track 13 might then be used for the lead vocal, followed by double-tracked harmony vocals on tracks 14 to 19.

Mixing down to create more tracks is sometimes necessary. Here the harmony vocals are mixed down to stereo and sent to tracks 20 and 21, leaving tracks 14 to 19 clear for strings and horns. It is good to have a track available for afterthoughts, such as the piano overdub added on track 22. Track 23 is often left clear because it is prone to pick up sound from the SMPTE code recorded on track 24.

Mixing down to two-track stereo gives producer and engineer the opportunity to create a very personal interpretation of the sound. Echo and other effects are added, tone adjusted and the sounds panned to their desired places in the stereo picture. Tracks 1 to 22 excepting track 11, the guide vocal, pass through the mixer to be recorded on a two-track stereo tape.

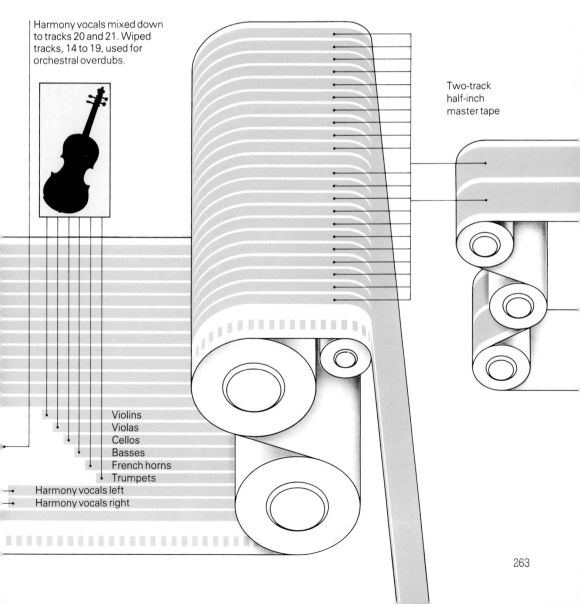

Harmony vocals mixed down to tracks 20 and 21. Wiped tracks, 14 to 19, used for orchestral overdubs.

Two-track half-inch master tape

Violins
Violas
Cellos
Basses
French horns
Trumpets
Harmony vocals left
Harmony vocals right

263

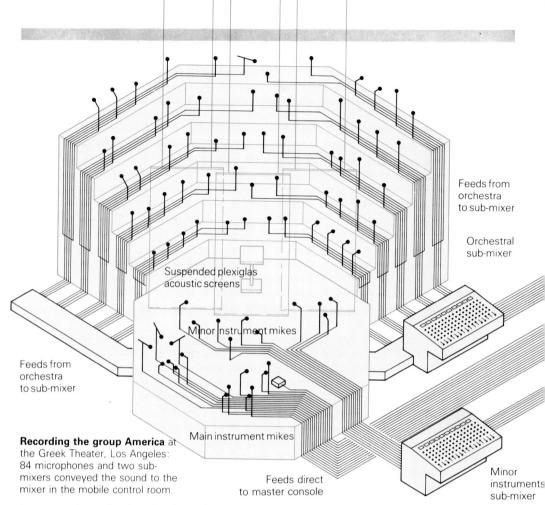

Feeds from
orchestra
to sub-mixer

Orchestral
sub-mixer

Suspended plexiglas
acoustic screens

Minor Instrument mikes

Feeds from
orchestra
to sub-mixer

Recording the group America at
the Greek Theater, Los Angeles:
84 microphones and two sub-
mixers conveyed the sound to the
mixer in the mobile control room.

Main instrument mikes

Feeds direct
to master console

Minor
instruments
sub-mixer

because of an afterthought about the overall construction of the song, or you might want to segment the song as a chorus-verse rather than a verse-chorus. Or, if there is a better solo section from one take to another, you might splice it into the master, taking into account the tempo and whether the musical ins and outs of the edit will work. It can also be great fun to experiment with what you think are impossible edits and discover that they will actually work.

Location recording

This is by no means the easiest of recording tasks, and all your studio experience and techniques will at some point come into play. The rule is: always be prepared for the unexpected.

One of the most complicated location recordings I ever did was with the group America at the Greek Theater in Los Angeles, where we had to do everything, right down to the stage setting. Because the group was backed by an orchestra of 60 musicians (conducted by Elmer Bernstein), my first problem was how to achieve good separation between the orchestra and the

group. The stage was not terribly large, so we decided to stack the orchestra in tiers at the back of the stage and hoist huge perspex sheets in front of them, to act as acoustic screens and prevent the orchestra from being picked up on the group's mikes and vice versa.

I decided to use a close mike technique for the orchestra whereby each instrument was individually miked. Obviously, this meant we were using a huge number of microphones: with the group and the orchestra combined we had a total of 84. Because no mixing console can accommodate that many microphone inputs, we use two big mixing consoles at the side of the stage. One console was used to submix the orchestra to give me the various orchestra sections. This was then fed to the master console in the mobile studio and combined as a stereo picture to two tracks of the multitrack. The second console was used to submix all of the percussion, and the minor instruments used by the group only. For all of the main sounds, such as vocals, drums, guitar and keyboard, the mikes came as direct feeds to the master console in the

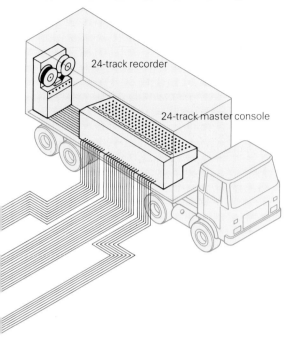

24-track recorder

24-track master console

Microphones develop faults and there may be many cables that will pick up interference from the lighting system. This is why, wherever possible, you should try to give yourself a separate earth.

A location recording of this size requires simplicity. For example, you wouldn't want to use 15 microphones on the drums, but instead you might use two overhead snare drum mikes, a bass drum mike, and, perhaps, a few spot mikes on some of the toms.

A second engineer will handle the PA and would normally use his own microphone set-up, which means that every instrument will have two microphones. To avoid cluttering the vocalist's face, the PA engineer and recording engineer will sometimes share the same vocal microphone; the cable will be split at a point away from the stage enabling both engineers to add their own separate equalization.

Some hints on location recording would include the following: be careful with equalization; remember that you are in strange surroundings and do not try to be clever because you can do that on the mix. When you return to the studio you will probably discover that you need some overdubs, such as patching the lead vocal track. This is why separation is so important: if there has been too much leakage of, for example, the vocal on to the orchestra mikes, you would still hear the live vocal against the one you have overdubbed in the studio.●

mobile recording studio. This meant that there were two recording engineers on stage listening to their submixes on headphones. We also had our own communication systems plus video link-ups so any problems could be quickly rectified.

For this type of work a positive approach is required — there is no time for experimentation.

Mobile control room and studio: a handful of companies on either side of the Atlantic produce custom built mobile control rooms. Some of these include small studios, useful for overdubbing vocals after a live recording. Many have two 24-track recorders, giving 46-track capability. Pictured right is Mobile One, whose features include remote controlled video cameras enabling those in the control room to see what is happening on stage, a small studio and air conditioning. Cables are stored and connected to inputs and outputs between the wheels.

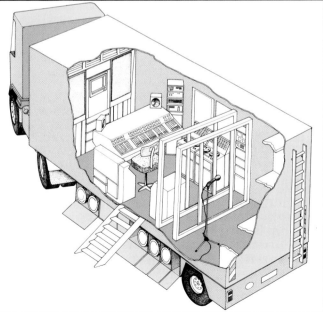

Record Production

In those dim post World War II days, when rock 'n' roll was uttering its first lusty cries, the term "record producer" was never used, and if it had been, it would not have applied to more than a score of people in my country. So my first tentative efforts to control sounds on wax from 1950 carried the title of Artistes and Recording Manager. Of course, recording has changed, and with it the functions of those who influence it. Nowadays it seems that every fourth person I meet is a record producer or at least aspiring to be one. (They also say that one person in four has some form of mental instability, but that's another matter).

But what does a record producer do? Well, his lonely responsibility is the final sound of an issued record. The way he goes about getting that sound is a very individual matter. There is no particularly right way to make a record, but many different routes to the same end. And horses for courses, one type of record requires different handling from another. The late, great, Goddard Lieberson left us many gems from the world of the original cast album, but I doubt that he would have had much joy producing a group such as Led Zeppelin.

The first and most important thing for a producer is to find and work with an artiste whom he likes and believes in. If he has not got faith in his charge, no amount of technique will make a great record. Enthusiasm is a *sine qua non*. Likewise the material must be right, and he should be convinced it fits the artiste perfectly. I cannot stress this too much. Content is everything. If the producer is handling a singer who does not write songs, he must search and search until he finds the right number for that person. And if the singer has a favourite song that the producer believes is wrong for him, he must use every trick in the book to ensure that the right one is recorded. With a singer-songwriter, selection is a different kind of problem, for it is all too easy to bruise egos, and even the greatest composers write "dogs" at times. The creator is not necessarily the best judge of his own material. You know the old saying – the best thing about a spoilt child is that he is never in your own family.

So we come to the first requirement for a good producer – tact, diplomacy, call it what you will – it is the ability to have your will prevail without

making it obvious. If you make the artiste believe he has chosen well, that it is his idea to do what you want, you have made a big step forward. Of course, you had better be sure your judgement is good because, if it is not, you might as well forget about record producing. It is not the glamorous job it seems. It is painstaking, worrying, lengthy, and sometimes downright boring. But if you're good at it, it is immensely fulfilling.

Tact in handling highly talented people means getting on well with everyone. A firm rapport in the studio is a must in my opinion. I know of certain producers who go for the opposite, and believe that a certain aggressiveness leads to greater performance. Well, it doesn't work for me. A highly charged atmosphere is no place for the creation of great music. I like a cool environment to work in. That is not to say that excitement is missing. It is wonderful to feel electricity generated by creative people working in harmony. But a serene delight is the perfect aim. And that means getting your groundwork right.

Let us assume we have a great song for our artiste. Whether we have acquired it after hours of listening to rejected material or whether we have even insignificantly been part of the process of its creation, we have arrived at our choice. The chapters in this book written by the most illustrious of songwriters reveal the extent of the craft, and how meticulous and painstaking is a song's origin. Rarely does a masterpiece tumble out of the brain of its creator in an instant. And the producer should understand that work, encourage and foster it and, if he dares, guide it and alter it. But again, a note of caution. Often, when I get carried away with an idea of changing a song for the better, I question my nerve. Who are you, I say, a musician who has never actually written a No. 1 hit, to criticize and suggest alterations and improvements to a work written by someone who has spent his life creating great songs? Such arrogance! It is a chastening thought, and, suitably reflective, I answer by saying that it is necessary for everyone to listen to another voice. That voice may not be accepted, but it serves to question, even to strengthen, the creative process. No-one should be afraid of it.

Preparing for recording

This participation, if enacted with tact and warmth and lack of conceit, can be fruitful and lead to the development of the song in its arrangement. The shaping of the material is very much a matter for the producer along with the composer and the arranger. A consensus of good taste is required from all parties, and it helps to get all this sorted out before one puts a foot in the studio. Invariably the writer will have made a cheap demo record of the song which serves as a springboard for ideas. Do we have a written score? Shall we start with a basic rhythm track and add an orchestration later? Shall we group together some favourite musicians and make "head" arrangements in the studio? We must work it out in advance and prepare accordingly. The studio itself has to be chosen and booked along with the engineer of one's choice; the right musicians selected and a suitable date found for the coming together of these talents. The system of recording has to be decided on, whether it is 8, 16 or 24 track multitrack or even digital. The professional producer will have his organization so effective that all the apparently mundane but vital necessities fall into place imperceptibly smoothly. An efficient and understanding secretary who does all the leg work is a must, and I have been blessed with immense help from that quarter.

I have stressed the importance of rapport with the artiste. There must be a firm bond between the producer and the performer – as Quincy Jones puts it, a kind of loving trust that will shine in the final performance. Similarly, a bond must be forged with the recording engineer. As years have passed we have seen the emergence of the engineer/producer, a self-contained production unit where the two jobs are combined. Some are very good and make wonderful records. But I am old fashioned enough to believe that two heads are better than one, provided they work as one. For many years I have worked in harness with Geoff Emerick, who has the best pair of ears in the business, and we know each other so well that we do not talk much in the studio. Our relative roles have been forged over so many sessions that we complement each other naturally. Of course, we like and trust each other so that occasionally we do overlap. I might question some aspect of Geoff's equalization or ask him to alter the ambience of an instrument, and likewise he could bring my attention to a dubious bass tuning or a "froggy" vocal note. It works wonderfully well. I know that Quincy has a similar partnership with Bruce Swedien, and I was delighted and surprised to find out how similar were our ways of working.

This does not mean that I do not work with many other fine engineers. Indeed, it is necessary, for Geoff produces many valuable records of his own, and if our dates do not coincide we

obviously go our own ways. Interestingly, when Geoff produces, he sometimes prefers to have an engineer working with him for, as I do, he believes in the separate roles.

Getting to the soul of the artiste

Empathy with the artiste goes beyond a mutual respect. The producer must get inside the very soul of his charge, and bring out the depth of feeling that lies beneath the surface. And if the artiste is the writer of the song, the producer must probe his mind to find out what he means and how he wants the song to sound.

Some creators are more articulate than others, but most people do not really know what they want until they hear it, so a lot of guessing and intuitive reasoning must be employed in the design and the construction of the records. Paul McCartney was always definite in his ideas, and it is true to say that most creative thoughts in The Beatles came from him. John Lennon, on the other hand, lacked the dogged persistence for thinking out detail, and one had to search for his ideas. But his songs were inherently so full of atmosphere that the construction of their recordings became almost like an archaeological dig, and equally rewarding. When John first presented me with the song *Being For The Benefit of Mr. Kite* for instance, I had known its origin. John would often take his inspiration from the written word, be it newspaper, slogan, or in this case an old Victorian poster that he had hanging on the wall in his house.

The word imagery in the song required an imaginative frame to convey the atmosphere of a circus of olden days. One had to be able to smell the sawdust in the ring and be dazzled by the swirling lights of the fairground. I reasoned that the most characteristic sound of a fairground or circus was that of the calliope – the steam organ of olden times. To get this effect I needed three sounds. First, I used a bass harmonica within the rhythm pumping away on the first and third beats of the bar. Dear old Mal Evans, The Beatles' faithful roadie, jumped at the opportunity of being able to play this part. The next and more important line was that of the melody at the end of the first vocal refrain, where the music goes into "Harry the horse dancing the waltz". John wanted the tune to take over in a kind of swooping and swirling sound as he described it. So I

Overleaf
The original arrangements by George Martin for *Eleanor Rigby* and *I Am The Walrus. Eleanor Rigby* has two violin parts, a viola and a cello. *I Am The Walrus* uses horns, violins, cello and bass clarinet. Lyrics are written in, including Lennon's "Goo goo goo joob".

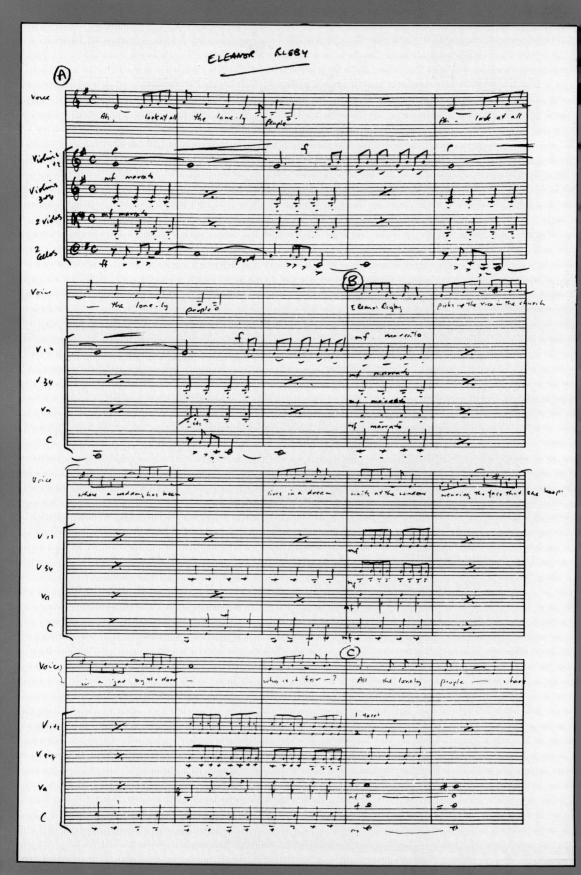

ELEANOR RIGBY

got John to play the tune on one organ while I played very fast chromatic runs on another for a kind of rotary swirling effect. But I couldn't get my runs fast enough for what I wanted, so I used the old and simple method of changing the tape speed to raise my speed of playing. By switching the 30-inch machine down to 15-inch and getting John to play an octave lower at half the speed, I had twice as much time in which to complete my chromatic runs, and when brought back to normal speed the effect was really scintillating!

So far so good, but I still needed a little bit more to give that circus sound. Nowadays, of course, we would probably use a very sophisticated synthesizer but they just hadn't been invented at that time. I asked my secretary to do some research and dig up old steam organ recordings. They operated on the pianola principle and were driven by paper rolls with holes punched in them. There were quite a few recordings still in existence, but they were all of well known tunes – marches by Souza and so on – and I didn't want to run into any copyright difficulties nor did I want identifiable tunes anyway. So I transferred one or two of these recordings to tape and then got the engineer to chop up the tape into little pieces about 15 inches long. When he'd done that I told him to throw them all up in the air and mix them up. He obviously thought I'd gone a bit bonkers, and even more so when I asked him to splice them together again in a random order. It's amazing how when you want to get a random effect, life plays tricks on you. A lot of the pieces came back together in the right order, but by reshuffling, and turning things back to front and so on, I eventually ended up with a tape that bore no resemblance to any tune at all but was unmistakably a steam organ. This was my background "wash" and by pasting it in the back of the sound, so to speak, I finally clinched the circus sound. John was delighted with it and he wasn't an easy person to please.

Translating an idea into sound

So we come to the next important attribute of a producer: I have already mentioned tact, empathy with the performers, and organization, taste, and technique. A producer has to develop the ability to translate an idea into sound alone. His or her imagination must be used to its maximum extent. There is a great palette of sound colours that we can dip our brush into, but we must use taste and discretion in doing so. As with oil painting, if one heaps too many colours on the canvas, either the result is a bizarre mess that confuses the eye or, if the colours run, we end up with a very muddy picture; so in sound, too much

"colour" can be self defeating and result in confusion. I have heard so many records guilty of being over produced because too much has been attempted. The producer must learn how far he can go in complicating his sound before the effects begin to cancel each other out. He must always remember that the voice must be heard and the song given a clear interpretation.

Experience, of course, counts for a great deal in record production and, while it is perfectly possible for a raw producer to get lucky with a hit, the craft can only be mastered by continual work with different artistes. It is useful to work in different studios too, as each has its own characteristics and there is no better way of learning than by experience. There is inevitably an overlap with the producer's role and that of the engineer, and our budding hit-maker should learn about the acoustic and technical problems that the engineer has to cope with. I had the advantage of growing up with the development of the industry and so I began in the days before multitrack recording existed. Let us consider the sessions in those days. Originally, the ideal recording was that which most faithfully reproduced the original sound, so the producer would concentrate on getting the best arrangement from the band and the best performance from

the vocalist. The engineer had to obtain the finest balance of the whole ensemble in one go, using microphones which had little discretion in their pick up; so that his balance was essentially a *blend* of sound. Every microphone was picking up a great deal of sound, not only from the instrument it favoured, but to a lesser extent all the other instruments as well. The art of recording was very much a matter of using the acoustics of the studio and careful placing of the instruments to obtain a natural balance.

I had worked a great deal in the enormous No. 1 Studio at Abbey Road and had made many a fine classical recording there with only one or two microphones. I remember trying this technique with the Basil Kirchin Band – a heavy brass and saxophone line-up with drums and timbales. Getting separation in that studio was almost impossible, but it was a useful lesson in microphone placing.

Nowadays, of course, even very loud instruments are close-miked or directly injected into the board so that the separation is not a problem, and the multitrack layering technique means

Abbey Road, No. 1 Studio: one of the largest, specialized recording studios in the world and the scene of many historic recordings, classical and popular, including *Sergeant Pepper*.

that all the separate sounds are clinically clean and free from the sound of any other instruments. While it makes life easy, it is also tedious and time consuming, and can lead to a sterility in sound. You know how in painting by numbers one is able to paint a picture by filling in delineated areas with separate colours. It is easy and effective, but I doubt if Rembrandt would have approved. Similarly, if our sounds on our musical canvas are too detached from each other, we can end up with a very mechanical and detached effect, and the clever engineer will deliberately use spill and ambience to improve the sound.

Young engineers and musicians are coming to realize that the "live" quality of a multi-performance recording adds tension and excitement to the sound, even if it is more difficult to handle.

From four-track to multi-multitrack

From the early days of mono, stereo and two-track recording, progress was painfully slow, so that when I came to produce the *Sergeant Pepper* album (which in truth began with the *Strawberry Fields/Penny Lane* recordings), I had still nothing better than four-track equipment to use. People have said to me with an almost holy reverence, "How did you manage to do it on only four tracks?" Well, the snappy catch answer was that I had no option! But in many ways it helped. First, one had to be very disciplined in the use of those tracks, and I had to plan ahead mentally whenever a new track was started. I became used to recording on one four-track machine from another, but obviously this ploy could not be used too frequently without serious loss of quality. Quite often we would put bass and drums together on one track, guitars on another, lead vocal on the third and we would preserve the fourth track for "extras" like lead guitar, or backing voices, or whatever. In more complicated songs, where we obviously needed more tracks, we would transfer our four tracks to two on another four-track machine and then fill up the two virgin tracks. *A Day In The Life* required the massive orchestral effect, and I used several four-tracks, and worried about fitting them together later. In 1967 we had no locking facilities between tape machines, so syncronizing was very much a hit and miss affair. If you

Overleaf
The control room at Cherokee Studios, Los Angeles: Paul McCartney looks on while Geoff Emerick and George Martin operate the mixing console. The two small speakers are Auratones, which give an idea of how a recording will sound on radio. (Photograph by Linda McCartney)

listen to *A Day In The Life,* you will hear the orchestra slightly out of time in places, but it doesn't matter.

When eight-track came along it was like manna from the gods, and the promise of 16 tracks was beyond belief.

Parkinson's law works here as in everything; if one has 24 tracks available one tends to use them.

Overdubbing a vocal track

One of the benefits of using a large number of tracks comes when one is attempting to produce a superb vocal track by overdubbing. Once the singer is comfortable with the studio, headphone balance and so on, and the engineer has made his adjustments to give the voice a good sound, I like to keep every performance I can. Sometimes a beautiful phrase will occur in an otherwise dull rendition, or the artiste will manage a new twist to a line that had not emerged before. By assembling five performances alongside each other on the multitrack I can then select the best part of each performance by bringing up the relevant fader. In this way a complete performance can be assembled that is the product of many "takes", all without editing and retaining the original backing.

A note of caution regarding the way we listen to a multitrack recording: the effect of 24 tracks in a good control room can be pretty impressive but one must never forget that, eventually, it has to be boiled down to two simple tracks, and will be heard in a wide range of listening conditions.

Balance and volume

I continue to be astonished at the extraordinarily high levels of sound that are experienced in many control rooms. Naturally, there is excitement in hearing fine music played loudly, but it can be deceptive and, of course, physically damaging if sustained for too long.

I make no apology for saying yet again that noise levels are too high – particularly in concerts. The levels pumped out by huge monitors are staggering and close proximity to them is bound to lead to damaged hearing. The sinister thing about impairment of hearing in this way is that its effect is often delayed by as much as four years. In the same way moderation is desirable in the control room too, not only for one's health, but because the balance can also be affected. I like to vary my level of listening, sometimes loud on the big JBLs, sometimes quietly on the little Auratone speakers, sometimes in between. The brain can act like a limiter and, at extreme levels, alter the balance of a sound, filtering out

AIR Studios, Montserrat, West Indies.

the "nuisance" elements and changing the interpretation.

Multi-multitrack recording

Of course, multitrack recording does nothing to improve the sound. It certainly increases tape noise, and it merely delays the moment of truth when one has eventually to commit everything to stereo. What it does do is to give one greater flexibility. In recent years I have been spoiled as a producer by having at my command the best recording facilities in the world. In London, at AIR Studios, and at my AIR Studio on the West Indian island Montserrat I am able to lock two 24-track machines together and this facility gives one an unlimited number of tracks.

The *Tug Of War* album with Paul McCartney, The Little River Band album, *Time Exposure,* and Ultravox's *Quartet* album were all produced

using this useful facility.

This is how the technique works. We begin in the ordinary way on one 24-track machine, laying down the backing track and being extravagant in the use of tracks. It is perfectly possible to use seven tracks on drums alone, two on bass guitar, two on piano or stereo synthesizer, two more on double-tracked guitar and so on. When one is using a locking pulse, one track has to be retained for the SMPTE code and it is advisable to leave the adjacent track clear also. And if a Linn drum track is used (even for a guide), it is very easy to find that all 24 tracks have been filled fairly quickly.

Right, now suppose I need to add an orchestra at a later date; a "slave" tape is then made up, with a coded track to lock it to the master, and a roughly mixed version of the master on six or seven tracks. The remaining tracks can now be filled, yes filled, with the orchestral addition. Suppose I want backing voices with a choral sound, but only using three people? Another slave is made up in the same way as slave 1, and the empty tracks are filled with voices (twelve to sixteen lines of voices make a great sound).

And so the process goes on, extravagantly using new slaves for each batch of sound. When it is perfect each one is mixed down to stereo and inserted on to a "master" slave. Only when the final mix is ready do we permanently run two multitrack machines in harness, and we mix any number of tracks up to 46 down to two.

It is a luxurious process, surprisingly quick and effective, but it requires great discipline from the engineer and his assistant, and meticulous book-keeping. It is all too easy to get confused with many different tapes and scores of tracks, and a clear head is vital at all times.

There are a number of technical advantages. First, there is little wear on the master track of rhythm sounds. On conventional multi-track recordings the original tape is played time and again during the overdub process, and you would be surprised how many times the tape passes to and fro across the heads. Wear is inevitable with a deceiving loss of quality. Not so on the multi-multi system. Once the original rhythm is complete it is not touched again until the final mix.

An added bonus which we had not bargained for was a decrease in background noise. I can only agree with Geoff Emerick on this, who believes that, as the final mix comes from separate sounds on the multitrack machines, the only sound common to both machines is the background tape sound which sometimes phases itself if not out, then certainly lower. The result, using 30 inches per second tape speed and Dolbys on selected tracks (like bass guitar, for instance), is very clean indeed, and is about the ultimate until one gets to digital recording.

Digital recording

If description of techniques in recording sounds unartistic, remember that it is all part and parcel of the process that the good producer must have at his fingertips. Not only should he be able to advise the artistes on musical matters, he must be fully conversant with everything that goes on in the studio. There are so many "toys" available in studios nowadays. Outboard equipment is being produced in ever more novel forms, and each time I see something new I ask, "What does it do, and does it do it better than its predecessor?" I have yet to find a really great noiseless harmonizer that will pitchchange a large interval without a tiresome glitch, but quantum leaps are being made in the manufacture of all these instruments of effect, and no doubt perfection is possible at a price.

Which brings me to digital recording. It has been a long time coming, and even today very few studios have multitrack digital recording. Personally, I like it, although I know many musicians who are uneasy with it. The absolute ceiling of 20 Kilohertz in frequency range may have something to do with that, but my personal aural equipment is not capable of hearing such high frequencies (very few people are blessed or cursed with a receptivity beyond 16 Kilohertz), so digital presents this one with no problems.

Many people are mystified by digital recording. They have heard it is better, but they have no idea what it is about. Let me give a brief explanation. Ordinary recording stores the electrical impulses (which have been converted from the pure aural vibration by the microphone) on magnetic tape as magnetic variations in the coating.

Digital recording on the other hand, analyzes the frequencies constantly and stores the information as a binary code on tape in the same way as a computer operates. If you can imagine "stop-framing" a slice of sound, analyzing it in terms of frequencies, converting the information into numbers to store on tape and doing that fifty thousand times a second, that is what a digital recorder does. And on playback, a reverse process takes place, with sound being reconstituted from the codes on tape. There is no background noise of tape hiss or interference between tracks, no distortion and very high signal to noise ratio. It is virtually impossible to distinguish between live sound and a digital recording. So what's the drawback? In a word, expense. The system is very expensive to buy – more than twice the amount of a conventional system and there is little likelihood of the price coming down, because of its complexity. In effect, it puts an extra 3000 dollars a week on to a recording project, and not many artistes or record companies want that overhead these days. It will, of course, be thrown into sharper focus when the compact disc becomes popular, for the present system of vinyl pressings offer such inferior average quality, alas, that ultra-superb recording quality makes little difference.

Tricks of the trade

As we know, multitrack gives us the opportunity to overlay one sound many times, so that theoretically one could make a symphony orchestra out of a string quartet. Well I am sure the Musicians' Union would not smile on that idea, but it is very useful to record multitracked background voices. A live choir gives a particular sound that is good but quite often not the personal blend that is required, while the same voice recorded many times is able to duplicate the inflections and nuances perfectly.

When producing *Tug Of War* I found that Paul, Linda and Eric Stewart's voices blended very well together if they sang the same note. Building up a background choral sound became a matter of designing the part and then recording the three singers singing unison on each part three or four times. I would thus use sixteen to twenty tracks on any one piece. And where a long sustained note is to be sung it was possible to overcome shortage of breath by "dropping in" on the tracks. I would record a line as far as they could go before the voices became unsteady, then run the tape back a beat or two and re-record from that point. By dropping in on the tracks a continuous sustain could be achieved. Of course, there would often be a slight bump in the sustained sound where the drop-in occurred, which meant that a different place in time had to be selected for each drop-in. But when 16 or more tracks were played together these blemishes could not be detected. Listen to *The Pound Is Sinking*. There is a very long backing vocal which ends in a low hum that is quite impossible to do "live", even for a trained singer. I think it sounds good.

Harmonizers are very useful tools in the studio. The addition of a harmonized version of a guitar track to the original, if subtly treated, can give a 12-string effect that is pleasant, and it can of course be used to correct faulty tuning. I have occasionally patched just one note in an otherwise perfect phrase using a harmonizer to correct the pitch. And a harmonizer with a wide pitch change – say about a third (about 25 per cent increase or decrease) – can do weird and wonderful things to the spoken voice, making one sound like Minnie Mouse or Elliot Gould with a cold.

Noise gates are very useful, too. Sometimes I like to do what I call musical stencilling. On one occasion, during the recording of Paul McCartney's *Hey, Hey* track, I wanted the rhythm guitar to play a very brittle, fast and complicated rhythm. When it became obvious he was not going to get it with enough precision, I quickly wrote the rhythm down – it was a two bar phrase – and gave it to Steve Gadd who, without batting an eyelid, played it perfectly first time over the passage in question, using a stick on a cowbell. This sharp sound was not meant to be heard on the track, however. Instead, I got Paul to get a good sound on the Yamaha CS80 and play a sustained series of chords. Then I used the cowbell sound to trigger the release mechanism of a Kepex gate which allowed the Yamaha to be heard only when the cowbell was triggering. We were in effect punching holes in the silence – hence my description stencilling – and the result was a very tight sophisticated rhythm in impeccable time. The same technique works with any sound, even voices.

These ideas are great fun to do, but one must never use them for the sake of it – only if it is right for the song. I make no apologies for saying once again that all this modern trickery only puts the gloss on the production but it is not important by itself. The music and the performance are supreme. That we must never forget.

Sequencing

Once all the recording is finally complete there is an important task still remaining: all tracks need to be put into a running order (sequencing). This has a significant effect on the way a listener hears a record, particularly for the first time. Imagine starting the *Sergeant Pepper* album with *A Day In The Life*; there would be nothing left after the first track. We must attract attention in the beginning, sustain interest in the middle, end the first side with a feeling of satisfaction yet leave the listener wanting more. The second side is similar, although the need for a good opening is not as great as on side one, and the finale should ideally clinch the whole album with its last notes.

One always tries to have a good number of single tracks in an album and if I had five tracks out of ten that I thought were hits I would probably place them at one, two, five, six and ten to get maximum effect. But, leaving commercial considerations aside, the flow of the album is by far the most important factor.

Distances between tracks, too, have to be considered. Some pieces require a little silence before the following track starts. (Although in Jeff Beck's album *Blow by Blow* I deliberately chose to overlap the tracks with each other, running the album almost like a disc jockey to maintain the pace.)

There is a final small consideration. I try hard to make each side last the same amount of time – as far as is possible. For one thing, keeping playing time down to 20 minutes per side gives me a chance to make the record sound louder without distortion. Also, when that album is issued on cassette, an even running time avoids an embarrassing wait at the end of the tape for the "turn over" side to finish running – another commercial consideration.

Conclusion

Looking back twenty years, I remember recording The Beatles first album in a single day. It was direct recording to stereo, of course, but in eleven hours we recorded ten songs – finished. Today people spend months creating albums and, if a project is completed in three weeks, the suspicion is that something is wrong with it. And yet I can listen to those early records and not be ashamed, so I ask the question, "Have we progressed a great deal?". Well, certainly one can never go back, and competition is so keen today that the product has to be impeccable, technically and artistically. What is more, it must have soul. It must lift the emotions of the listener. It must come from the heart.●

Producing Records

I was a violinist – a child prodigy, I'm afraid – who started working in studios because I wanted to play jazz. My first job was in a demo studio – sweeping the floors. At 17 I started making demos with two friends. We did them for next to nothing, working very fast and cutting lots of corners by doing everything ourselves, right down to the background vocals and harmonies. None of the sophisticated equipment was around then. If you wanted echo there was nothing with which to make it; this was in the days before plates. I remember Les Paul's studio, which was at his home, had a tunnel under the yard which he used for recording echo.

Starting out as an engineer

I became involved in the technical side of music because the speed at which we made the demos meant that we each had to do more than one job. The bass player doubled as the singer, and so on. The quicker we worked, the better editor I became. After a couple of years I decided to risk everything on a studio of my own. A & R began in 1960. It was a small three track studio with a good ambience that became pretty popular. I spent the rest of the decade there as an engineer. I suspect that quite a few of my chances to break into production were thwarted because my partners thought it wasn't right for me to do so; it would have been competing with the clients.

My first real studio experience was cutting acetates – at that time the intermediate stage between tape and disc – which taught me more about things like sibilance and bad echo than anything else. The first echo plates weren't terribly good. Then we got two monos and started using echo delay. I began playing around with delay after hearing it on all the Columbia recordings. It was such a special sound that I used to sneak over there and watch people like Streisand recording in an effort to discover the secret. It turned out the engineer was using reverb and splitting the sound by mixing the echo and the reverb. I was always using reverb after that, mainly to compensate for the small size of my studio, which was by no means an orchestral room, although on occasions we crammed as many as 50 musicians into the place.

A good reverb man was worth his weight in gold. Most people didn't know how to use the plates and broke the springs. The metal of the plate has a pitch that shouldn't be changed once it's right. You're better off with four chambers at different lengths, if you can afford them, and isolating the vocals from the band. This was popular in stereo around then because it created the effect of the band having dimension and the singer a much shorter sound.

At the end of the 1960s everybody was expanding and A & R was involved in building various studios around the country. Then somebody from *Billboard* convinced A & R to go into the record business – just in time for the big slump of 1970. Well, at least I got to produce my first legitimate record, a hit that went down the toilet because of bad distribution. It was a real disappointment. I decided, if I couldn't produce records my own way, to stay an engineer. It didn't turn out like that because young people kept approaching me to do demos at weekends, and build new acts. The time in between was spent training new engineers.

Musicians were always asking about the latest sound and recording techniques. I gradually built up a tremendous rapport with them, especially because a lot of producers never bothered to show up for recordings. I didn't really care about the credits or the royalties. The magic of the studio was enough.

Studio techniques

As a musician I know how unnatural it can feel playing in a studio. Separating the sounds often means physically separating the musicians, which is not how most of them are used to playing. I always maintain eye contact with them even though this means abandoning the screens that prevent spill.

In fact, spillage gives tremendous atmosphere. We first realized this on the old Bacharach/Dionne Warwick recordings. We never shut down the string mikes, even when they weren't playing, because it lent an extra dimension to the record. When the strings did come in they really were there rather than suddenly being introduced from a dead spot.

Recent recording fashions have preferred to keep everything separate and clinical. Fortunately, it's going the other way now. More and more artists want that explosive sound, especially from the drums, that you can never get from an isolated atmosphere. We used to copy Gus Dudgeon's drum sound, which was unique in that way, with none of the fatback snare popularized by Motown. In the States people still talk about "English drums" and I love that sound when you open everything up.

I rarely put anything around the drums, even with an acoustic piano, which is about the hardest thing to record. With Billy Joel we put his piano about six to eight feet away from the drums. The pressure from the two instruments sounds like a hundred tons spilling into each other, it's terrific. If you isolate the instruments you never get any competition between them. And how much isolation do you really need?

Contact with the musicians is all important. Working with headphones you might as well be in a different room. Earphones give a certain amount of feeling but they don't tell you when the atmosphere in the studio is really cooking. It's better to sit in with the musicians because in the control room you don't hear what's in the musicians' headphones. You can use a monitor, but it's not exactly what they're hearing because of the vibration of the studio itself.

I'm a nut about the musicians' headsets. I cue, limit and set them before the musicians arrive, subdividing them into whatever groupings we're using depending on the variety of the mix. Years ago we built a cue system based on multiples of two tracks running live which enabled us to sweeten the two track directly into the musicians' 'phones so they could listen to what the producer heard. Billy Joel loves hearing the effect on his voice while he's singing. It makes him perform differently. If you've got an echo on his voice he can hear it. I'm told John Lennon always put an echo on his voice and it made him elated just to hear it. Everyone's got different tastes too. If I set a mix for Paul Simon and give him what he wants, he'll still make his own adjustments. When you plug your headphones into his set it sounds quite different.

Getting the right take

Artists aren't comfortable with strangers in the studio. I discourage visitors, even family, because musicians often start showing off for them. All phone calls are blocked, except emergencies. I'd rather stay nine hours in the studio and have food sent in than break the concentration. Once it's gone, the atmosphere evaporates.

I hate rehearsing probably because of my early days doing demos three or four at a time, fixing them as we went. I like musicians to know the song long before we record. Normally you find your model in the freshness of the first few takes while everyone still feels spontaneous. The heart of the record is often in those early

takes. It's rather like being able to refer to a demo to remind yourself why you originally wanted to do a song. A demo can have something you've overlooked and lost by mistake in the recording.

If nothing has happened after an hour or so I suggest moving on to something else, which can be rough on the artist. But if you don't get something in five takes you're unlikely to get it in 20. You just end up sitting around wasting time. With repetition musicians can get too slick and intellectual, resorting to the same licks, the things they've heard and think you want. Sometimes when two guitarists get together it causes what I call guitarrhea. They have a great thing going playing off each other that's nothing to do with the song. Such excess is better avoided as it unbalances the other musicians. Then I'll cut in with other instruments, which can annoy a musician if he feels you're interrupting his ego. This can be awkward because one of the main functions of a producer is to encourage and reassure musicians' egos. It's the only way to keep them on top of something.

We'll roll three or four takes in a row, make a mix of the best, then try it a couple more times. I always do vocals live with the band unless it's clear that the singer will perform more freely alone later. Then I'll overdub. It's preferable to bring up different tracks rather than editing different takes or dropping in overdubs. It's hard cutting together different takes and you'll still need an overdub.

If something's wrong – like bad phrasing or someone out of tune – we cut the track again rather than trying to fix it. If just one person's out then you can repair it. The bass player might say, "I'm tired. I'll shoot it once more and if you still don't like it, I'll come in again tomorrow when I'm fresh." If you have the confidence of the musician you can get that kind of co-operation.

I make mistakes too. Stuff ends up in the garbage can. But basically it's cheaper to recut rather than trying to patch it up. You can easily lose something or get distracted with the sweetening. It's important to remember that sweetening is just that. It won't disguise deficiencies in the original. Better to do it again.

Edit as you go along. It's easy to leave something in because you might use it later. The danger is that you'll forget about it, so it's best to cut immediately. It's like adding percussion or treble to a mix: suddenly it sounds more interesting, a usually false impression that can get you sidetracked later. Anyway, it's always possible to interlock the section into another machine for later reference. The great advantage of editing

Billy Joel

as you go is that it forces you to think about the gaps and discourages commonplace or second rate ideas from sneaking through too easily. Experimenting first on a synthesizer can be useful: it gives you a feeling about something without the need to commit yourself.

Producers and artists

Billy Joel and I always laugh at the way his band listens to a finished record: they hear the groove but they don't listen to the whole unit. A producer is someone who has to try and imagine that complete unit from the beginning.

The fundamental point of being a producer is the relationship with the artist. First you have to convince a band or singer that you're not going to put your stamp all over their work. It helps to know an artist's work and to discover their strong points before recording. Rapport is better if someone knows they can speak to you. If I have a fault it's that I cater far too much for the musicians. I drop my ego in the studio, but I do like to feel free to say what I think.

Producers should never cramp artists. At the same time you have to convince them of your editing ability. It's a delicate balance. After a couple of flops where I had no control, I decided not to go into the studio with any act until we'd spent a couple of weeks checking each other out. If artists' egos are in the wrong place you can tell after a couple of meetings. It's like being out on a first date: they might tell you they love your records; what they don't tell you until the second

or third date is that's not what they want. Often they're after something you did in the past, something with which you're no longer comfortable because it's too easy. Or worse, they ask you to start sounding like someone else.

There's a different kind of egotism around today than there was ten years ago. Now everyone seems to think they know how they should sound. And you can easily end up doing a service job; they don't really want your touch at all. (This isn't to say that producers should have a recognizable trademark. In fact, I go out of my way not to repeat myself.) I love working with the big stars so long as they don't have preconceptions about how they should sound. I don't want to be a service producer and would much rather be able to make a fresh approach.

Artists usually want a producer because they like the way he did a particular record. But they don't want to sacrifice the control they've had, or feel they ought to have. If you don't manipulate them in the wrong direction, or play games with them, it's possible to manoeuvre most artists around to your way of thinking.

Pre-production is mainly a matter of gaining confidence and respect. This is most important with singer/songwriters who invariably are overprotective towards their material. I'm not a publisher and I'm not looking for a credit on the song, but I do like to help with the writing. Hardest of all is letting artists know that criticism of a song they've written isn't personal. If a song is really terrible, it's up to the producer, as a kind of

Phil Ramone

Barbra Streisand in *A Star Is Born*

helpful mirror to what's happening, to say so. That can be difficult on first acquaintance. If the singer's in love with the song, let them go ahead until they trust you enough to know that you're not out to clobber them. I work just as hard on the duds and stress the importance of getting the vocal right, which helps take the artist's mind off any basic criticism. Insecurity shows in a recording. In the end the duds eliminate themselves when they're laid alongside the good tracks.

A Star Is Born

Marrying film and music is perhaps even more exciting than working in the studio. In 1976, when I did the movie *A Star Is Born* with Barbra Streisand, we decided to record the whole thing live. I didn't want Barbra to lip-sync at all, which meant that the musicians had to perform live for every take. We did this on two 16 track machines linked together. The movie – whether it's a masterpiece or not – was an extraordinarily ambitious undertaking from the sound angle and we really succeeded in capturing every little bit of that live quality. There was very little sweetening apart from some dummy strings in a couple of scenes which we did later on a synthesizer.

Roger Kellaway did the recording. Before we started I advised him to carry a cassette recorder with him everywhere because I knew Barbra would be constantly changing the arrangements. There were four copyists and four orchestrators always on hand in anticipation of what was about to happen. Sure enough, there were as many as three or four arrangements for each song. I had every piece of information stored on different tracks.

Barbra has so many ideas and is such a perfectionist that you have to be incredibly together to keep up with her. I made her carry a cassette recorder too, on which to note all her ideas. Nearly always she came up with a variety of approaches to every song: she has an incredible way with a line.

On one occasion it was three days before she accepted a take on one piece of scoring. The band stood up and applauded. I admire her attitude and perseverance. Better that than working with the kind of artist who loves something on the day and loathes it a month later. One thing about Barbra, and Paul Simon too, is that she suspects something if it's too easy. When a recording goes down too quickly she insists on finding out everything else that can be done to it before finally making up her mind.

Strangely enough, Barbra couldn't understand that the musicians needed time too. "The band has to be right too," I'd tell her. "Well, I sang

okay," she'd say. I pampered her to the point of spoiling her. She wouldn't like the strings in one part, then she would, or she'd ask for the backing singers to be dropped, then she'd want them back again. I had multiple tracks rolling all the time. I used a maglink and interlocked everything, and, as it was all done live, we had to keep incredibly close checks on what was happening. Barbra is fantastic singing live with the rhythm section on stage in the movie. What you see is what we recorded.

Our only argument during filming was over the closing song. Her first attempt was a magnificent combination of acting and singing: she cried, she did everything right, except something was missing. She was furious when I told her. Luckily, the director, Jon Peters, backed me up. The next morning, before the set was dismantled, Barbra went back and did another take. She was so moving that we were all in tears. It's all in the movie. Originally Barbra intended to play the song over images from the film. I told her to stay with her singing the song using just the centre camera on her face. Her face and what she was feeling as she sang said far more than anything else could have done. I'm very visual as a producer and that's what I try to get on record: pure performance.

Making the artist perform

Inspiration is the vital factor in producing. I always look for it in the performance. There must be an emotional connection that you have to get down on the record. It's got to come off the disc every time you hear it. Singers really get to me if they have that ability to perform on record.

If the singer plays an instrument the best way to record them is to let them play. Paul Simon has no confidence in his vocals unless he's accompanying himself at the same time. With Billy Joel we put a couple of blankets over the piano and let him pound away because he sounds completely different singing on his feet. He may look creased and awkward hunched over the piano, but that's the way he performs best.

If it feels right, you can be totally crazy and break all the rules. Once with Mick Jagger we put four speakers on screaming, gave him a hand mike and let him run around the room. It's not his style to stand still in front of one microphone. It worked fine, even with all the bass and drum leakage – that's the way their records sound. If you know what you're doing technically, you can cover just about anything.

That animal energy of live performance – with the singer roaring and the drums screaming: I'll go to any lengths to capture that on record.●

Producing Records

I had no ambitions to become a record producer; it was all an accident. I had only a vague idea about what a producer did.

I was known mainly as an actor although I'd done some solo work with Mickie Most on his RAK label, which was when I found production starting to fascinate me more than writing. I was playing in *Jesus Christ Superstar* with Paul Nicholas, who was keen to make some singles, when Robert Stigwood – who had heard one of my songs – suggested that Paul and I work together. In those days a role in *Jesus Christ Superstar* qualified you for a pop single. We found two writers, Bugatti and Musker, and recorded three titles that were instant hits. It was a very easy way in for me.

The performance

Most producers either have an engineering background or are musicians. Being an actor as well as a singer – I do all the backing vocals on my records, and I play guitar – really helps me producing hit singles. A single must have a sense of theatre. Rather like a one-act play, it opens, gets immediately to the point, then ends. A sense of performance, because of the atmosphere it evokes, is almost as important as the tune itself. Glynis Johns can't really sing but she "performs" *Send In The Clowns* so well that there isn't a dry eye in the house. Sung better the song would probably lose its honesty.

A recording of mine that deliberately aimed for a strong, spooky sense of theatre is *Dancing In The City*, which was a big European hit for a duo called Marshall Hain. It was particularly pleasing because it was the first British record to use syn drums. In almost all my work this theatrical frame of reference is there in the background. I'm sure it helps singers and players to give good performances.

Nine to Five

Nine To Five first came to our attention as a demo. It was a miserable failure because, as with many demos, the structure was incorrect. They'd started with the bridge, which was all wrong. But there was this great hook which, in true demo tradition, either came in too soon or too late, and stayed too long or not long enough. And this great big hook, with a dirty sounding saxophone

like something from an old Emile Ford number, reminded me of the frog in *Pinky and Perky*. I kept on seeing this frog! The best way I could describe it to the sax player, whom I'd never met before we came to record, was to ask him to play it like Lord Rockingham. "Yes," he said, "I was in Lord Rockingham."

The song was for a new girl signed by EMI about whom the BBC were doing a documentary. Her name was Sheena Easton. She was delightful, like a breath of fresh air; she even made the tea. We played her the old version of the song only once, then the arranger/pianist who was with us played her the restructured version, which was much simpler. By working to a note in the bridge of the song, which is its "ceiling", we found the key in which she was most comfortable.

First the bass, drums and keyboard were laid down. We used lots of tracks for vocals and bounced them down to a stereo picture. After the basic rhythm sections were completed, I did all the "oohs and aahs" and the big hook vocals, bounced them down, then added the guitars and all the sequences. Sheena was the last thing to go on. Because she was a novice it was important that she should have a record to sing to rather

Sheena Easton

Christopher Neil

than having to imagine the sounds accompanying her. So we made the record for her, got a nice balance in the cans for her to listen to, and then she sang.

It doesn't always work like that. With some singers you can take the best of several performances and edit them together, redoing a line or a section here or there and dropping it in. Someone like Sheena, who goes for the take and gives it everything, finds it difficult to leap into a performance half-way through a verse. With her background in pubs and clubs she really only understands closing her eyes and starting from the top.

Style

I suppose every record producer has a style, although I'm not sure that's necessarily a good thing. The advantage of anonymity is that you can keep ahead of the fads, so the public never has the chance to say, "Oh, that was last year!" Recognizable styles easily become passé. As for style reflecting taste, I hope that my tastes are still changing enough for me to not make the same kind of records all my life.

In the end, it all comes down to instinct. You get a gut-feeling when an arrangement is right. Like we say, 'It feels like a record, it sounds like a record.'●

Producing Records

I like to approach every project like I've never done it before and will never do it again. It's best to rely on the same intuition and instinct you used the very first time you produced a record. I try not to get too hung up on a big, extensive pre-production process because it often turns into a very sterile affair. Keep everything fresh and don't look back at what you've just done, whether or not it was successful. Also keep from getting into rigid routines so that every time is like opening a little Pandora's box. You have to play psychological games with yourself so you don't freak out each time. A lot of movie directors, when they try to get a picture together, imagine themselves sitting in the front row on opening night watching a film directed by somebody they don't really like too much. You really get to be moved in that kind of situation.

Working with artists

The better you know the artist as a person, the easier it is to develop a musical sense. Michael Jackson is truly a *friend* and I think we know each other pretty well both personally and musically. Michael is one of the finest artists and human beings on this planet. We talk about everything all the time, not only music. On the last album, *Off The Wall,* we felt "Okay, Michael, it's time to grow up, not to be a little bubblegum singer anymore, to go out and feel everything you're supposed to feel at 21 years-old". So I asked myself, as though I wasn't involved as a producer, what I'd like to hear Michael sing that would move me emotionally. You can try to guess the commercial potential of a record but the best way is to please yourself and trust the goose pimples and that old gut feeling. That's really the basis of producing. Training and past experience as an arranger/producer/conductor/ composer all come into play, but it's best to lead with your instincts and support them with your craft. Film scoring experience doesn't hurt either, because pop records can only be enhanced with a theatrical and/or dramatic touch.

Music is the result of what we are as people; I've always felt that. If it's not magical to you, nobody else'll like it. So you're always waiting for those special moments, trying to produce magic from a chemistry between people, in whatever situation is right for them. Some artists need to be uptight to really perform, with their adrenalin at its peak, others need to be relaxed, yet in the end there's no guarantee that 28 to 29 takes will necessarily produce that magic. In fact, the entire entertainment industry is about trying to "bottle lightning". There's also a saying we have in the studio that goes: you have to leave space, after you've done your homework, to let the Lord walk through the room.

Collaborators

I use the same team of people a lot of the time, which helps. Every now and then I stray off, but I always run back to the family, as I call them. Most of the group are very flexible. My engineer, Bruce Swedien, who has been with me for 23 years, was there at the beginning when we worked with Dinah Washington, Sarah Vaughan and Billy Eckstine in Chicago; then he went off with the Chicago Symphony for 11 years. Working with people from a similar background, whether pop or classical, counts for a lot. If you can get brilliance out of a classical piccolo trumpet, maybe you can use that to good effect recording Patti Austin, James Ingram or Lena Horne.

It's great to work with a combination of intuitive and trained musicians because they're both going in the same direction but coming from a different source. The trained musician needs his paper in front of him with every demi-semi-quaver written there; the intuitive one uses private little codes and learns how to notate everyone else's code. Rod Temperton doesn't read or write music, yet he is one of the few songwriters I know who also understands arranging. He has an innate contrapuntal sense, whether it's for vocal backgrounds or accompaniments, and when you listen to one of his pieces you can hear as many as eight independent melodies going on outside the main lead. Even though he doesn't write music, he manages to put down what he wants in a way both he and I understand. That's all it's about – relating. By the way, he's also a beautiful human being.

Not reading music scares some musicians into seeing it as a big academic, intellectual mystery. I try to encourage young guys to learn because it's really no more than an alphabet. Reading music simply enables everybody to know what's going on at the same time; it's communicating the mathematics of musical feeling, or more simply, it's just a way of letting everyone know what you want to play without resorting to humming. I work a lot without written music, but if you've got 109 musicians in the studio, there's no way to proceed except with the written note. It depends on the situation; if musicians can really feel the music, you can't tell the difference.

I was taught to read music by Ray Charles when we were growing up together. I'd started singing in a gospel quartet when I was about 13, then I took up the trumpet. Ray was very concerned that I learned to read music so he taught me in braille. I began arranging and composing with the trumpet before moving on to all the other brass instruments. Ray and I used to play a place called The Rocking Chair in Seattle. Well, Seattle's not exactly New York so we ended up playing everything from polkas to bebop and pop to *Claire de Lune*, depending on the crowd. I'm still criticized for being so eclectic, but that's how it is, I happened to come up that way.

You have to remember that music was very

George Martin and Quincy Jones

different in the early 1950s, not necessarily simpler, but much more polarized. Pop music didn't express its feelings too boldly in those days. Songs like *Mule Train, Doggy In The Window* and *Davy Crockett* were just cute little melodies that didn't involve any emotion. At first only black people listened to R & B. It's like it never occurred to most people to really *feel* music. Until then songs were for remembering and singing along, but not for really responding to, especially not with your body. Then in New York they started listening to all the doo-wop groups. So the cultures started merging, which was very healthy because a lot of great music came out of this fusion.

I remember the day everything changed. It was 1955. I was arranging for the Tommy and Jimmy Dorsey Band in New York City when they were featured on the television show "Saturday Night Bandstand", which was the summer replacement for the "Jackie Gleason Show", when

Quincy Jones and Michael Jackson

the young guest artist Elvis Presley came in and sang *Hound Dog*. Hip-shaking Elvis started the equivalent of what England went through in the early 1960s: an emotional revolution. It was the first time a white performer was singing black music on nationwide television in America.

Jazz

Most musicians and arrangers have had a foot in jazz some time or another. I came from a jazz, R & B and gospel background. As kids we listened to Charlie Parker, Ray Brown and Dizzy Gillespie; we all wanted to play solos like them. I also used to listen to Duke Ellington's sax section, then write down the parts to see what they were playing. It was an incredible ear training experience.

Jazz and improvisation help teach you not to freak out if everything doesn't go as you expect. That helps when you're producing – nothing throws you a curve. Say a singer likes to sing on top of or behind the beat, and doesn't have a very good feeling of tempo, you can ride with it and adjust. Jazz helps your perceptions to become more acute, whereas classical music is more interpretative and very cut and dried, unless you're dealing with someone like Stockhausen or Cage. Some of the best musicians combine both backgrounds. The greatest woodwind players I've worked with, like Phil Woods or Hubert Laws, are jazz players with classical training. These two are so ambidextrous they could sit comfortably with any symphony or jazz group in the world.

Electronics

Right after Stevie Wonder recorded *Super-woman,* around ten years ago, he asked me if there was an instrument which would translate what he played into a score because he couldn't write music. I told him he was crazy. But there is

one now, the Synclavier, which'll do anything, even print scores. You can program an entire orchestra into a 16-track machine and it'll play back sounding exactly like an orchestra. You can change anything you like, put the notes in and change the colours afterwards – create a French horn, a violin or a clarinet texture and then change them all individually. It's an absolutely revolutionary machine. The only problem is staying on top of this technology, or it will get on top of us. The evolution of electronic music and instruments is accelerating at an alarming rate of speed. Still these instruments will never replace acoustic sounds. They are just a beautiful addition to the vocabulary of the orchestra.

You've got to be scientific in your approach. And you've got to stay curious. I used to bug musicians to death when I was little, asking a million questions about everything. Stevie Wonder is the only person I know who is even more inquisitive than I. His curiousity about the synthesizer eventually led him into all the beautiful things he did with *Innervisions* and *Music Of My Mind*.

I first got into synthesizers around 1965 when I was working on film scores. I used to go and ask Paul Beaver – the man we call the grandfather of electronics – what kinds of tricks and interesting sounds he had. I was doing a pilot for the television show "Ironside" when he suggested trying something I'd never seen before, which turned out to be a synthesizer (as far as I know this was the first time this instrument was ever heard by the public). This was well before Wendy Carlos did *Switched on Bach*. Next time I went back to him with another problem, for the same show, he said again, try the synth. When I told him I'd already used it once, he said, you don't understand – we're dealing with infinity, 40 million sounds, if you like. Paul told me I'd better learn to understand the synthesizer because it was going to be around a long, long time. How right he was. Paul Beaver was also a beautiful human being.

Advice for beginners

One piece of advice I'd give to young musicians would be to try to create an affinity with the best of all kinds of music, depending on your taste. I've always enjoyed a broad menu. We're very fortunate today in having had a lot of people who came before us, like Beethoven, Charlie Parker and Duke Ellington, who eliminated the need for us to re-invent the wheel all the time. An enormous amount of love and hard work has gone into music. What's interesting is that we all use the same material, even in 12-tone music. It's always those same twelve notes.●

The Music Business

" . . . if you stand still, you're
going backwards."
SIMON DRAPER

The Record Industry

Music became a business because it had to. Originally, all musical entertainers, from the wandering troubadour and the court musician – the ancestors of the singer/songwriter and the session player – through Mozart up until the very early music hall artistes, played in person to small audiences. They were paid for these performances, and their music and songs, if popular enough, were then passed on to other performers, without any charge being made.

The birth of the music industry

It was the concept of copyright, designed to protect the originators of the music, that turned music into a business, and today's copyright for recorded sound originated from copyright in written music.

The works of classical composers were being published over 200 years ago. Music publishers were increasingly needed to publish songwriters' work in the form of sheet music, and the publisher became the person responsible for registering the copyright on what had been written. Without this, of course, there was nothing to stop someone else from saying that he had written the music, nor would the writer be able to make money from other people performing or, later, recording his work.

In Britain the Music Publishers Association (MPA) was formed in 1882, which shows how long music publishing has been in existence as an identifiable business. In the United States the National Music Publishers Association (NMPA) was founded in 1917, when the record industry was barely in its infancy. When records were first produced, copyright existed for recordings of published songs as well as for the original version, on the grounds that each rendition of a piece of music by a certain singer or group of musicians constituted in itself another creation, and that creation had to be registered with a copyright.

Royalties to musicians

Record companies therefore grew up as people who registered and owned the copyright in the recorded music, and they in turn paid the artists and musicians a percentage, or royalty, on what that recording earned. This came from various sources, but most notably from the sale of records.

Originally, by far the largest royalty on the sale of a record went to the publisher and the songwriter, while the recording artist received very little. In England in 1910 the Mechanical Copyright Licensing Company was formed in anticipation of the 1911 Copyright Act which instituted the payment of "mechanicals" – the percentage of the price of a record paid to the publisher and writer of the material used on that record. This company later became the Mechanical Copyright Protection Society (MCPS) which is today responsible for collecting mechanicals and distributing them to their rightful recipients. In the United States the Harry Fox Agency undertakes this responsibility.

In 1914 the American Society of Composers, Authors and Publishers (ASCAP) was formed and in the same year the Performing Rights Society (PRS) was created in England, to collect and distribute royalties paid each time a work is performed, live or on record. Payments go to the copyright holders – the composer, lyricist and publisher – one or all of whom may also, but not necessarily, be the artist. In 1940 Broadcast Music Inc. was set up by a collective of radio station owners in the United States; it is now in competition with ASCAP.

The artist becomes a star

Only relatively recently – over the last 10 or 20 years – have artists begun to receive an appreciable, and in many cases huge, percentage of the money made from a record. This may be because until then the value was thought to lie in the song itself, rather than in the artist's rendition of it. Today, however, the reverse seems to be the case.

Before the existence of records, the composer was the most important person in the music industry (such as it was) because, apart from hearing a piece performed live in a theatre, the only way anyone could enjoy a song was by buying a copy of the composer's sheet of music and playing and singing it for himself; in the old days, therefore, it was the songwriters, not the performers, who were the stars. Very few records were bought in the early days, and income from them formed only a small part of a band's or artist's total income; a song was more likely to be heard sung by a variety of artists, either in live performance or, after 1912, on the radio.

It was the appearance of record charts and the hit parade – especially in the United States – that caused a great change in the way recording artists were viewed. Unlike the early days, where the demand was for the songs, the deliberately developed, or manufactured, pop star became the norm until, today, the aim of most record companies is to find the right artist rather than the right song.

The traditional image of the naïve pop performer, duped by a grasping manager and record company, who finds himself a penniless has-been after his fame and luck have run out, is very much outdated. Just as the publishing and recording of music grew to become a business, so artists and writers became more business-like, and today record company executives spend a great deal of their time talking to lawyers, accountants and artists about the legal and financial aspects of the business.

The business becomes more efficient

It was the record business itself that encouraged this attitude: there was no longer room for the kind of disorganization which the industry had exhibited in its infancy, when people did not make, or expect to make, much money. Nowadays, record companies have to invest a fairly heavy sum in an artist or band to get them off the ground. Making records has become such a refined art that better and more creative producers are required. Such creative people are in demand and are therefore expensive, and record companies are no longer prepared to spend that kind of money on artists who are not likely to prove long-term investments.

Once a record has been made it must be promoted and marketed and this, too, is expensive. There are now, for example, many radio programmes on which a record must be played if it is to have a chance of being a hit; at one time playing a record on one family programme would have been enough.

Apart from needing a certain amount of airplay, the record must also be promoted to the popular press, television producers and a wide variety of other people. Nowadays, video films are an essential part of promotion, too, as is putting the artist on the road to play live dates. In the old days this could be done at very little cost; indeed it was possible to actually make money by going on the road. The prohibitive cost of sophisticated sound systems has now made this impossible, however. Putting on even a small concert these days costs a considerable amount of money, added to which, if there is no public demand for an artist, the record company has to bear the cost of touring until such a demand is created. Even when that has been achieved, the artist still has to be broken (made commercially successful) internationally which usually – if the artist is European – involves being sent to the United States, and this can be hugely expensive.

All these factors are indications that, at some point in the development of the music industry, the tail had, perhaps, begun to wag the dog, and accountancy to rule artistry. This is now, to a large extent the case – particularly in the United States.

At first this was detected only by people within the industry itself, but later the public also gradually became aware of it, and in the late 1960s and early 1970s – just after the spread of hippy culture – people were beginning to say that "music should be free". They were paying $8 or $10 for concert tickets and were beginning to question whether this was right; they were also paying a lot of money for records while at the same time they saw that record companies were making a great deal of money, and that music itself had become a big business.

Later, as they also began to see that artists were staying in the best hotels and were flying around the country in private planes with a bevy of lawyers and accountants, they awoke to the fact that artists were not necessarily creative people being manipulated by "fat cats", as was once generally thought, but were, in fact, part of the same "music business" syndrome.

Artists go into business

In many cases, the artist was not content to simply be a part of the music business, but became a businessman in his own right by making himself a record company executive and setting up his own record label and/or publishing company. Much of this was due to ego: most of the early artists' labels were started as a way of simply demonstrating the artist's importance, and few were actually commercially successful.

Some artists, it is fair to say, have more right to own a record company than many of the people who actually do own them. Owners and managers of record companies have to have judgement – the ability to differentiate between good commercial ideas and purely personal whims. Some artists may start their own labels because they have an ability in that particular area; others, on the other hand, may not even question their motivations or qualifications, but simply make up their minds that they want their own label. So the next time their contract is up for review, they stipulate that this is what they must have.

Apart from self-gratification – more a feature of artists' reasoning some years ago than it is today – it must be said that a great many good products have been generated by such labels, and some of the newer labels have been more successful than the older ones. One of the most successful in recent years has been the artist-run, artist-controlled 2-Tone. When one considers the groups that it found and signed – Madness, Selector, The Beat – it is no wonder that other record companies were so envious of its success.

Famous artists labels

Perhaps the most famous artist label of all was Apple – set up by The Beatles for a variety of reasons, of which ego gratification and a genuine desire to play a Svengali-type role towards new recording talent were the most obvious. This label ceased to operate in any significant way in 1980, and has subsequently ceased to exist altogether as a record label, although it still survives as a royalty-collecting office. It's interesting to note that, of the individual members of the group, Paul McCartney – the most commercially successful of the four – has always put his recorded product through the same major company, EMI; John Lennon, the most determinedly individualistic, never set up his own label; George Harrison has his well-established, but hardly prolific, Dark Horse label, which is an outlet only for his own material; and Ringo Starr started, but has had little success with, Ring-O Records, which no longer operates as a record label.

The Rolling Stones – shrewd and well advised in business matters – also set up their own label, Rolling Stones Records, which, though used mainly for their own records, has an occasional release from a favoured protégé.

Elton John's label, Rocket Records, has experienced several ups and downs – one particularly difficult period being alleviated by the artist signing himself on to his own label – having previously kept his own recording career and his label quite separate. Similarly, Led Zeppelin's Swan Song label has, on occasion, seemed aptly named, with regular rumours of the group's demise. Although its development has been marked by long periods of inactivity, it is still very much a viable venture licensed to WEA.

Rolling Stones Records, Swan Song and Rocket Records are all, like Apple, the business/creative ventures of seasoned world-famous artists with a great deal of personal wealth. They all have, or have had, offices of their own, and function chiefly as adjuncts to the careers of the artists who set them up.

Of the three, neither Rocket Records nor Swan Song can claim to have found and developed new artists with great success, with a few isolated exceptions – most notably Rocket Records' recent signing up of the talented and reasonably commercial singer/songwriter, Randy Edelman, and Swan Song's early success with Dave Edmunds, and subsequent signing of the already famous Bad Company and the talented Maggie Bell. And The Rolling Stones' label has hardly even tried, save for one LP by reggae artist Peter Tosh, which, unfortunately and unfairly, got more notice for its scratch 'n' sniff cannabis-scented cover than for its music. Grunt, the label owned by the group Jefferson Starship, is similar to Rolling Stones Records – a vehicle for the group's own output.

Independent labels in Britain

The impact of artists' labels on the music business has been minimal, apart from their contribution to the creative mix and spread of talent on record. But independent labels collectively have had a profound effect on the business, especially in England and particularly in the second half of the 1970s and on into the 1980s.

Stiff Records heads a list of small, streetwise British record labels which have acted like yeast on the dough of the record business. Now a fully fledged part of the industry, it continues to build on a past which witnessed the launch of artists such as Nick Lowe, Elvis Costello, Lene Lovitch and Ian Dury with some, if not quite all, the adventurousness of former times. Other independents ("indies") with solid reputations include Chiswick and Beggars Banquet (with a knack for spotting commercial sounds which led to releases as diverse as the sinister electronic futuristic music of Gary Numan and the airy sweetness of a group of South American pan pipes players). There are also specialist independent labels such as Highway, Leader and Topic (folk music), Word (Christian music), Old Gold (re-releases of old rock and pop singles), and Greensleeves (reggae), as well as numerous specialist jazz and blues labels.

However, it is the huge number of very small independent labels mostly spawned by the anti-establishment solo entrepreneurial spirit synonymous with punk and New Wave music, which have done the most to give the record business an overall new look. Serving a youth market which was, and still is, largely alienated from the image and output of established record companies, they are enterprises with low overheads, low turnovers and low success rates (in terms of the proportion of chart entries compared to overall number of releases). Most have as little use for the traditional kind of licensing, pressing and distribution deals with major companies as large manufacturers have for them.

But, as the independent label boom reverberated (and continues to reverberate) through the music business, the services it needed grew, and are still growing, with it. Independent distribution networks like Spartan and Pinnacle; small, cheap, low-tech studios where even a one-man label could afford to make recordings; independent sales and promotion companies, and companies offering custom record pressing, label and sleeve printing – all burgeoned with the independent label explosion.

Independent labels in the United States
It is harder for independent labels to become nationally significant in the United States, simply because the country is so large. However, there have been some success stories and in recent years the greatest of these is probably A and M Records, which was founded by Herb Alpert and Gerry Moss largely with money derived from Alpert's hits with The Tijuana Brass. This is now an international company with several leading artists signed to it.

The Geffen label, founded by David Geffen is also extremely successful. At one time Geffen handled John Lennon and Elton John; he has recently signed Simon and Garfunkel and Asia.

Chrysalis management meet to discuss a new project, involving representatives from all departments: A & R, production, marketing, press, promotion and sales.

His output is distributed by Warners. The Planet label which was set up by producer Richard Perry distributes through RCA and includes The Pointer Sisters among its artists.

Smaller labels than these – to an extent comparable to those which grew out of the punk movement in England – include Slash Records, which is a phenomenon on the west coast but as yet not a force nationally; and Ze which records Kid Creole and the Coconuts. Backstreet Records was formed to launch Tom Petty and the Heartbreakers, and the Scotti Brothers label has Survivor, who had a hit with *Eye Of The Tiger,* the theme song of the movie *Rocky 3.*

Thus, as the recession of the late 1970s and early 1980s sank its teeth into the financial fat of the record business, the rise of the independents brought the talent and vitality of small enterprise to the capital and expertise of big business.

Among the many effects the independent labels have had is to cause many very experienced record company executives to look back on their own humble beginnings, and question whether or not there are lessons to be learned for the progress of the big companies they now own or work for.

Chrysalis
There are distinct parallels between the development of my own company, Chrysalis Records – and now the Chrysalis Group – and the development of the pop music business in general.

Chrysalis began as an agency that booked groups for live performances, mostly for colleges. Terry Ellis and I started with the groups

we liked, and had no investment at all. As we expanded, we took on more artists and had to build an organization to service them. Then we began to sign bands we did not know – unknowns, in fact, in every sense of the word. Some we believed to be potentially great and some we signed simply to feed the system. Once you have a record company, you have to keep putting out records; you can't simply say to your staff, "Well, I'm sorry but we haven't any records to sell at the moment because the artists we like have decided not to make any for a while." You can't have people sitting around in offices, factories and distribution depots twiddling their thumbs, so you sign artists who have marginal appeal rather than not signing any at all. Then you start oiling the machine and spending a lot of money. The whole organization becomes increasingly pressurized, and requires much more attention to detail.

When Chrysalis first became a record company the first Ten Years After album took us three days to record and cost virtually nothing to produce, but it sold because the group was popular. It wasn't even a particularly well-recorded record, but in those days that didn't matter. Nowadays the competition to get a record played on radio is so great that, without a highly professional finished product, you stand no chance at all.

The music business today

The music business has always had the same public image as all branches of the entertainment industry: not too solid in a financial sense, and people with rather odd and colourful characters. However, recently – and particularly over the past few years – the music business has made great efforts to become more responsible and appear more of an institution, especially as far as the financial sector is concerned. There has been a deliberate attempt to demonstrate maturity, and today the business is run by people who are much more intelligent and serious-minded than in the early days, though they are perhaps slightly lacking in creativity. The business actually changed some years ago; what we are trying to do now is to change the image to match the reality. These changes are not merely cosmetic, but reflect a gradual and deep-seated change in the way the business works. In short, it has become more business-like.

Investment

The differences between now and 1966, when I entered the record business are enormous. From the point of view of investment, it didn't cost anything to set up a record company in those days. You could go into business simply with an office, and one man and a dog to run it. This couldn't happen now – or, at least, not in the same way.

Much more capital is needed now, and because of this there has been a reversal of trends, towards very cheaply run independent operations which do things quite differently, and put out a totally different product from that of the larger, well-established labels which were able to form the music business of the 1960s and 1970s from small beginnings. Anyone starting out now would therefore handle things very differently.

Larger companies may, of course, require substantial investment from outside. Assessed as a prospect for investment, as a venture that a large corporation or bank might want to put money into, the music industry is still seen as volatile, and investors are wary of it. Their wariness is justified, as this is definitely not a business in which anyone can predict volume from one year to the next because it is entirely dependent on hits, which are unpredictable at the best of times. Nevertheless, it is an illusion that other areas of entertainment, such as films, are more financially viable than the record business; they are, in fact, no more stable.

While dark-suited money men may eventually respond favourably to the more sober, executive-style image of the music business, it can be argued that the trend away from the happy-go-lucky, artistically eccentric image of the industry – more obvious at the senior management end – is keeping some highly creative, but not especially business-like, people out of executive positions. It is perfectly possible to combine a business sense with creativity, however, and there are many people in the business who do. Anyone who has started, or would like to start, their own record company must combine both or expect to fail.

Creativity versus profitability

The lack of creative talent in executive positions is most marked in the big multinational companies: very often the creative head in such a company is not given time to turn his part of the company – or his national company, if he is managing director of one company in a multinational group – round to the expected profit level. It can sometimes take two or three years to bring an artist's career to fruition, and during those years the corporate body – the creative head's employer – often gets panicky. Regardless of whether or not the person they have employed has, in the long run, the business acumen to make a success of the company, the multinational will look at the current figures and see that the artist who was supposed to become commercially successful has not done so. In fact, the creative executive and others involved with the artistic side of the business may know that the artist's career is, in fact, in very good shape, but this will be irrelevant if it is not reflected in the figures.

The creative executive is therefore elbowed out and replaced by a lawyer or an accountant. That way, the corporate body feels that at least the business side will be run properly, and that the company will turn in a profit, or, at worst, not make a huge loss. This may be so, but it will not get anywhere, either.

In my view, one of the big problems with the music business these days, especially in the United States, is that it has become too formalized: too much power has been given to lawyers and accountants who sign artists and make records merely to service existing demand from radio stations, instead of taking chances on more creative artists. In fact, record sales in the United States are not as good as they should be partly because the business has been slow to break some of the more interesting artists. This is not so true in Britain where creative people have been allowed a little more room to express themselves.

A global view

The legitimate music industry exists only in the industrialized nations of the world. Throughout most of Africa and the Far East, South America and in some Mediterranean countries – notably Greece – the record industry is a pirate industry. This means that people take records put out by bona fida labels and, regardless of copyright, tape anything they like, in any combination they like, to produce a record. For example, someone might put The Police on one side of a record, Abba on the other, with maybe a few Blondie cuts thrown in, and then sell the finished result.

The legitimate record industry is currently in decline. This is due partly to economic recession, but also to the march of home entertainment technology, which offers the consumer several relatively new items: video; cable television; much more radio programming; and the hardware that has caused the record industry its biggest headache – cassette recorders and music centres. People no longer have to buy their own records – they can tape a friend's.

Home-taping is a problem in all countries and the principal reason for the record industry's serious decline in recent years. Worse still, the decline has become self-perpetuating: since record companies are not making profits, the money for investment in new artists – who, as I have said, may take two or three years to repay the initial investment with commercial success – is not readily available. Therefore, record companies become more conservative, and start to concentrate more on established record-sellers, thus inevitably losing out on creativity. Home piracy is an international problem, although it is less prevalent in countries with healthy economies, where more people still prefer to buy their own records.

International markets

In order to grow successfully, a record company must have access to the entire international market. This doesn't necessarily mean that it has to set up its own offices in different countries – it can operate through foreign licensees. It must have these outlets, however: although every company must look to its home market first, it is difficult for any developing company to make a profit by selling to its domestic market alone. (The British market, for example, is only 8 per cent of the world market; the remaining 92 per cent must be taken into account as well.)

Marketing territories

A marketing territory is a set of countries in which there is a spill-over of interest or appreciation of certain bands, or kinds of music, from one country to another. France, for example, remains a law – and a marketing territory – unto itself, because the French tend to be chauvinistic: they will not, for example, listen to German radio just because they happen to be close to a German transmitter. Similarly, Spain and Italy are also markets on their own. The biggest spill-over is between German Switzerland and Germany, and both ways across the Dutch border, to Germany and Belgium. The Scandinavian countries hold together as a market, as do Australia and New Zealand, which is thriving despite the recent downturn in sales. Japan is the second largest market in the world, though this is misleading, since much of its market is for domestic repertoire. However, if an English-language record becomes a hit in Japan, it will sell a huge number of copies. The United States is, of course, the biggest market in the world and for most types of popular music spills over into Canada.

Developing markets

There are problems regarding those marketing territories which are, as yet, undeveloped.

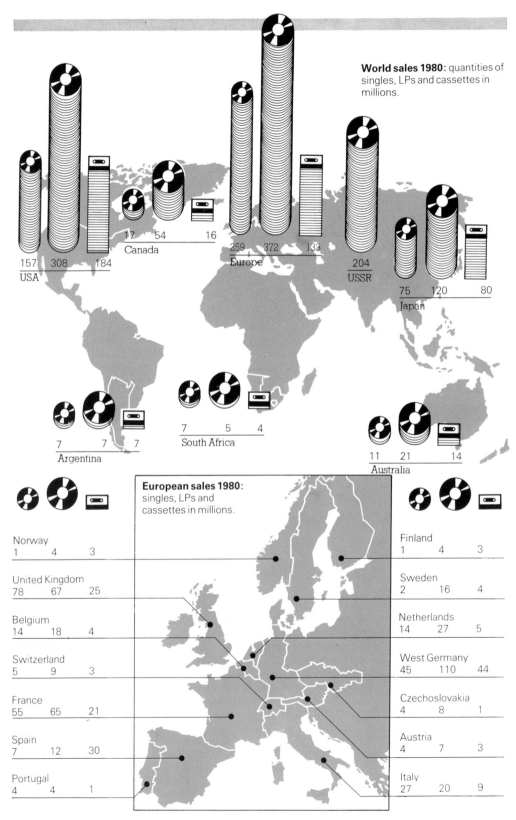

World sales 1980: quantities of singles, LPs and cassettes in millions.

157 308 184
USA

17 54 16
Canada

259 372 133
Europe

204
USSR

75 120 80
Japan

7 7 7
Argentina

7 5 4
South Africa

11 21 14
Australia

European sales 1980: singles, LPs and cassettes in millions.

Norway
1 4 3

United Kingdom
78 67 25

Belgium
14 18 4

Switzerland
5 9 3

France
55 65 21

Spain
7 12 30

Portugal
4 4 1

Finland
1 4 3

Sweden
2 16 4

Netherlands
14 27 5

West Germany
45 110 44

Czechoslovakia
4 8 1

Austria
4 7 3

Italy
27 20 9

People have often tried to make money in South America, for example, but, besides the problem of piracy which is widespread, they are also faced with rampant inflation. Several record companies have set up in Brazil in an attempt to try and tap their economic growth, but even there the inflation rate is 120 per cent. Since record companies operate on a three-month billing system, by the time a company gets paid for the records it has sold, it is already losing money on them.

The Iron Curtain countries are potentially a vast market, since they have no piracy or counterfeiting, and, in addition, it is possible to bring money out of them, although at poor exchange rates. The insatiable demand of the Iron Curtain market is in fact very tempting – if it were opened to the record industry, the world market would increase by about 25 per cent overnight.

The problem lies in the controls imposed by the non-capitalist system. Capitalism works on the basis of supply and demand: if you make more of something than the public wants, you have to throw the surplus away; if the public want more than you initially manufacture, however, you simply make more of the product in question and set your price according to the demand – at a point where you make a profit. Most Communist countries, on the other hand, are committed to a planned economy. If there is a manufacturing capacity for, say, 10 million records in the Soviet Union in a year, the number of records of each type of music will be planned in advance. The divisions might, for example, be classical, popular, and the spoken word. The "popular" category may then be broken down into folk, jazz, ethnic and international; and then international will in turn be divided into various sections as well. There may eventually turn out to be an allocation for 235,329 Western pop records for the year; that is the number they will make – they will price them at the equivalent of $10/£5, although they could get ten times that for them, the demand is so high – and that is the number they will sell. Understandably, this system has created a widespread black market.

Some indication of the potential size of the record market in the Communist block was given by the immense success of Western records in Czechoslovakia and Poland until their moves towards a more open policy were crushed.

There is also a huge demand for records in India, but again much of the produce is pirated, and the biggest demand is in any case for Indian music. The third world as a whole could be a very good market from which the record industry might gain growth, but, even if the piracy problem in these countries could be curbed, the resulting sales would be mainly for home-produced repertoire. This offers the multinational companies little incentive.

Milestones

A number of milestones have marked the development of the established music industry: the invention of stereo recording; the LP coming to dominate a market that was originally intended for singles; San Francisco and Monterey – events which started an entirely new kind of music; Woodstock, which pinpointed how strong music had become in youth culture; and then, in Britain, The Sex Pistols letting the industry know it was not always going to be that way; the advent of the cassette; and, most recently, the cassette's victory over the eight-track cartridge in the United States, which has meant that the American industry has, belatedly relative to the British, had to start living with the home-taping problem.

The future

To a great extent what is affecting the business now is competition from other forms of entertainment, and this is growing despite the fact that records represent such great entertainment value. In radical comparison to the cost of other consumer goods, record prices have only doubled in 20 years, and in terms of the cost of other forms of entertainment that increase is tiny. This is despite the fact that the vinyl from which records are made is a petroleum by-product, and oil prices have soared. To confront this competition the music business is diversifying – into video, for example, including video games. Such diversification needs great capital resources, however, and many companies cannot afford to turn to these new lines of business.

Before long the music business will reach a new equilibrium, and will exist at a steady level relative to other forms of entertainment. There will be fewer record companies and fewer recording artists providing music for a diminishing market. It will be a very demanding market – and is already much more so than it used to be – in terms of choice and quality.

Record companies will have to afford all the new technology; if the public wants it they will have to provide it. The compact disc, though much more expensive to produce, will eventually take over from the vinyl LP because people will want the high quality of sound and longer playing time. But seven-inch singles and pre-recorded cassettes are nonetheless here to stay.●

How a Record Company Works

Record companies come in all shapes and sizes. Whatever form they take, however, their success largely depends on the talent of the people who run them, the quality of their staff and, of course, the odd bit of luck. The music business is a volatile world – its history is littered with the corpses of companies that have waxed brilliantly only to wane miserably – and, like many of the artists it promotes, a record company's success may be short-lived.

The talents of the people who run record companies will vary according to the size of company they are involved with. A large company, for example, will place very different demands on its top people than a small one. Many small companies are started and run by people who simply have a flair for spotting new talent and an ability to promote an artist almost single-handedly. A large concern, on the other hand, will require people with organizational skills and financial and legal know-how – qualities that are usually only developed with experience, and therefore unlikely to be possessed by an entrepreneur in the early stages of his career.

However, whether a company is a large international group employing thousands, with the inevitable bureaucracy that this entails, or a small, entrepreneurial concern fighting for success, certain job functions will be common and essential to all of them, although the division of these functions will vary.

In a small company one person may be responsible for two or three functions, whereas in a large company the same responsibilities may be handled by two or three departments. This generally happens when the larger company has many artists producing a wide variety of music, and a huge catalogue of past recorded work. Large companies, in fact, often break down the functions of their personnel even further. For example, they may have a production department in which certain managers are responsible only for printing cover sleeves, or ordering from back catalogues or dealing with singles, while others deal only with albums. Small companies, on the other hand, may have only one person responsible for production and will look to larger companies for distribution and sales.

Corporate structure

Like other commercial and industrial concerns, most record companies have a board of directors with a managing director and chairman or president responsible to that board for the day-to-day running of the company. The board has a collective responsibility to its shareholders for the current and future success of the company, and for ensuring the best possible return on the shareholders' investments. Sometimes the directors are actually employed by the company, or, alternatively, they may represent a single shareholder or group of shareholders: major record companies are often subsidiaries of large commercial groups, while many smaller ones are owned and run by the people who started them.

It would be impossible to define the structure of one record company and then simply present this as a blueprint for all the others, since the structure of a record company is ultimately determined by the imagination, skill, energy and idiosyncracies of the people involved in it. However, certain job functions are common to all these companies and it is possible to place these in a representative order.

Artists and repertoire manager (A & R man)

All record companies are in business to sell recorded music, and the department which acquires the rights to the music they sell is known as Artists and Repertoire, or A & R. The A & R manager's job is to find and persuade artists to sign recording contracts with his company. He needs a wide range of contacts, which consist of managers or owners of music clubs, journalists and musicians – anyone, in fact, with a love of music.

Few good A & R men have really catholic tastes. They are generally attracted to music and develop a deep interest in it, through their own love of a particular type of music. There are, in fact, many cases where A & R policy has created a distinct image in a record company. The most obvious example of this is Tamla Motown. Others include companies as diverse as Atlantic, which had a great reputation for R & B and Soul through the 1950s and 1960s; Stiff, with its irreverent roster of artists; and Island, which, more than any other company, brought reggae to world-wide recognition. All these companies reflect the tastes of the A & R people responsible to them: in each case the A & R decision-makers were trailblazers who, through their beliefs, foresight and tenacity, succeeded in popularizing much-maligned and ignored styles of music.

A word of warning to anyone with ambitions in the A & R field: the hours can be long and arduous. Apart from the paper work which is an essential part of the A & R man's job, a great deal of his time is spent in studios, going to gigs and rehearsals, and talking to bands – often late into the night. In addition, the pressures on him can be enormous, since A & R men are often squeezed between bosses looking for talent and instant success and bands complaining about faults in the company. A tough constitution and sufficient self-discipline to avoid indulgence in drink and drugs is essential: that disastrous path has been trodden by too many talented artists and A & R men alike.

Finding the artists It is the A & R man's aim to find artists who have the potential to make music that will sell, and in doing this he is faced with strong competition from other A & R men. His methods of finding new talent include going to gigs, building up and keeping in touch with his contacts, listening to demo tapes and talking to band managers, agents, and musicians.

A record company with a good reputation has many musicians beating a path to its door, and the top A & R men rarely have time to listen to the enormous number of demo tapes sent to them. Instead, they may prefer to listen to people with a good track record in the business – a successful band manager with a new act, for example. Good managers are important to the A & R man: Island Records developed a fruitful relationship with a management partnership run by David Enthoven, John Gaydon and Mark Fenwick, signing first their band King Crimson and, later, Emerson, Lake and Palmer and Roxy Music.

Signing deals Once an A & R man has found a band he wants to sign, he must persuade them that his is the best company to work for. This won't be difficult if no one else is interested in the band, but sometimes a number of companies are eager to do a deal, and the band consequently demands higher advances and royalties. It's important from the outset to establish a feeling of trust with a band: a sensible band with a sensible manager does not always sign the best cash deal if they feel that some other company has a better understanding of how to record and promote their music.

Negotiating a deal with a band involves the A & R man in consultation with the company's business affairs head and, usually, the president, or managing director and the financial director. Only the most trusted A & R men have a free hand to sign whatever bands they choose, and

even then they are restricted by tight budgets. The entrepreneur with his own company, however, may well be able to take such decisions entirely on his own, depending on the amount of capital he has available.

Ideally, a recording contract should be tailored to meet the needs of the band as well as the financial interests of the company. An unworkable contract, no matter how cast-iron, will inevitably end in a welter of recriminations and lawyers' letters and, at worst, in court. It is the A & R man's responsibility to ensure that a band has sufficient funds to make good records; it is the managing director's, or president's, and business affairs manager's responsibility to see that a contract does not expose the company to too much risk.

Recording Signing on a new band is really only the beginning as far as the A & R man is concerned. He then has to work closely with the band and their manager, to plan them a successful recording career. Most bands are eager to start recording almost before the ink on their contract has dried. In the case of inexperienced artists, however, this isn't always a good idea, even when the best producers and recording engineers are available. Any music the band may have composed must first be judged and then either kept or discarded according to its merits. If the artists don't write their own material, good songs have to be found for them to record.

It is the A & R man's job to make sure that a band is well rehearsed and their material sufficiently strong before allowing them anywhere near a studio. He must also ensure that they have a producer who understands and appreciates what they are trying to achieve musically. This will be particularly important if he himself is unfamiliar with the type of music they play. A talented band with a strong manager will make life considerably easier for an A & R manager, but he will still be held ultimately responsible if anything goes wrong.

Promotion Once the decision to start recording has been made, the A & R man makes sure that the sessions go well, and, in the meantime, plans the release date of the single or album with his colleagues and discusses the sleeve design with his art director.

The A & R man's main role in the area of promotion, however, is to act as a link between the band and the record company, and to make sure that each is aware of what the other is doing. He discusses the record company's promotion plans with the band's manager, and reports to his superiors on the general progress of the recording sessions. He also informs them about the band's touring schedules – always an important factor, since records are issued to tie in with a band's promotional activities. The band's manager keeps him informed of these and will ask his advice if necessary.

The A & R man and his colleagues are aware of the band's long-term plans, but it is the relatively short period around the release of a record that has every other department in the company working hard.

The production head

It's the production head's job to order sleeves, labels and records or tape cassettes, and to organize the mastering of the final tape for pressing. When the exact week of a record's release has been decided, after consultation with the A & R man, the marketing, sales and promotion directors, the production head sets everything up so that the records are manufactured and ready for release on time. This involves: making sure that the art director has the artwork for the record jacket completed in time for printing; coordinating the pressing factory and the jacket printers; making sure that the details on the sleeve and labels are correct and that the business affairs head has all the necessary copyright details; and, finally, planning for the availability of advance copies for those that need them.

Production pitfalls Once a record is released, it is usually the production head's responsibility to see that as far as possible supply equals demand; ideally stock should not go unsold. This is difficult, since the precise demand can only be guessed at. When Island signed on Bob Dylan, for example, we had to rush-release his album *Planet Waves* and, in our enthusiasm and excitement, completely misjudged the album's potential, ending up with thousands of unsold copies. Too many mistakes like this will quickly give a company a serious cash flow problem. The production manager must therefore also study figures, discuss their progress with the sales manager, and keep abreast of all promotional activity – a difficult job at the best of times.

The marketing director

While all this is happening, the marketing director is arranging advertising schedules, together with the design and manufacture of advertisements, posters, shop display material and other promotional pieces – all of which will have previously been approved by the band's manager and the marketing director's superiors. Frequent meetings will take place between key personnel to make sure their work is effectively coordinated, and the marketing director will liaise with the sales director and his sales force to make certain that shop display material is ready on time. Most important of all, however, he will think, think, and think again about his promotional campaign to try to ensure its total success.

Advertising is rarely effective on its own, however, and the marketing manager will also have to see that his plans coincide with promotional activities undertaken by the band, such as tours and concerts. He will be responsible for working within a strict budget and for getting as much for his money as he can, without overspending. He must also aim to get the best-placed advertisements in the music papers and make sure that there is no wastage of posters and promotional material.

The publicity manager

The press, or publicity, manager may well have started his side of the operation long before the band has even gone into the studio, and the results of his work begin to take effect as the record release date approaches. His most important task is to get press coverage – whether national, musical or local – and to do this he must know the relevant journalists on all the national and musical papers, and be able to judge which of them are likely to present the band in the most favourable light. He may already have some indication of this from past reviews of the band's performance. If, however, few journalists have had a chance to see or hear the band, his job is considerably harder.

Although it is generally accepted that bad publicity is better than no publicity, the last thing a press officer will want is a bad review, and he will therefore have spent a good deal of time with the band, their manager, and the A & R man, discussing the best ways of getting good publicity. He will advise the band on how to handle interviews and, if any of the band members have strong opinions, will try to seek out journalists who share them. On the whole, he will try to find writers who will be fired by the band's talent and who will in turn fire their readers' interests. His task is a delicate one because he can never

The departments within a record company are all involved with the development of a band and the release of its records. Quartet was the third album that Ultravox released after signing with Chrysalis and the first to be produced by George Martin. The roles played by the different departments are described on the following three pages.

A & R DEPARTMENT

Artists are usually brought to the attention of a record company through its A & R (artists and repertoire) manager. He arranges to hear the artists in performance or on a demo tape (sometimes acting on information from journalists, managers and musicians) before signing them up. In Ultravox's case a concert date, *below*, through a recommendation from two respected managers in the music business, led to their recording contract with Chrysalis. The first single they submitted – *Sleepwalk* – soon became a hit record and was featured on their album *Vienna*.

PRODUCTION DEPARTMENT

It is very difficult to calculate how many copies of a record to manufacture. The production manager, after consultation with other departments must try to ensure that supply does not exceed demand. This becomes easier once a group have become established because the market can be identified. If a second single is to be taken from an album and is expected to enter the charts, such as *Hymn* from Ultravox's *Quartet* album, there is a great possibility that there will be renewed interest in the album, and that it will sell in large numbers for a second time. The production manager must try to take this into account when placing his order for pressing albums, *below*.

MARKETING DEPARTMENT

Once a band has signed a recording contract, the marketing manager is responsible for promoting the band with advertising campaigns, store displays and so on; in short, making sure the band gets noticed. Ultravox's image is as important as their music and the design of their albums has to reflect this. Nearly all the posters and promotional material such as the store display, *below*, reflect this design. If an advertising campaign is successful, another – using the same visual concept – may be planned for a different medium, television for example.

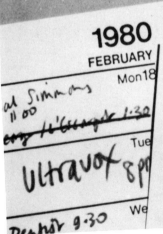

really be sure of a terrific review. On the other hand, he should be able to gain enough support to ensure that the band appear on the right pages at the right times.

The promotion manager

The promotion manager's role is to radio and television what the publicity manager's is to the press, and, just as the publicity manager must know his journalists, so the promotion manager must know the right programme producers and disc jockeys. Although a television appearance brings a band much wider recognition than weeks of slogging around the country playing a small club, the promotion manager's most important task is to get enough air-play for singles to give them a chance of becoming a hit. A hit single is still the best way of quickly making a

PUBLICITY DEPARTMENT

Extensive and favourable coverage in the music press is essential for any band. The publicity manager needs to be familiar with all the journalists on the major music papers and ensure that they get to know the band. At first, Ultravox's music had to compete with the fading punk movement so it was necessary to find journalists who were sympathetic to their electronic style of music. After a band's initial success, it is up to the press manager to keep interest alive in the music papers. He must also liaise with the band about the best way to handle interviews. The best thing that can happen is for a band to be featured on the cover of a mass circulation paper.

PROMOTION DEPARTMENT

Exposure on television and radio is vital to a band's success: three minutes' air-play can lead to a record in the Top 50. This in turn may lead to a television slot which is likely to send the record much further up the chart. The promotion manager's job is to persuade programme directors and disc jockeys to play his band's record. Advance pressings of records are sent to managers of clubs and discotheques and they are asked to fill in a "Reaction Report", like that for Ultravox's *Reap The Wild Wind, below,* the first single to be released from the *Quartet* album.

SALES DEPARTMENT

The task of selling records to the retail stores is up to the sales manager and his force. He will take orders and supply records to stores around the country, sometimes using promotional material such as stickers, T-shirts and posters. His job is to make sure that the stores have adequate stock when a record is released. With a new group, special promotion may be needed and the sales manager will concentrate his efforts on shops with a good reputation for promoting new records. Once a record gets into the charts, *below,* the sales team have little difficulty selling it; their problem then is to keep the shops adequately supplied.

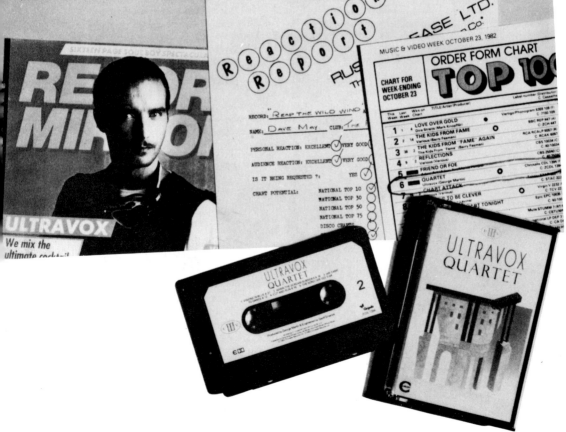

INTERNATIONAL DEPARTMENT

Nowadays, international recognition is very important for an artist's career and most companies therefore have distinct international departments. The international director negotiates with foreign record companies, who may take on all the domestic company's list or just the recordings of one artist, or even a single record. He arranges foreign media coverage for his artists, and has to be constantly aware of differing and changing music trends all over the world.

CREATIVE SERVICES DEPARTMENT

The visual images of recording artists have become increasingly important in recent years – so much so that in many recording companies the Art Director, someone responsible for sleeve and poster design, has become part of a new department, often called "Creative Services", whose job is to oversee all visual imagery and to ensure visual co-ordination. One of the Head of Creative Services' main responsibilities is video – seeing that a band's video promos fit in with their overall image. Video films can help boost record sales enormously and, in many cases, are more effective than live performances on TV, providing more optical possibilities. Nearly all of Ultravox's singles have been accompanied by video films, written and directed by them and incorporating an imaginative use of lighting, mood and effects.

band known to a wide audience (it will then be the A & R man's responsibility to see that the band aren't just "one-hit wonders"). In fact, if a promotion manager knows his job and the right programme directors, he may even make a significant contribution to the choice of the single from a band's album.

The promotion manager has one of the hardest and most competitive jobs in the record industry because vast quantities of singles are released every week, but only a handful get air-play.

Entry into even the lower reaches of the Top 50 can open many doors, however; and if a band are lucky enough to have a hit on the radio, television appearances will invariably follow. If these are successful and the band's single continues to be a hit, they can look forward to playing to larger audiences and attracting an increasing number of fans. All this places an extraordinary amount of pressure on the promotion manager, who must be a resilient and gifted salesman if he is to succeed at his job.

The sales director

The sales director and his staff are responsible for actually selling the records. Albums are usually sold to shops a month before their release date; advance orders are solicited so that, once the album is released, all the shops receive their stock at approximately the same time. Some companies have sales forces that deal only with singles. These call on a select number of shops more frequently than those selling albums; they sell singles in advance of their release dates and continue to promote them once they are released.

The sales director provides his staff with promotional material and any other sales aids that are available to him. He sets targets for his team, and holds regular meetings with his staff when he will threaten and cajole them until the targets are met. He also keeps in regular contact with the shops.

Important store chains and wholesalers are the sales manager's main priority, but individual shops with good reputations for promoting new records are also singled out for special attention. The members of the sales team are responsible for seeing that the shops allocated to them order adequate stock, and for informing the shop managers of any national or local campaigns which may be relevant. They must also see that the dealers receive any additional promotional material that is available, such as posters, stickers, buttons, badges and T-shirts.

Another important part of the sales director's task is to plan sales campaigns for back-catalogue albums, and, together with the marketing manager, he will organize incentive schemes for the shops and advertising campaigns to help the dealers sell the stock they buy. Thus the sales director must constantly deal with the new albums being released by his company as well as keeping up the volume of sales on back-catalogue albums.

The international market

It is generally accepted that a record company and its artists will never be successful unless their records are distributed and promoted around the world, and while the United States and Britain have traditionally provided more world-famous musicians and singers than any other country, this is now changing because record companies in other countries are creating strong, international sales and promotional teams.

Cases where a record company can consistently make a profit from an artist who only sells in his home country are rare. Usually an artist will achieve his initial success in his country of origin, and from there tries to gain world-wide experience. The Beatles gained valuable experience and solid support in Germany, but it was in Britain that they had their first break.

The United States has traditionally been slower to tour artists abroad; even those singers, such as Elvis Presley, who already had huge record sales in Europe might have doubled them had they undertaken a European tour. Companies are now aware, however, that music is a worldwide business and most companies now have an international manager or director responsible for liaising with and hustling a company's overseas affiliates. He also plays an important role in planning promotional tours and gigs in other countries and in relaying information and sales figures from abroad.

The international director

It's the international director's job to secure record releases in as many territories outside the domestic market as possible, and to break records internationally. This initially involves negotiating with a record company in every foreign country with a sizeable record market. These negotiations might be for, say, the rights to release his company's entire catalogue, or the repertoire of one act, or even one record title. When the terms are agreed upon, a licensing agreement for the right to release the records or catalogue is drawn up between the domestic record company (the licensor) and the foreign record company (the licensee).

As well as negotiating for the release of a record company's repertoire worldwide, the international director must also ensure that the foreign record companies are supporting new records and artists with appropriate marketing campaigns, and that the records are being given maximum media coverage. The international director builds up an information service for the foreign licensees keeping them aware of all the domestic record company's activities, including new artists' recording plans, release dates, tours and chart ratings. The international director also keeps the licensee supplied with items such as master tapes for pressing from, sleeve films for printing from, photographs, press cuttings and promotional videos. It is sometimes his responsibility to encourage the artists to tour in foreign countries, whether to make live and television appearances, or to attend interviews and press conferences.

The financial director

The financial director of any commercial concern plays a vital role, and every record company has an accountant on its board. In the music industry, where such vast sums of money are spent, proper financial control and administration are crucial for effective decision-making; the financial director determines the amount of money available for investment, and does everything he can to keep costs down.

Another important aspect of his job is the administration and payment of artists and of their publishing royalties – inaccuracies and late payments can ruin a company's relationship with an artist, and easily lead to expensive legal proceedings.

Royalties paid to artists are often complicated by such matters as different rates for different countries, and deductions for payments to producers; accounts staff must therefore be aware of the royalty rates that apply to every artist.

A good financial director will enable a company to weather bad sales periods or economic recessions that might otherwise force it out of business. Depending on the size of the company he is employed in, he will usually have a team of accountants, book-keepers and accounts clerks to administer accounts and analyze sales and expenditure figures.

The company lawyer

The increasingly complicated contracts required to safeguard the interests of both companies and artists have created a need for legal expertise. It is the company lawyer's responsibility to see that a company's contracts are correctly drawn up, and that the artist has no conflicting contracts with other companies. He must also keep the appropriate people within the company informed of the details of artists' contracts. This type of information will be particularly important to accounts staff responsible for royalties, since all payments, advances and royalties must be supported by a contract to safeguard the company's interests.

The head of creative services

Ever since the late 1960s, record companies and their artists have become increasingly aware of the importance of the packaging and presentation of their records. This, combined with the increased importance of the artists' visual identity, has meant that companies and artists alike are paying more and more attention to this area, which has traditionally been the responsibility of the art director.

As his province has expanded, so too has the art director's job definition changed; nowadays the person responsible for the visual side of a company's efforts is sometimes known as the head of creative services.

"Creative services" covers not only single and album sleeves and advertising and display, but also video, which is used for in-store promotion, as a domestic and international sales aid, and for television promotion.

The importance of the promotional video cannot be overlooked; many artists and companies invest huge sums in videos intended to establish a strong identity for an artist or record.

The head of creative services is responsible for all the many visual images necessary to promote his company's artists. To do his job successfully he has to use the very best creative people he can find and keep himself fully abreast of the changing needs and style of the marketplace in which the artist is competing.

Job opportunities

Many of those in the top jobs within record companies began humbly. An efficient postroom has been the start of many a successful career. Denny Cordell who signed J.J. Cale and Tom Petty and the Heartbreakers to his own label, started out as a dogsbody and tea-maker at Island Records in the early years – positive proof that people with initiative, flair and tenacity can always make it to the top in the record industry.

Conclusion

The music business is ever-changing and varies from country to country. In the United States, for example, where there are thousands of radio stations, the record companies have many more radio promoters than in European countries. Most record companies now have video departments which make promotional clips for use on pop shows, cable television, or in sales and international conferences.

The record business is volatile because tastes change so quickly and companies that are quick to spot new trends can just as quickly find themselves bankrupt or dealing only in catalogues from an earlier, more successful period.

At present, the music business is absorbing new audio and video technology, and indeed new ideas from all branches of communications technology. Whatever the future holds, it promises to be every bit as exciting as the past. One thing is clear: the record companies will always have room for talented people.●

The Search for Talent

Virgin Records' policy and the qualities it looks for in artists, have both changed consistently over the years. The only thing that has remained the same in our search for originality, because this is a vital consideration for us.

When we are considering whether to sign an artist, we look for a complete package of different attributes: a strong image, because that's an important factor in Britain, a little less so in the United States; a distinctive, original sound; and good songs. In different times and circumstances some people would say, "forget all that, you just need good songs," but in our experience we need all of these elements and we look particularly for style and image.

A band with an image

We don't try to impose an image on a band. We look for a band that already has a strong sense of its own image. Groups who start off by discussing

with us what sort of image they should have and whether they should change their name put us off straightaway, because we're interested in bands who already have insight into what's going to make them successful; they've got to want to be successful. It would be patronizing if we, who are old men in our thirties, set ourselves up as experts on youth culture; but what we can do is recognize some of these qualities in other people and draw on our experience in the music business as a whole.

Phil Oakey of The Human League knows better than we do how his band's sleeves should look, and to some extent he probably knows better than we do what kind of records they should put out. He relies on us to give advice and to act as a sounding board, but the inspiration for The Human League's success comes entirely from him. All that we have contributed is a sympathetic ear, patience through two years of nothing much happening and the facilities that the band have needed. We are good at listening to suggestions from our bands and we don't take a hard, doctrinaire line, recognizing that sometimes, although not always, the artist knows best.

Helping bands to improve

Once a record company has signed a band, they should provide them with the means to improve,

Culture Club with their vocalist Boy George on left

enhance and elaborate because quality and sophistication are more acceptable today than they were four or five years ago. There is a feeling that the public are beginning to want something different again. Elastica, who we've just signed, have an original and different sound; whereas Culture Club have a sound that's in the mainstream of last year, but they have good songs and an extraordinary image. The first thing that attracted us was their image – especially their lead singer, Boy George – because the first two songs they gave us were not particularly impressive.

We signed China Crisis in the middle of 1981. Their image wasn't terribly strong, but I thought the group had a good, identifiable sound. They also had some interesting songs, but they were rather unstructured, unworked-out, and so they've spent most of this year improving the way their songs hang together and how they work as a whole. Eventually the whole thing falls into place and we think, "well we've got a very good chance with this band."

Virgin has a roster of artists, 60 per cent of whom are commercially and financially successful. We do a tremendous amount of work with our successful bands to get them to maintain their success or to move upward over a long period; constantly forcing them to evaluate themselves and to improve. Then we have to look at the other bands and decide whether they're going to get somewhere, or whether we should let them go and look for new ones to supplement the label. Obviously, we're always looking at the current trends.

Finding new artists
We try to use our record stores and everybody we know or meet to give us advance information of anything that's happening that we should be aware of. We look at the hot news items and also, in an almost academic way, we look to see whether, within our limits, we should add someone different to our roster. This isn't as calculated as saying to ourselves that we *need* a heavy metal band, although something like that happened in 1980 when we signed Ian Gillan. This year we signed Gary Ward, another heavy rock act, and Shooting Star, but we've also got some high-quality mainstream artists such as Phil Collins, Toto-Coelo and Toni Basil. Because we're not especially good at handling artists of that type, we have a deal with a small-label production company who look after them for us and we handle distribution and overseas licensing. That's one way that we're expanding the company.

Sleeve designed by band member Phil Oakey

A small record company starts out on a wing and a prayer and then, if they're lucky, they suddenly find they've got a successful band and are making lots of money. Then they have to decide what to do when the inspiration has worn off, because once you become established your business doesn't work in quite the same way.

We set up Virgin in 1973 with just one person, Simon Draper, working full-time. His job was to sign bands and then work out the market and how to distribute them. Mike Oldfield's *Tubular Bells* was our first signing. The basis of the company was Virgin retail and so some of the artists we signed came directly from our experience in retailing, such as the group Tangerine Dream. We knew about their potential as a result of our mail order operation. People were writing to us asking for German records that no one had ever heard of, so we started importing them, discovered that they sold well and realized that we had a specialist knowledge of this kind of band. Most independent labels begin as the result of some specialist knowledge; for example, Stiff was started by people who had a knowledge of and perspective on punk; and further back Berry Gordy – who, incidentally, also owned a record store before starting a label – had great experience of R & B when he founded Tamla Motown.

This year we hired a young guy who knew a lot about dance music and he's brought a bit of expertise that we didn't have before: a good perspective on, and insight into, dance hits. He has come up with some very good things, some soul and some disco. This is bringing us a new range of artists; we have to keep evaluating and trying to expand our range even further without creating too large a roster of artists, which can be dangerous.

The trend now

The tendency today is for bands to become more chart/single oriented and generally more sophisticated. Style, production and imagery are of paramount importance, and we seem to be moving back to the days of the manufactured pop star. A group will come out of nowhere, be successful instantly – almost without having done any gigs – and suddenly they start making these super-gloss albums. Everyone is aspiring to be ABBA rather than The Velvet Underground or The Rolling Stones.

This is a trend away from what was happening in the late 1970s, when the last big change in the British record industry was brought about by punk. At that time – around 1976 – a new generation of young musicians came through who had far greater control over what they were doing. Their music was relatively unsophisticated, and they didn't seem to require the services of professional producers, engineers and art people; they didn't even seem to need the professional pluggers to anywhere near the extent that most popular music does, because their music had been given life by the street and the kids.

Punk was a natural phenomenon and the major record companies were completely thrown, because they couldn't understand or come to terms with it. The groups didn't seem to need them; they simply needed their money and their distribution – distribution is always the bottom line. This caused a change in attitude within record companies and in the way they worked; yet, inevitably, those same companies and the people who work for them are now returning to their previous position.

The small label phenomenon

Along with punk came independent record companies, because people realized they could make a record cheaply, get it pressed, the sleeves printed and put it out themselves. Small companies proliferated, but the problem they all shared was distribution. When Virgin started, the only functions we didn't feel competent to undertake were distribution and selling; so we did a deal with Island records whereby we paid them for the use of their distribution system and access to their manufacturing and sales force, while we did all of our own marketing promotion.

Some of the small independents, such as Rough Trade, Spartan and Pinnacle, began to set themselves up as distribution companies to act for themselves and others; and so small-labels became a phenomenon.

The small labels thrived on idealism, and they could get away with a certain amount of inefficiency because everyone wanted product. But when it came down to the realities of business – efficient distribution, aggressive selling and comprehensive coverage – many of those who had been running the champion labels suddenly realized they needed better knowledge and control of the business sides of their companies.

Surviving by signing the right artists

The lifespan of many independents are determined by their specialist knowledge and interest. A company has to grow in order to survive and it has to grow in the context of the record industry; if you stand still, you're going backwards. Thus successful independent record companies inevitably become less and less like independents and more and more like majors; a lot of people today refer to Virgin as a major record company, but the distinction is that Virgin is a private company run by two individuals. We've had to go through the same changes as everyone else and, after the first three or four years, we realized we had to try something completely new – become more of an all-round record company and more professional. We had exhausted our specialist knowledge, which used to be called "underground" music, so we started to sign mainstream acts such as The Motors, XTC and then, with punk, The Sex Pistols. Since then we have tried hard to stay with the trends, and occasionally, perhaps, we have helped to form them.

In time the independent movement began to run out of steam and, because of competition, the entrepreneurs looked increasingly to producers, engineers and professional pluggers. The major companies absorbed many of the independents and began to control them. Once they begin to regain a measure of control, the major record companies tend to try to get more.

While it was easy to start an independent record label in 1977, it was not so easy to continue to exist unless you had been lucky enough to sign some very good acts and had been able to adapt to changing market conditions. This is why we have tried to become as efficient as possible, and why we take a great deal of trouble over signing the right artists and helping them to improve. ●

Management

When we're looking for a new band, commercial considerations are obviously important – will they sell? However, they have to interest us as well, otherwise we wouldn't get any enjoyment from working with them, and you can't market a product successfully if it doesn't interest you.

One particular group, for example, have repeatedly asked us to manage them, but we've always refused – partly because it would be morally wrong for us to take them on since we couldn't give them the service we know they deserve, but also – and more importantly – because they don't have any particular interest for us, even though we know their product is commercially viable. This is important. If you are telephoned at, say, three in the morning by an artist you believe in, you don't mind and you're on their case immediately. But, if you find it a bore from the start, you have a negative reaction, the artist gets upset, and things go from bad to worse.

Managers and artists

As a manager it's important not to start getting any egotistical ideas about being a member of the band: once that happens you won't be able to give an unbiased criticism of the band's performance, and will inevitably get wound up in the band's publicity machine. You have to remain detached, like a referee, in order to deal with the inevitable personality clashes that occur within a band.

Although as far as the public is concerned the manager should be purely a businessman with no involvement in the musical or personal side of the group, it is important for a band to feel that they can look up to the person that represents them as someone who has the say, not only on legal matters, but on other things as well. The relationship between manager and band must, to some extent, be on a personal level: the band should respect you as a friend as well as a business manager, which means you have to be on call at any time of the day or night to give any advice that might be needed.

Bad and good management

Some managers represent too many artists; only a few of their clients become successful and receive any financial benefits from the arrangement. Although the manager will benefit from all his artists, he cannot provide a proper service for every one of them and so some will inevitably lose out. Even though such bands may eventually leave him, he will still continue to make money from their future earnings.

A good manager does not operate like this, because it's immoral and unethical. He wouldn't consider taking someone on if he didn't think he could give them the service they deserve; and any musicians, who have the sense to realize they've reached the point where they need someone to look after them, have a right to that service.

The need for a manager

It's very important for a band to accept the fact that they need management. Sometimes you get a group who think they can manage themselves and take on a manager only because they can't get the contract they want from a record company; working with such people is like constantly banging your head against a brick wall, because there is a constant conflict of interests.

Successful musicians know their limitations. If you really think you've got a chance of making it, then go all out, but you've really got to get a team together, because an artist can't manage himself – Julian Bream and Bill Wyman are rare exceptions. Very well-established groups, such as Pink Floyd and The Rolling Stones, can manage themselves successfully simply because they don't really need management any more, but very few artists ever reach that point.

It's much easier for a manager to deal with record companies than for the artist to do so, because, as a rule, record companies only like to deal with artists from the musical point of view, although there are some that think they can run the artists as well: most record companies are full of frustrated managers and artists. A good manager is someone who advises, enjoys managing, and is in the job because it's what he really wants to do, and not just because he's been frustrated in some other ambition.

When to get a manager

It's not essential for a band to have a manager just as soon as it is formed. First the members must get together as a unit of people and prove to

Squeeze, managed by David Enthoven and Mike Hedge

themselves that they're "worthy of management".

There's usually one member of the band who's so hungry for stardom that he'll work out for himself that the band need somebody to help them deal with contractual problems, and then he will persuade the others that they must seek management. But they must work that out at the beginning; they have to get together as a group and decide that they want to make it: if the desire isn't there, they will never get anywhere. A lot of artists don't actually want stardom – by stardom we mean success – if they stop to really think about it, and they've got to want that more than anything, even before the manager comes on to the scene.

Only very rarely can a band put something together on their own, unless they're musicians who have been around for a long time, have been through the mill, and can therefore get themselves together and go all out on a commercial level. They can succeed because they've been through it; they know what they want and they're going to capitalize on their experience before they get too old.

But it is very different for a band that's just starting out. They will have to scratch the money from wherever they can, do a gig whenever they can. Once they have made a demo tape, however cheap, it's time to bring in a manager, who can then negotiate with the record companies as required.

A new band should sign with a manager only when they are independently represented by a lawyer of their own choice, and until that happens they shouldn't sign anything. The lawyers in this business are aware of all the pitfalls and there are plenty of good music lawyers around. The band's first signatures should be on a management contract. Once that has been settled, all other contracts can be left to the manager to deal with.

Finding a manager

A new band should look for honesty in a manager above all else. Unfortunately, there are some dishonest people in this business because such vast amounts of money are involved. Any potential manager should be checked out with other people in the business. Try to find someone who has had a square deal from their manager. Shy away from managers with a lot of artists because you'll just be another name on their list. They might be doing a lot of business, but at the end of the day they will have to unscramble a mess of contracts that haven't done them any favours in the first place.

When a band is getting together, it's essential that they don't sign anything until they have management, which is why honesty is so important in a manager – not just because an unscrupulous one may rip you off, but because you need honesty in his reactions and his honest belief in you as an artist.

Becoming a manager

There are no hard-and-fast rules for someone wanting to go into management. You have got to know the trade well enough to be able to advise the people who are in it, and there's no simple way of learning that – you can only do it by experience.●

311

Session Musicians

When one hears a recording of a well-arranged song and appreciates the exciting beat, the subtle string sound, the dramatic brass punches or any other skilful effect, it is natural to award credit to the artist or band and their producer – and rightly so. However, it must not be forgotten that much of the music industry's success depends on the work of backing, or session, musicians. If, for example, you look at any recent album produced by Quincy Jones or Gamble and Huff, where the concept of the album is built around one artist or a small group, there is invariably a list of performers' names on the album sleeve telling you who the drummers, guitarists, horn players, string players and the rest of the back-up musicians are.

Session musicians are hired to play for recordings and live gigs, and they have to perform with maximum efficiency. For a small band, prepared to rehearse by ear at home, time is of little consequence, but when, say, twenty or thirty musicians are assembled to record together, they must all be extremely professional in their approach. They are usually good readers, able to carry out on the spot whatever is asked of them in terms of altered phrasing or variations in the arrangement. They must have a wide musical vocabulary and few musical prejudices.

A good professional session player does the job in the way which will best suit the track; he will adapt to the producer's wishes and get what is wanted on to tape with the minimum of fuss. Most young musicians who become session players nowadays will have had a formal musical education and will have eventually gained a place at a music college. After completing their studies they will move on to gain experience in whatever field they choose – anything from rock groups to symphony orchestras – gradually achieving a very high standard of musicianship. Generally speaking a musician will have made a name for him or herself in a band or orchestra before attempting to get into sessions. Sessions will probably bring higher financial rewards, give the musician the opportunity to play more varied styles of music and work alongside the élite of the music profession.

Many of the top session musicians of today have not had the benefit of a formal musical education; some are self-taught, having played in the local dance hall or club and possibly later joined one of the big bands on the road; others will have played in groups. Some cannot read music but make up for this in other ways. Such players are limited as to the type of session they can do; they are likely to be booked for sessions where time is not important and their special talents can be exploited. With plenty of hard work and a bit of luck a good musician can make a career as a session player. Although you can make it if you can't read music, you are much better off if you can.

Session fixers

The majority of sessions are arranged through a so-called fixer (orchestral manager to be polite)! This is someone, like myself, who puts together an orchestra, band, or rhythm section – in fact any combination of instruments and singers that anyone might require. A fixer should have a wide musical background because he will have to book musicians for many different styles of music; unless he is familiar with as many as possible, one day he will come unstuck! Over a period of time in the profession he will have gained considerable knowledge of most aspects of the music business: dealing with musicians, composers, arrangers and producers. There is also a lot of paperwork involved: contracts, union agreements, distributing fees and residuals – so it's not all glamour.

Whatever type of session a fixer is booking, a lot of work and thought will go into it. He will decide the type of musician required and gradually work through lists of players he knows until he gets the right one. If it's a busy day, then there is an opportunity to try someone new. Once everything is completed, he will go along to the session to make sure everything runs smoothly and that the client is happy with the result. After the session, all he has to do is send the company the bill. If for any reason the company defaults, the fixer is still responsible for paying the musicians. He is the one who carries the financial can.

Types of session

Master sessions Session musicians are most frequently hired for studio master sessions at which recordings are made. Most recordings feature freelance session musicians, although some small bands use no extra musicians. The session player is paid a fee for playing on a track whether or not it is released. He will rarely be paid royalties, even if the record is a big hit, because the producer and/or record company is taking the risk and will have paid the musicians in advance of the record's release. There are occasions when session musicians earn "points"; if an especially well-known player adds an important ingredient to a recording, he may demand a small percentage of the production points, such as a half of one per cent (half a point) or one per cent (one point). If, for example, a sax player is noted for his solo work and a solo sax is an essential element in the hit potential of a record – Gerry Rafferty's *Baker Street* or Billy

Session musicians, *below,* from the London Symphony Orchestra. Professional players often supplement their orchestral duties with studio work, which can encompass anything from demo sessions, music for TV movies and signature tunes, to advertising jingles.

Joel's *Just The Way You Are,* for example – then the player may claim a point on top of his session fee.

Some recording companies in the United States have a house band. These musicians work regular studio hours and are paid a fixed wage, perhaps with extras in the form of points or bonuses for big commercial successes.

In England, if a player plays two or more parts in the same piece of music in the same three-hour session, for the first playing he gets the standard fee, for the first overdub he gets 125 per cent of his initial fee in addition, and for the second overdub he receives 140 per cent in addition. So, a fast player can make a good sum in three hours. The union has arranged matters so that it's more expensive to use one player to do three parts than it is to use three players. However, for convenience, recording studios

will frequently use one player for two or three parts, and for guitars and keyboards they will often do this so that the feel is consistent. In the United States musicians receive an all-inclusive fee per session, regardless of the number of overdubs they perform.

Demo sessions Demonstration, or demo, sessions are similar to master sessions in that they take place in a recording studio. A demo tape is recorded when a song must be heard in a basic form by, say, a publisher. He might hire three or four musicians – usually a rhythm section – to record a simple version without frills and not intended for commercial release. In some states of the United States there is a fixed lower rate for demos and an electric "beep" occurs on the tape every 30 seconds to ensure that it remains a demo and is not sold commercially.

TV sessions There are specific minimum rates for live performance on television, and if the musician appears on camera a higher scale of fees operates. Repeat fees are paid if a television recording is broadcast more than once. In England, performers at signature tune sessions are paid more highly than they would be for normal TV recording sessions; this is because the television companies pay repeat fees for all music except signature tunes. Again in England, once a television commercial has been used for a period of three years, the musicians get a repeat fee; and if a record is produced from a television film score they will receive recording fees as well as the initial television fee.

In the United States payments for TV sessions are more complex, although signature tunes are not considered a special case. For home television, excepting commercials, musicians are paid a one-time session fee, and receive a percentage royalty only if the programme is repeated in another medium – such as videotape; royalties are paid through the Special Payments Fund of the American Musicians Union.

Session musicians who record on to videotape for later transmission on television are paid a different scale of fees, which vary according to the programme in which the music is included and the time of day at which it goes out. No repeat fees are paid unless the programme is repeated in another medium.

Producers of made-for-television movies negotiate fees with the musicians; there are no set rates.

Musicians are paid a set fee for playing on a commercial, which can be used up to three times every hour for a period of 13 weeks. Thereafter the musicians are paid a royalty every time the commercial goes on the air.

Jingle sessions In the United States all the musicians involved in the recording of a jingle are paid repeat fees, known as residuals. In England, a musician who performs on a jingle is usually just paid a fee for the session. However, jingles are often written, recorded and produced by the same person or group of people. Such people can opt for one large fee, or a smaller initial fee and repeat fees every time the jingle is played.

Live sessions For live work – concerts, gigs or cabaret – musicians are paid a performing fee for, say, backing a singer in a show or playing in a classical concert. If a concert is recorded live so that records can be produced, an additional recording fee is due to the performers. Session players frequently go on tour with bands or singers, especially around their own country with singers from another country; an overall fee for the tour will normally be negotiated.

Playing sessions

As long as everyone follows instructions – and seasoned session players will always do this – sessions are usually straightforward. On expensive productions session players may have a fair amount of rest time, while other instruments are being overdubbed. The best studios have comfortable resting rooms, with television and video, and good canteens. Most recording sessions are well organized, so that the player can arrive, play his piece and any necessary overdubs and go home again reasonably quickly. If he is playing on several tracks of an album, he may go into the studio for a number of days in succession.

Advice for beginners

A musician wanting to break into session playing should first of all contact a fixer, arranger or composer; he should describe what he does and send a cassette. A composer or arranger will often only use people he knows, and so unfortunately musicians acquire most of their contacts by word of mouth. However, beginners should not despair; if an arranger cannot get any of the, say, pianists he normally uses, he will have to try someone new and his decision could be based simply on having heard a demo tape that day.

The budding session musician should have talent and a good attitude. Just play well, get on with people and try to get your name around because, like every other business, this one requires luck. Some of the best players never get in because they are not the right type – perhaps they are inflexible or awkward. It's a matter of the right time, the right place and the right attitude.●

Music Publishing

Thirty years ago, the music publisher was much more important than he is today. In the "old days" a publisher would create opportunities by finding a manuscript, going to a producer to record a song and becoming directly involved in the commercial aspects of promotion. In the late 1950s and the 1960s the publisher would place writers under contract and give them a living wage, and if he believed a writer had some talent and commercial viability, he would be willing to gamble a certain amount of money.

Today the role of the publisher is very different. The number of large publishers is declining because many artists are now forming their own companies and becoming their own publishers. There has been a movement, especially in the past few years, to break the hold that publishers have had over musicians in the past. Sting of The Police, for example, recently set a precedent in music publishing by "taking back" the copyright on one of his songs. This type of non-traditional behaviour is certainly a potential problem for many large publishers, and it will not come as any surprise if a number of artists decide to follow the trend. Music publishing is still big business, but fewer and fewer artists are willing to negotiate deals whereby the publisher receives massive cuts from their income.

Cynics of the music world claim that the music publisher spends most of his time in an expensive office with calculator in hand, totalling artists' gains and losses. In some ways this is true because the publisher's main role today is one of administration; he is similar to an agent who receives a cut for performing certain duties. Because the trend is towards self-sufficiency, many groups arrive on the publisher's doorstep with a ready-made kit of songs written and recorded, and a manager. More often than not they are simply looking to the publisher to act as an administrator of legal arrangements and financial deals, who also happens to own them.

The ideal publisher, however, will be more than just an administrator. He will listen to the tapes sent to him and, if the song is good but the artist is not, try to place the material with suitable artists and recording companies. If the artist is both a writer and performer, the publisher's job is made easier because he can then sell him or

her as a package. Most publishers, however, do not do this because it is more a responsibility of management than publishing.

The economics of publishing

Music publishing has also changed from the economic point of view. Twenty-five years ago, a 50-50 division of profits between publisher and artist was the norm. Now, most writers expect a minimum of 75 per cent of all income and if the writer has had any success in some other venture – for example, if he is a member of a successful group and because of the group's name is able to write for other artists – he might demand and receive 85 per cent of the income.

Music publishing used to be a risk business; the only risk today is if a writer or his manager demands guarantees on top of the artist's income. For example, an artist tells his publisher that, although he is due to receive 85 per cent of his income, the amount must at least equal a definite figure. If the 85 per cent turns out to be less than that figure, the publisher must bring the artist's income up to the agreed sum.

When The Rolling Stones became successful I was approached by their manager, Gordon Moves and realized I had to do something I believe nobody had ever done before. My arrangement with the Stones was that they would receive 85 per cent of the royalty income on their own recordings, and I added that they were to receive a 50-50 division of other recordings initiated by myself. In other words, I was saying that they were entitled to the lion's share of the records they created, but I would like to be a partner in those things I helped to create as a result of their initial efforts. The 15 per cent I was to receive might sound like a huge sum, considering the group in question, but in fact that amount was barely enough to cover my publishing costs. A fair agreement nowadays is usually a 70-30 or 80-20 split. There is a 50-50 split only in rare instances, for example when an artist records a song written or performed by a successful group, as when Marianne Faithful recorded *As Tears Go By*.

Income division

How the income from a song is divided depends upon the type of song; a piece recorded by a rock group has no real life other than its own recording by the artist. In England, six and one-quarter per cent of the retail selling price is fixed as a statutory royalty and is divided between, for example, the writers of the 10 or 12 songs on each album. In the United States it used to be two cents but is now four cents per title on an album or single, which is a substantial income for an artist who has written all of his own material and sold a million albums. The change in the law, which doubled the royalty, was hard fought for and there is still resistance from the big recording companies, but the United States has become the major territory in terms of income on mechanical records, as opposed to performing rights.

How that four cents is divided depends entirely upon the arrangement between the publisher and the writer. More often than not the writer is also the publisher. If he is not, the norm in the United States today is a 75-25 division, or sometimes 80-20; the writer retaining three of the four cents.

Your rights

Young artists are often confused about their rights and the complex legalities of music publishing, and for good reason. As much as an artist may wish to act on an entirely independent basis, it would be foolish not to seek advice from organizations that can help sort out some of the more complicated technicalities such as copyrights, royalties and all the fine print.

There are a number of associations available to the songwriter that will ensure his or her rights. In England, these include the Songwriters Association, the Performing Rights Society (PRS), and the British Association of Songwriters, Composers and Authors (BASCA). In the United States the equivalent associations are the American Society of Composers, Authors and Publishers (ASCAP) and Broadcast Music, Inc. (BMI). ASCAP and BMI are competitors and it is a matter of intuition as to which an artist chooses to join. ASCAP is the older of the two and BMI more aggressive, although this seems to be levelling off.

To avoid being taken advantage of, a writer in England who finds it difficult to get a contract with a publisher, but through his own efforts is able to record his work, should definitely join the Mechanical Copyright Protection Society (MCPS). MCPS also performs the useful function of collecting all the small sums due which a publisher is unable to monitor, such as from the Third World where even the largest international companies do not have affiliations. In the United States, the Harry Fox Organization provides the same services and also has the right to audit record companies and, as a result, pass on huge sums of money to its members. MCPS are

beginning to do this in England as well.

In America, if a young writer has a song which he or she feels has potential and is approached by a manager asking for the copyright, ideally the artist should first form his own company as a basic protection for his own rights. With a recording in hand and his company, which also owns the rights, as security, he could then approach a legitimate publisher and make an arrangement based on what the publisher could contribute to the venture in terms of further sales.

Film, television and advertising

With film music and advertising jingles, the situation becomes more difficult because a new writer is rarely allowed to walk into a film company and write music; the process usually takes place in stages. He might, for example, start by writing for television and slowly become recognized, developing contacts in the process. At this point, if he wishes to spread his field of recognition, a publisher becomes a great advantage.

Once the writer has reached this stage, there are certain points he must be aware of. Anyone who writes a jingle or television music is entitled to a commissioning fee, however low or high, based upon his reputation. That fee gives the film or television company exclusive rights to use that piece of music within a film, without interfering with the artist's other rights. In short, it is an exclusive right for that film in perpetuity – however successful the film is – and that is why the film company will pay a fee. The fee can range from an inconsequential sum to thousands of pounds or dollars. To ensure that the appropriate fee is arranged and that the contract is fair, a person with negotiating experience is required. It has happened more than once that a film company has taken half of an artist's rights, put the contract in a drawer, and the artist is lucky if he or she is then able to collect.

It is an unfortunate fact of life that an artist must give 50 per cent of his earnings from other sales of the music to the film company. Most television or film companies have their own publishing association and even people like Dave Grusin (*On Golden Pond*) probably co-published with the film company's publisher and received perhaps 75 per cent; 50 per cent as writer and 25 and co-publisher. Vangelis (*Chariots of Fire*) would certainly have had to give his rights to the film company as part of being commissioned. Depending on the size of the film and the budget, the commissioning fee for films is huge compared with television, but the rights you are required to pass over are exactly the same.

With advertising jingles, however, there is no

(hereinafter referred to as "the said work(s)") TO HOLD the same unto the Publishers their successors and assigns absolutely AND the Assignor(s) hereby agree(s) on demand to execute and sign any other documents and to do all other acts and things which may hereafter be required of the Assignor(s) for vesting in the Publishers the premises expressed to be hereby assigned AND the Assignor(s) hereby warrant(s) and declare(s) that the said work is a new and original unpublished work and does not infringe the copyright in any other work and that he (they) the Assignor(s) has (have) good right and full power to assign to the Publishers free from all encumbrances the premises expressed to be hereby assigned and every of them in the manner aforesaid. AND IT IS HEREBY CERTIFIED that the transaction hereby effected does not form part of a larger transaction or of a series of transactions in respect of which the amount or value or the aggregate amount or value of the consideration exceeds £5,500 (five thousand five hundred pounds). The Publisher undertakes to use its best endeavours to Publish and otherwise commercially exploit the said works.

AS WITNESS the hands of the parties hereto the day and year first above written.

THE SCHEDULE ABOVE REFERRED TO:

SHEET MUSIC ROYALTIES

(   ) per cent) of the marked retail selling price of all copies of the said work(s) sold (except as hereafter provided) but so that no royalties shall be payable on sample copies issued of the work(s).

(   ) per cent) of all sums received by the Publisher on the sale of foreign and colonial editions of the work(s).

The Publisher shall have the right to include the work(s) in any album folio or newspaper and to license others to make similar use and shall pay Fifty (50%) of all sums received by the Publisher in respect of the inclusion thereof in such album, folio or newspaper.

MECHANICAL ROYALTIES

(   ) per cent) of all Royalties received by the Publishers for reproductions of the said work(s) in connection with the manufacture of records (other than for use in or in connection with cinematograph films and television films) for sale to the Public.

SYNCHRONISATION FEES

(   ) per cent) of all Royalties and Fees received by the Publishers for the right to use the said work(s) in or in connection with any cinematograph film or television film.

PERFORMING BROADCASTING AND REDIFFUSION FEES

These are collected by the Performing Right Society Limited (and its affiliated Societies throughout the world) and are paid direct to its members in accordance with the Rules laid down by the Society and it is agreed that the Assignor(s) share shall be 50% (fifty percent) and the Publishers share shall be 50% (fifty percent).

If the Assignor(s) is (are) a Member(s) of the Performing Right Society Ltd., the rights hereby assigned are assigned subject to the rights of the said Society arising by virtue of the Assignor(s) membership of the said Society or otherwise but include the reversionary interest of the Assignor(s) in such rights expectant upon the determination by any means of the rights of the Society as aforesaid, subject to the payment to the Assignor(s) by the Publishers of the Assignor's(s) share of all performing right fees received by the Publishers, such share to be not less than the share previously payable to the Assignor(s) by the Society.

This Assignment may be regarded as the Assignor(s) certificate for the purpose of Paragraph (a) of the Performing Right Society's Rule 1 (O) authorising the Performing Right Society to treat the Publishers as exploiting the said work(s).

GENERALLY

All Royalties and Fees payable by the Publishers to the Assignor(s) by virtue of this Assignment shall be divided between the Assignor(s) in the following manner and shall be paid within 60 (sixty) days after June 30th and December 31st in each year:-

_____

SIGNED by the Assignor(s) _____

in the presence of _____

_____

SIGNED by _____ For and on behalf of _____

in the presence of _____

Publishing contract

requirement to assign a copyright to the company commissioning the jingle. It is likely, for example, that Chris Gunning still retains the copyright for his Martini commercial and would only have given the advertising agency the right to use his music in any form of advertising that they did. The logic behind this is that the advertising agency cannot publish or promote; they seek only a special piece of music to be written for a specific assignment.

Printed music

Thirty or forty years ago, a music publisher survived largely on profits gained from recording and from printing and publishing sheet music. Today, printed music does not have a very large slice of the publishing pie, although a useful source of income are the compilations that have replaced the single sheets. The percentage on these is negotiable. Ten per cent of the retail selling price used to be the norm, but anyone with a reputation will probably receive up to 15 per cent, on a worldwide basis.

In the past 20 years the music industry in the United States has surpassed the gross national product increase of the entire country. There is a great deal of money to be made in the business – and a great deal to be lost if the artist is not informed of his or her rights. Most music publishers are not out to take advantage of the small guy; it is to their advantage as much as it is to the artist's to have an agreement that is fair to both parties. The legalities of music publishing, however, can become complicated and it is thus in every artist's interest to have the attitude that he is responsible for his own welfare. There is a wealth of information and advice available – all you need do is ask for it.●

Promoting Concerts and Tours

There's always a great element of risk involved in promoting concerts and tours, and that applies just as much to the larger, well-established acts as to the smaller and newer ones. You can't leave anything to chance, as has been proved recently by Blondie and many other artists; you can't be too clever. Two things to be very careful about are fixing the correct price for a concert ticket, and finding the right place for the artists to perform – getting the right act in the right venue at the right price is half the battle. Naturally, there are exceptions to this: some acts puts on such extravagant shows – with enormous sets and immensely complex lighting – that the choice of venue is greatly restricted from the outset. A typical example is a band like Pink Floyd. They are one of the few acts that can use a place like Earls Court – the rent alone costs £175,000 ($280,000) a week.

Every decision you make requires careful thinking beforehand. You must be able to trust your instincts, and be flexible in accordance with the size of the act you are dealing with. With big acts it may simply be a question of the right time, the right place, and the right money. Newer acts, on the other hand, may require more active involvement on your part. Sometimes you'll win, on occasion you'll lose. We manage to win most of the time, and that is because we're careful.

The role of the promoter
Your role as a promoter will usually depend on the type of act you're handling. For some acts you may have to do everything: design the sets; put the show together; decide on the time and place of the performance and what sort of advertising to use; make arrangements about the hotels, trucking, transport, sound, lighting – even put the crew together if necessary. The larger, more sophisticated acts tend to deliver a great deal of the equipment themselves; other acts may not have anything at all.

Once I get involved with an act, I usually work on a one-year plan with them; as well as their concert tours, I help to plan the timing of their studio sessions. We have followed this system with acts like Eric Clapton and, more recently, Asia and Pink Floyd. Every act is different, however, and no two concerts are ever the same.

Choosing acts
When deciding whether or not to promote an act, I use two basic criteria: first, is it good entertainment? second, does it have long-term potential? I've never really been interested in one-hit wonders. Longevity is an important consideration in this business, and many concert and tour promoters probably take a five-year view of the acts they work with. Entertainment value is important too, because it is live music that you are primarily promoting on the stage – if the band has a hit record, that's simply an additional bonus. Hit records are a more important consideration these days, because of growing competition, but when we began promoting concerts in the 1960s they were irrelevant. Although many of the acts we started out with became very successful recording artists, their records only became popular once they had achieved success as live performers.

Starting in promotion
I began in this business as social secretary at college, which meant that I hired bands for college dances and concerts; by the time I had ended my three years there I was looking after the social side of five different colleges. During that time I worked with and started developing several different acts, including Family, The Move, The Moody Blues, Eric Clapton, Spencer Davis and Manfred Mann.

When I left college and started with a few colleagues handling promotions independently, I didn't particularly want to deal with tours, and so I began working on special events. I became involved with the first free concerts at Parliament Hill, London, with The Beach Boys, Fleetwood Mac, Procol Harum and Status Quo, and then did several shows at The Roundhouse in north London. We then got permission from the Greater London Council to use Crystal Palace and started putting shows on there, and it was then that the touring started, although at that stage it was still on quite a small scale. We began by simply helping out at events like the Great Western Festival at Lincoln and the Hollywood Festival: we produced shows for the people who were actually putting on the festivals. Later, I worked with Manfred Mann and The New Seekers, and began touring them; that's how we got involved with touring on a large scale.

Whenever we put on especially big shows for certain acts they would then ask us to handle a tour for them. We started working with artists

The Rolling Stones concert at Leeds in July 1982. The promoters are responsible for everything running smoothly and have to deal with numerous people from the local authority and the police to television crews and the support act, in this case The J. Geils Band.

like Genesis, Yes, Black Sabbath, Lou Reed, Van Morrison, David Bowie, The Who and The Rolling Stones, and slowly but surely we developed into a major touring company. We have always been particularly interested in special events, the big shows – and we still are. They are what I enjoy the most and they give the business a lift.

Tips for would-be promoters

A good organizational sense is essential. You must be able to handle the administration, but you must also have a good instinct for the music and be able to distinguish a good performance on record from one on the stage: a good hit record may not always translate into a good live performance. I always consider an act as a live proposition. Is it good? Does it entertain? Does the music work on stage? If you've got those elements together and have got your figures right, there's no reason to be foiled by the opposition.

I never get involved in bidding wars – I don't believe in them. I always put in my best offer for an act and if someone else offers twice as much good luck to them. I know my limitations – a vital consideration in this business. You should never take on more than you can handle.●

Press and Publicity

In previous chapters you have read about how music is produced, in all its various forms. Though many people are drawn to play music for their own pleasure, most young groups cutting their teeth in the local clubs and dance halls have an inner ambition to be the next Beatles, Jacksons or Sex Pistols. Thus, what I intend to do in the following chapter is to explain the methods by which music reaches the public – and the stark contrasts that exist between Britain and the United States.

The press in Britain

In Britain, the launch of a new artist has often been set in motion by one of the four major consumer magazines – *Sounds, New Musical Express, Melody Maker* or *Record Mirror* – *before* the artist has even signed a record company deal. *Sounds,* for example, often gives a boost to young bands by featuring them on the front cover before they have released a record.

The British music press, mainly staffed by young and enthusiastic music fans, is often more efficient in searching out new talent than the "A and R" departments of the major record companies. The four main weeklies sell on average about 200,000 copies a week each, and, as each has a committed, record-buying readership, they therefore hold an extremely influential position when it comes to getting a new group off the ground. For an aspiring band, a review of a gig or of an independently-released single in the music papers can be far more influential in attracting record companies' attention than any amount of phone calls, letters and tapes.

Thus, it is clear that music public relations men (PRs) will spend most of their time trying to get their new band written about in the music papers – though, conversely, when the acts are established, the PR may expend just as much energy trying to keep them out! I can think of many major bands who refuse to allow the music press to review their records or concerts. A few vitriolic reviews and comments in the *New Musical Express* have bruised many an over-inflated ego. In fact, a consistently hostile music press can do much to dent the career of an established band, though many an old warhorse has kept going despite this animosity.

No other country in the world has such a lively

and popular music press and Britain therefore contrasts vividly with the United States, where radio is all-powerful and where it is virtually impossible for a band to receive any significant recognition without major radio play.

The British music press' influence has built up since the early 1960s, although the situation now seems to be changing. *Sounds* recently overtook *NME* in the circulation battle, and has achieved its success by a populist approach – covering everything and anything. However, it is not without its blind spots and is not averse to giving a bad review. In contrast, *NME*'s attitude has meant that artists are reluctant to expose themselves to a possible mauling. It remains to be seen whether its approach will change, though there is already some evidence of this.

Meanwhile, *Melody Maker,* once giant of the music press, sadly went into decline in the late 1970s and early 1980s – but recently a change of staff and a new look has meant it is slowly gaining back its respect. The remaining popular weekly, *Record Mirror,* has steadily increased its circulation by concentrating on artists in the charts, although it has recently encountered competition from a bi-monthly magazine called *Smash Hits,* a lively, well-presented mixture of pin-ups, songwords, gossip and some serious comment which has cornered a huge market within a very short space of time. *Record Mirror* recently changed to a magazine-sized, colour pin-up format in a bid to challenge *Smash Hits.* In short, the music press seems to be realizing the economic reality that it needs to reflect public taste, as much as influence it, in order to survive.

Radio in the United States

In the United States an artist's effort is directed at radio and achieving maximum airplay. It is discouraging that many American stations are sticking to increasingly conservative playlists, in line with advertisers' demands to upgrade the demographics of their listenership. This explains why much new music fails to break through in America. In fact, often the only exposure for new bands that do not fit into US radio's acceptable moulds is on cable television, college radio and in trendy clubs in the major cities.

The American press, meanwhile, tends to follow the fashions rather than setting them.

Traditionally, British radio has always offered very limited possibilities. There exists one major network, the BBC, which broadcasts in the main on three different stations, covering three separate areas of taste. Radio 1 is the pop/rock music station, Radio 2 is a more middle-of-the-road/easy listening station, and Radio 3 caters for lovers of classical music. These stations broadcast all over the UK and Radio 1 almost dictates what records are in the charts. A network of commercial radio stations was established in the early 1970s – and new ones are still opening – but these have not proved to be influential in helping records to sell.

Pluggers

Most bands, either independently or through their record companies, have both press agents and what are known as "pluggers", who help them to gain exposure in the press and on radio. Pluggers spend their time visiting radio stations and trying to draw the attention of producers and disc-jockeys to the merits of the records that they are pushing. In the main it is the producers, or "programmers" at the stations who decide what records are going to be aired. Disc-jockeys, especially the big names, do have some influence on what is played, however.

Pluggers usually rely on a good personal relationship with both the producers and the DJs and aim to build up a respected reputation. Record companies rely on regular, heavy airplay to push records into the charts. The most-played records on Britain's Radio 1, for instance, receive between 14 and 20 plays a week. By the same token, quite a few records become "turntable" hits in that they receive heavy airplay but still fail to get into the charts. In the USA, a record company will aim to get a record into "heavy rotation" meaning 5 to 7 plays a day.

Then, of course, there are a few records that receive little or no airplay, but for various reasons, whether it be notoriety or sheer weight of other media interest, become hits. A case in point is the Sex Pistols' *God Save The Queen,* which stormed to the number 2 slot in the summer of 1977, within a couple of weeks of its release – despite being banned by every major radio station.

The importance of radio play is emphasized by the sometimes ridiculous lengths which record companies go to in order to draw attention to their product. Here at Chrysalis, for instance, we have delivered records in full biker's gear, on horseback, and with various accompanying gifts and gimmicks. On one occasion, while launching a band called Icehouse, we hit on the idea of freezing the records inside a block of ice – and then delivering them. But there was nowhere in London that could offer the proper freezing facilities – and we ended up freezing only two records, one-at-a-time. These eventually ended up in London record stores, delivered on flat bed trucks because they were so heavy, and customers were asked to estimate how long the ice would take to melt. The resulting flood was such that the fire brigade had to be called to pump away the water! And after all that, Icehouse still failed to get a hit with that record.

Such gimmicks may point to the fact that the old days of bribery and corruption are over, but there is no doubt that here and there, there is someone who might be susceptible to a free lunch or a bottle of wine – most promotion and PR people have fairly large expense accounts!

In America, promo-men, or pluggers, vie with each other to get their records onto the playlists of the local stations, pulling favours wherever they can. If a record does not fit immediately into the playlist mould, then the record company will aim at the smaller stations, and use any success in terms of people phoning in and requesting the record to influence the more important stations.

The scope of American radio is indicated by the fact that *every* city has several radio stations. These cover all areas of musical taste, usually split into rock (known as Adult Orientated Rock or AOR), easy listening, black-orientated soul, Top 40 and Country. The record companies try to determine which areas a record will appeal to – and attempt to sell it to the relevant stations. Many records will span more than one area; for example, Queen's *Another One Bites The Dust* went to the top of the soul charts and also received play on the rock stations. It is not impossible for a record to be featured across three or four different formats.

Recently a new format has arisen which is becoming known as "urban contemporary". This has sprung to life mainly in the big cities and features a mixture of black and white dance music. This format has allowed some exposure for the new forces in British music, and helped The Human League to start breaking *Don't You Want Me Baby,* eventually a number 1 single. However, in the main, the new wave of British music was not accepted in America because it did not fit into any of the established moulds. AOR would have seemed the natural outlet, but due to a shrinking market the stations came under increasing pressure from advertisers and adopted extremely conservative playlists. This explains the proliferation of bands which sound the same and often appear faceless. The list includes Loverboy, Styx, Journey, Foreigner, REO Speedwagon, Quarterflash, Asia and Kansas. There has recently appeared a slightly-sanitized version of the British New Wave encompassing such names as Joan Jett, The Motels and Huey Lewis and The News, which seems to be catching on.

The press in the United States

As regards music press, most of the major American cities have their own local music papers – *The New York Rocker,* for instance – but obviously these carry influence only in their local catchment area. There are a few national music-based publications, such as *Trouser Press* and *Creem. Rolling Stone* has moved increasingly into a more general area, covering politics, cinema and other areas of cultural interest. It is often a struggle for music papers to survive and they tend to concentrate on already-established artists and give little space to the up-and-coming.

The British national press

Another important area of concentration for the British music PR is the national press – a phenomenon unknown in the US, where newspapers are very regionalized. In the main the British national press gives good coverage to music. Britain boasts more national daily newspapers than any other country in the world – and it is in this area that the art of PR needs to be most finely-honed, for there is much competition for what is in effect very little space. To the popular tabloids, such as *The Sun, Daily Mirror, The Star, Daily Mail* and *Daily Express,* the PR will always try to supply interesting "angles" on an artist – be they tied to fashion, a zany photograph or the artist's outrageous personality – all the time seeking to stimulate interest from the pop pages and achieve maximum coverage.

The more serious daily and Sunday newspapers, such as *The Times, Sunday Times, Guardian, Daily Telegraph, Sunday Telegraph* and *Observer,* offer a more studied coverage and feature live and album reviews plus the occasional feature. They do not demand the strong "angle" sought by the tabloids.

The skilled PR will carefully gauge a balance between what should go into the music press and what should receive mass exposure through the dailies (*The Sun,* for example, has an estimated daily circulation of 4 million). It can be a long battle to get even a small write-up in a national paper on a new band, while an established star demands coverage right across the board and presents the PR with a continual struggle to supply the various "angles" and to keep the tabloids supplied with different and eye-catching pictures.

In Britain the PR can also direct pictures and stories at a variety of glossy "teeny" magazines, which are aimed at a younger audience and concentrate on the romantic boy/girl aspects of pop music. The titles include *My Guy, Jackie* and *Oh Boy!,* which all carry pin-up pictures, songwords and relatively light prose.

Television and video

Television is becoming an increasingly important means of exposure for new bands. In America, Cable Television has become very popular among young people and one cable station, MTV, is devoted exclusively to pop and rock music.

In Britain, one play on *Top of the Pops,* BBC1's weekly review of the charts, is enough to make a record a hit – though to qualify for inclusion on the show the record has to be already in the charts, something of a "Catch 22" syndrome. Channel Four, the new national channel, promises much coverage of music of all types and that it will provide a major stimulus for new bands.

The most recent important development in rock has been the utilization of video. In fact, recent sales in the UK suggest that hits have been made more by the quality of the promotion video than of the record itself. The public are thus coming to expect sophisticated and entertaining visuals to accompany records, and record companies are responding.

Many British bands have already established reputations for their first-rate and imaginative videos, among them Visage, Ultravox, Spandau Ballet, The Human League, Duran Duran, Adam Ant and Madness, and even the established superstars have come to realize the medium's importance. For example, would Barry Manilow's *Let's Hang On* have been so big a hit, had not the accompanying video been so stylish and witty?

Both in Britain and America, there are many opportunities for rock videos to be used on television. In the USA, Cable Television airs promotional videos extensively – and in Britain, *Top of the Pops,* other pop programmes and kids shows are using videos increasingly.

A three-to-four minute video is an expensive proposition for a new band, and unless they have a millionaire manager, record company backing is required. It is, however, possible for a new band to go into a cheap studio and make a relatively unsophisticated video, which can at least be viewed by record company A & R men without them having to leave their own office. Believe me, this can only be an advantage to all concerned.●

Video and the Music Business

Television programmes have always been an important means of selling records. It isn't always possible, however, for an artist to appear live on a television programme. An artist living and working on the west coast of the United States, for example, can't always be immediately available on, say, the east coast or in England or Australia, nor even, sometimes in his own locality. To meet this need films of artists were made which could either be sent to different countries for showing on their pop music television programmes, or used in the artist's own country if he were unavailable for a live performance.

Video "promos"

With the advent of video technology, making films became a more immediate and less expensive process than before: video can be edited on the spot, as the film is being made – something that was not possible in traditional film-making – and it allows for many optical effects which have grown alongside the technology itself. In time, artists and record companies began to think they should try to make interesting films of the artists, rather than just putting them on stage and pointing a camera at them. They decided, therefore, to try to introduce imagination, stories and high production values into their video films, and this is how the film became the video-clip.

Once the record companies began to use talented, independent directors, they discovered that their videos were, in fact, far more effective than live appearances of their artists on pop music television programmes: they had far greater control over production values and could therefore make the artists look much better. Something that is visually attractive is a great sales weapon: if people identify with an artist visually they will become more involved with the music, and are therefore more likely to remember a song. At Chrysalis we first became aware of this with Blondie, because their lead singer, Debbie Harry, was exceptionally photogenic; any television appearances she made – and even photographs of her – greatly attracted people's attention to the group and their music, and consequently helped to sell their records.

Video therefore became an important promotional vehicle in the music industry, on both sides of the Atlantic. In England and most countries in western Europe, video promos are shown on television pop music programmes.

In the United States video is beginning to have a big effect. The new MTV cable television music station that plays videos 24 hours a day, offers a unique opportunity to familiarize the public with new artists and retain their interest in those they already know – an opportunity which as yet does not exist in any other country.

"Promo" techniques

Originally, the video system was rejected by serious film-makers as kids' promotional stuff. Early videos were certainly very basic, with a minimal amount of production technique. Since then, however, as budgets have grown, and the quality of the films has increased, people have come to realize that there is a great deal of skill involved in creating a good three- or four-minute video promotion film: the time restriction means that a great deal must be packed in to make it interesting. Getting the pace of the film right is a vital consideration: while it shouldn't be too fast, it must have interesting elements flowing in and out so as to maintain the viewer's attention. No matter how quick and busy a video film is – or, for that matter, how expensively produced – if it doesn't flow well and isn't directed and edited properly, it just won't work.

Frequently, enormous sums of money are spent on videos – you can usually tell how much, just by looking at them. However, you don't have to build a huge set and hire a cast of thousands to create an interesting visual – Bryan Ferry made a very successful video with just himself sitting on a chair against a white background. The joy of video is that all kinds of artists, whatever their visual image, can use the system successfully. Debbie Harry is very dynamic and jumps about; you don't have to take a lot of trouble – you just put her in front of the camera and tell her to sing. As long as we get the face, hair and movement, that's all we really need. The group Ultravox, on the other hand, are static, slow, rhythmic and automated, and their presentation on stage is not especially visual. Nevertheless, they have a well developed sense of production and a great deal of imagination; they write and direct their own videos very successfully, and have managed – using lighting, mood and effects – to create impressive videos, in which they, as individuals, play only a small part. Video gives recording artists an opportunity to extend their abilities into another medium: it is a further mode of expression for them.

When to make a video

With a group like Blondie, once an album had been made, you immediately start thinking about making three videos as quickly as possible of the most obvious singles for different countries of the world (Germany, for example, won't necessarily choose the same single from the album as, say, the United States). In fact, if Blondie simply made their album and videos and then stayed at home, everyone would be perfectly happy, because that video would be far more useful than having the group tour or do interviews.

When an artist who is well-known on the singles charts releases a new album, you are fairly safe to make videos right away, because you know you will have some demand for the videos and will get air-play for their records. With a new artist, however, you have to wait until the record begins to move in the charts to see whether you're likely to have any success. Once you do get some interest, and people begin to ask for videos, you must move quickly, which fortunately is very easy with the video system. In any case, it's a good idea to have a director or producer on hand working on a few ideas, so that you can move into action at very short notice should the need arise.

There's a danger of wasting a good deal of money with videos: many good video films have never been seen because the record they were made for has not gained enough prominence to warrant television exposure. It's a classic chicken and egg situation: you can't assume that, because you've got a terrific video, a song will be successful; you've got to get to the point where someone likes the music enough to want to show a video film on television in the first place.

The visual age

The advent of video has changed the entertainment industry by creating a new means of promotion and of exposing a product to the public, and it has also made people think a little more about their music. I believe that we're in a visual age, and that eventually people will become so used to the visual aspect that they won't want to buy a record unless they've first seen the video on television and have therefore been seduced by the visual image. This adds an entirely new element which the music industry must work with. Music that would previously have sold simply on its sound, now has to sell visually as well.

To sell records with the aid of video, you have to create something that will sell essentially on its visual content, not just on the music: in other words, you need a visual accompanied by music, and not the other way around. Pop music which requires visual accompaniment is rare. The song *Mickey* by Toni Basil is an example of a hit record that actually needed a visual image. The song is based on an American cheerleader, but people don't realize that until they see the video film with all the cheerleaders jumping up and down. In that instance, it was definitely the visual that sold the record.

Toni Basil in the video for *Mickey*.

Video albums

In my view video albums are not a viable commodity. The sense of novelty, and the attraction of a new industry caused many people to move out of the music business and into video. However, they didn't really stop to work things out; they simply accepted that this was where the future lay, and that this was therefore the right path to follow. Unfortunately, many of them have now fallen by the wayside. In the early days of video, everyone said, "Well, here's a whole new area to work in – naturally there will be video albums".

Chrysalis was the first company to make a video of an album, again Blondie. We took a bit of a risk, because we didn't know how big the market would be, although there did seem to be some demand for it. We did know that we had a very visual artist in Debbie Harry so we spent a little more making videos of each track for a video album. It worked for us and we made money from it, because we were the first ones to do it; it was still a novelty at that time.

A big question mark hangs over the entire video industry, not just over video albums. Video recorders do seem to be becoming an increasingly established part of the lives of certain people – those with fairly high incomes.

Debbie Harry of Blondie

However, what do these people actually do with their video machines? What do they play? Where does video fit into their lives? If they have the time, they use them to watch films and recorded television. My main interest in video is that I can have someone record the races while I'm out doing something else. I don't think many people really want to sit and watch video albums, whether they're on disc or cassette. People who buy records are presumably interested in listening to music, not watching it. Music alone fits into people's lives more easily, because they can listen to it while they're doing other things: they can listen while they're doing the dishes or driving the car; they can dance to it; and they can have it on when they're chatting to someone they don't know very well to fill in the gaps in the conversation.

In fact, music can act as a background for most things, but people don't actually want to stop and look at it. Perhaps someone who likes opera might sit at home and put on their video of *Don Giovanni*, but I don't think many people do that.

The future of video

The most logical direction for the video business is into rentals, and this is already happening. While people are not going to hand over a size-able chunk of money for a video disc or cassette that they will probably only watch once every five years, they are more likely to be prepared to pay a smaller sum to be able to watch the video, and send it back the next day. It follows that if something is going to be viable on a video cassette then it's also got to be viable for television, which is why I think the video industry will deal mostly in movies and items which are already on television. In this way the industry will get two bites of the financial cherry: payment for the television sale and residual income from the sale of video cassettes to rental companies.

The video industry is still in its infancy; we're just learning to crawl, and let's hope we will all learn to walk, and, perhaps one day, to run. It's still a small industry which has a long way to go before people can start driving about in Rolls Royces on the strength of it. I have no idea where we'll be once we've learned to run. Fortunes are frequently made by the people who watch other people discover where the future lies, and then copy them: it's usually the second person in line who makes the money, not the first. The first person makes the mistakes and loses their money, while the second person takes advantage of the lessons that have been learned. This could well be true of the video industry too.●

The Jingle Business

One of the most appealing facets of writing or producing music for commercials is the variety of shapes required: the need to design each piece to answer very specific needs. Each new assignment necessitates a new design. The design of a jingle includes: the style of music; the form (full lyric, partial lyric, instrumental); the orchestration, which is very often conceived before the piece is written; the sound, a combination of many elements that may also be envisioned prior to composition; the time allotted for the music (is it used throughout, or spotted in the commercial?); above all – the market you are trying to reach and the type of product you are selling.

Music to convey a message

The purpose of advertising music is not just to entertain: it must help to create an atmosphere which will make the product more appealing to the consumer. Producing such music is not abstract creativity. Elsewhere in this book some extremely accomplished artists discuss their creative habits, and reveal the subjectivity of their approaches. The objectivity required of the jingle writer is in direct contrast. We cannot simply present a song that we dig, or that "says something we want to express". Instead, we must home in on a target and "get the message across".

An advertising agency comes to us and says, "We have this point of view about our product. This is how we are positioning that product. Here is our creative strategy. This is the situation we are creating. Our market research shows this or that to be our key product strength. Here is what our consumer looks like. This is how our product answers a perceived need. Now go write!"

Then, we must take our tools – words, music and sound – and mould them into a message that answers the assignment. No matter how great a song we write, no matter how innovative a sound we produce: if we don't fill the assignment, they *won't buy* and we have failed. The major difference about our work is that we must deliver on demand and operate in a directed or regimented creative atmosphere.

Jingle writing: a very special skill

Thus, those who write advertising music have to develop the discipline necessary to compress musical thoughts and to do it with style; this is a very special skill which is not easily acquired. In the 'hundreds" of years I've been in this business, I have found that it is always those writers who concentrate their talents and hone their skills to our particular needs who consistently turn out the best product. This skill takes time to develop: it can be taught and it can be learned, but it is a unique skill. There are a rare few who can handle being both a successful songwriter and a successful jingle writer.

An ability to compress thoughts and ideas is essential. It is very difficult to write successfully in the short form. Wasn't it George Bernard Shaw who once wrote, "Please excuse the length of this letter. I didn't have the time to write a short one." We work, primarily, with a 30 second commercial – 30 seconds in which to establish a relationship with the viewer, fight off all the other distractions and set a message in his head. The song has to get him in, hold him, sell to him and leave him entertained and receptive to hearing that message again and again – not a small talent!

Life as a jingle writer

It is difficult for jingle writers to transfer to writing other forms of music. The decision makers in other fields seem to be reluctant to give full recognition to the talents in the advertising business. Many commercial film directors have worked hard for a long time in an endeavour to get into motion pictures or television, and the percentage of successful transitions there is not very high. Several songs have come out of commercials to be successful in other areas, but it is nonetheless rare for those who write commercials to make the transition over to writing for the regular music business. And, of course, there is a deterrent: a writer of commercials, who is really good, is making excellent money at his craft and is also getting his creative kicks. Why does he need the horror of those other fields?

He may not make as much money as the top writers of film scores or the leading artist-writers in the pop field. However, in the long run he does very well and is constantly active. This is not a "one hit" business: you make your money by consistently writing hit after hit and cumulatively "making the buck".

Payment for jingles

The notion that enormous sums are paid for any one piece of music is false. Normal creative fees range from a low of $1500 (£900) to a high of $15,000 (£9,000). Occasionally an artist might be paid $25,000 (£15,000) or more if his name is used in the campaign, both internally to company employees and to the general public.

Some composers receive repeat fees, or residuals. Many composers take on several other roles in the production of a jingle; it is not uncommon for a composer to be paid and to receive residuals as player, arranger, contractor, conductor or any combination of slots. Singing is where there is an enormous amount of dollars. It is common practice for the writer – if he has the talent – to sing his own song. In Los Angeles I am involved with LA/NY Music. One of the partners, Mark Vieha, is an outstanding composer/lyricist and is also much in demand as a singer; he not only sings on his own commercials but is called upon by our competitors to sing on theirs as well. Jay Kennedy, another partner, is a fine arranger/

Herman Edel

conductor and is paid in both categories; it is cumulative effort that can bring about success and high earnings.

Advice for beginners

Getting into this business, like any other, is difficult. You must know the intricacies of music, film, television, radio and, above all, the advertising business. The positive side is that we are always searching for that new talent, that unique ability. Every production house is looking for the "new voice". Whether you are in London, Los Angeles, New York or Tokyo – any major advertising centre – there are production houses that you should contact. Some writers start in agencies, others in recording studios. The response to the ageless question, "How do I break in?" is the same as in all industries. There is no one answer other than persistence. It also doesn't hurt if your father is the senior partner in the law firm.●

Creating a Commercial

Writing music for commercials demands not only the composition talents of the composer but also the ability to work to a very tight "brief". The brief gives the guidelines within which the music must be written. Often, before the composer is even contacted, the advertising agency creative team may have written the lyrics, talked over the words and musical concept with the client and in Britain they will have had to submit the script, words and outline picture details to the I.T.C.A. (Independent Television Companies Association Limited) for initial approval under the British Code of Advertising Practice. In the United States the Federal Communications Commission plays a similar watchdog role, although material is not submitted to it at this early stage. Thus several people's ideas and thoughts will have been integrated in the brief and the composer must work within these considerations.

At the first meeting the "brief" has to be discussed in detail. The musical direction for the composition must be decided: pop or classical, and is there a specific form within the generic area, say electropop or middle of the road (MOR). Sometimes music of one particular recording artist may be discussed to illustrate the direction. If there are lyrics, should they be sung by a solo boy or girl or a group of singers? Background information to the campaign is most important. Is there a specific age group that the advertiser wishes to appeal to? Probably more than any other advertising device music can help underline this point. Up-to-date pop will not help to sell a savings plan to retired couples, but it would certainly be suitable for selling the latest fashion make-up to teenagers.

An adaptable tune

When developing a melody it is sensible to consider the adaptability of the tune. A memorable tune the construction of which lends itself to re-arrangements is a most valuable asset to an advertiser. Music can provide a link between various advertising campaigns giving the product a corporate image. For example, the now world-famous British Airways theme written by Jake Holmes has been re-arranged in many, many different ways (more than 30 to my knowledge) and provides a most memorable corporate image for this airline internationally. McCann Erickson on behalf of Martini commissioned Chris Gunning to write a theme for them over ten years ago. The Martini tune is another excellent example of a melody which can be adapted and arranged in many different ways to suit the visual theme.

On which medium will the music be used: radio, television or movies? Music for radio commercials often has to paint the entire sound picture, whereas a soundtrack for a television or movie commercial should complement and reinforce the visuals.

It is most important to consider the "left hand" side of the script, which is a synopsis of the visual plot. The art director may have prepared a "storyboard", drawings of key frames from the film which help us to understand the concept at the initial briefing. In some cases music is commissioned after the film has been shot so that we are working to a finished visual.

The final, but vital, question is, "When would you like to hear a demo?" And the answer is often, "Yesterday if possible!" The music for a commercial is nearly always required at very short notice.

To illustrate the realization of a jingle we have re-printed the script for a commercial for The TSB. The composer, Graham Preskett and I attended a meeting at the advertising agency JWT with the agency's producer, copywriter and art director. We were to work on a script called New GT, which was to form part of a series of scripts all based on the same music brief: a catchy melody with a sung logo, with words in between spoken in rhythm.

We discussed the brief further, commenting that the hook, "TSB, the Bank that likes to say yes", would need to be instantly memorable and should be in direct contrast to the "sung/spoken" section.

Recording a demo

After a briefing session for a new tune, a demo is nearly always recorded so that the agency can hear the melody and an outline of the style of the arrangement. In some cases, as with TSB, the demo is also used for research. Extensive market research is carried out in the advertising industry to ascertain the effectiveness of an advertising concept in which music plays a major role. Can people remember the melody? What *was* the product?

The TSB jingle was first recorded in a multi-

Script and music for a TSB commercial: the music, *left,* has to be synchronized to the split second with action and voice over specified on the script, *right.* To produce the music for this 40-second commercial, extensive planning and market research (using a demo tape) has to be undertaken before the master can be recorded.

track studio using a small rhythm section and two singers. Demos are not often recorded in such a sophisticated form. However, this track was to be presented to the client and then researched; the agency, Graham and I all felt confident that this could form the basis of the final recording.

Recording a master

Commercial music is recorded in the studio, using all the techniques available to the record industry; the only difference is the time scale. In England the basic studio jingle session with musicians, as arranged with the Musicians' Union, is one hour, during which we not only have to listen to all the instruments and put the sounds together, but also rehearse and record the track. The average length of a jingle session overall is four hours, including vocals and over-dubs, at the end of which we walk away with a mixed down final tape.

We frequently work with material as complex as many record productions, but the budgets do not allow us the luxury of several days in the studio. We are, however, fortunate in being able to work with some of the top musicians and singers in the world. During the recording of vocals for advertising music great attention must be paid to the clarity of the words; after all our aim is to sell the product.

The TSB commercial was adapted slightly from the demo, following excellent research

results. The campaign was definitely going ahead and we went back into the studio to add more instruments to the track and to record the verse sections (the speak singing) with the jazz singer George Melly. However, we kept all the chorus vocals from the first session. The final vocal recording was made in a multitrack studio with picture facilities so that George Melly could see the finished film as he spoke, and so that we could ensure that the words were synchronizing with the pictures.

Advertising music provides a major challenge to composers and producers, because every brief is different and contains its own problems which have to be overcome. It is an exciting world; the pressure is constantly there, whether you are involved in writing a tune lasting 30 seconds within 24 hours of the briefing, or working in the studio to the highest standards of sound production, producing final tracks in perhaps four hours which might have taken a recording artist days to accomplish. There are however no compromises in commercials: the same standards must apply as with feature films.●

A Career in Recording

The recording industry has never really rationalized its attitudes to training. If you ask people who work in recording studios, you will find that hardly any of them received a formal training in recording techniques. A few will have studied music, physics or maybe even electronics at school – but for the most part they have had to pick up the specialized knowledge needed to produce good recordings by looking over the shoulders of others. You could argue that this learning-on-the job system works pretty well and, of course, many of our top engineers and producers came up that way. But it takes time to learn the difference between good and bad sound, and beginners run the risk of picking up the bad habits of their elders along with the good, before they learn to discriminate for themselves. Now that studio equipment has become very complex, a basic knowledge of electronics is needed so that the gear can be used to its full creative potential. At the same time, those who work in the control room need a working knowledge of music so that they can manipulate the sounds in a musically creative manner.

The word "creative" is at the heart of the matter. Most people can see immediately that a maintenance engineer really does need a detailed training in electronics and circuit troubleshooting techniques. Otherwise he could never make fast repairs or align the equipment properly. But producers and balance engineers are working with sounds and ideas: how do you train them to be creative? Well, the answer is, you can't. Yet it is helpful for them to have a proper understanding of how musical instruments generate sounds, how the studio acoustics

John Borwick demonstrates a mixer to a group of students

modify the sounds, how different microphones perform and how console controls, level meters, add-on processors, loudspeakers, and even the human ear and brain affect the sounds we hear. Understanding the tools of our trade makes it easier to use their full potential, and this leaves us free to get on with the important creative element.

In most other professions a basic set of knowledge and skills has been established over the years. This has resulted in the setting up of formal training courses. So, if a young person wants to enter one of these professions, he can be told, "Go and study the course in XYZ: when you get the degree, diploma, certificate or whatever, you will be well on the way to a career in your chosen profession." The establishment of agreed standards of training generates a whole literature of textbooks and specialist journals. Newcomers know what they need to study, and existing practitioners know where to look for information that will keep them abreast of new developments. At the same time, this training superstructure raises the status of a profession, generates an atmosphere of confidence amongst potential employers and simplifies recruitment procedures.

In-house training

The absence of a tradition of formalized training in the recording industry is compensated to an extent by the in-house training which some of the larger studio organizations have set up. In England the BBC and EMI lead in this respect, and many engineers and producers throughout the industry freely admit that they learned the basics of the job at one of these establishments before moving to other employers or setting up on their own. The IBA companies have also built up good training facilities to cover sound as well as video theory and practice. These larger employers demand a certain educational standard from their recruits – even if it is only a few modest grades at "O" or "A" level – enough to enable them to undertake the in-house training. There may also be facilities allowing the recruits to attend outside courses during their first year or two of employment.

In-house training has the great advantage that its relevance to the job is never in doubt; trainees can immediately relate each piece of theory to a real recording task. Many of the instructors are people who actually do the job, and practical training can include "hands on" balancing, mixing, sweetening, editing, and so on. The equipment used in training can be the same up-to-date gear used in the studios, with additional units willingly loaned for the purpose by suppliers keen to promote the unique features of their designs.

The danger is that in-house training can be too localized and parochial. The instructors can only pass on what they themselves know or have found useful. A broad over-view of the art of recording may be missing.

Formal education

In both the United States and Britain there are recognized training courses, at universities and colleges. Recruits can acquire an in-depth training which will command respect wherever they go.

In the United States courses range from four-year degree courses, available at New York University and Berklee College of Music, Boston, to several courses lasting a few weeks or even less. A few of these last are of doubtful use in furthering a career, offering "full 24-track 'hands-on' mixing in two days." In between there are several worthwhile one- and two-year certificate courses; a good one-year course is that offered by the Institute of Audio Research in New York. Most courses of any length include periods of training on the job in commercial studios.

In England the best known university course related to recording is the 4-year Bachelor of Music (Tonmeister) course at the University of Surrey. Some may consider this course over-long and over-detailed given the present level of training in the industry as a whole, and yet it only mirrors the serious attitude to education adopted by other professions. Candidates competing for the eight entry places each year must have good "A" level grades in Music and Physics, with Mathematics as a preferred third subject. The students are therefore musicians with a technical bias and the course itself is divided almost equally into musical training, acoustics and electronics theory, and recording techniques.

Several other universities and colleges run courses covering the musical or technical aspects separately so that, by working on the missing element in his own time, a student can acquire a good foundation for a career in recording. For example, the Polytechnic of North London's B.Sc degree course in Electronic and Communications Engineering covers all the right subjects in electronics and physics, and has an acoustics option very useful to aspiring recording engineers.

On both sides of the Atlantic certain universities, music colleges and business schools offer courses covering the business side of recording studios and of the music industry in general.●

CHRISTOPHER SMALL

Music in Education

There is no such creature as a totally unmusical person; those who appear so are usually people whose musical sensibilities are as yet unawakened or, due to negative experiences, have become inhibited. It is a shame that the split in western music today – a split crudely represented as "classical" and "popular" – has caused so many young people to be cut off from their musicality and from any real musical experiences while still at school. The split is not a natural one; it took on its present form probably only in the early years of this century, and is as much social as musical in origin.

Classical music: a minority art

Despite, or perhaps because of, its high status, classical music remains very much a minority art, viewed at best with indifference and at worst with hostility by the majority of students. Many pupils do enjoy their own musical activity outside school but, for many more, spontaneous musical expression is allowed to atrophy or is even discouraged.

The fact that the majority of schools are committed to classical rather than popular music is not surprising. In both formal and musical education there is an insistence upon the sacredness of the written word; in both there is an extended period of formal instruction during which the pupil is completely dependent upon the knowledge and skills of the teacher; and in both, examination and certification are required before a pupil is regarded as a true practitioner of the art. Even the behaviour of an audience in a concert hall is the same as that expected in the classroom: silence, stillness, attention and respect for authority.

Popular music within formal education

Popular music, on the other hand, is by its very nature opposed to the spirit of formal education and, not surprisingly, some of the greatest musicians have made their way without formal instruction, learning their skills instead through performing and imitation. The entire culture of popular music is at odds with the kind of standardization on which examinations are based. Popular music does not encourage stillness, isolation and intellectual concentration, but movement, group involvement and ecstasy – all of which are considered out of place in the classroom.

It is often argued that the exclusion of popular music from the classroom is no bad thing, as much for the "health" of the music as for the peace and conformity of the school; the example of certain schools of jazz, which reputedly turn out dozens of competent tenor saxophonists who all play exactly like John Coltrane, is often quoted as a cautionary tale.

Schools where popular music flourishes

There are, however, schools in which popular music flourishes and, remembering that the acts of creation and performance are not separate in popular music, it is interesting to look at the circumstances in which this is allowed to take place. First, there is usually a teacher or other person who carries some weight in the school hierarchy (maybe a janitor or a senior pupil) who values music for its own sake rather than as something to amuse the less academic pupils, or as a means of dealing with difficult groups ("if I listen to your music, you can listen to mine"). Secondly, this person does not dominate, or impose his or her own values on the young musicians. In the nature of things – and in contrast to classical-music culture – pupils usually have their own values and standards which, contrary to the assumptions of establishment musicians and music-lovers, are not mere reflections of peer group pressure, fashion or commercialism – Benjamin Britten, after all, was as carefully packaged and marketed as Elvis Presley. If this person is a competent performer in one or another popular traditions, so much the better, because the ability to practice what one preaches is always a virtue in a teacher. However, the best thing he or she can do is to provide physical and psychological space – which may include defending the musicians' activities against attack from colleagues – and encouragement.

Those who would like to introduce popular music into a school find themselves in a contradictory position, since on the one hand they wish to establish it as an accepted topic of study in the curriculum, with appropriate allocation of time and resources, while on the other the terms of such acceptance run counter to the very nature of the music. It is up to each individual to decide the extent to which compromise on this is possible.●

Glossary

Words followed by an (♦) are themselves listed in this glossary.

A Cappello Music sung without instrumental accompaniment.

Acetate Reference or demo disc, usually cut (♦) for technical evaluation purposes.

Action The ability of a musical instrument to respond to a player's technique, which depends on many different factors according to instrument. Guitar action is largely determined by the height of the strings from the fingerboard and may therefore be "high" or "low". Keyboard action refers to the degree of sensitivity of the keyboard to the player's touch; touch-sensitive synthesizers, for example, react to the velocity and pressure of a player's hands for different effects such as *crescendo* (♦), and *vibrato* (♦). Piano action describes the reaction of the mechanical parts of the piano to the player's touch.

Active circuitry A powered circuit, such as a synthesizer, electronic piano or studio mixer. Also a component included in some electric guitars and basses, enabling wider frequency control and boosting facilities than are available in passive (♦) instruments.

A/D converter Device which converts analogue waveforms into binary language for storage in digital form on tape or disc.

Ad libbing Improvisation.

ADSR (Attack, Decay, Sustain and Release) (also known as an envelope generator) Module which is present in all synthesizers, enabling them to simulate the manner in which instruments make their sound. It can, for example, set up an attack (♦) like a piano's (short, sharp), and the appropriate decay time, (♦) sustain (♦) time and release (♦) switch, which fixes the end of the note.

ADT (artificial double tracking) An electronic studio device for simulating the effect of a double-tracked (♦) voice or instrument from only one track or source.

Ambience The acoustic characteristics of a room or area with regard to reverberation. A room with a lot of reverberation is said to be "live"; one without is "dead".

Analogue delay An electronic device for delaying a signal by using "bucket brigade" integrated circuitry. Can also be obtained by using a tape machine. See Tape echo.

A & R (Artist & Repertoire) The A & R man of the 1950s and 1960s used to be reponsible for finding a repertoire for artists to record. Nowadays, however, this is usually handled by producers, while A & R departments tend, for the most part, to be involved with talent spotting and record release/promotion.

Assigning (also known as routing) Switching technique used with multitrack (♦) mixers whereby the engineer directs any input (♦) to any or all output (♦) channels. Normally all circuits are wired to a routing, or assigning, switch on the desk. (♦)

Attack The way in which a musical note begins. "Fast attack" is very sharp, like the sound of a snare drum or piano being struck hard; "slow attack" on the other hand, is best achieved with sustaining (♦) instruments such as the violin and flute.

Attenuator A level control which may be switched or smoothly varied to reduce the gain of an electronic circuit. See Potentiometer.

Audio range (also known as audio spectrum) Range within which human beings can detect sound (roughly 20Hz-20kHz). The audio range diminishes with age; average range is about 40Hz-15kHz.

Backbeat The second and fourth beats in music written in even time (i.e. 2/4, 4/4 etc). In 3/4 time, or other more complex time signatures, the last beat of the bar.

Backing track (also known as backing rhythm) Recorded instrumental track which forms the basis of the accompaniment for vocals or lead instruments.

Backline The amplifiers used for individual rhythm instruments on stage; they are usually placed behind the players.

Baffles (also known as gobos) Studio screens – usually on wheels – which are used to reduce leakage (♦). They can have either soundproofed or reflective surfaces, to suit different ambiences (♦).

Band pass filter An electronic filter which limits the effect of frequencies either side of a desired frequency range.

Baroque Originally meaning bizarre or highly ornate, this term is now used to refer to an era in European music from *c.* 1650 to *c.* 1750, when counterpoint and harmony were of great importance. Nowadays, a "baroque arrangement" may be either similar to Bach or Handel in style, or heavily contrapuntal, as in Quincy Jones' arrangements or The Beach Boys' vocal counterpoint.

Bins Term for bass speakers on a PA (♦) rig; large, acoustically designed speaker cabinets.

Blowing see Jamming

Bluegrass A type of country music from the south of the United States, usually played without any percussion instruments. All instruments in this type of music are string, and include the fiddle (violin), guitar and the obligatory five-stringed banjo.

333

Board see Console

Bop (also known as Be-bop) Mid-1940s to mid-1950s style of jazz, epitomized by such legendary figures as Charlie Parker, Dizzy Gillespie and the younger Miles Davis. Generally performed by small groups, this jazz form stretched the boundaries of twentieth-century rhythmic music more than any other music of the time.

Bottleneck guitar (also known as slide guitar) A technique originally used by the old blues guitarists who would tune the guitar to an open chord (usually D major or C major), place the neck of a bottle over one finger of the left hand, and slide this over the frets, while playing, to produce a crude lap-steel or Hawaiian guitar effect. Nowadays the bottleneck itself is usually a steel or glass tube.

Bottom The lower end of the audio range with regard to response or bass presence.

Bouncing (also known as ping-pong) A technique used in multitrack recording. Extra tracks are obtained by sending two or more pre-recorded tracks to be recorded on to one spare track.

Brass 1. The term for those instruments which are made of brass and played with a metal tube mouthpiece, such as the trumpet, French horn, trombone and tuba. **2.** Term often used to describe the horn (♦) section of a group, which frequently includes saxophones – not technically brass instruments because they have a reed mouthpiece, although they are usually made of brass.

Break 1. An instrumental passage in a song, as in, for example, a "horn break" or "guitar break". **2.** Term used by music businessmen to mean make an artist successful and well-known in a given territory: normally achieved with a hit record.

Bridge 1. That part of a stringed instrument which stops the sounding length of the strings. It is placed somewhere between the nut (♦) and the tailpiece (♦) at the point where most accurate tuning is found. **2.** The middle 8 (♦) of a song, or the link passage between, say, a verse and chorus, which may be only two bars in length, sometimes more.

Bug Jargon for contact mike or pickup used on acoustic guitars, violins, saxophones etc.

Bus/Buss Jargon for the routing of an input (♦) signal to one or more output (♦) channels. The bus control is used to assign (♦) an instrument to a particular track; for example, a harmonica coming into a desk (♦) on, say, input 1 may be bussed to track 4 on the tape recorder.

Busking see Jamming

Calibration The process of lining up tape recorders or any equipment in terms of frequency response and level.

Calibration tones Sine wave tones recorded at the beginning of reels of tape in order to facilitate alignment.

Chart 1. Published ranking of records in terms of sales; **2.** Jargon for written music part, or chord symbols (♦), as opposed to printed music.

Chops Jazz vernacular for skill, as in: "That horn player has great chops."

Chord symbols Symbols in letter form which are a shorthand method of indicating the chords which are to determine the harmonic structure of a piece. G7, for example, means a G major triad with a minor 7th (dominant 7th), the notes being G, B, D and F natural. Chord symbols are used mostly in rhythm section music, for the piano, guitar, and bass.

Chorus 1. Main body of a choir. **2.** Refrain of song. **3.** Jargon for sequence of chords in an instrumental piece, as in, "Take two choruses." **4.** Electronic device which creates the effect of more than one sound from a single source by combining a short delay (♦) (usually between 5 and 30 milliseconds) with slight deviations in pitch.

Chromatic scale A scale taking in all 12 semi-tones of the octave.

Clavinet A stringed keyboard instrument with a bright cutting sound; similar to the harpsichord, but with a hammer – rather than a plucking – action.

Clef A sign often found at the beginning of each line of written music, and used to fix the position of middle C on the staff (♦). The common forms are the treble and bass clef. To avoid using too many ledger lines the clefs are often adjusted to suit the range of particular instruments. In general, the higher the range of the instrument, the lower the position of middle C on the staff. Hence, the alto clef, where middle C is the centre line, is used for the viola because the middle of its range is from around middle C to the octave above. The range of the cello is lower, so the tenor clef where middle C is higher on the staff is used. Conversely, the violin's middle range is from G above middle C to an octave above that, so middle C is placed below the treble staff.

Click track 1. A rhythmic guide track consisting of a series of clicks (usually semi-quavers) used to assist in time-keeping during recording; **2.** Clicks recorded in order to start or cue (♦) synthesizer sequences or electronic drums. The clicks can be used to trigger a number of different sequences recorded at different times while still keeping them all in synchronization.

Compressor An electronic device for reducing the range of dynamics of an audio signal.

Concept album An album with an overall thread running through it, which may be musical, lyrical or thematic. Examples are *Desperado* by The Eagles, and *War Of The Worlds* by Jeff Wayne.

Concert pitch The internationally agreed tuning of a particular note. This is determined by the frequency of its sound waves, which is measured in cycles per second, or Hertz (Hz). Concert A above middle C is 440Hz.

Console (also known as board, desk, mixing console) The piece of equipment through which inputs (♦) and outputs (♦) are routed either to or from a tape recorder, and with which adjustments in tone, level and balance are made.

Course A pair of strings struck together and considered as one, a characteristic of certain stringed instruments, notably the mandolin (each pair in unison) and the 12-stringed guitar (each pair may be in unison but the lower four pairs of strings are usually in octaves).

Cover (also known as cover version) Subsequent recorded version of an original song; there are, for example, over 1,000 covers of the Lennon-McCartney song *Yesterday*.

Crescendo Growing in force; getting louder.

Crossover 1. An electronic splitting device used between amplifiers and speakers to divide the sound into two frequency bands. The "highs" will be sent to the horns (♦ 3) and the "lows" to the bins (♦). **2.** Term used to denote that an artist's style is a blend of two main streams of music; for example, a soul/Afro-Cuban crossover is soul music mixed with West Indian and Latin American rhythms.

Cue (also known as foldback, talkback) Part of the circuitry of the mixing console which enables: (a) the engineer in the control room and the musicians in the studio to communicate via headphones; (b) previously recorded material to be fed to the musicians so that they can play in sync when doing over-dubs (♦); (c) Direct injection (♦) instruments to be monitored via headphones while recording is in progress.

Cut Making a master disc (♦) from which finished records can be pressed: so-called because the master tape sounds are transferred on to a lacquered disc by a cutting machine which uses a needle to draw the sound patterns into the acetate.

Cutaway The spaces left when portions of the electric guitar body have been cut away to allow better access to the frets. A guitar with a chunk removed both above and below the neck is known as a "double cutaway".

Da Capo Term used in written music, meaning back to the beginning (literally, "from the head").

D/A converter A device which converts digital binary numbers back into continuous analogue wave forms. See also A/D converter.

Dbx The trademark of a popular noise reduction system used with multitrack (♦) tape machines.

DDL see Digital Delay Line

Decay 1. The dying away of a note. **2.** In synthesizers, part of the ADSR (♦).

Decay time The time (in seconds) which it takes for a sound to decay to a level 60 decibels below its original level. It is normally known as RT60.

Decibel (dB) The unit of sound measurement. OdB is taken to be the threshold of hearing, while 130 dB is the threshold of pain. A normal speaking voice is about 65-70dB.

Delay To slow down the arrival of a signal by electronic means. See Analogue Delay and Digital Delay Line.

Demo Abbreviation for "demonstration", usually referring to tapes or records used for marketing or testing. See Acetate.

Desk see Console

Digital Delay Line (DDL) Similar to analogue delay (♦) except that the effect is achieved by means of digital circuitry. This involves converting signals to digital impulses, which can be recreated any number of times to produce the delay.

Direct injection (DI) System by which the sound produced by electronic instruments can by-pass microphones and go direct to a mixing desk (♦), thus eliminating the risk of leakage (♦).

Divisi Literally meaning "divided", the term is usually used in string writing to indicate a subdivision of a single section; for example, first violins playing three separate parts.

Dolby The first, and still the most widely used, tape noise reduction system – invented by Dr Ray Dolby. During recording this device raises the high frequencies (where most background hiss is present) above normal. On playback these are reduced to normal perspective once more and the hiss is greatly reduced.

Double 1. Repeat the same instrumental or vocal part on another track when recording (see Double-tracking). **2.** Term for a musician performing on more than one instrument; for example, a wind player may be hired to play on saxophone, and double on flute.

Double-tracking Recording the same musical part twice on separate tracks to produce a fuller sound, brought about by the slight variations and mis-match between the performances.

Downbeat The first beat of the bar; the opposite of backbeat (♦) and upbeat (♦).

Drawbars Tone controls on Hammond organs which take the form of bars with numbers along their length. They allow the player to mix fundamental (♦) tones with harmonics (♦), thus enabling greater control when mixing (♦) complex timbres.

335

Drop in see Punch in

Drop out Loss of tape signal due to a faulty tape or poor contact with the tape recorder heads.

Dry (also known as dead) Term applied to sound which has no added reverb or echo. See Ambience.

Dub 1. Abbreviation for overdub (♦). **2.** To add sound to film or video. **3.** A style of vocal delivery associated with reggae music, involving extensive use of echo (♦).

Echo 1. Distinct repetition of a sound until it dies away naturally. **2.** Distinct or indistinct repetition of a sound produced and controlled in the studio for effect, mechanically or by means of electronic processors. See Delay, DDL, Analogue delay, Digital delay, Tape echo.

Echo chamber A live room containing speakers and microphones used to simulate natural reverberation (♦).

Echo plate An electromechanical studio device which produces simulated reverberation (♦) (but not delay echo) by means of a large metal vibrating plate.

Echoplex A tape device which uses a tape loop and five recording heads to create echo effects. The recording heads are movable to enable echoes to be produced with any desired delay.

EMT Brand name of a well-known echo plate device.

Envelope generator see ADSR.

Equalization (EQ) The adjustment of the frequency response of an audio signal to obtain a desirable sound.

Equalizer An electronic device for cutting or boosting selected frequencies – simply a sophisticated tone control.

Expander An electronic device for increasing the range of dynamics of an audio signal.

Fade (also known as fade-out) Jargon for gradual fading of a signal to nothing. Usually used at the end of a number or recording as an alternative to an abrupt end.

Fader Term for the volume control on a mixing console (♦), which is usually a sliding control rather than a knob.

Feedback 1. Howl or squeal produced when a microphone or pickup is too near its speaker, thus picking up its own output and re-amplifying it. Correctly called acoustic feedback. **2.** Used in electronic circuits to return part of the output signal to the input in order to cancel out some of the circuit's deficiencies.

Filter Electronic device which boosts or cuts certain frequencies, one of the main parts of an equalizer (♦).

Finger pick A plectrum which fits over the player's finger. It is used a great deal in country and bluegrass (♦) music.

Fixer 1. A contractor who "fixes" or books people for recordings or concerts. **2.** American production jargon for a re-recording of a poor performance.

Flange Outer rim of tape spool.

Flanging A similar effect to phasing (♦) except that a wider variation in tape speed is used, giving the effect of a slight pitch deviation.

Flat 1. The lowering of a pitch by a semi-tone. **2.** Sound which has not been equalized.

Flat pick Plectrum held between the player's thumb and forefinger.

Flutter Small rapid variations in tape speed, causing pitch variation. They are often due to a faulty tape transport (♦) or turntable mechanism.

Foldback see Cue

Forte Loud.

Fortissimo As loud as possible.

Fundamental The lowest frequency of a note in a complex wave form or chord.

Fuzz box A device which breaks up the sound passing through it, causing a distorted sound simulating that of a valve amplifier being overdriven. It is particularly favoured by guitarists.

Gain Amount of increase or decrease of volume.

Glissando Sliding quickly between one note and another without any perceptible pitches in between. A true *glissando* is best obtained on instruments like the violin, trombone or timps, where the production of continuous sound is not impeded by keys or frets.

Gobos see Baffles

Graphic equalizer Equalizer (♦) using small linear faders which permits manual control over a wide range of selectable frequencies.

Great stave see Staff

Harmonics Vibrations of frequencies that are multiples of the fundamental (♦).

Harmonizer A device which electronically changes the pitch of a signal without affecting tempo.

Headroom Technical jargon for the safety margin allowed for peaks in volume without distortion.

Headstock The section at the top end of the neck of a guitar which incorporates the machine heads (♦).

Hertz (Hz) Unit of measurement denoting frequency. Originally measured in cycles per second (CPS), 1Hz = 1 cycle of a sound wave per second. See KiloHertz (kHz).

High end Term denoting sounds with a frequency higher than 5kHz.

Hook A musical phrase – vocal or instrumental – which is repeated a number of times in a song to literally "hook" the listener. Instrumentally it is often synonymous with riff (♦).

Horns 1. Abbreviation for French horns. **2.** General term in musical jargon for the brass and/or wind section of a band or orchestra. **3.** The treble or high frequency portion of a PA (♦) speaker system. The horns work in conjunction with mid-range and bass bins (♦) to give high-quality response over the entire audio range.

Hum Low-pitched drone coming from electronic equipment. It usually derives from the mains supply.

Image Jargon for the stereo panorama of a recording.

Inboard equipment The term for modules and devices that are a built-in feature of a recording/mixing console (♦); the opposite of outboard equipment (♦).

Input 1. The point at which an audio signal enters a recorder, mixer or signal processor; the opposite of output (♦). **2.** A signal received by a recorder, mixer or signal processor.

IPS Inches per second.

Jack plug A signal connector used on electric instruments to connect them to an amplifier via a lead, referred to as the "jacklead".

Jamming (also known as blowing, busking) Playing along with other musicians without the aid of written music.

Joystick A controller for modulating sounds, mostly used on synthesizers (♦) in place of pitch and modulation wheels, but can also be used as a pan-pot (♦) for multiphonic sound systems.

Kepex A type of noise gate (♦).

KiloHertz (kHz) Hertz measured in multiples of 1,000: i.e., 5kHz =

5,000Hz. In studio jargon they are usually referred to simply as k: i.e., 5k rather than 5kHz.

Lay back Musicians' jargon meaning to relax and not rush the tempo.

Layering 1. Synonym for overdubbing or recording one track at a time. **2.** Adding layers of sound or having one part doubled by several instruments to create a fuller sound.

Leader tape Coloured PVC tape used at the beginning and end of magnetic tape or between tracks for the master tape (♦) of an album.

Leakage 1. Pickup of the sound of one instrument on other mikes in the studio at random. **2.** When the sound of one track spills on to another on recorded tape. This usually occurs between adjacent tracks on low quality recording machines.

LED (light-emitting diodes) These are incorporated into VU meters (♦) to reflect transient peaks of volume.

Legato Sustained, controlled, or joined together; the opposite of staccato (♦).

Level The amplitude, or volume, of a signal.

Lick Jargon used to describe a musical phrase, usually with reference to a particular instrument, as in, for example, "guitar lick". See Riff.

Limiter A signal-processing device that reduces volume peaks without colouring the overall dynamic range as much as a compressor does.

Lipsync Mime the words of a song on a TV show or film.

Low end Frequencies below 100Hz; the opposite of High end (♦).

Machine heads (also known as tuning heads) Geared mechanisms on the headstock (♦)

of a guitar around which the strings are wound; they are used for tuning.

Manual Keyboard or set of keys. A theatre organ may have as many as four manuals or keyboards.

Master disc see Cut 2

Master mix The final mixdown, the one that will be used in cutting the disc.

Master tape The final multitrack recording or the two-track stereo ¼ inch tape which carries the final mixdown from the multitrack (♦) tape and from which the master record is cut.

Microprocessor The control section of an IC (integrated circuit) chip – a small computer. It is used in sophisticated digital outboard equipment and units such as sequencers and drum machines; also in automated or computer mixing desks.

Middle 8 Synonymous with bridge (♦ 2.) Originally always eight bars in length it was a section of a song which contrasted with the verse and chorus. Nowadays, it is used, like bridge, to mean a linking passage, not necessarily eight bars long.

Mixer A device which mixes signals in terms of level and/or tone during recording or playback.

Mixing (also known as the mixdown) The process of balancing and adjusting existing tracks on a multitrack machine and transferring them on to two-track tape.

Modulation Changing from one key, or tonal centre, to another.

Monitor 1. Loudspeaker used in studio control rooms to determine quality or balance. To monitor is to listen to such a speaker in order to make appropriate adjustments, or to listen through headphones while playing overdubs (♦). **2.** Loudspeaker used by performers on stage so that they can hear themselves.

Monitor level The volume of speakers in a studio.

Monitor select A set of switches which enables a recording engineer to monitor certain sounds in isolation or together.

Multicore A single cable containing a number of separately insulated wires. When used with a stage box (♦) it keeps the routing of microphones tidy and easy to locate, especially over long distances.

Multitracking Recording on to more than one track of tape.

Multitrack tape Tape on to which music is recorded on several tracks and from which the engineer or producer mixes down the ¼ inch master. Multitrack tape usually contains between 4 and 24 tracks according to the format of the machine and the width of the tape.

Mute 1. Any device which reduces the level (and usually alters the tone in some way) of an acoustic instrument, such as a trumpet or cello. **2.** A switch found on some recording consoles (♦) which reduces the overall monitor level (♦) by more than half.

Noise gate An electronic device which cuts out audio signals below a threshold selected by the engineer.

Noise generator A device used in synthesizers (♦) for producing high frequency sound effects.

Noise reduction The use of a compressing or expanding device which reduces unwanted tape hiss. See Dolby.

Notch filter An electronic device which can remove unwanted frequencies with only minimal disturbance to those on either side.

Nut The plate at the top end of the guitar fingerboard, usually made from plastic or brass, over which the strings pass before being inserted into the machine heads (♦).

Octave divider An electronic device which produces higher and/or lower octaves of a given signal. It is used by guitarists and, occasionally, horn players – such as The Brecker Brothers – when playing electric sax and trumpet via a bug (♦).

Ostinato Persistent repeated pattern of notes or musical figures creating an effect or structure on which to build. See Riff.

Outboard equipment (also known as toys) Effects devices and signal processors which are not part of a mixing console's inherent features, such as flangers, harmonizers, and chorus pedals.

Out of phase Two signals are "out of phase" when certain frequencies are cancelled due to the reversal of polarity of one signal relative to another.

Output 1. The point from which an audio signal leaves a recorder, mixer or signal processor. **2.** Signal sent out by a recorder, mixer or signal processor.

Overdubbing Adding new sound to previously recorded material on a spare track, or tracks, of multitrack tape.

Panning Positioning a sound's source within a stereo panorama to left and right. This is done with a pan-pot (♦) (potentiometer) or a joystick (♦).

Pan-pot (panoramic potentiometer) Control knob on a studio desk (♦) used for placing tracks within the stereo panorama (left/right).

Parametric equalizer Equalizer (♦) which differs from a graphic equalizer (♦) in that the frequency bands selected can be continuously varied (narrowed or widened) instead of falling into predetermined steps or sections.

Passive circuitry A non-powered circuit. Standard electric guitars and basses usually have passive circuitry, although in recent years

active circuitry has been introduced in several models.

PA system Abbreviation for Public Address system, the loudspeakers directed at concert audiences.

Patching Connecting two elements in a circuit by external wiring.

Phase shift devices Devices in which the input signal divides and recombines to produce phasing (♦).

Phasing An effect produced by feeding a signal into two tape recorders and recording the combined outputs on to another machine. The effect produced is a swishy tonal sweep achieved by varying the speed of one of the input tape recorders.

Pianissimo As soft as possible.

Piano Soft.

Ping-Pong see Bouncing

Pink noise Noise containing all frequencies in equal proportions.

Pitchbend A device which enables a player to bend the pitch of a note on a synthesizer, usually with a pitch wheel, strip or lever.

Polyrhythmic Several rhythms occurring simultaneously.

Potentiometer Continuously variable level control for varying the signal in an electronic circuit; can be rotary or linear (fader). See Attenuator, Pan-pot.

Preamplifier Amplifier used to boost signals before they reach a main amplifier so that low level signals can be brought up to a volume that can be handled by the main amp.

Presence A control on many amplifiers which boosts mid-range frequencies.

Punch in (also known as drop in) The system whereby a fresh part is added to existing material on tape by switching from "Play" to "Record" while the tape is moving.

Quadrophonic sound Sound which reaches the listener from every side with instruments positioned all around the panorama (see Panning). It is used most successfully in live concerts, by bands such as Pink Floyd, where sound travelling effects are used with great imagination.

Rap Rhythmic speech. The term refers to a technique first used by disc jockeys on black radio stations in the USA whereby they record fast, rhythmically spoken lyrics over an existing backing track. Hits include *Rapper's Delight*, to the backing track of Chic's *Good Times*, Blondie's *Rapture* and the highly successful *Don't Push Me ('Cause I'm Close to the Edge)"* by Grand Master Flash.

Reed instruments Those wind instruments whose sound is produced by a vibrating reed, such as the clarinet, saxophone, harmonica and harmonium. The "double-reed" instruments – such as the oboe, cor anglais and bassoon – are so-called because the mouthpiece is formed from two reeds stuck together.

Reeds Generic term in musical jargon for reed instruments, including the saxophone. See Brass **2.**

Release The last in the four parameters of an envelope generator, or ADSR (♦). It governs how much a note rings on after a key has been released.

Reverb/Reverberation The sound characteristics of a room: a "live" room has a lot of reverb, usually from highly reflective surfaces; a "dead" room has less. Reverb devices are used to simulate ambience (♦).

Ride Move a fader (♦) up and down to find the optimum level.

Riff A musical phrase, usually repeated for a whole section of a song, which gives the song its flavour and sometimes its hook (♦). Riffs are most frequently played on guitar and/or bass, occasionally by other instruments.

Rimshot A drumming technique which involves hitting the skin and rim of the drum simultaneously, thus producing a distinctive sound.

Roll off Technical jargon for reduced high frequencies.

Rough mix Any mix of a song or piece which is used for reference purposes, but is not the final or master mix (♦).

Routing see Assigning

Royalty A small percentage of the wholesale or retail price of a record, tape or sheet of music paid to an artist, writer or producer on each copy sold.

RT60 The normal abbreviated form of decay time (♦).

Saddle Strip of hard – usually metal – material in the bridge assembly of a guitar, over which the strings pass. It is usually adjustable for string clearance and intonation. See Action.

Scat singing Vocal improvisation without words, usually in jazz, commonly known as scatting.

Scratchplate Plastic or metal plate attached to the front of a guitar body to prevent pick scratches.

Sel-sync Abbreviation of selective synchronization, a recording process whereby monitoring (♦) comes from the record head itself, enabling overdubs to be "synced" with tracks already recorded.

Separation The effect of minimizing leakage (♦) when recording.

Sequencer A digital or analogue device, similar to a recorder, which uses control voltage and gate pulses, recorded on tape, to play a series of pre-programmed notes and impulses on a synthesizer (♦) or several synthesizers.

Shell The body of a drum, without heads and fittings.

Ska Early bluebeat (pre-reggae) Jamaican music.

Slide guitar see Bottleneck guitar.

Spillage see Leakage

Splice Join two pieces of tape, usually when editing.

Staccato Short, sharp individual notes, not played in a linked or sustained way; the opposite of *legato* (♦).

Staff (also known as stave) The five ledger lines on which musical notation is written. In the case of music for instruments such as the piano, harp and organ, two staffs (treble and bass) are used, known collectively as the "great stave".

Stage-box A shielded box into which several microphones can be plugged and connected to a multicore (♦).

Stave see Staff

Strobe tuner An electronic instrument tuner which utilizes stroboscopic light.

Sustain Elongation of a note, either by playing technique or by electronics.

Sync-lock The use of a synchronization signal to connect two or more tape recorders.

Synthesizer Instrument which produces a wide range of sounds electronically, using voltage-controlled oscillators, filters and amplifiers and an envelope generator, or ADSR (♦).

Tailpiece The piece on a semi-acoustic guitar or any instrument of the violin family through which the strings are threaded and held in place at the lower end of the instrument.

Talkback see Cue

Tape echo (also known as tape

339

slap) A means of delaying the repeat of a sound by adjusting the time lapse or delay between the record and playback heads of a tape recorder.

Tape transport The motorised mechanism which moves the tape evenly across the record and play heads. Recorders with high speed tape transports play at 15 IPS (♦) or more.

Thumb pick Pick which slips over the player's thumb.

Tine A slim steel rod forming the tone bar in a Rhodes electric piano. Tines act like the strings in an acoustic piano, and are struck by felt-covered hammers.

Toys 1. Musical jargon for extra instruments used to enhance an arrangement which are not essential to the structure of a piece of music; e.g., tambourine, glockenspiel. **2.** Synonym for outboard studio equipment (♦).

Transducer Device which converts energy from one form to another. For example, a microphone turns sound energy into electrical signals which can be boosted and turned back into sound via an amplifier and speaker.

Transients Instantaneous changes in dynamics producing steep wave fronts.

Transpose Alter the key of a song or piece of music. For example, songs written for female singers will often have to be transposed to a lower key for a man.

Transposing instruments Instruments which play in a different pitch from that of the music written for them. Instruments have usually been transposed to bring about a standard system of fingering for instruments of the same family – such as saxophones or clarinets – which differ widely in range. If none of the saxophones, for example, were transposed, players would have to learn several different fingerings in

order to play different instruments within the family; and would have to concentrate hard to remember which saxophone they were playing at any one time. Transposing certain members of a family of instruments enables players to play any member of the family – and to switch from one to another – with ease. Clarinets, flutes, double reeds and all brass instruments have at least one transposing instrument within their ranges.

The double-bass, piccolo and certain tuned percussion instruments, such as the glockenspiel, will sound either an octave lower or higher than the music written for them; and in some cases, the difference may be as much as two octaves. These are also transposed but simply to save the use of ledger lines. See Staff.

Tremolo Fast repetition of the same note with no pitch change.

Tremolo arm Strictly speaking, a vibrato arm, a lever which fits on to the bridge of an electric guitar and is employed to instantly raise or lower the pitch.

Trill Rapid alternation of two notes.

Trim see Attenuator

Truss rod A strengthening bar used in the necks of some guitars to avoid warping, or, if warping occurs, to facilitate easy repair.

Tuning head see Machine head

Una Corda Literally "one string", the direction found in written piano music indicating use of the soft pedal.

Upbeat 1. Second or last beat in a bar. **2.** The last beat of the bar in an introduction to a piece of music, before the downbeat of the first full bar.

VCA Voltage-controlled amplifier. See Voltage control.

VCF Voltage-controlled filter. See Voltage control.

VCO Voltage-controlled oscillator. See Voltage control.

Vibrato The up and down oscillation of the pitch of a note by use of: the diaphragm for singers and players of wind instruments; or the fingers for players of bowed and other stringed instruments.

Vocal Jargon for voice part.

Voice box Device which sends the output of an instrument through a tube which fits into a player's mouth. The sounds can be altered by the player's mouth movements and then reamplified.

Voicing The way in which a musical chord is structured.

Voltage control The basis of musical synthesis first discovered by Dr Robert Moog. Each note on a synthesizer keyboard produces a different voltage, so that the pitch is said to be "voltage-controlled". Other parameters of sound such as tone, attack, envelope (see ADSR) can also be affected by voltage control.

VU meter Volume unit meter, a device which indicates volume. Each channel of a mixing desk, recording console (♦) or multitrack (♦) machine has its own VU meter.

Wah-wah pedal A pedal which produces a "wah" effect by sweeping the tone from bass to treble and back

Wall of sound An amplifier, or amplifiers, stacked on top of two or more speaker cabinets.

Washed out Term used to describe sound which lacks definition owing to too much reverberation.

Wet Reverberant-sounding. See Ambience and Dry.

White noise Noise containing all frequencies rising in level by 6dB every octave.

Wow Slow deviation in tape speed causing long slurring alterations in pitch. See Flutter.

Recommended Reading

General

Harrison, Sidney *Enjoyment of Music* (EMI London, 1953)

Hindemith, Paul *Elementary Training for Musicians* (Schott, London, 2nd ed. 1949)

Jacob, Gordon *How to Read a Score* (Boosey & Hawkes, London, 1944)

Sachs, Curt *History of Musical Instruments* (Dent, London 1942)

Spence, Keith and Swayne, Giles (editors) *How Music Works* (Macmillan, New York, 1981)

Wade, Graham *The Shape of Music* (Allison and Busby, London 1982)

The History of Popular Music

Betrock, Alan *Girl Groups* (Delilah, New York, 1982)

Carr, Patrick (editor) *The Illustrated History of Country Music* (Doubleday/Dolphin, New York, 1980)

Cohn, Nik *Pop from the Beginning* (Paladin, London, 1969; Stein & Day, New York, under the title *Rock from the Beginning*)

Coon, Caroline *1977: The New Wave Punk Rock Explosion* (Omnibus, London and New York, 1982)

Ellington, Duke *Music is my Mistress* (Quartet, London, 1977)

Frith, Simon *Sound Effects* (Pantheon, New York, 1981; Constable, London, 1983)

Gillett, Charlie *The Sound of the City* (Souvenir & Sphere, London 1969)

Grissim, J. *Country Music: White Man's Blues* (Paperback Library 1970)

Haralambos, M. *Right On: From Blues to Soul in Black America* (Eddison Press, 1974)

Hindley, Geoffrey *Larousse Encyclopedia of Music* (Hamlyn, London, 1971)

Marcus, Greil *Mystery Train* (Dutton, New York, 1975; new edition 1982; Omnibus, London)

Marsh, Dave *Born to Run* (Doubleday/Dolphin, New York, 1979)

Martin, George *All You Need Is Ears* (Macmillan, London, 1979)

Miller, Jim (editor) *The Rolling Stone Illustrated History of Rock & Roll* (Random House, New York, 1980: Pan/Picador, London, 1981)

Murray, Albert *Stomping the Blues* (Quartet, London, 1978)

Rolling Stone (edited) *The Rolling Stone Interviews 1967-1980* (Rolling Stone Press, 1981)

Russell, Ross *Bird Lives* (biography of Charlie Parker) (Quartet, London, 1973)

Whitcomb, Ian *After The Ball* (Penguin, London & New York, 1972)

Writing and Arranging Music

Bazelon, Irwin *Knowing the Score: Notes on Film Music* (Van Nostrand Reinhold, New York, 1975)

Del Mar, Norman *The Anatomy of the Orchestra* (Faber & Faber, London, 1983; California University Press)

Jacob, Gordon *Orchestral Technique* (Oxford University Press, London & New York, 1982)

Lees, Gene *Modern Rhyming Dictionary* (Omnibus, London & New York, 1981)

Limbacher, J. L. (editor) *Film Music: From Violins to Video* (Scarecrow Press, 1974)

Lovelock, William *The Elements of Orchestral Arrangement* (Bell & Hyman, London, 1968)

Mancini, Henry *Sounds and Scores* (Wise Publications, London & New York, 1962)

Manvell, R. and Huntley, J *The Technique of Film Music* (Focal Press, 1974)

Palmer, King *Teach Yourself Orchestration* (English University Press, 1964)

Piston, Walter *Orchestration* (Gollancz, London, 1955; Norton, New York)

Read, Gardner *Music Notation* (Gollancz, London, 1974; Taplinger/Crescendo, New York)

Rundel, Don Michael *Harvard Concise Dictionary of Music* (Belknap, Harvard)

Sachs, Curt *Rhythm and Tempo* (Dent, London, 1953)

Thomas, T. *Music for the Movies* (A.S. Barnes and Tantivy Press, 1977)

Weissman, Dick *Songwriter's Handy Guide* – 3 parts: *Melody Writing, Lyric Writing, Selling Your Songs* (Alfred, Sherman Oak, California, 1980)

Wood, Clement *Rhyming Dictionary* (Collins, London & World, New York, 1976)

Performing Music

Anderton, Craig *Electronic Projects for Musicians* (Guitar Player Books, Saratoga, California, revised edition 1980)

Bacon, Tony (editor) *Rock Hardware* (Blandford Press, Poole, 1981)

Baines, Anthony *Brass Instruments and their Development* (Faber & Faber, London 1976; Scribner, New York)

Baines, Anthony *Woodwind Instruments and their History* (Faber & Faber, London 1976; Norton, New York)

341

Bartolozzi, Bruno *New Sounds for Woodwinds* (O.U.P. London & New York, 1982)

Bateman, Wayne *Introduction to Computer Music* (Wiley, London & New York, 1980)

Bevan, Clifford *The Tuba Family* (Faber & Faber, London 1978)

Blades, James *Percussion Instruments and their History* (Faber & Faber, London, 1974)

Bone, P. *The Guitar and Mandolin* (Schott, London, 1954)

Brindle, R. S. *Contemporary Percussion* (Oxford University Press, 1970)

Brymer, Jack *The Clarinet* (Macdonald, London, 1963)

Chamberlin, Hal *Musical Applications of Microprocessors* (Hayden, Rochelle Park, N.J., 1980)

Crombie, David *The Complete Synthesizer* (Omnibus, London & New York, 1982)

Denyer, Ralph *The Guitar Handbook* (Pan, London, 1982; Knopf, New York, 1982)

Devarahi *The Complete Guide to Synthesizers* (Prentice-Hall, London & New York, 1982)

Galway, James *Flute* (Macdonald, London, 1982)

Goosens, Leon and Roxburgh, Edwin *Oboe* (Macdonald, London, 1977)

Graham, Bruce *Music and the Synthesizer* (Argus, Watford, 1980)

Gregory, Robin *The Horn* (Faber & Faber, London, 1969)

Gregory, Robin *The Trombone* (Faber and Faber, London, 1973)

Holland, J. *Percussion* (Macdonald, London, 1979)

Husler, F. and Rodd-Marling, Y. *Singing: the Physical Nature of the Vocal Organ* (revised edition Hutchinson, London, 1976)

James, Philip *Early Keyboard Instruments* (Holland Press, 1967)

Kentner, Louis *Piano* (Macdonald, London, 1977)

Langwill, Lindesay G. *Bassoon and Contrabassoon* (Ernest Benn, London, 1963; General Publishing, Toronto, 1963)

Legg, Adrian *Customising Your Electric Guitar* (Kaye & Ward, London, 1982)

Lhevinne, Josef *Basic Principles in Pianoforte Playing* (Dover, New York & Constable, London, 1972)

Mackay, Andy *Electronic Music* (Phaidon, Oxford, 1981)

Menuhin, Yehudi and Primrose, William *Violin and Viola* (Macdonald, London, 1976)

Peterlongo, Paolo *The Violin* (Paul Elek, London, 1979)

Quartz, J. J. *On Playing the Flute* (Faber & Faber, London, 1966; The Free Press, New York)

Rendall, F. Geoffrey *Clarinet* (Macdonald, London, 1977)

Rensch, R. *The Harp* (Duckworth, London, 1979)

Rose, Arnold *The Singer and The Voice* (Faber & Faber, London, revised edition 1971)

Russell, R. *The Harpsichord and Clavichord* (Faber & Faber, London 1973)

Ryan, Lloyd *The Complete Drum Tutor* (Duckworth, London, 1981)

Schrader, Barry *Introduction to Electro-Acoustic Music* (Prentice-Hall, London & New York, 1982)

Sumner, William Leslie *The Pianoforte* (Macdonald, London, 1966)

Tortelier, Paul *How I Play – How I teach* (Chester, London, 1976)

Turnbull, H. *The Guitar* (Batsford, London, 1974)

Williams, Peter *A New History of the Organ* (Faber & Faber, London, 1980)

Recording Music

Anderton, Craig *Home Recording for Musicians* (Guitar Player Books, Saratoga, California, 1978)

Borwick John (editor) *Sound Recording Practice* (Oxford University Press, Oxford, 2nd ed. 1980)

Lambert, Dennis & Zalkind, Ronald *Producing Hit Records* (Schirmer, New York, 1980)

Nisbett, Alec *The Technique of the Sound Studio* (Sagamore, Plainview, N.Y.)

Rosmini, Dick *The Multitrack Primer* (Teac, Montebello, California, 1978)

Tobler, John & Grundy, Stuart *The Record Producers* (BBC, London, 1982)

Tremaine, Dr Howard M. *The Audio Cyclopedia* (2nd ed) (Howard Sams, Indianapolis)

Business

Dann, Allan & Underwood, John *How to Succeed in the Music Business* (Wise Publications, London, 1978)

Rapaport, Diane Sward *How to Make and Sell Your Own Records* (Quick Fox, New York, 1979)

Shemel, Sidney & Krasilovsky, M. William *This Business of Music* (Billboard, New York, 1979)

Zalkind, Ronald *Contemporary Music Almanac* (Schirmer, New York, published annually)

Training and Education

Self, G. *New Sounds in Class* (Universal Edition, 1967)

Small, Christopher *Music, Society, Education* (John Calder, London, 1977; Riverrun Press, New York, 1982)

Vulliamy, G. and Lee, E. *Pop Music in School* (Cambridge University Press, 1976)

Index

double-reeds 187, **187**
double-stopping 190
double-tracking 261, 262
doubling 171, 185, 235
Drake, Pete 151
Draper, Simon 307-9
Dreadlock Holiday 175
Dreamer 111
Drew, Martin 158
drum 23, 24, 37, 48, 78, 158-62, **159**, 198, 203, **259, 262**
  playing 160, 163-5
  recording 278-9
  tuning 158-60
drums:
  African talking 175
  bhaya 169
  bongo 83, 168-9, **169, 198,** 200
  cassa 83
  conga 83, **166,** 168
  electronic 160-2, **160**
  steel **174,** 175
  tabla **168,** 169-70, 203
  tabor 199
  timbales 170, **170**
  timpani 174-5, **175**
  tumba, *see* conga
drum grips 158, **159,** 163
drum heads 158
drum machine 96, **122**
drum sticks 158, **159**
dubbing 93, 336
Dubliners, The 199, **199**
Dudgeon, Gus 278
Dukas, Paul 187
duos 198-9
Duran Duran 322
Dury, Ian 292
Dvorak, Antonin 187
Dylan, Bob 35, **35,** 53, **53,** 58, **60,** 61, 151, 196, 197, **197,** 300
dynamic microphone 240, **241**
dynamic range 228

E

Eagles, The 54, 103, 199, 334
ear, human **227,** 333
Earth, Wind and Fire 82, 103, 175, 179, 181, 202, **202, 213**
East Thirty-Second Street 127
Easton, Sheena 284-5, **285**
Ebony and Ivory 62
echo 103, **122,** 143, 204, 230, 234, 251, **251,** 278, 336
echo chamber 137, 336
echo plate 234, 336
Eckstein, Billy 286
Eddy, Duane 137
Edel, Herman 326-7, **327**
Edelman, Randy 292
Edison, Thomas 126
editing 261-4, 279
Edmunds, Dave 292
education 332
  formal training 331
  musical 312

Edwards, Bernard 155
El Ibanez 132, 133, 144
Elastica 308
Eldridge, Roy 178
Eleanor Rigby 58, 79, 82, 102, 190, **267**
Electric Light Orchestra 191, **192,** 213
electronic music 35, 43, 126-8
electronics 43, 288
electropop **43,** 203-4
Ellington, Duke 88, 106, 178, 288
Ellis, Terry 293, 323-5
Emerick, Geoff 256-65, **257,** 267, **271,** 276
Emerson, Keith 115, 117, 127, 213
Emerson, Lake and Palmer 38, 127, 299
EMI 23, 42, 292, 331
Emmons, Buddy 151
Emotions, The 103
Empty Garden 115
EMS synthesizers 119
EMT reverberation devices **251**
Emu Systems 119, 120, 130
Emulator 124, **125,** 130
engineer, recording **242,** 256, **259,** 267, 278
Eno, Brian 127
ensembles, small 197
Enthoven, David 299, 310-11, **311**
Entwistle, John 203
envelope generator 118, 119, **119,** 333
equalization 256, 265, 336
equalizer 234, 235, 242-4, 336
  graphic 216, **252**
Ertegun brothers 23
euphonium 176, **177**
Evans, Gil 178
Eventide H949 harmonizer **252**
Ever So Lonely 203
Everly Brothers, The 101, 102, 151
Everything's Coming Up Roses 75
Evil Genius 185
expander 235, 336
Eye Of The Tiger 293

F

Faddis, John 181
fader 244, 274, 336
fade 184, 336
Fagan, Donald 98
Fairfax, Ferdy 90
Fairlight CMI synthesizer 124, **125,** 128, **128,** 130, 131
Fairport Convention 190, 199
Faith, Adam 190
Faithful, Marianne 315
falsetto 98, 99
Family 318
farsifa organ 48

Federal Communications Commission 328
Fenwick, Mark 299
feedback 35, 127, 134, 152, 336
feedback mixer **259**
Feldman, Victor 171
Fender, Leo 133, 134, 144, 149, 154
Fender bass 47, 152-4, 156
  G & L 154
  Jazz Bass 154, 155
  Precision Special **152,** 154, 155
Fender guitar, 47, 134, **134, 135,** 139, 154
  Stratocaster 134, **134,** 139
  Telecaster 47, **135,** 154
Fender Rhodes 48, 63, 83, 110, 115, **117**
Ferguson, Al 85
Ferguson, Maynard 180
Ferry, Bryan 323
fiddle 199
film music 50, 84, 86, 89-93, 138, 171, 283, 316
  electronic 128
financial director, recording company 306
Findlay, Chuck 181
finger cymbals, *see* crotales
Fire 117
Fisher, Matthew 113, 117
Fitzgerald, Ella 100, 105, 184
fixer, session 312, 336
flanging 230, 235, 336
Fleeson, Martin 140
Fleetwood Mac **44,** 318
Fleta guitar 140
Flock, The 190, 203
Flowers, Bruce 180
Flowers, Herbie 175
flügelhorn 176, **177,** 179, 180
flute 83, 118, 180, **186,** 196, 197, 198, 202, 203
  "grunt" flute 186
Flying Burrito Brothers, The 151
Flying Lizard 230
foldback 234, 244, 335
folk 35, 55, 100, 190, 192, 197
  duos 198
  folk-rock 199, 203
  line-ups 199
  urban 35
For Free 185
For No-one 83, 179, 203
Ford, Emile 284
Ford, Mary **47**
Ford, Tennessee Ernie 151
Foreigner 321
form (of song) 56-7, 78
Fortunes, The 94
Fosse, Bob 222
Fostex, A4 recorder **233**
  A8 **233**
  Multitracker **238,** 250
  150 **238**
  350 mixer **234**

fotdella 197
Four Freshmen, The 101, 102
Four Tops, The **28,** 29
François, Claude **60**
Frank Lloyd Wright 133
Franke, Chris **121**
Franklin, Aretha 32, **32,** 99, 103, 182, 207
Frap contact microphone 187
Fraser, Andy 155
Free 155
Freed, Alan 23, 24, **24**
french horn 82, 83, 176, **177,** 178, 179, 202, 203
French Lieutenant's Woman, The 89-90, **91**
frequencies 227, **228**
fretless bass **152,** 154, 155, 157
Friend or Foe 222, **222**
From Me To You 66
Fry, Tristan 171-5, **171**
Fuller, Jesse 'Lone Cat' 197, **197**
Fullerton, George 154
funk 41, 43, 154, 171, 179
Furth, George 77
fuzz-box 47, 137, 200, 336

G

G & L bass guitar 154
Gabrielli Brass 181
Gadd, Steve 158, 160, 163-5, **164,** 277
Gallup, Cliff 146
Gamble and Huff 312
gamelan gong 187
Gang of Four, The 20
garage rock 42, 43
Garfunkel, Art 103
Garrard, Maggie 328-9
gating 251
Gaucho 98, 185
Gaydon, John 299
GB 10 guitar 133
Gee Officer Krupke 77
Geffen label 293
Geffen, David 293
Geils, J., *see* J. Geils Band, The
Geldorf, Bob 61
Genesis 20, 203, 319
Gentle On My Mind 61
George, Boy **307,** 308
Getz, Stan 182
Geyer upright piano **110**
Gibson guitars 132, 134, 142, 148, 149, 152
  Byrdland 133
  ES335 133, **133,** 139
  Les Paul 47, 134, **135,** 139, 142
    Les Paul Custom **135**
    L5 slimline 133
    RB250 194
Gillan, Ian 208, 308
Gillespie, Dizzy 178, **178,** 288, 334
Gillett, Charlie 23